OPENING MEN'S EYES

MICHAEL CARDO was born in Durban in 1977 and went to school at Kearsney College. He studied English, History and French at the University of Natal and in 2003 gained a PhD in History from the University of Cambridge, which he attended on a Cambridge Commonwealth Trust scholarship. He has worked for the Democratic Alliance since 2003 in a variety of capacities: as Director of Research; as Helen Zille's speechwriter during the 2009 election; and currently as a policy adviser. Between 2006 and 2008, he was a Visiting Research Fellow at the Helen Suzman Foundation, while he researched and wrote *Opening Men's Eyes*. This is his first book.

OPENING MEN'S EYES

*Peter Brown and the Liberal Struggle
for South Africa*

Michael Cardo

JONATHAN BALL PUBLISHERS
JOHANNESBURG & CAPE TOWN

This edition first published in trade paperback in 2010 by
JONATHAN BALL PUBLISHERS (PTY) LTD
P O Box 33977
Jeppestown
2043

ISBN 978-1-86842-392-7

Cover by Michiel Botha, Cape Town
Typesetting by Etienne van Duyker, Cape Town
Design and reproduction of photo section by
Triple M Design & Advertising, Johannesburg
Editing and index by Alfred le Maitre, Cape Town
Printed and bound by CTP Book Printers, Cape Town
Set in 11 on 14 pt New Baskerville ITC

To my parents, for everything, and
to Francis, for being on the side of the angels

Contents

Acknowledgements

Not long after Peter Brown died in 2004, some of his friends and former colleagues from the Liberal Party suggested that a book be written examining the liberal tradition in South Africa and Brown's place in it.

The idea gestated for a while, and in 2006, Francis Antonie, then Senior Economist at Standard Bank and currently Director of the Helen Suzman Foundation, put my name forward to write it.

It soon became clear that the nature of Brown's contribution to the struggle *against* apartheid and *for* liberal democracy – assiduously documented at the Alan Paton Centre and Struggle Archive at the University of KwaZulu-Natal – warranted a full-scale political biography.

I am grateful to Francis Antonie for his wise advice and warm friendship during the course of my work, and for introducing me to Brown's widow, Phoebe. Together with Colin Gardner, Randolph Vigne and David Welsh, they got the ball rolling on this project. All gave unstintingly of their time, interest and expertise. All read draft chapters and offered valuable criticism.

Phoebe Brown spent countless hours with me, patiently answering my (sometimes impertinent) questions with equanimity. She eased my path in innumerable ways, and I am deeply grateful to her for her kindness and generosity.

I owe Randolph Vigne a huge debt of gratitude. He read each chapter after it was finished, as well as the completed manuscript. He offered helpful editorial suggestions, pointed out errors of fact and was an indispensable resource in every way. He put me in touch with many of Brown's friends and associates in South Africa and the United Kingdom, and was consistently solicitous and supportive.

This book was made possible through the material support of the Oppenheimer Memorial Trust and the Brown Family Trust. The Helen Suzman Foundation kindly awarded me a Visiting Research Fellowship while I researched and wrote about Brown's life and work. I am particularly grateful to the Foundation's former Director, Raenette Taljaard, and two of its Trustees, Doug Band and Richard Steyn, for this opportunity.

I find the detective aspect of archival work especially satisfying. My detections were undoubtedly made easier by Estelle Liebenberg-Barkhuizen and Jewel Koopman at the Alan Paton Centre. Ever friendly and ready to go the extra mile, they made researching at the Centre a real pleasure.

My thanks also go to the archivists and librarians at Michaelhouse; the Killie Campbell Africana Library in Durban; the Manuscripts and Archives Department at the University of Cape Town; the National Library of South Africa in Cape Town; the William Cullen Library's Department of Historical Papers at the University of the Witwatersrand; the National Archives in Pretoria; the United Party Archives at the University of South Africa; the Borthwick Institute for Historical Research at the University of York; and Jesus College, Cambridge.

It is a measure of the esteem in which Peter Brown was held, and the fondness and devotion that he inspired in those who met him, that so many people were so ready to help me with this book. I would like to thank them all, especially the following people who gave me access to their private papers, letters and photo collections, and who shared their memories of Brown with me on more than one occasion: John Aitchison, Anton Brown, Christopher Brown, Vanessa Brown, Catherine Brubeck, Christianne Carlisle, Sam Chetty, Dot Cleminshaw, the late David Craighead, David Evans, Liz Franklin, Adelaine and Walter Hain, Eric Harber, Steve Hayes, the late Sir Raymond 'Bill' Hoffenberg, Douglas Irvine, Derick Marsh, Olga Meidner, Pat McKenzie, the late John Carlyle Mitchell, John Morrison, Neville Rubin, Simon and Joy Roberts, Peter Rutsch, Jack Spence, the late Helen Suzman, Beryl Unterhalter,

Leslie and Pessa Weinberg, Jill Wentzel and Daphne Zackon.

In Pietermaritzburg, I was fortunate to share the reading room at the Alan Paton Centre with Norman Bromberger for several months. I owe much to him for the series of interviews he conducted with Peter Brown in the 1990s, the tapes and transcripts of which are lodged at the Alan Paton Centre. I spent many hours picking Norman's brain about Peter Brown, the Liberal Party and the political and intellectual history of liberalism in South Africa. His probing intellect and good company spurred my labours.

In London, Wolf Hamm allowed me to make copies of over a hundred letters that Brown wrote to him over a forty-year period. He was also a gracious host and answered my numerous questions patiently and thoughtfully.

I would like to acknowledge Chizuko Sato, who sent me two chapters of her unpublished DPhil thesis, 'Forced Removals, Land NGOs and Community Politics in KwaZulu-Natal, South Africa, 1953-2002' (University of Oxford, 2006), which helped contextualise Brown's land activism.

Thanks are due to the team at Jonathan Ball Publishers: Jonathan Ball, who took on the manuscript and galvanised me in his inimitable humorous and congenial way, and Jeremy Boraine and Francine Blum, who expertly saw the book through production. I am also grateful to Alfred LeMaitre for the scrupulous and professional manner in which he edited the manuscript and compiled the index; to Michiel Botha and Kevin Shenton for their design work on the cover and photo section respectively; Etienne van Duyker for the design, layout and typesetting of the book; and Valda Strauss for meticulously proofreading the book and patiently accommodating my changes.

Finally, I would like to thank my family – especially my parents for all their care and generosity on my research trips to KwaZulu-Natal – as well as my friends in Cape Town, who provided me with welcome distractions from writing. Without their support and encouragement this would have been a much harder book to write.

Cape Town
August 2010

PROLOGUE

Three weeks after his release from jail in 1990, Nelson Mandela travelled to the strife-torn province of Natal, where members of the Inkatha movement and supporters of the United Democratic Front (UDF) were engaged in a bloody civil war.

Addressing a crowd of over 100 000 people, Mandela relayed his powerful message: 'Take your guns, your knives, and your pangas, and throw them into the sea. Close down the death factories. End this war now!'

Throughout his speech, Mandela returned to the theme that was later to become the leitmotif of his presidency: unity in diversity.

Speaking in Zulu, he said that no one could boast more proudly of having 'ploughed a significant field in the struggle against apartheid' than the people of Natal. And that struggle had won the participation of 'every language and colour, every stripe and hue'.

Along with Zulu elders who had provided leadership to the African National Congress (ANC), like John Langalibalele Dube, Pixley ka Isaka Seme and Albert Luthuli; together with members of the first black political organisation in Africa, the Natal Indian Congress (NIC); and with the workers from Durban who flexed their industrial muscle during the strikes of the 1970s, 'Whites, too, [had] made a contribution to the struggle in Natal':

It began with the lonely voices of Bishop Colenso and his daughters who denounced imperialist injustices against the Zulu people and who campaigned vigorously for the free-

dom of their leaders. The Natal Liberal Party waged stead-
fast campaigns against removals, and its work has been continued into the present by people like Peter Brown.[1]

Mandela saluted their 'proud and courageous history'.

Four years later, as President, Mandela again paid tribute to
Peter Brown when he invited him to attend a 'luncheon in honour
of the veterans of our struggle for freedom' at the Union Buildings
in Pretoria.[2]

Who was Peter Brown, to whose role Mandela made special reference in one of his first, and most important, speeches as a free
man? And why, over the course of the following decade, until his
death in 2004, was Brown's contribution allowed to fade from the
nation's collective historical consciousness?

Reflecting on a visit to the Apartheid Museum in Johannesburg in 2003, the historian and journalist, RW Johnson, noted
that there was 'one old election poster of [Helen] Suzman's about
a foot from the floor but no pictures of Alan Paton, Peter Brown
or any other white liberals who suffered and fought against apartheid'.[3]

The only white faces shown as part of the struggle, he observed,
were communists. Was this a case of white liberals being deliberately
airbrushed from the historical canvas?

To be sure, in death, Brown was paid handsome tribute by his
friends and former colleagues in the Liberal Party (LP), which he
helped to form in 1953 and which he led between 1958 and 1964.
Memorial services were held in South Africa and England, and
obituarists at home and abroad sketched his life and work.[4]

In life, too, Brown did not go altogether unrecognised: in 1997,
the University of Natal conferred on him an honorary doctorate,
and in 2000, the Pietermaritzburg-Msunduzi local council awarded
him a civic certificate of commendation for 'his dedication to justice, the selfless work he [had] done over decades in a variety of
different fields, and the quiet influence that he [had] exerted on
a large number of people'.[5]

Yet there has been very little real understanding and appreciation, both in the past and the present, of the nature and importance

of the part played by liberals like Brown in opposing apartheid and forging non-racial democracy. Winnie Mandela once recounted to Brown how, when she visited Robben Island in the 1980s and mentioned his name, she was 'shocked to receive a whole lowdown on your quiet but most impressive political history', adding that she 'had no right not to know it'.[6]

The reasons for Brown's relative obscurity are partly personal, partly ideological and partly political.

Brown was a modest man. Born into a Natal family of Scottish descent, country traders on his father's side and farmers on his mother's, he inherited two abiding characteristics.

The first was a heightened sense of community awareness, shaped by an appreciation for the rhythms of rural life and an allegiance to the soil. Land and community were Brown's two great concerns. They are the golden threads that connect his liberal activism in the 1950s and 1960s, when he opposed the state's programme of 'black spot' removals, through his chairmanship of the Association for Rural Advancement in the 1970s and 1980s, to his development work with African farmers in the 1990s.

The second was a natural Scots reserve, a diffidence that was occasionally pierced by his teasing, dry wit, which made Brown entirely indifferent to matters of reputation and veneration.

Even so, personal reticence alone does not explain why Brown's contribution has gone largely unheeded. In post-apartheid South Africa, the ANC has inevitably sought to remember its own heroes. In the process, many others have been forgotten. This trend has been abetted by various currents in writing about South African history since the 1970s, beginning with the ideological dominance of the so-called 'Marxist-revisionist' school of that time.

The Marxists were hostile to liberal scholars, whose 'conventional version' of South African history they wished to overturn, since, in their view, it elevated race over class as an analytical tool and misunderstood the relationship between capitalism and apartheid. More than that, the revisionists viewed liberal history as an apology for British imperialism, whose material interests, they claimed, lay at the heart of racial discrimination. Such views served to marginalise liberal historians from the centre of public debate and to disparage the role of political thinkers and activists steeped in the liberal tradition.

Invigorated by the rising tide of social history in the 1980s, which overlapped with a move to write 'history from below', revisionists were further disinclined to engage with the history of (white) 'high politics' or to examine the life histories of individual politicians.

Liberalism itself – as a reformist, anti-apartheid political ideology and project – was deemed to be a subject unworthy of serious interrogation. Whatever their other achievements, the revisionists did South African history-writing a great disservice by vilifying liberalism as a mere adjunct of imperial conquest, racial segregation and capitalist exploitation.

Political factors, too, have played a part in pushing liberals to the periphery. Under apartheid, the word 'liberal' was a term of abuse, employed with equal venom by opponents on the left and the right. To the Nationalist government, the epithet signified sedition and, when prefaced with 'white', race treachery. To those in the ANC, which had its own liberal tradition, increasingly from the 1960s liberalism meant submission to white trusteeship and paternalism, and a commitment to gradualism that stunted the revolution.

In 1962, the ANC President, Chief Albert Luthuli, wrote in his autobiography that the Liberal Party had been able to speak with 'a far greater moral authority than other parties with white members' because of the quality of people at its head – people such as Alan Paton and Brown.[7]

Luthuli congratulated the LP for taking its stand on 'principles and not on expediency'. He welcomed its policy of non-racial membership as 'an act of courage', and he expressed the hope that the Progressive Party would follow its example. His views typified those of an older generation of African leaders.

A younger generation, centred on the ANC Youth League and among whose notables were Nelson Mandela, Walter Sisulu and Oliver Tambo, were more dismissive. Their reservations were reinforced by a more explicitly leftist intellectual critique, often quite polemically powerful, that can be traced back to the Trotskyite

Non-European Unity Movement in the 1930s and 1940s, and which fed into the thinking of the Congress of Democrats (COD) – the white, communist-leaning, section of the Congress Alliance. Prefigured by the Pan-Africanists who broke away from the ANC in 1959, Black Consciousness activists likewise denounced white liberals in the 1970s and 1980s. They insisted that the liberal identification of non-racialism with colour-blind integration served to keep the basis of the apartheid social order – white privilege – intact.

Ideological mistrust of liberalism has persisted in post-apartheid South Africa, fuelled by opposition to so-called 'neo-liberal' economic policies (which the ANC accuses the official opposition of advocating, and which, ironically, the ANC's own alliance partners charge the government with pursuing). The new black political elite, girded by a resurgent Africanism, accuses 'liberals' – which it uses in a loose and imprecise way, much like the apartheid definition of 'communists' – of subverting its transformation agenda. The ANC believes it is faced with a major ideological offensive, 'largely driven by the opposition and individuals in the mainstream media', whose 'key objective' is 'the promotion of market fundamentalism to retain the old apartheid economic and social relations'.[8]

Even a non-Africanist ANC leader like Kader Asmal (now since resigned from active politics) denigrates the history of white liberals by arguing that they waged a McCarthyite cold war against the ANC's alliance partner, the South African Communist Party (SACP). Asmal believes that liberals were sanctimonious about the ANC's recourse to violence. He claims they acquiesced in PW Botha's murderous states of emergency and aggression against neighbouring African states in the 1980s.[9]

Peter Brown's life and work present the clearest refutation of such claims. It is true that some Liberals, like Patrick Duncan, had a virulent dislike of communists, which on occasion bedevilled relations between the LP and the ANC and which prevented closer cooperation between the two organisations. Brown was wary of, but by no means antagonistic towards, communists. Distancing himself and his party from Duncan's controversial 'Open letter to Chief Luthuli' in 1959, in which Duncan accused the ANC of being in

thrall to communists ('the worst oppressors of the modern age'),
Brown wrote that 'the communists among its [the ANC's] members ... have been in the forefront of those who have put up the
most spirited defence there has been of fundamental democratic
rights'.[10]

He pleaded for liberals and communists to sink 'our ideological
differences for the moment and get on with the job of disposing of
the devil we know'.

In part, Brown's pragmatic approach owed something to the
fact that the COD (formed in 1953 as a front for the banned
SACP) lacked the kind of presence in Natal that it had in the Cape
and the Transvaal. However, it was also a measure of Brown's
common sense: dismissive of dogma, he sought to bring together
different interests, traditions and organisations in the anti-apartheid
cause. His liberalism was of the practical, not the purist, variety.
Always focused on the promotion of social justice and non-racial
equality, Brown's liberalism was nurtured by close personal friendships and interactions that transcended racial and ideological
divides.

Although Brown abhorred violence, he never judged those,
both in his own party and in the ANC, who turned to arms. He
believed that violence was 'forced on reluctant people by the failures of the past'.[11]

In this way, he was quite unlike his friend and mentor, Alan
Paton, whose exegeses on violence did indeed bear something of
the self-righteousness of which Asmal complains.

The magazine *Reality*, which Brown edited after his ban was
lifted in 1974, vigorously condemned the states of emergency
imposed in the 1980s and the apartheid government's contempo-
raneous incursions into neighbouring countries.

Brown's life history, which spanned the rise and fall of apartheid, may offer the chance to re-evaluate some of the criticisms
that have been directed at liberals. Brown's biography is also a
political history of the times: in particular, it encompasses the history of a remarkable party, which, despite a brief life, left an enduring legacy.

Forced to disband in 1968 by the state's Prohibition of Political

Interference Act, which forbade blacks and whites from belonging to the same political organisation, the LP worked to make the common society a reality. The ideas and values it promoted are today enshrined in the South African Constitution, having displaced both the Marxism-Leninism and exclusive Africanism with which liberalism vied for space in the marketplace of ideas.

Through his leadership of the Liberal Party, Brown played an early and crucial part in articulating an alternative vision to the racial exclusiveness of apartheid: this was at a time when other anti-apartheid organisations in South Africa, such as those that formed the Congress Alliance, were racially compartmentalised. In some ways, the Liberal Party marks a rupture in the history of South African liberalism. In style and substance, there are important discontinuities between the Liberal Party and the political tradition associated with nineteenth-century Cape liberals that preceded and nourished it. There are significant differences, too, between the activist extra-parliamentary liberalism of the LP and the parliamentary liberalism of the Progressive Party in the 1960s. The Liberals launched as a non-racial party, whereas the formation of the Progressives in 1959, Brown noted, 'was an all-white launching and the policy decisions were all-white decisions'.[12]

The Progressive Party only reopened its membership to blacks, in defiance of the Prohibition of Political Interference Act, in 1984.[13]

While the Liberals advocated universal suffrage from 1960, the Progressives continued to support a qualified franchise until 1978. Where the Progressives rigidly adhered to 'constitutional' means of protest, the Liberals advocated boycotts and sit-ins. And, as the Progressives focused on civil rights, the Liberals campaigned for socio-economic rights, proposing various forms of regulation and redistribution to deracialise the economy.

By drawing attention to these distinctions, it is not my intention to praise one kind of liberalism at the expense of another: both hastened the end of apartheid, and both shaped the kind of society in which we now live. I do wish, however, to puncture some of the misconceptions that exist about the history of South African liberalism.

As chairman, Brown presided over and guided the radicalisation of liberalism in the Liberal Party. In his influential *African Profiles*, published a year before Brown's ban in 1964, Ronald Segal called Brown 'a figure of considerable political intelligence and realism' who was 'substantially responsible' for attuning the Liberal Party to the 'changing nature of political resistance to apartheid'.[14]

What follows is an attempt to understand how Brown applied this intelligence and realism to work for change, to show the significance of his contribution and to provide a documentary record of his life's work, both during his years of involvement with the Liberal Party and after his return to public life in 1974.

PART
ONE

Origins and childhood
1924-1938

By the time Peter McKenzie Brown was born on 24 December 1924 at his parents' Musgrave Road home, Monaltrie, high on the slopes of Durban's tree-lined Berea, the Union of South Africa was a troublesome teen.

Fourteen and a half years earlier, on 31 May 1910, the Act of Union came into effect. It welded the two former British colonies, Natal and the Cape, and the two Boer Republics, Transvaal and the Orange Free State, into a single national polity. General Louis Botha, the man who fought heroically on the side of the Boers in the bitter South African War (1899-1902), was installed as Prime Minister with General Jan Smuts as his right-hand man.

Together, under the umbrella of the South African Party (SAP), they attempted to defuse old ethnic and linguistic rivalries by uniting Boer and Briton in a shared sense of nationhood. The fulcrum of their project was white supremacy: going into Union, all the provinces, with the exception of the Cape – where the nineteenth-century liberal tradition still prevailed – rejected black voting rights. With Botha and Smuts at the helm, a slew of segregationist legislation ensued. New laws imposed a job colour bar on the mines, restricted African land ownership to the 'native reserves' and controlled the influx of blacks to urban areas.

Botha and Smuts's efforts to promote a shared national identity, based on Anglo-Afrikaner unity, were circumscribed by imperial notions of belonging. South Africa was still a British Dominion. The symbolic armour of Empire – 'God Save the King', the Union Jack and English itself – was brandished in public life in a way that rankled with those who had waged war against Britain. They had struggled for self-determination and resented this easy assumption of British superiority.

The adolescent nation was showing signs of fractiousness. Spurred on by their opposition to Union participation in the First World War, and galvanised by what they viewed as Botha's heavy-handed subduing of the 1914 Boer Rebellion, those so aggrieved began to reassert themselves politically. Their message of cultural affirmation and national sovereignty was articulated not in the language of their forefathers, Dutch, but in the confident cadences of modern Afrikaans. They rejected British overlordship and wanted a more rigorous native policy to protect white interests.

In June 1924, the organisation that embodied their voice, the National Party, came to power by forming a coalition with the Labour Party. The Nationalist leader, General Barry Hertzog, was sworn in as Prime Minister. South Africa's political trajectory was set to change decisively. Six months later, Peter Brown entered the world.

These, then, were the currents that were to determine the course of Brown's public life and work: the fall of empire, the rise of Afrikaner nationalism, the legal codification of racial discrimination and their combined effect on black resistance to the Union's racial politics.

* * *

59 Musgrave Road lies at the top of the Berea, the ridge which descends steeply into the Durban city centre below, and which, on a clear day, affords commanding views of Africa's busiest port and out to the Indian Ocean beyond.

In the 1920s, as it is now, Musgrave Road was a prestigious address. Most of the gracious Victorian homes have given way to modern townhouse developments and apartment blocks, but the location still marks itself out as a place of privilege.

Framed by rows of palms and flamboyants, the Browns' home, 'Monaltrie', was built in 1897 for the consul of Belgium and the Austro-Hungarian Empire, William Auerswald. Designed in the Queen

Anne revivalist style, with red face-brick, white-painted balustrades, half-timbered gables, several verandas and an entrance portico, the two-storey villa was set on a large property that extended all the way up to Essenwood Road above. Today it is a national monument.

Brown's father, Hugh, was a keen polo player, and he wanted space to stable his ponies. Many of Peter's earliest memories were of time spent on the polo fields with his father and his two older siblings, Craig, born in 1917, and Elizabeth (known to the family as 'Bet'), born in 1920.

Hugh Brown was born in 1886 to William George ('WG') Brown and his first wife, Dollie. WG Brown moved to South Africa from Scotland in the late 1870s and opened a trading store in a small settlement called Rietvlei, above the densely forested Karkloof Valley in the Natal Midlands. From there he settled in Pieter-maritzburg, the capital of the Crown Colony of Natal, and became a minor importer and wholesaler. As his enterprise grew, he decided to relocate to the commercial hub of the colony, Durban, where he opened WG Brown & Co. The business supplied country stores with what was then called 'Kaffir truck' – goods such as blankets, copper wire, cheap cutlery and basic foodstuffs.

WG Brown was a tough Lowland Scot. (In later years, when Peter was asked whether he was conscious of his Scots descent, he replied: 'Certainly, but more from my mother's side than from his [WG Brown's]. I think his was sort of Lowland, west coast of Scotland, whereas as they were true blue Highlanders.').[1]

WG Brown was an astute businessman. His second wife, Elizabeth, a music teacher from Aberdeen whom he married in 1922, identified in him a 'hard-headed Scottish capacity for driving good bargains'.[2]

He was as parsimonious as he was plucky, and he was unsenti-mental in his personal relationships – both with his son and his clients. But then relations between the traders of 'Kaffir truck' and their consumers were hardly based on charity and compassion.

For all that, Hugh, who took over the prospering family busi-ness and ran it until he died, became a businessman with a social conscience. Educated at Michaelhouse and Jesus College, Cam-bridge, he was a kind and temperate man who combined his business interests with active civic engagement and philanthropic pursuits. He was especially concerned with education and social welfare: he served on the Board of Governors of several Natal schools, and was a patron of St Martin's Diocesan Home for Children in Durban.

Peter described his relationship with his father as 'good', and added, on reflection, that 'it hadn't reached the stage of any great intimacy' by the time Hugh died on 21 August 1935.[3]

Hugh Brown died pursuing his passion: polo. He worked hard to establish polo as a sport in South Africa, as chairman of the South African Polo Association between 1930 and 1935. And he was a keen and able player (nicknamed 'the Wizard' for his control of the ball) and manager, having captained the South African team during a tour of Argentina in 1933.[4]

His death, in a semi-final at the South African Polo championships in Pietermaritzburg, was the result of an accident: he collided with two other players, was thrown off his pony and hit the back of his head on the ground. Hugh Brown was rushed unconscious to Grey's Hospital, but it was too late to save him: his skull was badly fractured and he died of internal bleeding that night.

The *Natal Witness* ran a glowing tribute to Hugh Brown, noting that he had been the driving force behind polo in South Africa and 'its most energetic proselytiser'.[5]

More than that, he was 'one of those great and luminous souls … filled with a wide and abiding sympathy for the misfortunes of others'. His generosity was hidden behind a 'modesty which was the outstanding trait of the man, a gentle unassuming manner which cloaked a character both rich and rare'. In his private life, he 'was one to whom all in sorrow, need or happiness must gravitate, one who formed a centre wherever he was'. And, although he was a generous benefactor to good causes, the sum total of his benefactions would remain untold because 'so many were unknown except to the recipient …'

Nearly seventy years later, when Peter Brown died, the *Witness* (as it had become) expressed similar sentiments about Brown junior. Peter inherited from his father a deep sense of civic duty. He also inherited a substantial amount of money. His father's estate was valued at over £200 000, and part of it was used to set up a trust which, according to him, his mother 'proceeded to administer very effectively' with her brother-in-law, a Durban-based attorney named Jim Hathorn.[6]

Brown later reflected that he was financially independent, even during his mother's lifetime, 'as a result of that bequest'.

Brown's mother, Helen Mary (affectionately known to family and friends alike as 'Maisie'), also came from an affluent family. She was born in 1890 to a second-generation descendant of a Byrne settler,[7] Archibald McKenzie, and his wife, Helen Jessie Weddel. Maisie was the fourth child in a family of ten daughters and one son (he was the first-born) – a rather expansive brood, which explained her father's nickname of 'ten-to-one McKenzie'. Maisie's father was one of the first pupils at Hilton College, the elite private school in the Natal Midlands, which was founded in 1872, and where he excelled academically. He qualified as a medical doctor at the University of Edinburgh, to which he had been awarded a scholarship. On returning to South Africa, McKenzie set up a practice in Durban with a fellow Edinburgh alumnus, Sam Campbell, whose son Roy would go on to become a famous poet. Together they founded the Berea Nursing Home.[8]

Schooled in England, Maisie was a bright, lively and quietly forceful figure. Asked whether she read to him much, or steeped him in literary culture, Brown remembered his mother as a 'detective novel reader' rather than an 'intellectual': 'she was much more a practical, down-to-earth person, I think.'[9] He characterised their relationship as 'close, but not demonstrative'.[10]

Peter never really got to know his brother well. Craig went up to Cambridge when Peter was still only ten years old, and then joined the navy when the Second World War broke out. His sister Bet was an eccentric girl, who battled with anorexia as a teenager, and although Peter had a soft spot for her, their relationship could at times be difficult. Bet died in 1977, in the psychiatric hospital at Town Hill.

Maisie did many good deeds for the community: she volunteered in old age homes and orphanages and she shared her husband's concern for social welfare. But although her interests were wide-ranging, they were not, according to her son, 'cross-colour line interests'. In fact, as far as the Union's racial politics went, Brown's parents assumed – in his view – that 'the order of things was as it should be and that it would continue to be like that'. He explained: '[A]s far as everyday talk was concerned, I don't think that black politics was a subject that came up at all. I think they were sort of benevolent, not quite despots, but benevolent masters, as it were.' [11]

In fact, neither Hugh Brown nor his wife was particularly political. On Maisie's side, though, the family was not entirely unfamiliar with political controversy. 'Ten-to-one' McKenzie's brother, Major (later Brigadier-General Sir) Duncan, was one of the main protagonists in the relief of Ladysmith during the South African War. Another brother, Peter, wrote several polemical socialist tracts, which was fairly unusual for the son of Nottingham Road farmers. Maisie's sisters were politically divided when Smuts's South African Party fused with Hertzog's National Party to form the governing United Party (UP) in 1934, in the wake of the crisis triggered by the Great Depression. Some, like her sister Winifred, who married the *bloedsap* (as diehard SAP supporters were known) judge, Johannes Christiaan de Wet, stood by Smuts. Others, appalled by Smuts's rapprochement with the Nationalists, supported the jingoist breakaway organisation, the Dominion Party.

Hugh and Maisie Brown were probably middle-of-the-road United Party supporters. Although they were public-spirited and took their civic responsibilities seriously, the world in which they operated was all white. If they were liberals, their liberalism wasn't defined by their progressive attitude to the Union's so-called 'native problem'. Their attitude wasn't progressive by the conservative standards of Natal's Anglophone settler elite; it was entirely run-of-the-mill. Their younger son was to develop his particular brand of liberalism independently of them. And some of his earliest influences came from school.

2

MICHAELHOUSE
1938-1942

If Brown's family life gave him little exposure to the everyday lived experiences of ordinary black South Africans, so too did his schooling. He attended private boarding schools in Natal – first Cordwalles Preparatory School for Boys and then Michaelhouse – where the pupils all came from similar privileged middle- and upper-class backgrounds. They were all white, all male and predominantly English-speaking. By and large, the teachers tended to support, rather than question, the racial status quo.

Modelled on the English public school system, these institutions were 'liberal' in the broad sense of the word: they sought to inculcate values like tolerance and compassion, and the education they provided was directed towards the cultivation of the mind for its own sake. As the founder of Michaelhouse, James Cameron Todd, noted in his Speech Day address in 1897, the year after the school was founded: 'Our aim is to make, not accountants, not clerks, not clergymen, but men; men of understanding, thought and culture.'

Yet for all their emphasis on a liberal-humanist education, the ethos of these two schools was conservative – socially and racially. As outposts of 'Little England on the Veld',[1] as Peter Randall describes private schools in South Africa, they schooled the scions of the white settler elite in the rituals of Anglicanism, masculinity and Englishness. The worldview they helped to fashion could easily accommodate – and sustain – the traditional racial order in South Africa: the belief that white was superior to black.

However, Brown did receive from Michaelhouse what he later identified as 'a very strong liberal input' which 'had quite a substantial influence' on him.[2] This was the paternalistic liberalism of the 1930s – the idea that the role of the white man was to act as trustee for the 'natives' by providing them leadership with justice – which Brown would in due course reject. It was a long way from the non-racial liberalism, with its core belief in the common society, which Brown would embrace in the 1950s and 1960s.

The teachers at Michaelhouse made a far greater impression on Brown than those at Cordwalles. He felt that his schoolmasters at Cordwalles were 'pretty remote', although he did recall the headmaster – a 'rather fearsome character called Jack Besant, of whom everyone was dead scared'.[3] In the 1960s and 1970s, by which time he had retired, Besant used to visit Brown while he was under banning orders. Brown was touched by this expression of solidarity, for he had 'never … dreamed that there was something like that in him from my experience of him at school'.

In 1938, the year before the Second World War broke out, Brown entered Michaelhouse. The official school history notes that: 'By 1938, Michaelhouse evinced an unmistakable air of maturity.' The grounds and buildings were a growing source of pride, sound standards of scholarship had been established, there was a committed core of staff, and pupils enjoyed a varied programme of extracurricular activities. 'The standing of the school was … more secure than it had ever been and its reputation more widespread' – thanks in part to the *Illustrated London News*, which had profiled Michaelhouse in a series of articles.

The following year marked the arrival of a new Rector, Frederick Rowlandson ('FR') Snell, whom Brown credited with bringing a liberal influence into the school. Snell had been schooled at Winchester and had read chemistry at Oriel College, Oxford. He had been a senior science master at Eastbourne College before he was appointed Rector of Michaelhouse. Snell was politically aware and civic-minded. In England, he had served as vice-chairman of the Eastbourne Unemployment Council and been a councillor for the Distressed Areas Association.

Snell's major innovation during Brown's time at Michaelhouse was to introduce an exchange programme with Adams College, the oldest school for black pupils in Natal, and the second oldest in South Africa after Lovedale in what is now the Eastern Cape. Situated south of Durban in Amanzimtoti, Adams was founded as a mission school in 1853 by Dr Newton Adams of the American Board of Missions. By the 1930s it comprised a teacher training college and an industrial school, as well as primary and secondary schools.

Adams College boasts several distinguished alumni and former staff members, many of whom went on to play prominent roles in public life. Many of them became active in the ANC. The three Natal ANC leaders whom Mandela identified in his famous speech in Durban in 1990 – John Dube, Pixley ka Seme and Albert Luthuli – were all at Adams. ZK Matthews – the anthropologist who went on to an illustrious academic career at the University of Fort Hare in the 1940s, served as provincial president of the ANC in the Cape in 1949 and was a key initiator of the Congress of the People at which the Freedom Charter was adopted in 1955 – was head of the high school between 1925 and 1932. In 1934, Edgar Brookes took over as the principal of Adams College.

By then in his late thirties, Brookes was already a pillar of the liberal establishment and a name to be conjured with in academic and political circles. He was to become one of the guiding lights in Brown's life. He influenced the subject choices Brown made as a university student, helped Brown to find his first job and later formed an integral part of the Pietermaritzburg liberal network.

By the time he joined Adams, Brookes had undergone a Damascene conversion politically. Born in England in 1897, Brookes came to South Africa with his parents when he was four years old. Educated at Pietermaritzburg College, he was precociously bright, matriculating at the age of 14. His ambitions at that stage, as he wrote in his memoirs, 'fluctuated … between becoming an Anglican priest and becoming prime minister of South Africa'.[4] As it happened, unable to finance full-time university studies, Brookes took a job as a clerk in the Department of Customs and Excise in Durban – he was later transferred to Pretoria – and read for his Bachelor's degree as an external student at the University of South

Africa. In 1920, he entered the Transvaal University College (TUC) – the intellectual stronghold, along with the University of Stellenbosch, of Afrikaner nationalism – where, in his own words, he 'fell in love with the Afrikaner legend'.[5]

While at TUC, Brookes, a historian with an interest in contemporary politics, wrote his Master's thesis on the workings of the South African constitution during the first ten years of Union, and completed a book, *The History of Native Policy in South Africa from 1830 to the Present Day*, for which he was awarded a DLitt in 1924.

On the strength of his book, Brookes, the quintessential English gentleman who had grown up in that most English of provinces, Natal, was appointed to the chair of Public Administration and Political Science at TUC. *The History of Native Policy* defended racial segregation. It was subsequently used by the newly installed Prime Minister, Barry Hertzog, to give ideological legitimation both to the package of segregationist bills which his Pact government wanted to steer through Parliament and to the broad thrust of its 'native policy'. For a time, Brookes became a darling of the Afrikaner Nationalist establishment. In September 1927, General Hertzog appointed him as a South African delegate to the Assembly of the League of Nations.

A research trip to the United States that same year made Brookes question his earlier support for segregation. His experiences there taught him 'the salutary lesson that the black man was capable of considerable achievement in a milieu of white civilisation'.[6] And so he began a 'spiritual pilgrimage' which took him from separate development to an inclusive liberalism. He soon recanted his views on segregation, and became active in liberal bodies like the Joint Council of Africans and Europeans and the South African Institute of Race Relations (SAIRR; formed in 1929), from where he championed the idea of incorporating an acculturated class of blacks into 'white civilisation' in the 1930s and 1940s.[7]

Anchored by his Christian faith, Brookes was warm, wise and gentle. Although he went on to enjoy an active career in liberal politics – first as a Senator representing Natalian Africans in Parliament between 1937 and 1952 and later as national chairman of the Liberal Party after Brown was banned in 1964 – Brookes was neither a political animal nor an instinctive liberal. He described himself as a 'natural conservative' who became 'a liberal in South African circumstances almost in spite of myself'. His real gift was as an educator, and it was an inspired decision on his part, as principal of Adams College, to allow the exchange visits with Michaelhouse.

Looking back in 1979, Brown recalled the dramatic impact of his visit to Adams College:

> I first knew him [Edgar Brookes] as a schoolboy. When he was principal of Adams College I went there with a party from my school on an exchange visit. Such visits, between a white school and a black school, were a revolutionary concept in the Natal of 40 years ago. And my visit had on me the effect they were no doubt intended to have. It shattered the accumulated stereotypes about black people with which I had grown up.[8]

Brown would recall that, at Michaelhouse, he 'certainly had more of an interest in the race question than probably most of the others did', and this was in part fuelled by his visit to Adams College.[9] However, the radicalising effect of the Adams visits should not be overestimated. For some pupils, it reinforced the natural order of things. An entry entitled 'Impressions of Adams' by 'NTA and HWM' in the *St Michael's Chronicle* for 1942 records the impressions of two boys who spent a week at Adams. Their conclusion is telling: 'As a result of the unselfish work of both European and Bantu staffs, and the cooperation of all, Adams is proving a great success, and catering for two of South Africa's most pressing needs – native teachers and cheaper skilled labour.'[10]

Michaelhouse offered 'race relations' as a subject in post-matric. The school also tried to stimulate among its pupils an interest in 'native' culture. For example, Hugh Tracey, then Durban branch manager of the South African Broadcasting Corporation and later one of the major figures of modern ethnomusicology, gave a lecture on 'native music' to the Music Society in Brown's matric year (1941).[11] The Debating Society, of which Brown was a

member, also paid attention to 'native affairs'. The Society met on
6 September 1941 to debate the motion that 'The present difficulties between the two European races of South Africa will be sub-
merged in the face of the growing Native Problem'. During the
general discussion that followed, the House was addressed by
Senator Brookes. The first vote was narrowly lost by 14 votes to 16,
and the second, on opinion, was won by 19 votes to 17.[12] The Debating Society did not always address such lofty concerns. In 1941,
the motion, 'In the opinion of this house pets lead to effeminacy',
was carried by 32 votes to 22.[13]

Michaelhouse got Brown thinking about race relations. As an
alumnus, he would get very upset when he thought the school was
lending support to the government's racial policies. He would frequently fire off a letter of protest to the Rector and Board of
Governors when Michaelhouse invited to address its Speech Day
someone Brown found politically dubious. In 1963, it was CH
Rautenbach, Rector of the University of Pretoria and Chairman of
the state's Education Advisory Council.[14] In 1965, it was the Administrator of Natal, Theo Gerdener, who had formerly served as a
Provincial Councillor for the Nationalists. 'Who next?', wrote Brown
to Chairman of the Board, 'Mr Vorster [the Minister of Justice],
perhaps? Dr Verwoerd [the Prime Minister]?' By the 1960s, he felt
that 'the school [had] become so closely tied to the established
order in South Africa that it no longer produces, in any significant
number, men who will see and fight the evils in that order'. 'Does
the school serve the purpose for which it was founded?' he asked
the Chairman of the Board of Governors.[15] And the uneasiness persisted over time: for instance, he took issue with Hendrik Verwoerd's obituary in the *Michaelhouse Chronicle*[16], and he viewed with
'the gravest misgivings' the invitation to Rhodesian Prime Minister
Ian Smith to address the boys.[17]

For the most part at school, Brown remembered going 'along
with the defined path of trying to pass matric, playing games, and
so on'. Having been moved up a class at Cordwalles, he was in a
higher age cohort at Michaelhouse. He recalled being 'quite good
at passing exams – not so good at remembering what I learnt a year
later'. In his matric year, Brown was made a prefect in Pascoe

house, along with his cousin Henry Barnby. Barnby, whose mother was Hugh Brown's sister, was a good friend, as were Bud Chaplin, Duchesne Grice and Rex Pennington, alongside whom Brown later saw active service; and Simon Roberts, with whom Brown played first-team cricket.[18] Both Roberts and Grice were to become life-long friends. Pennington would go on to become Rector of Michael-house between 1969 and 1977.

In his post-matric year, 1942, Brown was made head boy. With characteristic self-deprecation, he would later ascribe this to hav-ing 'been there longer than anybody else'.[19] That year he was elected captain of the squash team and awarded colours.[20] At Speech Day on 1 October 1942, Lord Harlech, the guest of hon-our and then British High Commissioner in South Africa, appealed to the boys to 'make a sacrifice' by eschewing a 'security job' in commerce and industry. Instead he urged them to go into the 'nation-building professions', such as the civil service, public administration and professional politics. He also predicted that the war would produce a swing to the left from which South Africa could not isolate itself. He urged the boys: 'We have got to have far greater social unity; we have got to have better conditions for all races so that slums and the like are no longer tolerable, that bad public health is intolerable, while racial relations have got to be put on a better footing.'[21]

The official history of Michaelhouse claims that, for the boys, 'the war was a swirling mist, sometimes clearing so that it was hardly noticeable, occasionally so enveloping as to halt them in their tracks, mostly evident as a bank ahead, beyond which lay university or careers and the questions of a new order and peace'.[22] It is difficult to reconstruct Brown's personal experience of the war, or to weigh the importance of Lord Harlech's speech in his decision to join up. Certainly, by his post-matric year, a number of Brown's older peers had enlisted. His brother Craig had joined the navy at the begin-ning of war and was stationed in the Far East for the duration. All of these factors must have influenced Brown's decision to visit a recruiting office in Durban in October 1942, where he signed up and was assigned to the Tank Corps.

A few months short of his eighteenth birthday, Brown took the decision without hesitating. To him it was the 'obvious thing to do'.[23] Despite never having been drawn to the military life – his father was a conscientious objector and he had hated cadets at school – for Brown 'there was no question that that was what one wanted to do as soon as one got out of school'.[24]

3

WAR
1942-1945

The outbreak of the Second World War in September 1939 polarised South Africa. On 4 September, the Prime Minister and leader of the ruling United Party, General Hertzog, moved in Parliament that the House should adopt a position of neutrality. His deputy, General Smuts, moved an amendment to Hertzog's motion, calling on the Union to declare war on Germany. Smuts's amendment was carried by 80 votes to 67. The following day, Hertzog resigned his premiership and rejoined the National Party. On 6 September, the Governor General, Sir Patrick Duncan, asked Smuts to form a new government. And so South Africa went to war.

The war had some immediate political consequences domestically: it led to a reunification of Afrikaner nationalists in the *Herenigde* (Reunited) *Nasionale Party* and a hardening of attitudes – towards empire, towards English-speaking South Africans and towards blacks – among the Afrikaner nationalist right. The war also seemed, for a time, to tilt the United Party in a more liberal direction. The wartime imperative for increased production led to rapid industrialisation and increased African urbanisation, which in turn catapulted segregation into crisis. Economic integration was leading to social integration between the races, and in 1942 Smuts himself told the liberal South African Institute of Race Relations that segregation had 'fallen on evil days'.[1] That same year, the Smit Report on the social, health and economic conditions of urbanised blacks recommended the administrative recognition of African trade unions and the abolition of pass laws.[2] The pro-democratic climate created by the fight against fascism, which led many liberals to engage more directly with notions of egalitarianism, universal franchise and the common society, also acted as a fillip to South African liberalism in the 1940s.[3]

These, then, were the prevailing political winds as Brown journeyed one Wednesday afternoon in October by train to Cullinan in the Transvaal, and from Cullinan to his new temporary home – a training camp at Kaffirskraal, near Klerksdorp.

Life at Kaffirskraal was monotonous. Describing his daily activities in a letter to his mother, to whom he wrote once a week with only irregular interruptions throughout the war, Brown noted:

> We have breakfast at 6:30 and fall in for the day's work at about a quarter to eight. We then have two periods [of squad drill] of about an hour and then break for tea at ten o'clock. We then have another three periods before lunch which is at about one. We get an hour off for lunch and then start again. There are only two periods in the afternoon and so we are finished by about 3:45 and then are free until the next morning unless you have extra drill, which is fairly easy to avoid.

Life at Kaffirskraal was made more bearable by the company of his cousin and friend, 'Archie' McKenzie, with whom he played tennis and drank beer in the canteen, Wednesday night 'bioscopes', grills at the YMCA recreation hall and occasional weekend visits to one of his mother's sisters, Nancy Brayshaw, in Johannesburg.[4] In Johannesburg, in the company of his cousins, Brown would meet civilian friends and go dancing in Orange Grove.

Late in 1942, Brown and a number of others who had joined the Tank Corps were reassigned to the Signal Corps. Theirs was the 'rather unromantic' job, Brown would later recall, 'of stringing [the] infantry platoons together with telephone wire'.[5] He told his mother that he 'hadn't the least desire to become a signaller, but the majority of the Rookie Depot were taken by force and dumped in it, so I suppose I will have to make the best of it'.[6] At the end of

January 1943, the signallers were sent to Piet Retief for further training. They stayed at a camp where the conditions seemed luxurious compared to Kaffirskraal: bungalows and beds made a decent change from gravel floors and leaky tents.

The transition was short-lived, however. In February, they were sent back to Kaffirskraal, and later to a camp called Balloon, where they waited with growing impatience to be incorporated into the 6th South African Armoured Division and sent 'up north', as military service in North Africa was known. By March, Brown had 'had just about a stomachful of this signalling racket' and the never-ending wait to join the '6th'.[7]

But in April, events began to gather momentum. From Balloon, Brown's unit was taken to the Hay Paddock camp in Pietermaritzburg, from where, one night, they were taken by train to Durban, put on the troopship *Ile de France* and dispatched to Egypt, where Brown was 'plonked right in the middle of the desert with just about nothing to be said in its favour'.[8]

Brown's letters to his mother from Egypt suggest a heightened sense of introspection and a nascent concern with the direction in which his future studies might lead him. In one of his first letters home, he asked her to send him books of poetry ('Keats, Rupert Brooke & De La Mare'), a Zulu dictionary, a grammar book and one or two Zulu stories, and some books on native affairs.[9] For the rest, his letters home tell of his sporting activities in camp (cricket and hockey), gatherings at the YMCA, leave periods in Cairo, and they inquire after the welfare of his sister, Bet, and his three mares stabled at Nottingham Road.

Brown's network of family, friends and associates from Natal, including 'Bud' Chaplin, Duchesne 'Doosh' Grice, Murray Otto, Rex Pennington and his cousins Henry Barnby and Archie McKenzie, helped him withstand the boredom and gloominess sometimes induced by long periods of inactivity in camp. Brown celebrated his nineteenth birthday with them in December. He recounted to his mother, who had sent a cake and £5 for the occasion, how, 'with the aid of a little alcoholic stimulus', the group was soon 'exercising our vocal chords in grand style'. 'I showed distinct promise as a soloist', he boasted, 'and the chorus had volume, if nothing much else. Further entertainment was provided by Barnby's recitations and Otto's Zulu war dance. A grand success!'[10]

In Alexandria, where he took leave with Henry in November, Brown met with the Whitfields, a couple whose son had been a contemporary of his at Michaelhouse. Whitfield was the chief of police in Alexandria, and he and his wife entertained Brown and Henry Barnby to lunch and dinner. But despite his privileged background and social connections, Brown experienced the war as an ordinary soldier. Looking back on his wartime experiences towards the end of his life, he felt that one effect of the war had been to 'establish a sort of other rank/officer, sort of class conflict', adding that 'I was on the lower – the bottom – end of that class conflict, and that probably didn't do me any harm either'.[11] One of his best friends during the war was a white miner, someone who Brown probably would not have met during the normal course of life, and whose acquaintance he found 'a broadening experience'.[12] Brown remained a private throughout his wartime service and claimed that it 'would have bothered me if I had been promoted'.[13]

His contact with Africans and Coloureds was more limited, but the Union's racial problems played very much on his mind as he struggled to work out his views from afar. Commenting to his mother on an article by Senator Brookes, he said:

> Personally I think the most important problem at the moment is to improve the Native's living conditions and his health, before you even think of raising his educational and social standing. But, on the other hand, education may be the best way in which that can be achieved. Our European population is so small as compared with the Native that I'm pretty sure that the only way in which we can improve their conditions is by giving the Natives themselves a chance to help themselves. And the only way in which that aim can be reached is through education. Heaven knows! I'm completely out of touch, so that bit of blurb is mere guess work.[14]

In his first letter of the year for 1944, Brown asked his mother to send him a copy of *The Black Man's Burden*.[15] Published under the authorial pseudonym of Jan Burger but penned by the historian Leo Marquard, who served as the Deputy Director of the Army Education Services during the war and who later became the Liberal Party's first national chairman, this tract was widely read by South African servicemen.

Marquard punted a left-liberal line. He lamented the withering of liberalism under the United Party. In part the UP's failure to effect liberal reforms to native affairs, he argued, was a result of the fusion in 1934 of its two constituent parties – Smuts's South African Party and Hertzog's National Party. Marquard claimed that:

> The union of the two major parties ... had a dampening effect on liberalism, since the Government was strong enough in numbers to be able to ignore so scattered a vote, and weak enough, inherently, to be afraid of offending the right wing of its party. Further, the United Party professed to unite English and Afrikaners; but the union was pre-carious, and any suggestions for reform were rejected on the convenient grounds that they might imperil the rela-tions between English and Afrikaners. The result is that lib-eralism is fighting a gallant rear-guard action, and all it can do is to try to prevent the forces of reaction from having it all their own way. It is, indeed, apparent that the limits of reformism have been reached, and that any further improvement in the living conditions of the non-European proletariat will have to be achieved along the lines of indus-trial action rather than by liberal influence in politics.[16]

Marquard, the liberal disillusioned with liberal parliamentary poli-tics, came to the conclusion that the establishment could only be changed by 'an indigenous socialism purged of the colour bar – a socialism based on class and not on race'.[17]

Brown read *The Black Man's Burden* with great interest. He told his mother that 'provided the people who read it attempt to carry out a little of what he [Marquard] advocates things may begin to look up a little'. Warming to his theme, he continued:

That's not enough though. Unless we start a nationwide
campaign against disease, malnutrition, ignorance and the
thousand and one other evils which beset the Native I'm
afraid our whole system is going to come back on us. I've
been doing a bit of heavy thinking lately & plans are beginning to formulate themselves. If I ever get the chance to put
them into practice they'll probably land me in gaol, but
even that might be quite an experience.[18]

What exactly Brown was thinking he did not elaborate, but his
words were prophetic: sixteen years later, he would be imprisoned
for his 'plans'.

Brown's letters to his mother in 1944 reflect a growing interest
in politics. In February, he wrote: 'This week's local UDF [Union
Defence Force] paper was brimful of Parliament's activities and
especially the new social security Bill. The paper disappeared before I had a chance to study it in any detail but, at least, it does look
as if they are beginning to face up to our problems at last.'[19] In
November he informed her that he was 'immersed' in a book
called *Colour Conflict*. He felt that whenever the author compared
South Africa with some of its neighbours, 'we seem to come off a
very bad worst'. But Brown was hopeful that 'the country is at last
beginning to awaken to its responsibilities'.[20] Not all his letters
home were equally high-minded. At one point he told his mother
that he and Bud had decided that their life's work was to set up a
nightclub 'on an unprecedented scale of luxury in Durban'.[21]

In May 1944, Brown's signal unit, which by that time was
attached to an infantry regiment (comprising the Imperial Light
Horse and the Kimberley Regiment) in the 11th South African
Armoured Brigade, was sent to Italy. Brown spent most of the
winter of 1944/1945 in the Apennines; moved slowly north of
Florence across Italy; and took part in the last offensive, ending up
near Milan, where the German forces in Italy surrendered on 29
April 1945. On 8 May, Winston Churchill announced that the
German high command had surrendered. The war in Europe was
over.

Brown wrote to his mother that the German surrender had

'come as a shock' but that there was 'no particular excitement' when he heard the news: 'The main feeling is one of relief that there will be no more ducking and diving or crawling out of bed in the middle of the night to go and do a job ... I can't help feeling that our little group has been extremely lucky not to have lost more than it did.'[22]

Soon after the fall of Milan, Brown went to the coast at Rapallo where, he advised his mother, he 'spent my pleasantest four days since Henry and I made use of the Whitfields in the old Alexandria days'.[23] Later that month he stayed at a 'badly run' hotel in Maggiore.[24] In September, Brown and a group of friends went on a 'Venice pass'. They made it to the Austrian border and ended up in Munich and Berlin.[25] Brown would later evoke 'the terrible devastation in those places ... the terrible poverty of those people who had nothing to eat ... and ... dressed in rags most of them'.[26]

While he was in Italy, Maisie made enquiries about sending her younger son to Cambridge. Both his father and his older brother had been at Jesus College, and Maisie was determined that Peter should follow in their footsteps. At the time, Brown was undecided about his future plans. Faced with a demobilisation questionnaire, he told his mother: 'I think I shall just tell them that I'll be continuing my education, and they can battle with that. The more I think of it the more convinced I become that the farm is the place for me.'[27] In the event, he indicated that he would go to university to study either Agriculture or Arts, and he named Rhodes University as his first choice, though adding that his training might take him overseas.[28] What Brown later identified as 'footlooseness'[29] may have attracted him to Cambridge, or at least made him acquiesce, initially, in his mother's wishes. Not that freedom from family ties would have been his overriding concern; having learnt that his cousins Archie and Henry were also likely to go up to Cambridge after the war, he noted with satisfaction that 'things promise to be quite homely'.[30]

However, as the demobilisation period wore on, Brown became increasingly uncertain about his postwar prospects. In August he wrote to his mother: 'I'm damned if I can think of any job ... that stirs me with the slightest interest.'[31] In September he told her that he hoped she had not got 'too far' with 'this Cambridge business', because 'however I may have felt about going to a University a year ago, I'm very much against it now'.[32] And if he did decide to pursue a career that required a degree, he told her, he would prefer to attend a South African university. The family business did not hold much appeal, since that would be 'too much like walking into a livelihood that came as the result of Dad's & Grandpa's & Craig's work'. Instead, Brown wanted a job that he could succeed in through his own efforts, preferably something 'out in the open' that offered 'spice and variation'.

The concern which he had shown for race relations at school, and which he occasionally expressed in his wartime letters, seemed, for the moment, to have given way to indifference and ennui. In later years, Brown would offer the following explanation:

> ... [A]t school this race relations thing had become an interest of mine. I certainly came back [from the war] and thought: 'Well, to hell with it, this world now owes me a peaceful life.' And I, initially anyway, had no urge to get involved in that kind of thing again. And, I suppose I had to be shaken out of that, before I did begin to get involved again.[33]

So when Brown set sail for South Africa, on 5 January 1946, it was with no firm grasp of what the future had in store for him. Any thoughts of public service were far from his mind. All he wanted, after the tumult of the previous three-and-a-half years, was peace and quiet. He found it on his mother's property in Mooi River, where he began to learn how to farm.

4

CAMBRIDGE AND THE AFRICAN AWAKENING
1946-1948

B rown had always been interested in farming. In 1858, the original McKenzie settlers, Duncan and his wife Margaret Campbell, had bought a farm in the Fort Nottingham area from Ste-
phanus Johannes Maritz – brother of the Voortrekker leader,
Gerrit Maritz – and it had remained in the family. Hugh Brown's
sister was married to a man who farmed at Nottingham Road.
There was also a cousin who farmed at Lion's Bush. Brown spent
part of many of his school holidays with his cousins on these farms,
and this instilled in him a lifelong love of the countryside – as well
as a curiosity about farming.

Before Hugh Brown died, he bought a small farm at Mooi
River, 'Brownstones', where he sent his polo ponies to rest. During
the war, Maisie Brown made it her headquarters and handed over
the Musgrave Road house to Bet. It didn't take much to convince
Peter – freshly demobbed, in no rush to take up university studies,
and in search of a life 'out in the open' – that farming might be his
calling. Reminiscing about his return to South Africa after the war,
Brown remarked: 'Well, I thought, that's a good life for me, I'll go
and farm and that will be it'.[1]

Although Brown took to livestock farming naturally, and settled
in easily at Brownstones, he was eventually persuaded by his
mother that he needed a degree to his name, and that the Faculty
of Agriculture at Cambridge was the best place to earn it. Perhaps
feeling a little restless after a few months back in South Africa, this
time he didn't resist. Nine months after his return home, he set off

abroad once more. He left for England at the end of September 1946 with his cousin Henry Barnby, who was going up to Oxford. A desert storm forced them to stop over in Cairo, where they revisited their wartime haunts. When they arrived in London, Brown was picked up from the air terminal by his brother, Craig, and almost immediately the pair set off to buy saddles, bridles and bits at the 'horsey shops'.[2]

Brown arrived at Jesus College, Cambridge, on 5 October. His first impressions were not favourable. A day after his arrival, he complained to his mother in the tones of the barefoot colonial that he had 'never seen so many peculiar looking creatures, gathered together in one place, in my life before'.[3] A week into his course, he wasn't 'very much impressed with either the course or the lecturers so far'.[4] He took four main subjects: Agricultural Botany, Soil Science, Agriculture and the History and Economics of Agriculture. The first two he described as 'pure Greek' but the second two were 'at least intelligible even if they are beyond me'.[5] Brown regretted that there was nothing 'practical in the way of crops or stock' on the course, and only two weeks into his spell at Cambridge he predicted: 'I don't think I'll come back next year.'[6]

Brown disliked Cambridge and he never settled, despite the fact that a number of his closest South African friends were at Cambridge (Bud Chaplin and Simon Roberts) and Oxford (Henry Barnby and Rex Pennington) at the same time. Almost immediately his thoughts turned to how soon he could leave. He wrote to his mother in November: 'As far as this place goes there isn't really a great deal to say. I wish I could say that I liked it, but honestly Ma, I think it's quite awful.'[7] The passage of a miserable northern hemisphere winter steeled Brown's resolve not to return. He informed his mother in January 1947:

> There isn't a single thing I like about this place other than a few of the buildings to look at and a few of the people to talk to. I'm afraid that even in time I wouldn't come to like their public school regulations and not even in a hundred years could I come to like the twirps [sic] who go to make up the Faculty of Agriculture. The more I see of the course

the more convinced I become that it's all very well for somebody who intends to take up research, but for my sort I
don't think it's so good. We honestly haven't learnt a single
thing of practical value since we started.[8]

Brown enjoyed inspecting cattle on the University farm – he told
his mother that he thought Herefords were the breed for him[9] –
but he found the theoretical aspects of his course tedious and
impractical. A hands-on man, Brown quickly became impatient
with abstract notions. He was a doer, and whatever he learnt he
sought to apply: he would, in due course, adopt the same approach
to politics.

The December vacation provided some welcome relief from
Cambridge. Brown got together a group of about fifteen friends
to go skiing in Pontresina, Switzerland. The contingent included
several South Africans who were studying or living in England,
among them Barnby, Pennington, Gavin Relly (who, after his
studies at Oxford and a brief stint working for the then UP leader,
Sir de Villiers Graaff, started his career at Anglo American in 1949
as Harry Oppenheimer's private secretary and later succeeded
Oppenheimer as chairman in 1983) and Brown's cousin, Christianne 'Chris' McKenzie. Chris was related to Peter on both his
mother and father's sides: her mother, Helen Mary Brown (who
coincidentally bore the same name as Peter's mother), was a first
cousin of Hugh Brown's and had married Maisie Brown's brother,
Archibald McKenzie. Sixty years on, Chris recalled the holiday as
being a 'great success': 'The first night everybody was a bit reticent
about dancing, but Peter started the whole thing off by dancing
with the barmaid.'[10] Brown was the jester of the group. He got
going backwards down a slope one day and couldn't stop. He came
to an inelegant end in a cow barn under a house. 'All down the
road, Chris reminisced, 'the maids were shaking out pillows on the
roofs, and they found it hilarious'.

Brown found Cambridge less conducive to mirth. Already at
the beginning of the Lent term, a plan had begun to take shape in
his mind. He wrote to his mother in January 1947, informing her
that he would see out the academic year, wander around England

in the summer, and then, 'provided truck & partners were forthcoming', travel back home overland through Africa. He told her, 'I
think it would be just the greatest thing & certainly the only way to
see a fair slice of Africa', but he knew she would be displeased. 'I
can hear your disapproval from here,' he wrote, adding, 'Still that's
the way I feel & unless something remarkable happens I can't see
myself coming back again.'[11]

Ever since his demobilisation, Brown had been drifting. The
idea of farming at Mooi River appealed to him, but he also wanted
to be footloose. When his mother raised with him the possibility of
going up to Cambridge again, he thought, as he would later phrase
it: 'Well, there's another escape for another year or two before I do
anything serious.'[12] His course at Cambridge failed to capture his
imagination, and, because he was by nature a serious and thought-
ful young man, he longed for something that would spark his mind
and give him a sense of purpose. Ironically, he found it at Cambridge, at a meeting addressed by the South African-born novelist,
Peter Abrahams. This was Brown's road to Damascus.

Born in Vrededorp near Johannesburg in March 1919, Peter
Abrahams was the son of a black African father and a mixed-race
French-African mother. In terms of South Africa's warped system of
racial classification, this made him 'Coloured'. His father died when
Abrahams was still a young boy, and his mother suffered from per-
sistent poor health. Abrahams grew up poor, and he worked from a
young age – as a tinsmith's helper, a kitchen worker and a dish-
washer – to put himself through school. A keen student of literature, he began writing short stories and poetry at the age of 11.
After school, he found it difficult to find work as a journalist in
South Africa, and so in 1939 he took a job on a merchant ship and
spent two years at sea before disembarking in England. Once there,
he became a regular contributor to the *Daily Worker*, a communist
newspaper, while he pursued a career as a literary writer. His early
works, including the short story collection *Dark Testament* (1942)
and the novels *Song of the City* (1945) and *Mine Boy* (1946), all
explored the hardships of life as a black South African and the har-
rowing effects of racial discrimination. *Mine Boy* brought Abrahams
to international attention and went on to become a classic.

It was Abrahams who, on a winter's day in February 1947, brought home to Brown the brutality and the injustice of the South African racial order, and rekindled in him the desire, which he had first experienced at Michaelhouse, to do something about it. The meeting addressed by Abrahams was organised by a group of communist students, and Brown had been encouraged by some of his white South African peers to go along and 'jeer or catcall or boo'.[13] But when Abrahams spoke, Brown was enraptured. He wrote to his mother in a state of great excitement about the meeting:

> This week I went to a meeting on the Colour Bar at home at which one of our Natives from home could, and did, get up and say how he and all the rest of them felt. It was a revelation of our own blindness, and it decided me. I reckon we've been patting ourselves on the backs and saying that things must be done, but they must be done slowly, for long enough. I also reckon that unless things start to move a great deal faster pretty soon there's going to be one hell of an explosion. There's also a lot of talk by people like ourselves about getting the right sort of people to go into it, but none of us are ever prepared to do it. Well, I can go in for it without even the risks of not being able to make a living out of it, so if I don't, I can't think of any reason why anyone else should. So there I am, and no amount of talking to my conscience will make it shut up so for my own comfort it's Native Affairs all over again, as it was before the war.[14]

When he was older, Brown became interested in the writings of the nineteenth-century Russian liberal thinker, Aleksandr Herzen, who campaigned for agrarian reform and the emancipation of serfs in his homeland. Brown took to heart Herzen's aphorism, 'We have to open men's eyes, not tear them out', and in his encounter with Abrahams he underwent that eye-opening experience. Brown, who as a white South African had grown up to accept the state of race relations, despite moments of doubt and questioning at school, was jolted out of his complacency by Abrahams. It was a revelation of his own blindness, and it decided him: he must make a career for himself in native affairs – although exactly what that might entail he was still unsure – to help head off the racial 'explosion' that seemed to him, two years before the apartheid government was even voted into power, inevitable.

In a long letter to his mother, Brown explained the circumstances that led to this moment of self-discovery. He tried to persuade her that that although farming would probably be the most pleasant job he could take on, it 'certainly wouldn't be the most useful':

> When the war came to an end and I eventually got home I managed to bluff myself into thinking that by risking my neck a few times I had squared off my debt to humanity and could sit back and relax and enjoy things in an easy comfortable way for the rest of my days. That was an error of thought that persisted, with occasional lapses until I left home ... Then the Christmas holiday and when I got back here I wasn't so engrossed in the course and began to think things over a little more rationally. That I should inherit money without having earned it has always been a weight on my conscience and I always reckoned it entailed its obligations. At first I thought that by farming well and importing stock and breeding good stuff which would be made easily available to the people who most needed it, I might fulfil that obligation ... All the time, though, I knew that the people who really had the greatest claim on me were the Natives, but I just didn't have the courage to admit it.[15]

Having found the courage, through Abrahams, to admit it, Brown asked his mother to inquire about an appropriate university course in South Africa and how long it would last. He concluded playfully: 'And then, by the time that's over I hope to heaven to have decided what my activities are to be and what direction they'll lead to. Probably a short-cut to hell, but it should be a pretty interesting short-cut.'

Maisie consulted Edgar Brookes, who suggested that Brown continue his agricultural studies and enter the agricultural section of the Native Affairs Department. There he would supervise the agricultural training of native farmers in the reserves, assist in the rehabilitation of the reserves and, possibly, ultimately rise to the directorship of Native Agriculture.[16] Alternatively, Brookes suggested, he could do a BA in Bantu Studies with Zulu and Social Anthropology or Roman Law as majors. An LLB would remove any barriers to the top of a department. 'In due course,' he advised Maisie, 'he would become Native Commissioner of a District and could with luck rise to the leadership of the Department.'

Maisie forwarded Brookes's letter to her son. Although he was excited to switch to a BA in Bantu Studies, the prospect of life as a Native Commissioner didn't fill him with enthusiasm. Instead, he told his mother, his plan was 'eventually [to] stir up my own little bit of trouble independently'.[17] She also sent him prospectuses for the relevant courses at the universities of Cape Town and the Witwatersrand. Brown inclined to Wits because there, he explained to Maisie, 'you have the full picture of the Native trying to adjust himself to urban life'. Besides, he had more friends in Johannesburg than Cape Town. In the end, however, on the advice of Brookes, Brown registered for a two-year Diploma in Native Law and Administration at the University of Cape Town (UCT) in 1948, and stayed on for a third year to obtain his BA.

His change of course having been settled, Brown elected not to write his end-of-year exams at Cambridge. Instead he focused his energies on organising his trip through Africa. He spent June and July 1947 punting on the Cam, swimming, playing cricket and holidaying in Italy, where he met up with Rex Pennington, Gavin Relly and Graham Boustred (who also went on to a career in senior management at Anglo American). Most of his time, however, was spent in London, trying to find a suitable truck and meeting potential travelling companions, to which end he placed an advertisement in the *Times* on Tuesday 10 June. Brown wanted five passengers. By Saturday 14 June he had already received thirty letters in response to his call.[18] After a few days of interviews, he excitedly informed his mother: 'My success has been something far beyond my wildest dreams and I think I should be able to get five people who will fit in together just about as well as possible.'[19] They included a married English couple of about thirty by the name of Hartshorn, and a young South African mechanic called Jack Caudron. By the end of July Brown had found a suitable old army truck.

The group intended to leave the United Kingdom on 9 September from Folkestone, travel along the French coast into Spain, cross into Morocco via Gibraltar and follow the coastal road to Algiers. From Algiers they would go south along the so-called Hoggar route across the Sahara into Niger, and then wend their way across Nigeria, Cameroon, French Equatorial Guinea, the Congo, Uganda and Kenya. From there, they would play the route by ear.

At the end of October, the troop was still holed up in Tangier, waiting on the authorities to process their visa applications for French West Africa and Equatorial Africa.[20] They eventually left Algiers on 27 November.[21] Brown found the desert heavy going: 'From [Laghouat] on there was no pleasure in driving,' he wrote home, 'it was just a question of some parts being not quite as bad as others ... It was really quite a struggle and I can't say I enjoyed it.'[22] The truck broke down frequently, and two days out of Algiers he contracted jaundice. But by the time Brown's party reached Kano in December, where they installed themselves in a spacious former officers' mess, things were 'just about as good as they could be', with everyone enjoying 'living in the lap of luxury'.[23]

On 16 January 1948, Brown reached Kenya. He wrote his last recorded letter home from the trip the following day.[24] Like the rest of his letters to his mother at the time, it is matter-of-fact. It provides few insights into the places he had travelled through, the characters (or even names) of the people he had been travelling with, and some of the more light-hearted incidents along the way. Only occasionally is it leavened with a flash of dry, self-deprecating wit. But it is, after all, a letter to his mother. Brown's trip through Africa, even if he did not articulate it, must have been, like his encounter with Abrahams, an eye-opening experience of its own kind. It was unusual in the 1940s for a white South African (most of whom still self-identified as 'Europeans') to want to explore and discover Africa in the way Brown did. The journey was also symbolic: it marked the end of Brown's postwar period of 'footloose-ness'. Now he was returning home to answer Abrahams's call.

INTO 'NATIVE AFFAIRS': THE UNIVERSITY OF CAPE TOWN
1948-1950

No sooner had Brown arrived back in Natal from his African trip than he had to make his way to Cape Town for the start of the academic year, at the end of February. The subjects he took in the first year of his diploma were Native Law and Administration, Social Anthropology, Economics and Xhosa. Having grown up in Natal, Brown knew a smattering of Zulu, so he was disappointed that only Xhosa was offered.[1]

He found Cape Town much more congenial than Cambridge, and quickly settled into the ex-servicemen's residence on campus, which was called by its occupants – in somewhat macabre fashion – 'Belsen', after the Nazi concentration camp, Bergen-Belsen. The counterpart for ex-servicewomen was likewise dubbed 'Buchenwald', and it was there that Brown's cousin Daphne McKenzie (Chris's sister) took up residence while she studied medicine. Brown took Daphne to the university dance for ex-servicemen and -women in April, so that, he reported home, she could 'have her toenails flattened'.[2]

Brown immersed himself in campus life. He joined the university's 'lowest'[3] rugby team, and proceeded to break his collarbone during a practice session. He took up squash once again, and it was on the squash court one particularly hot summer morning in 1948 that he met Bill Hoffenberg for the first time. Hoffenberg later recollected that they were both suffering from hangovers, which were seriously worsened by their exertions on the court, but which were rapidly relieved by the carton of beer that Brown produced from the boot of his car after their match.[4]

A medical student, Hoffenberg became one of Brown's closest and most enduring friends. He would later shadow Brown in his political involvements while pursuing a highly successful career as an endocrinologist. Hoffenberg introduced Brown to Antoinette 'Swaer' Swart, a young liberal Afrikaner from Tzaneen in the Northern Transvaal, who would go on to serve as the Minister of Health in Uganda before independence. She tried to involve Brown in setting up an 'International Club' at UCT – a forum for students of all races to meet and discuss topical issues, which never quite got off the ground.

Brown showed little interest in student politics, which in his recollection was aimed at 'trying to ensure that ex-servicemen got what they felt were their just deserts'.[5] The Student Representatives' Council (SRC) served as a lobby group for former soldiers, and it focused on the difficulties they experienced, financial and otherwise, in re-adapting to civilian life. Brown played no part in the SRC – 'it wasn't on my agenda',[6] he later said – nor did he take an active interest in Union politics in the way that some of his wartime letters home suggested he might. Although the war had pricked his liberal conscience and made him more aware of the political environment at home, Brown had little personal experience of Afrikaner nationalism. Like many other English-speaking South Africans, he didn't appreciate the depth of Afrikaner nationalist feeling, nor did he imagine that Smuts could lose the 1948 election. The result of the May election, which the National Party won, came as 'one most unpleasant shock' to Brown, who told his mother that he had hoped 'the war might have bred some sort of liberal outlook in this country'. 'Instead,' he lamented, 'we are to have "apartheid" and get on with the job of turning the clock back, just as fast as we possibly can.'[7]

His studies engaged him more than they had at Cambridge, and he did reasonably well at the end of his first year. He obtained a first for Xhosa, second-class passes in Native Law and Administration and Social Anthropology, and a third for Economics.[8] But he didn't find his time at UCT 'transformative'. Interviewed in his later years, he explained: 'I went there to try and pass exams. I suppose the only thing that was really of long term benefit was … that

I learnt enough about Xhosa to be able to convert what I learnt to Zulu.'[9] Few of his lecturers made a great impression on him, although the one that made Brown 'think most' was AC Jordan.[10] Jordan, whose son Pallo would become an ANC luminary, serving as a Minister in the administrations of both Nelson Mandela and Thabo Mbeki, was a distinguished academic and novelist. As a pioneer in Bantu languages and literature, the bulk of Jordan's creative output was written in his mother tongue, Xhosa, and he developed a new method of teaching Xhosa to non-speakers.

If Brown went through the motions to earn his degree, and if both student politics and national politics failed to engage his interest in a meaningful way, then his time at UCT was certainly transformative in one sense. For it was during this time – at the July Handicap race-day in Durban in 1948, in fact – that he met Phoebe Barlow, the pretty young daughter of the industrial tycoon, Charles Sydney 'Punch' Barlow.

The Barlows ran a corporate concern to be reckoned with. In 1902, Major Ernest 'Billy' Barlow formed Thomas Barlow & Sons in Durban, selling wool products and engineering components. In 1927, his son Punch, then an engineering graduate of twenty-two, sold the first Caterpillar tractor in South Africa. Thanks to Punch, Thomas Barlow & Sons became the official sales and service dealer for Caterpillar in South Africa. Punch proceeded to turn Barlow-rand, as the company was called after its acquisition of Rand Mines Limited in 1970, into a hugely successful conglomerate with diversified interests in mining, manufacturing and construction.

Punch Barlow was a hugely talented man. Educated at Caius College, Cambridge, he captained the Natal rugby team, was invited to the Springbok rugby trials of 1928, played county cricket for Somerset in England and was an accomplished golfer. He took up polo and captained the Springbok side to the Argentine Republic in 1952.

Punch and his wife, Cynthia, mixed in socially rarefied circles. Punch was a great friend of Harry Oppenheimer. In Johannesburg, the Barlows owned a house next door to Eric Gallo, who had founded the first South African recording company, Gallo Records, in 1932, and his wife, Kay. Punch would eventually divorce Cynthia and marry Kay, while Cynthia set up home at Vergelegen – the historic wine estate in Somerset West which Punch acquired in 1941 after the death of its previous owners, Sir Lionel and Lady Florence Phillips.

It was into this world of wealth and high society that Phoebe Barlow was born in 1930. When Bridget McCall married Harry Oppenheimer in 1943, Phoebe and her sister Dinah were bridesmaids. But, despite her privileged background, Phoebe, like Peter, had a social conscience and a genuine concern for those whose life circumstances were radically different to her own. When she met Peter, Phoebe was a volunteer worker for the Cape Flats Distress Association, which had been founded four years earlier to help alleviate the problems of poverty, disease and malnutrition on the Cape Flats.

Phoebe and Peter had in common a concern for the underdog; they shared a love for horses and polo (by now Peter was actively playing in tournaments); and they both knew wealth and privilege. Even so, Brown, who despite being warm and companionable could be shy and reticent, felt slightly out of his social depth and ill at ease with Phoebe's family. Phoebe remembers Peter as having a slightly 'wild' side at the time: after she met him at the July Handicap, their group went to the Cosmo nightclub in Durban. She was rather taken aback to see him take off his jacket and shoes, climb on the table, and start dancing frenetically. This was apparently his party trick. When Phoebe told her mother that she had met Peter, Cynthia, who knew of the Browns through polo circles, said: 'Oh, but he's a rather odd character, isn't he?'[11]

The August after Peter and Phoebe had met, he told his mother that he had been to 'rather a high class party out at the Barlows' last night'.[12] In September, he wrote to her:

> I seem to be elevating myself somewhat in the social scale these days. I can't quite think why. I found myself involved in a cocktail party at this polo-playing ... bloke's place on Tuesday night and out at the Barlows' today. I managed to survive the cocktail party somehow. I'm afraid I wasn't born to be a cocktail thing.[13]

In November he commented that he had 'just been very high class' and spent a few days at Vergelegen. But he confided to his mother: 'I don't think I was quite cut out to be a social success and having to behave reasonably well became a bit of a strain sometimes, but anyway I managed to survive.'[14] Brown found Vergelegen to be 'the most beautiful place', and he enjoyed riding, swimming and 'generally loaf[ing] around'. 'Phoebe is the name you must remember, Ma,' he gently chided. For their part, Punch and Cynthia welcomed Peter into their home, although they would become apprehensive about his politics in time to come – insofar as his politics took a toll on his home life.

Phoebe and Peter were married at the Anglican Church in Somerset West on 15 April 1950, and they held their wedding reception at Vergelegen, which remained in the Barlow family until 1987, when it was sold to Anglo American. Harry Lawrence, who had served as a minister in Smuts's government (first as Minister of Home Affairs between 1939 and 1943 and subsequently as Minister of Justice between 1945 and June 1948), gave one of the main speeches.

There were no signs yet that Brown himself, who was halfway through his final year as a student, was contemplating a career in politics. Yet with studies almost complete, and Peter Abrahams's dramatic testimony still fresh in his memory, he would have to give serious thought to how best he could apply his knowledge and 'stir up' his 'own little bit of trouble'. Brown was eager to return to Natal. So once more he approached Edgar Brookes for guidance, and that is how the newlyweds – back from their skiing holiday in Kitzbühel, Austria, in December 1950 – ended up in Pietermaritzburg the following year. There, Brown started his career at the Local Health Commission, which introduced him to the community of Edendale.

EDENDALE
1951-1952

The Browns moved to Pietermaritzburg in May 1951, and made their home in Mitchell Road – just off the Old Howick Road, which winds steeply up Town Hill towards Hilton. For two years they stayed on a property a few houses down from the residence that was to become their family home throughout their life together. The latter residence was Shinglewood, a large, sprawling house set on acres of land with neatly kept gardens at 14 Mitchell Road. Children arrived soon enough: first the twins, Christopher and Vanessa, on 31 December 1951, and then, four years later, another son, Anton, who was born disabled. Phoebe busied herself with child-raising while Peter immersed himself in his work at Edendale.

In the 1950s, Edendale, which lies a few kilometres outside Pietermaritzburg, was home to a bustling multiracial community. The settlement was started in 1851 by the Rev James Allison of the Wesleyan Missionary Society, on a farm he bought from the Voortrekker leader, Andries Pretorius. In 1860, the farm was subdivided into four parts: a residential area planned on urban lines that provided for a church and school, streets, water furrows and plots sold to Africans in freehold title; an agricultural area; commonage; and a marketplace and graveyard.

By the 1930s, conditions in Edendale were deteriorating. According to one historian: 'After many decades of no rubbish collection, no sewers, no housing standards, no regulations on animals, and no government support for good land husbandry, much of Edendale was a mess.'[1] There was extreme soil erosion, water pollution, residential overcrowding in the mud-and-wattle homes, and rampant disease such as tuberculosis. Edendale faced environmental collapse, a prospect that terrified the white residents of Pietermaritzburg, who viewed it as a risk to their own health.

In response, on 1 April 1942, the Natal Provincial Council proclaimed the 'Public Health Area of Edendale and District' and placed it under the control of the Local Health Commission (LHC).[2] The task of the LHC was to clean up the mess in Edendale without driving out the local population. In the 1940s, the LHC was run, in Brown's own words, by white 'benign paternalist[s], very concerned to do good'.[3] And their good intentions were translated into real achievements: by 1951 the LHC had built houses and clinics, bridges, roads, sewers and water mains.

Edgar Brookes thought that the LHC would be a good place for a young man like Brown to start his career, and he put in a good word on Brown's behalf with the Commission's chairman, TM Wadley (after whom Edendale's Wadley Stadium is named). Brown was stationed at the Commission's head office in Pietermaritzburg, but he spent much of his time fact-finding about conditions on the ground in Edendale. There, he met Henry Selby Msimang, one of five or six Africans who sat on the Edendale Advisory Board, which assisted the LHC in its work. Msimang was the Board's secretary, and he became Brown's political mentor and friend.

Selby Msimang was born in Edendale in 1886, and, after a varied career in Johannesburg and Bloemfontein as an interpreter, newspaper editor and labour organiser (at one point in the 1920s he was President of the Industrial and Commercial Workers Union), he settled back in Edendale in 1942. Msimang was one of the founding members of the South African Native National Congress in 1912 (the precursor to the ANC), and he served on its labour portfolio for many years. He was a prominent member of the committee that raised funds to send a Congress deputation to Britain in 1914, to lobby the British Parliament and the Colonial Office to repeal the Natives' Land Act of 1913. During the 1940s and 1950s, he was the ANC's provincial secretary in Natal. A titan of black resistance politics in twentieth-century South Africa – in addition to his political activism, he wrote prolifically condemning segregation and apartheid – Msimang was steeped in the non-racial tradition of Congress politics. He taught Brown a lot during the young man's brief stint at the Local Health Commission, and was a fixture in Brown's life until his death, four years short of his century, in 1982.

Brown did not stay long with the LHC because it decided, fairly soon into his employment, that he would be a good candidate to start a branch of the YMCA in Edendale, under the auspices of the Commission. Brown later recollected:

> I don't know how hard [the LHC] tried, but they didn't seem to be able to find a good practising Christian to start it and I eventually ended up getting that job. And we set up a YMCA in what was the old market at Edendale which had never been used ... because the people didn't grow enough, I suppose, to make it worthwhile. So that became the YMCA. And it was pretty fundamental stuff – it provided a venue for meetings and so on. Most of the activity, as it was, was centred around the schools and sports competitions and soccer league and netball league and that stuff.[4]

The LHC leased premises to the YMCA at the Georgetown Market Hall at a nominal rent of £1 per month. Their agreement was accepted by the Administrator of Natal in January 1952, but because of delays caused by structural adjustments and electricity installation, the hall was only officially opened by the Administrator on 26 June 1952.[5]

Brown seems to have started raising funds for the hall in November 1951. He appealed to the Pietermaritzburg Master Builders Association to donate benches, commenting in somewhat paternalistic fashion:

> The work I need hardly urge is one that must commend itself to all those interested in the development of the Bantu Youth ... The area is one which there is a danger of lawlessness unless the energies of African Youths are directed towards healthy recreation.[6]

In 1952, half of the Edendale YMCA's income came from a £500 grant given by the YMCA Natal Regional Council.[7] The LHC made a small contribution and Brown raised the rest, often tapping his old school for funds[8]. In 1952 he drew a modest annual salary of £450, but fortunately, he, Phoebe and the children didn't depend on it for their livelihood.[9]

As the YMCA's 'social worker' in Edendale, Brown's job was to run the social centre at the Georgetown Market Hall, which provided members with a variety of recreational facilities – including a cinema and a library, as well as various indoor games, boxing, table tennis and music and dancing. He also organised a sports programme for schoolchildren in the area. Every Friday afternoon during the school term, up to 500 children took part in football and basketball competitions. Brown enjoyed his work at the YMCA: it enabled him to indulge his sociable side; it offered him the 'spice and variation' which he sought, because he was not desk-bound; and, above all, it exposed him to life in a multiracial community.

There was quite a big Indian population in Edendale, and one of the people who Brown met during his YMCA days was Sam Chetty, a mild-mannered mechanic with a sharp sense of humour whose company Brown really enjoyed. Chetty was to provide Brown with one of his most valued and long-standing friendships across the colour line. Brown also met another of his closest black friends, Archie Gumede, at this time. Gumede, who was born in Pietermaritzburg in 1914, worked as a legal clerk and joined the ANC in 1949. He became the assistant secretary of the ANC's Pietermaritzburg branch, working alongside Selby Msimang, who was secretary at the time. In 1951, he was elected assistant secretary of the ANC in Natal. Later in the struggle against apartheid, he was the founding President of the United Democratic Front (UDF). Gumede was extremely fond of Brown and named his daughter Phoebe, after Brown's wife.

Men like Chetty, Gumede and Msimang opened Brown's eyes to what life was like for a black South African without rights of any kind. Their friendships helped to foster and crystallise Brown's deepening understanding of, and commitment to, non-racialism – the idea that your race should not determine your rights, responsibilities

and opportunities in life. When he delivered the second Alan
Paton Lecture at the University of Natal in 1995, Brown reflected
that 'it was at Edendale that I made my first real contact with black
Natalians, and began to learn something from which I had been
largely insulated up until that time'.[10]

Many of Brown's new friends and acquaintances were involved
in the ANC. They were politically well-informed and engaged.
Although Brown had at times in the past expressed an interest in
politics, he had never been actively drawn in, or sufficiently exer-
cised, to initiate his own participation. His experiences at Edendale changed that. But by 1952 it was also abundantly clear that
South African politics – and the role that liberal-minded whites like
Brown had to carve out for themselves – had been transformed by
the Nationalist victory in 1948.

Almost at once, the National Party set out to ensure complete
separation between black and white. The consequences for South
Africa were momentous. In the first three years of its rule, the
Nationalist government directed a barrage of racially discriminatory legislation through Parliament as it codified its policy of apartheid. The new laws included the Prohibition of Mixed Marriages
Act (1949); the Population Registration Act (1950), which entrenched racial classification; the Immorality Act (1950), which
prohibited all inter-racial sexual contact; and the Group Areas Act
(1950), which made residential segregation compulsory.

Participation by Africans, Coloureds and Indians in the body
politic was steadily eroded. The Natives' Representative Council
(NRC), established in 1936 to give Africans a semblance of representation by whites in Parliament in exchange for the elimination
of the Cape African franchise, and to which Msimang was elected
in 1948, was abolished. The Bantu Authorities Act (1951) replaced
the NRC with a system of government-sanctioned chiefs in the
reserves but made no allowances for African representation in
urban centres and 'white' rural areas. The Indian Representation
Act (1946), which the United Party had introduced to give Indians
white parliamentary representation, was annulled in 1950. In
1951, the Prime Minister, DF Malan, signalled his intention to
abolish the Coloured franchise.

The rigid separation of black and white, and the systematic erosion of black political rights, offended Brown deeply: they went
against what he was learning from his friends and experiences at
Edendale to be natural and fair and just. At the same time, he was
plagued by doubts about the real usefulness – to the residents of
Edendale and to 'race relations' generally – of his work for the
YMCA. The looming racial 'explosion', to which Peter Abrahams
had alerted him in 1947, and which Brown had forewarned in his
letter home, seemed to become more inevitable with the passing of
every day. Something had to be done. The LHC was an imperfect
vehicle. During his brief spell with the LHC, Brown had realised
that whatever liberal potential it had would be snuffed out by the
Nationalists; they would subvert the Commission and turn it into
an instrument of apartheid. Brown felt himself being pushed further and further into direct political action. Midway through 1952,
he finally took the step to which he had been building up, haphaz-
ardly and unconsciously, ever since he visited Adams College as
a schoolboy.

PART
TWO

7

THE PIETERMARITZBURG LIBERAL GROUP AND THE FORMATION OF THE LIBERAL PARTY
1952-1953

B rown's work at Edendale, and the contacts he made there, sensitised him to the plight of black South Africans under the Nationalist regime, and helped form his belief in the need for liberal, non-racial, opposition to apartheid. However, in the conventional arena of Union politics, Parliament, the voices of dissent were muffled.

The United Party, confronted with the apartheid juggernaut, submitted to creeping political paralysis. It timidly opposed discriminatory legislation here and there, while at other times it feebly mimicked the ruling party's language of white power. That small band of liberals in the UP caucus, heirs to the nineteenth-century Cape liberal tradition, thus became increasingly marginalised. In any event, the death in December 1948 of Smuts's deputy, Jan Hofmeyr – long regarded as a champion of liberalism in South Africa – dealt a decisive blow to mobilising whatever progressive forces existed in the UP.

The misplaced faith in Hofmeyr had a constraining effect on the liberal project in the period immediately after the end of the Second World War. Whatever his personal and political strengths, and he was endowed with many, Hofmeyr was not the man to rally liberals into action. That was to become the role of a new generation of leaders, like Brown.

* * *

The zeal with which the ruling party legislated to enforce white supremacy, assaulted civil rights and suppressed opposition was a spur to political action in the early 1950s.

There was a hardening of attitudes in the ANC, whose Youth League produced a Programme of Action in 1949 which shunned the conciliatory approach adopted by black activists over the previous four decades. The Youth League took a more militant line, advocating boycotts, stay-aways, mass action, strikes and acts of civil disobedience. The Defiance Campaign, launched by the ANC and the South African Indian Congress (SAIC) in June 1952 to protest against apartheid laws, manifested this altered approach to resistance politics.

Few white liberals had active links with the ANC at the time. Few understood the full import of African nationalism or could foresee how its growth would shape their own role in mediating between rival racial nationalisms. With the notable exception of Patrick Duncan, few white liberals joined the Defiance Campaign – and if they did, they tended to do so only towards its end.[1]

Even so, in white politics too it was a time of ferment. Many white ex-servicemen had been radicalised by their wartime experiences and by serving alongside black troops. Some had moved to the left through their membership of a socialist soldiers' 'trade union', the Springbok Legion. Others had imbibed liberal-democratic notions of inclusive citizenship through their encounters with the Army Education Services, whose second-in-command was the prominent liberal, Leo Marquard, founder of the National Union of South African Students (NUSAS) in 1924. For others still, like Brown, the fight against fascism had ingrained in them a profound aversion to tyranny of any kind.

Brown believed that the war had 'produce[d] a sort of special relationship between people who had been in it',[2] and this camaraderie was used to galvanise ex-servicemen into political action. The War Veterans' Torch Commando, for example, embarked on a dramatic campaign between 1951 and 1952 in defence of the Constitution. It staged torchlight rallies around the country in protest against the government's unconstitutional attempts to remove Coloured voters from the common roll.

The Torch Commando promised a new and radical form of political engagement, but this was stifled by the involvement of leaders and ordinary members whose primary interest was not the promotion of non-racialism. An older generation of liberals like Leslie Rubin, an attorney who later became a parliamentarian, was prepared to compromise for the sake of white political mobilisation; others, like Brown, were not.[3]

Brown attended the inaugural meeting of the Torch Commando in Pietermaritzburg, accompanied by a black school inspector he had met in Edendale, ABC Xaba. When the time came for them to join, however, Xaba was turned away. Unbeknown to Brown and Xaba, the organisation's membership was open only to whites. For Brown, the Torch Commando had 'abandoned [and] sidelined that particular [wartime] bond' between ex-servicemen of different races, and so he refused to enlist. In his undramatic way, Brown described the scenario years later: '… Xaba wanted to join, but they wouldn't have him, so I decided they wouldn't have me either'.[4]

Brown's political energies were soon to find another outlet. In June 1952, he invited a number of 'suspected liberals' to attend a gathering at his home. The invitation noted that 'if you are of liberal views you have probably been feeling rather helpless for quite a time and have been hoping for a lead from somebody in authority … there is no sign of that, so we will have to do it ourselves'.[5]

The immediate reasons for Brown's decision to assume the leadership mantle are not entirely clear. Although his outlook and sympathies had always been broadly liberal, and although he had a connection – through Edgar Brookes – to the liberal establishment, Brown had not followed a traditional liberal trajectory in any institutional sense. He was not involved in student politics at university; he never sought active involvement with NUSAS; and he was not yet a member of the SAIRR. There was a close-knit community of liberal intellectuals and political brokers in Cape Town – where Brown had been a student – centred around the Native Representatives in Parliament but also active in a plethora of extra-parliamentary initiatives like the Civil Rights League and the Institute of Citizenship. Brown was not part of this community.

Those who were to join the Liberal Party came to their liberalism in different ways. What is interesting in Brown's case is that he did so in a province, Natal, which, unlike the Cape, had no discernible political tradition of liberalism, nor one of non-racialism. There was an intellectual tradition, or strand of sorts, associated with thinkers like Edgar Brookes and Charles Loram in the 1920s, which, although styled as 'liberal' at the time, rejected the common society in favour of segregation. By the 1930s, Brookes, who became LP chairman after Brown was banned in 1964, recanted his segregationist views, but he had already helped to lay the ideological foundations of Hertzogite segregation.[6]

There was no network of quasi-political liberal bodies in the urban centres of Natal as there was in Cape Town, or even on the Witwatersrand, where the South African Institute of Race Relations was dominant. Men of Brown's class, background and upbringing – men of farming stock moreover – were more likely to be found supporting the conservative wing of the UP than seeking out 'suspected liberals' of a non-racial bent. Natalian farmer-politicians like George Heaton-Nicholls, the UP Member of Parliament who Paton described as a 'beetle-browed Imperialist' in his biography of Hofmeyr, usually combined conservative racial attitudes with a cloying jingoism.[7] Indeed, ever since Union in 1910, the major political preoccupation of white Natalians had been the maintenance of the imperial connection, which gave rise to endless tortuous debates about secession from the Union.[8]

Like-minded liberals often congregated together at the Anglophone universities. But Brown did not form part of that community of progressive academics, based at the Pietermaritzburg campus of the University of Natal, whose members formed a natural constituency for what was to become the Liberal Party, and from whose ranks a herder of liberal opinion might be expected to emerge. His decision to mobilise liberal opinion in 1952 may have been spurred by his experience with the Torch Commando. It was almost certainly influenced by his work in Edendale, where his contacts across the colour line and his experiences in a multiracial community sharpened what was to become the mainstay of his liberalism: a commitment to non-racialism. Even so, notwithstanding whatever personal traits may have impelled him to do so, it was by no means a given that Brown should take the lead in rallying liberal opinion in Pietermaritzburg in 1952.

Reflecting on the origins of his initiative several decades later, Brown stated that:

> ... initially it was just bringing in people one knew of because by that time we were beginning to see what the Nationalist Government was all about. And a general sense of disillusionment about the UP ever being able to do much about it. So, I suppose it was the ongoing impact of Nationalist rhetoric and the beginnings of them putting into effect their policies that provided us with the push to start wondering what we should be doing.[9]

The gathering to which Brown had invited 'suspected liberals' took place at his home on 21 June. No record exists listing those present, but Brown's old schoolfriend Simon Roberts, who at the time was serving his legal articles, was there. Ruth and Sally Lundie, both of whom were to become pillars of the local liberal community over the next few decades and who shadowed Brown in his later activities with *Reality* and the Association for Rural Advancement, were present from the start.

Years later, Brown recalled that 'the people involved were partly from contacts which I had made at Edendale – with Selby [Msimang] for instance'.[10] From the outset, the meetings took on a multiracial character. Another Edendale contact, Sam Chetty, who was to become a close friend of Brown's, was invited. So too was SR Naidoo, an elderly lawyer who belonged to the conservative Natal Indian Organisation.

At that first meeting in June, Brown observed that, through their absorption in the UP, liberals had become politically voiceless. He argued for 'the emergence of a liberal organisation on political lines in the Union'.[11] He felt it was vitally important to provide 'a new, non-colour-bar political home for non-white people as a counter to the developing tendency for them to consolidate into a solid bloc, and to regard all white people as belonging to an equally solid block in opposition to them'.[12]

The Communist Party, Brown remarked, provided a political home for non-whites by affording them full membership, and this was one of its attractions. There was no suggestion, at this stage, that non-racial liberalism should be promoted as a counterweight to communism. The battles between liberals and communists were to be waged later on, and even then they never assumed the fierceness in Natal that they often did in the other provinces. Brown motivated for a liberal organisation because 'white South Africa could not afford to let the alienation of non-white people go on any longer'.[13]

The group met again on 7 July. Brown suggested that the three main objectives of the proposed organisation should be to provide a rallying point for people of liberal outlook; to convince South Africans that liberalism afforded the best solutions to the country's racial problems; and to give 'the Non-European both hope for the future and faith that Black and White can combine to work that future out'. The organisation should fall 'somewhere between a political party and a discussion group'.[14]

Brown's discussion group met throughout the second half of 1952. It came to the notice of Alan Paton, whose novel *Cry, the Beloved Country* had brought the injustices of South African society to international attention when it was published in 1948 – a few months before the Nationalists won the election in May.[15] At the time, Paton was living in Bulwer while completing his second novel, *Too Late the Phalarope*.[16] He wrote to Brown, asking: '[W]hen is your meeting to be, because my wife & I would like to come to it.' He explained:

> I just have a kind of wish to be there; no one knows whether the formation of a Liberal Group will influence history or not, for it may be too late to do so; but it may well influence those who belong to it. For me it is a kind of step I am taking, which may or may not end a period of stagnation; & as it is therefore some kind of a holiday, I should like to be there, especially as it was in PMB that I was born.[17]

For Paton, whose pleas to his friend Hofmeyr for a greater role in public life had continually fallen on deaf ears, this first tentative step into political waters was to be anything but a holiday. It was to be the start of a lifetime's commitment to bringing about a common society – in deed as well as word. It was also, according to his biographer, the start of what was to become Paton's closest friendship during the second half of his life.[18] Indeed, Paton was much taken with Brown. In his autobiography, he recalled their encounter at the first of the meetings he attended, describing Brown as:

> ... a young Pietermaritzburg man ... [with] a social conscience about things like justice, equality and the rule of law, a conscience that was going to cost him dear. This conscience was outraged by the racial laws that were pouring out of parliament and was deeply troubled by the increasing racial alienation in South Africa.[19]

This was the first of many such words of praise written by Paton about Brown. It was through their joint leadership that liberalism came to be embodied politically, within a party, for the first time in twentieth-century South Africa. And it was through their doggedness that the liberal tradition, or a strand of it at any rate, came to broaden its scope and constituency by practising (rather than just preaching) non-racialism, and by appealing to blacks not as charges but as equal partners in a project for political change.

That was still to come, however. In the meantime, a number of liberal discussion groups similar to Brown's had emerged around the country – some quite independently of one another.

In Cape Town, Oscar Wollheim, an active member of the South African Institute of Race Relations and director of the Cape Flats Distress Association (CAFDA), where Phoebe Brown had previously worked, formed the South African Liberal Group (SALG). It aimed to 'bring pressure to bear on the United Party to revise its thinking' by adopting ten points.[20] These included: 'the elimination of all bars to the acquisition and utilisation of skill'; the entrenchment of non-racial property rights; 'the inherent right of all civilised men and women' to have a direct voice in the government of the country; and an adherence to 'constitutional and democratic methods'.

In Johannesburg, two liberal groups came into being: one,

known officially as the Johannesburg Liberal Group, was chaired by the historian Arthur Keppel-Jones. The other group was convened by the founder of the Springbok Legion and former Communist Party member, Jock Isacowitz, together with a young liberal advocate, Jack Unterhalter.

Keppel-Jones was a canny political commentator. His prognostication of life under 'a mythical Republic formed by the Nationalists in 1966', with the foreboding title of *When Smuts Goes*, was published in August 1947, and proved, in some instances, to be remarkably prescient.[21] Despite his standing as a distinguished liberal thinker and political writer, Keppel-Jones deferred, within this group, to Margaret Ballinger, the *grande dame* of contemporary liberalism, and the leader of the Native Representatives in Parliament. The formidable Ballinger – who was to say, when the Liberal Party was founded, 'I didn't join the Liberal Party; the Liberal Party joined me'[22] – gave her name to the group. It bore not only her name but also her stamp, in particular her attachment to an unreconstructed nineteenth-century 'Cape liberal policy', whose 'general principles', she felt, 'apply today as they did half a century ago'.[23]

Members of the group centred on Isacowitz and Unterhalter were more radical, more multiracial and more attuned to developments in black politics than their counterparts in the Ballinger group, who tended to view the former as somewhat less respectable than themselves. Along with what later became the Natal division of the Liberal Party, the Isacowitz–Unterhalter group and its sympathisers came to play an important role in radicalising Liberals and in shifting their liberalism beyond the strictures of the Cape liberal tradition.

In Pietermaritzburg, Brown maintained a regular schedule of meetings for his group and made contact with prominent liberals in other provinces, including Wollheim in the Cape and Julius Lewin in the Transvaal. Lewin was an up-and-coming lecturer in African Law at the University of the Witwatersrand and a member of the Ballinger group. Brown wrote to him, setting out the history and aims of his discussion group and inviting Lewin to address an audience in December. Lewin accepted the invitation for a later date, either in January and February, and pronounced, somewhat sententiously: 'Meanwhile, go ahead with your group. I'd advise self-education, i.e. getting a better grip on the *economics* of reform in SA.'[24]

Lewin was one of those liberals who continued to labour under the misapprehension that the United Party might yet be steered on to a liberal track. He told Brown: 'I had a talk with Desmond Craib [editor of the *Natal Witness*] and I hope he will have told you about our strategy of getting liberals to work *within* the United Party?'

Wollheim, on the other hand, rightly perceived that the UP was becoming 'more Nat by the day' and that the liberal ginger group, the Hofmeyr Society, had 'failed to make any impact on the UP from within'.[25] In his view, the UP was likely to lose the 1953 general election or else win it with a tenuous majority. This, he told Paton, would produce some sort of reorientation between the Nationalists and the UP and would pave the way for the South African Liberal Group 'to come out at once with a readymade machine'.[26] The time was not yet ripe for SALG to go public, however, as this would 'tend to drive the UP into even greater reaction and would give them a beautiful weapon with which to discredit this Group in the event of their not gaining a decisive victory in April'.

By November of 1952, Brown was eager to hold a public event, at which his 'suspected liberals' would formally announce their existence as the Pietermaritzburg Liberal Group and affiliate to the SALG as a branch.[27] Wollheim quickly discouraged the idea, joking that '[t]here are times when we in the staid and proper old Cape wish that you wild and woolly Natalians *would* secede from the Union to spare us further headaches'.[28]

While rejecting Brown's idea of a public meeting, Wollheim encouraged the paid-up affiliation of the Pietermaritzburg liberals to a proposed South African Liberal Association, which would amalgamate SALG with some of the other liberal groups that had sprung up in 1952. The Liberal Association would aim to build up a membership of 200 to 300 paid-up members of known liberal groups before opening up the membership more broadly. This was to avoid 'being inundated by cranks, long-haired types and other undesirables who might stack meetings and steer the thing in the wrong directions'. Instead, the Association was 'looking for the sort of liberal which respects the Institute of Race Relations and which has a practical, reasonable, intelligent outlook and no particular axes to grind'.[29] Thus spoke the imperious voice of Cape liberalism. And, once again playing to Brown's Natalian sensibilities, Wollheim joked: 'We shall be very careful not to tread on Natalian corns when the constitution is fixed as we know how many the Natalians have and how sensitive they are!'

Brown went ahead with a private gathering to inaugurate the Pietermaritzburg Liberal Group and to consider Wollheim's offer. The event was held in the Pietermaritzburg City Hall on 8 December and attended by 40 people of all races, including Brown (in the chair), Selby Msimang and SR Naidoo.[30] By this time Paton had moved to Anerley on the Natal South Coast and was busy starting a liberal group in Durban along with Bill Evans, a contact he had met through his involvement with the Toc H movement.

In his speaking notes for the occasion, Brown told himself to 'emphasise [the] moral aspect'. Few people realised how seriously race relations had deteriorated. It might be that the deterioration had 'gone too far', Brown's notes stated, but it was his personal view that 'one thing which might arrest it and put us back on the road to a peaceful future in SA would be the emergence of a LIBERAL political party with a policy of hope for all'.[31]

Looking back on the meeting just over a decade later, Brown wrote that Wollheim's idea of affiliation was received 'with certain reservations, some of them at least the result of Cape Town's rather easy assumption that it was the boss of the show and that other groups should show due deference and do what they were told!'[32] At the time, in a letter to Paton, he ascribed the reluctance to 'some rather childish form of Provincialism'.[33] Nevertheless, he was mandated to discuss Wollheim's proposal, on a forthcoming visit to Cape Town, before a final decision was taken. In the meantime, a committee was elected comprising Hugh Carey (a staff member at Brown's *alma mater*, Michaelhouse), Desmond Craib, Selby Msimang, SR Naidoo, Simon Roberts and Brown himself. The meeting also endorsed a set of five basic principles, which had been crafted and refined by Brown's discussion group between June and November 1952. The principles stated:[34]

1. We hold that all men should be equal before the law, and should enjoy free access to the Courts of Justice; freedom of speech, of the Press, of movement, and of peaceful assembly; freedom of religion; security of private property rights, and equal rights to acquire and own land; [and] the fullest possible development of innate capacities through appropriate education and training.

2. We hold that there should be no laws that discriminate solely on grounds of race or colour; and that all such laws should be abolished step by step. We recognise, however, that special laws are needed for the protection of those of all races who remain backward in civilisation or who are otherwise handicapped.

3. We hold that all men have a right to political representation, direct or indirect, in the organs of central government, and all who have attained an adequate standard of civilisation should enjoy the adult franchise and direct representation in Parliament, in the Provincial Councils and in local government.

4. Whilst we believe that members of the various races prefer their own social and community institutions, we are opposed to all forms of racial segregation not based upon consent.

5. We hold that Western civilisation is based on a belief in the value of the human personality; as such it can and ought to be enjoyed by all men who are able to uphold and maintain it, no matter what their race or colour.

With its emphasis on individual rights and the rule of law, the Pietermaritzburg Liberal Group's liberalism was of a conventional cut. In substance, if not in tone, there was not a great deal to distinguish its basic principles from Wollheim's ten points, although the latter paid more attention to education and the economy. The

approach to political change was gradualist, and the demands for
non-racial political rights and institutions, including the endorsement of a qualified franchise, were carefully couched in the language of upholding Western civilisation.

The principles pandered to the sensibilities of white Natal society by rejecting non-consensual racial segregation (and affirming
that different races preferred their own social institutions) rather
than promoting racial integration. As such, there was nothing
especially radical about the Pietermaritzburg Liberal Group's principles – they fitted quite comfortably into the parameters set by the
nineteenth-century Cape liberal tradition. However, most South
African whites in the 1950s would have balked at them. Indeed,
after the Group had met on 8 December, Brown received an
admonitory letter:

> I must tell you if I had come [to the meeting last night] I
> would have queried two of your principles as moving much
> too quickly. Under 1. 'and equal rights to acquire & own
> land'. I ask you would you like to have an Indian family liv-
> ing on one side of you and a native African family on the
> other?[35]

The writer cautioned further: 'The franchise for both Africans &
Indians should be most carefully guarded & only a very small &
select number allowed to qualify at first, I believe.' Another correspondent advised: 'Now the Nats are mistaken [and] misguided in
a hundred ways but I believe they are dead right in opposing purely
social intermingling of Europeans & non-Europeans.'[36] For that
reason, the Liberal Group's constitution should make it clear that
whites were prepared to meet 'non-Europeans' for political, business, religious and cultural purposes, 'but for purely social purposes
we consider it expedient and right to keep apart'.

Someone else who had been present at the gathering expressed appreciation for the 'moderation and sanity of the two
principal speakers', but thought 'the Indian, Naidoo, wrecked the
meeting'.[37] It was the writer's 'personal belief that non-Europeans
should not, at this stage, become members of the Group'. Indeed,

it was necessary for 'Europeans [to] lead and control the movement' if it was to succeed. Blacks should not occupy leadership
positions since 'nothing should be done which could be considered communistic'. The correspondent concluded haughtily:
'[T]he movement can only achieve results if it gains public support, which will be alienated if the Group is stampeded into flaunt-
ing its liberalism by giving office to non-Europeans, particularly if
the latter are not very carefully selected.'

These were the kinds of attitude which were to make the
Liberal Party's mission a difficult one. In the meantime, Brown visited Cape Town at the end of December 1952 and reported back
approvingly to the Pietermaritzburg Liberal Group on the course
which Wollheim's initiative was taking. Wollheim planned to hold
the annual general meeting of the South African Liberal Group
between 16 and 17 January 1953 in Cape Town. Four delegates
attended from Natal. From Durban went Alan Paton and a couple,
Ken and Jean Hill, who taught maths and classics, respectively, at
the local university. Geoffrey Durrant, Professor of English at the
University of Natal and one of many servicemen whose liberal politics had been shaped by the wartime Army Education Services,
represented Pietermaritzburg.

Out of this meeting was born the South African Liberal Association, which welded the disparate liberal groups from around the
country into a single entity with its own constitution, and which, in
May 1953, became the Liberal Party.

Although unable to attend himself, Brown told Paton that it
was his 'conviction that whatever else is decided [at the meeting],
there should be no hesitation about going full out into the political field after the election'.[38] He was concerned, however, by the
potential involvement of UP MPs like Harry Lawrence, Smuts's
former Justice Minister and later the founding chairman of the
Progressive Party, since he felt their participation was likely to
alienate non-white opinion.

At the inaugural meeting of the Liberal Association, Brown
and Durrant were elected as the interim Council members from
Pietermaritzburg. On 23 February, Brown chaired a meeting at
which the Pietermaritzburg Liberal Group voted to affiliate to the

Liberal Association. Durban followed suit on 26 February, accepting the Association's constitution – like Pietermaritzburg – with reservations.

Paton found the Durban meeting a trifle exasperating. Hans Meidner, a botanist from the University of Natal, was there – splitting hairs, according to Paton, about the pace at which political change should proceed. Meidner was a Jewish refugee from Germany. One afternoon in 1938, the story goes, the fourteen-year-old boy was riding his bicycle home when a friend appeared and warned him that all the other members of his family had been arrested. He turned around and kept riding, until he reached the Dutch border. From there he found his way to England, and eventually, with the help of Quakers, to South Africa.[39] He went on to serve in the South African Engineering Corps during the war. At one stage, when based in Greece, he was arrested by partisans because, he used to say, 'he was not a communist'.[40] While studying in South Africa, he had joined the Berea Mixed Branch of the United Party, thinking this was the start of a multiracial UP. As it turned out, 'mixed' referred to unisex membership.[41] Meidner was a great character, a forceful presence among Natal Liberals, and a good friend of Brown's – their friendship was to deepen during a spell in a shared prison cell in 1960.

Meidner's outspokenness irked Paton somewhat at the Durban gathering, as did Hilda and Leo Kuper (an academic couple from the University of Natal) 'pleading the claims of Bantu civilisation'.[42] Nevertheless, he felt himself being drawn ineluctably into the new political venture, and, in a sign of growing friendship with and trust in Brown, he confided some of his concerns: 'Must I go on writing? Must I get a job? Or must I join people like you & try to serve the country? These are my problems that I should like to have discussed with you.'[43]

Paton and Brown were soon to be working side by side. At a joint meeting of members of the Durban and Pietermaritzburg groups in Botha's Hill on 25 March, the Natal Region of the South African Liberal Association was formed, with Paton as its chairman and Brown as its secretary. Selby Msimang was elected vice-chairman.

At the time, the Association had still not launched in public. With the National Party triumphing in the general election on 16 April, a rising clamour of voices – especially among the Transvaal radicals – called for the Association to transform itself into a political party and to announce its arrival on the electoral scene. On behalf of the Transvaal Region of the Liberal Association, Jock Isacowitz requested that a meeting of the Council be held to discuss the matter.

The meeting took place between 8 and 9 May 1953 in the board-room of the *Cape Times*, amidst its fusty aura of old Cape liberalism. It was attended by nineteen delegates, including the Association's President, Margaret Ballinger, and Vice-President, Leo Marquard. Natal was represented by Brown and Msimang, who travelled to-gether to Cape Town in Brown's car. With Paton and Durrant being unable to attend, their proxies were held by Leslie Rubin and Brown, respectively.

Although Brown had told Paton, before the Liberal Association was founded, that the body should go 'full out into the political field after the election', he did not indicate whether it should do so under the banner of a political party or a political association. On the whole, the Natal members of the Association were reluctant to make the leap from association to party. At a meeting of the Natal Regional Council on 4 May, it was agreed that the Associa-tion should become a public organisation, but 'on the question of forming a political party it was agreed that this should not be done until a more detailed programme had been worked out. Instead an Association should emerge whose first aim would be to produce a political programme in order to emerge as a party.'[44]

Even so, when Brown and Msimang attended the meeting in May, they did so without a fixed mandate from Natal on the ques-tion of forming a political party. For Brown, two important factors shaped the discussion.

Firstly, Wollheim and Rubin told the *Cape Times* that the Trans-vaal and Cape Regional Associations were overwhelmingly in favour of forming a party. The newspaper ran the story on 6 May under the headline 'SA Liberal Party move', and named Ballinger, Mar-quard and Donald Molteno – grandson of Sir JC Molteno, Cape Prime Minister in 1872 – as the prime movers. This, in Brown's view, somewhat forced the Council's hand. As Marquard later recalled to Brown: '… to some extent Leslie Rubin jumped the gun by publishing our names and facing us with a *fait accompli* … Once that was done we had either to dissociate ourselves from the move or help found a Liberal Party.'[45]

Secondly, from the political rumour mill in Natal had come reports that the leadership of the Torch Commando was about to launch a new party, the Union Federal Party (UFP). Indeed, one of the UFP's chief architects was Geoff Durrant, who had given his proxy for the Council meeting to Brown with the strict instruction to vote against the establishment of a Liberal Party.[46] The Federals were likely to appeal to the imperial sentiments of English-speaking South Africans and punt a conservatively liberal native policy. Leslie Rubin, who had been a prominent member of the Torch Commando, argued that if a Liberal Party was to stand any chance of mobilising white support immediately it would have to pull the rug from under the Federalists by announcing its formation first. Other delegates at the Council meeting, realising that the political field to the left of the National Party might suddenly become somewhat crowded, were persuaded that the time to act was now. Liberals had gathered a great deal of momentum in the previous year and it would be difficult, further down the line, to rekindle the broad national commitment to the creation of a Liberal Party that currently existed.

This, at any rate, was the direction in which Brown's own thoughts were moving, and it was Brown who eventually moved, after protracted debates for and against, at the end of the first day: '(1) That this Association form a political party forthwith [and] (2) That a conference be called at an early date to formulate the programme of the new Party.'[47] Brown's motion, which in terms of the constitution required a two-thirds majority of Council members to vote for it before it was adopted, was narrowly defeated. After intensive overnight lobbying, the motion was reconsidered the following morning and was carried by 18 votes to 2. And so the Liberal Party was formed.

CONSOLIDATING THE HOME BASE: NATAL PROVINCIAL SECRETARY
1953-1955

Only two blacks had attended the Council meeting of the South African Liberal Association where the decision was taken to form the Liberal Party: Selby Msimang and the Rev SP Lediga. When the Party announced its leadership at the end of the meeting, it was all white: Margaret Ballinger was the President; Leo Marquard and Alan Paton were her Vice-Presidents; Oscar Wollheim was the National Chairman; and Leslie Rubin was Wollheim's deputy. Moreover, the Party's founders represented a hotchpotch of liberal opinion. Jock Isacowitz, the Transvaal delegate at whose urging the Council had been convened, was a former member of the Communist Party. His political past was regarded as something of a stigma by Margaret Ballinger. The fact that the Liberal Party provided 'a political home for younger and more radical elements', she would recall in her memoirs, 'was to form an inhibiting factor for many professing liberals, particularly in view of the banning of the Communist Party [in 1950]'.[1]

As it happened, the communists had no intention of infiltrating the new party, preferring instead to work through the recently formed white Congress of Democrats (COD) – from which vantage point they directed a steady stream of vitriol at Liberals over the years. But within the founding cohort of the Liberal Party there was a broad split between Transvaal radicals like Isacowitz and Jack Unterhalter on the one hand, and Cape conservatives like Oscar Wollheim on the other. The divisions cut across provincial boundaries: Ballinger was from the Transvaal, but she described herself as an 'old liberal of the Cape tradition'.[2] Whatever fissures were to emerge in the Liberal Party were partly provincial, partly generational and partly ideological. For a long time, they formed around issues such as the franchise (qualified vs universal) and how best to work towards political change (whether the Party should employ 'only ... constitutional means', as its founding principles demanded, or whether it might deliberately flout unjust laws in pursuing extraparliamentary avenues too).

In the early years, Brown tended to gravitate towards the centreright of the Party. This was true of the Pietermaritzburg Liberals as a whole. Durban Liberals like Ken and Jean Hill, Violaine Junod, Leo Kuper and Hans Meidner took a more progressive stance on certain issues. It was Meidner, for instance, who had balked at the Liberal Association's constitution because it promised equal political rights to 'all *civilised* persons'. The Liberal Party soon replaced 'civilised' with 'suitably qualified'. Like Meidner, Junod objected to the Party's assurance that it would 'employ only democratic and constitutional means to implement its principles, and ... oppose all forms of totalitarianism such as communism and fascism'.[3] For one thing, 'constitutional means' were not available to blacks, barred as they were from the body politic. For another, the government had rendered the term 'communism' meaningless through its Suppression of Communism Act (1950) – applying the epithet, as it did, to all opponents of apartheid – and Meidner and Junod saw no reason for Liberals to pander to such McCarthyism.

Brown's own radicalisation was to be swift, however. By the late 1950s, his political sympathies lay more with the Transvaal radicals than the Cape conservatives. By the end of the decade he would tell Walter Stanford – like Ballinger, a Native Representative in the House of Assembly – that it was 'becoming increasingly impractical to think and talk in terms of a qualified franchise in Africa in 1959. Africa won't listen.'[4] Certain individuals within the Party helped accelerate this political awakening. One was Jack Unterhalter, a constant friend, who Brown would describe as 'really the rock that held the Party together over the years'.[5] But by far the biggest factor in his moving to the Party's

centre-left was his work on the ground, in Natal, among disenfranchised blacks.

* * *

In their formal statement to the press after launching, the Liberals
affirmed: 'That no person be debarred from participating in the
government and other democratic processes of the country by
reason ... of race, colour or creed, and that political rights based
on a common franchise role be extended to all suitably qualified
persons.'[6] Such suffragist gradualism did not sit well with the ANC.
When, in March 1953, Wollheim sent a copy of the Liberal Association's constitution to the Secretary-General of the ANC, Walter
Sisulu, he received a politely dismissive reply: the ANC was 'committed to a definite policy and programme of action which flows
from the basic principles of universal suffrage' and could not
'advise the Africans to join other political organisations'.[7]

The Liberals' franchise policy dominated proceedings at their
first annual National Conference (later termed National Congress),
which took place between 11 and 13 July 1953 in the Britzius Hall
in Johannesburg. As Brown notes in his unpublished history of the
Liberal Party, 'there was no important body of opinion which, at
this Congress, argued for a policy of *immediate* adult franchise'.[8]
Most delegates accepted that the Party's initial policy should be to
introduce a qualified, non-racial, common-roll franchise, coupled
with compulsory education so that all qualifications could be met
reasonably. Rather, the debate centred on whether the Party should
adopt universal suffrage as its ultimate aim and, in the interim,
what qualifications should be imposed on the franchise.

Some felt that the Party should state clearly its intention to
work towards universal franchise; others saw no reason to look
beyond a qualified franchise and believed that the educational
qualification should be set relatively high, at Standard 8. During
discussions, regional fault-lines emerged. Transvaal delegates were
the most radical, having been given a mandate beforehand to 'vote
in favour of the inclusion ... of a clear statement to the effect that
our objective is universal adult franchise'.[9] Cape delegates, at least

those wedded to parliamentary liberalism and electoral politics, were the most conservative, seeking high qualifications and down-playing the inevitability of universal suffrage. The Natal represen-tatives, in Brown's opinion, occupied 'a position between the two extremes, but nearer the Cape'.[10]

On the Party's own terms, Natal's move to occupy the middle ground was well calculated: if the qualifications were set too high, potential black support would be alienated. If they were set too low, or if the Party unequivocally pledged itself to universal suffrage in the long term, white supporters (who, after all, were the ones with the power to make the Liberal Party a going electoral concern) might be deterred. The Party had to strike a balance between the fears and aspirations of its two constituencies while being careful not to polarise black and white even further. From the very begin-ning, the emphasis of Brown's liberalism had been on non-racial-ism. The Natal delegation to the first National Conference was multiracial. Even at this early stage, then, the Natalians' choices and actions were guided by a desire to promote inter-racial co-operation and goodwill. For that reason it sought to assuage white fears by plumping for qualifications, and to mollify black opinion by not setting them too high. For, in Brown's words, 'the effect of placing the standard [on the franchise] too high would be to disil-lusion all non-Europeans and to consolidate the present White and non-White blocs even more strongly'.[11]

After much debate, the Party resolved that it would seek to 'achieve the responsible participation of all South Africans in the Government and democratic processes of the country'. This was to be done by means of 'compulsory education for all South Africans and the extension of the right of franchise to all adult persons who have received such education'.[12] In order to ensure an 'orderly transition' to this goal, the Party would institute a qualified fran-chise for South African citizens over the age of 21, regardless of race, sex, colour or creed, on a common roll. The following quali-fications were stipulated: completion of Standard 6; an income of at least £250 in cash or kind *or* ownership of property valued at £500; and a special dispensation for persons aged 35 or older who occupied positions of 'special responsibility' or who had rendered 'meritorious service' to the community. Those who failed to meet these qualifications would be indirectly represented in the Senate.

The Party's franchise policy therefore represented something of a compromise. Nowhere was the commitment to universal suffrage baldly stated and qualifications for the franchise were set at an intermediate level. Yet even in Brown's own branch of the Party, these qualifications were controversial. In his report on the first National Conference, Brown acknowledged that there were members in Pietermaritzburg who would find the Standard 6 qualification 'much too low'.[13] Indeed, going into the Congress, the Pietermaritzburg branch had advocated a Standard 6 qualification, coupled with a further educational restriction. And at a Pietermaritzburg branch committee meeting shortly after the Conference, Brown's schoolfriend and branch chair, Simon Roberts, among others, protested against what he perceived to be too low a qualification. Roberts felt the franchise policy would estrange 'European' support and dent the Party's electoral prospects.[14] He subsequently resigned his chairmanship over the issue, but remained a member of the Party.[15]

At this stage, Brown, like Paton, was a qualified-franchise man. Paton had told Margaret Ballinger in May 1953 that 'whatever certain non-whites say about the universal franchise it will never be willingly granted by white people'. He personally 'could not honestly support the opening of the doors of our society to tribal Africans, Indian labourers, and the large depressed portion of Cape Coloureds'.[16]

At the National Congress in Durban in 1954, the franchise policy threatened to unravel Party unity once more. Late in the day, the Transvaal division submitted a resolution from its Kensington branch, which called upon the Party to achieve 'full franchise rights for all people in the minimum time'.[17] Meanwhile, the Party had already appointed a Franchise Commission, chaired by a radical Cape member, Jimmy Gibson, to advise on the franchise policy. Now, it just so happened that Gibson had unsuccessfully tried to pass the exact same resolution as the Kensington branch at a Cape Provincial Congress earlier in the year. In his capacity as Franchise Commission chair, he announced that, with the exception of the

liberal historian Rodney Davenport, the members of the Commission recommended that the principle of qualified franchise be
deleted from Party policy. 'The Party conservatives,' wrote Brown,
and on the franchise question he considered himself one of their
number, could be 'forgiven for feeling that they were being caught
up in a conspiracy.'[18]

In fact, together with conservative Cape liberals like Leslie Rubin,
Walter Stanford and Oscar Wollheim, Brown sided with Davenport's minority report. Brown argued that: '… it was undesirable to
change the Party's policy every year or so. To adopt universal adult
suffrage would have serious consequences in Natal.'[19] Curiously, he
was supported by Selby Msimang, who noted that, as things stood,
the Party was reliant on white voters for electoral success. As such,
'Africans must not make it difficult for the Party to make headway
by proposing things which the electorate would not accept'.[20]

In the end, the conservatives yielded ground and the Party resolved to 'extend the right of franchise on the common roll to all
adult persons'. However, provision was made for a 'transitional
period', so that the introduction of universal suffrage could be
'brought about by stages'. These stages were to be determined by
interim qualifications which might be educational, economic or
age-related. They would 'apply for the minimum period necessary
for a smooth transition to universal adult franchise'.[21] For all its
prevarication, this statement was seen as a victory for the franchise
radicals. Brown, for one, was riled by the way in which the whole
issue had been brought before the Congress. He was, in his own
words, 'by no means convinced of the overriding virtues of adult
franchise', and for some weeks afterwards he considered resigning
from the Party.[22]

Brown's avowed commitment to non-racialism and the common society therefore coexisted with a qualified commitment to
full political rights for blacks. It was an incongruity that was to
bedevil liberal politics in South Africa for years to come. In some
ways, the contradiction reflected a tension between pragmatism
and idealism in Brown's own makeup. In other ways, it simply
reflected the prevailing zeitgeist. As Brown reported back to
Pietermaritzburg Liberals after the 1953 conference: in a place like

Pietermaritzburg, 'where things move slowly and we do not feel any great pressure of events, we are almost bound to find ourselves on the Right, at the most, in the Centre. It is perhaps difficult for us to understand the deep sense of urgency which grips people in a place like Johannesburg.'[23]

At the 1953 conference, Brown had been voted onto the National Committee as a provincial representative from Natal, along with Paton and Hans Meidner. Brown, who was not yet thirty years old, had thus managed to insert himself into the upper echelons of the Party from the outset.

One of his main concerns about the new party was its lack of black leaders. The National Committee elected at the first Conference did not have a single black member. 'This Committee ... was conspicuous for its whiteness,' Brown was to say.[24] It was largely through his own offices, then, that at the National Congress the following year, the National Committee received an infusion of African and Indian membership. Dr DM Bassa, Selby Msimang and Mlahleni Njisane (who worked with Leo Kuper as a sociologist), all from Natal, were elected onto the Committee; the other provinces' representatives were all white.

In addition to serving on the National Committee, Brown had been elected the Party's Provincial Secretary at the first Natal Provincial Congress on 7 November 1953.[25] As Provincial Secretary, Brown built the Party's organisational framework in Natal. He traversed the province from the Midlands to the northern parts of Zululand, south towards the Transkei, and along the coastal regions. He signed up members, set up branches and communicated the Party's message to voters. Although at the end of 1953 Natal had the fewest paid-up members (201 in comparison with the Transvaal's 329 and the Cape's 380), by 1955 its membership had doubled to 420, and by 1956 it stood at 650.[26] Indeed, by 1956 Natal had the largest membership, the highest proportion of black members and a significant sway over the national leadership.[27]

As news of the Liberal Party travelled, sympathisers and potential supporters wrote to Brown to find out more about the organisation. Often, he would travel to towns where an interest had been expressed and address house meetings. Paton would usually be in tow, and once Brown had introduced the Party, Paton would deliver one of his stirring speeches. Brown made the arrangements for all of these visits, and followed up each one by sending a letter with further information about the Party. His drive and dedication came to the attention of senior members of the Party. In 1955, Walter Stanford told Brown that he was 'glad to see from your minutes the activity amongst the branches and the energy with which Natal is going along'. Natal was expending 'more energy than [the] other Provinces', and Stanford sent Brown 'many congratulations to you personally for your part in it'.[28]

By early 1954, the Natal division had established five branches in Durban, one in Pietermaritzburg, one in the Midlands and one in Edendale chaired by Selby Msimang. During the course of the year, Brown visited, among other places, Ixopo, Kokstad, Ladysmith and Stanger, and he held recruitment meetings in Raisethorpe and Plessislaer.[29]

It was through the formation of the Ladysmith branch that Brown met Elliot Mngadi, who became one of his closest friends across the colour line. Soon after the Party was launched, Brown had written to a young couple in Ladysmith, Walter and Adelaine Hain, at the prompting of a mutual friend, Jock Barnes. The Hains had recently returned from a stint in Kenya, where Walter worked as an architect, with their toddler son, Peter. (Peter Hain would rise to prominence in Britain as an anti-apartheid activist, and, later still, as a minister in Tony Blair's Cabinet.) Brown told the Hains about the Party, and asked if they might be interested in join-ing. They responded positively. As a result, he went to meet them in Ladysmith. They found him 'friendly' and 'sympathetic', with a sense of humour similar to their own – though they were a little taken aback to glimpse polo gear on the back seat of his car when they saw him off.[30] Soon afterwards, Brown organised a meeting at the Hains' home. Accompanied by Paton and Selby Msimang, he addressed a small group of people, who then decided to form the Ladysmith branch of the Liberal Party. Among those who joined the Party at that meeting was Elliot Mngadi, who remarked: 'This is the first time I've ever come through the front door of a white man's house.'[31]

At the time, Mngadi was working as a court messenger in Ladysmith. His job required him to travel across town, which he did on his motorbike. And because he found it more comfortable to ride around in riding breeches and glistening leather leggings, this was the garb he was wearing when Brown first encountered him. Mngadi cut a dashing figure. Brown remembered him as 'a bright-eyed, bristle-moustached, immaculately dressed ... young man'.[32] He was to play a pivotal role in recruiting black support for the Party through his work with the Northern Natal African Landowners' Association – a vehicle created by the Liberals in 1958, in conjunction with the ANC, to oppose so-called black spot removals.

Brown was determined to increase the Party's black membership. In July 1953, he received a letter from the national office in Cape Town remarking that it was 'especially interesting to find how much interest there is among Non-Europeans in Natal'.[33] In August, he broached the subject of the Party's 'one-sided racial membership ... elsewhere than in Natal' with Leo Marquard.[34] The position improved slowly: the lawyer Hyacinth 'Bill' Bhengu joined and was elected onto the Transvaal Provincial Committee in 1954. He would go on to become the Party's National Vice-President. In the Cape, Dan Tikili, a community leader and ANC veteran, recruited a number of residents from Langa. But it was really in Natal that the Liberal idea of non-racialism was matched, in practice, by growing black membership.

Letters sent to Brown in 1954 reveal that he was largely responsible for the Party's growth among Africans in rural Natal. He wrote to JZ Chamane, for example, expressing his 'delight' that Chamane had become a member, and telling him: 'If you know of any friends of yours who would be interested in the Party I would be very glad to have their names, as I would like to start a branch of the Liberal Party in Greytown.'[35] Lawrence Khanyile, from Georgedale Village, told Brown: 'I see no reason why I should not join the Party that aims at ameliorating our position politically in this country of our birth.'[36] Another recruit, A Maphanga, reported to Brown from Greytown that he had registered 13 members, 'leading men in our district', and assured him that '[w]e are very grateful to join the Liberal Party although most of us cannot read English'.[37]

The membership drive among blacks was bound to frighten off some whites, though. Mary Lee of Pietermaritzburg resigned her membership of the Party, and chided Brown for accepting 'Non-Europeans' to full membership: '... I have always felt that it is a mistake,' she wrote, 'to admit non-Europeans (all and sundry) to full membership ... when we have no means of knowing their real political allegiance.' She felt the Party was going to 'the sentimental extreme of valuing Non-European support more highly than that of the Europeans'.[38]

Brown's efforts paid off: by 1955, membership of the Natal division was approximately one-third African, one-third Indian and one-third white.[39] Some of this was achieved with the help of his old Edendale contacts, chiefly Chetty and Msimang, but the message soon spread beyond Pietermaritzburg. One distinguished Indian recruit was EV Mahomed, a great friend and personal aide to ANC President Chief Albert Luthuli. Mahomed joined the Liberals in February 1954, and built up a strong branch in Stanger. He went on to serve as the Party's National Treasurer, and was succeeded by Mngadi. Another new member was Manilal Gandhi, son of the Mahatma, who ran the settlement founded by his father in Phoenix, and edited a newspaper, *Indian Opinion*. In later years, Brown served on the board of the Phoenix Settlement Trust.[40] Long after Manilal's death in 1956, Brown felt that 'the memory of [his] warmth, and steadfastness and quiet strength remains as a support and encouragement to many of us after all these years'.[41]

In addition to his responsibilities as Provincial Secretary, Brown took over the editorship of *Contact* in October 1953.[42] Although the name was later appropriated by Patrick Duncan for his news magazine – launched in 1958 with George Clay as its first editor – *Contact* started life as a duplicated newssheet for the Liberal Association, and was edited by Hans Meidner. In November 1953, the National Committee decided to turn *Contact* into a national newsletter.[43] The first issue, edited by Brown, appeared the following January. He continued as editor until January 1958. In February of that year, when Duncan's organ was launched, Brown assumed editorial control of a newsletter, similar in format to the earlier *Contact*, first called *Sokhel'-Umlilo* and later, until it seems to have folded early in 1960, *Umhlanganisi*.[44] Since Brown wrote most of the leader columns for the early *Contact*s, these pieces, together with his 'Long View' columns in Duncan's *Contact* between 1959 and 1964 and his editorials for *Reality* between 1975 and 1993, constitute a documentary record of South African politics from a Liberal view over a period of forty years. Between 1964 and 1974, it was illegal to publish anything written by Brown, but, as editor of *Contact*, that was still some way off.

The early editions of *Contact* contained 500-word leader columns, a feature article of 1 000 words, a press survey and a digest of Party news from the provincial divisions. It was Brown's job to compile this, and to chase up the provinces for their news. In the Cape, he liaised with Jimmy Gibson and another radical, Peter Hjul. In the Transvaal, Michael O'Dowd, the future Executive Director of Anglo American, served as *Contact*'s point person for a period. The newsletter even found an international audience. A Party member who settled in England, Margaret du Manoir, distributed *Contact* to members of the Liberal International (LI) and English journalists on the *New Statesman*, *The Observer* and *The Times*. She told Brown that the editor of *The Times* was 'most sympathetic'.[45]

As editor, Brown was sometimes called upon to make decisions that might ruffle senior Party members. For instance, he rejected an article by Oscar Wollheim on the grounds that it might 'antagonise those members of non-European organisations with whom we are trying to get on friendly terms'.[46] This was something close to Brown's heart. At the beginning of 1954, he suggested that the Liberal Party should 'increase [its] knowledge of and strengthen connections with non-European political organisations'.[47]

When the Liberal Party first launched, the reception from the ANC and its fellow travellers – the South African Indian Congress (SAIC), the South African Coloured People's Organisation (SACPO) and the white Congress of Democrats (COD) – had ranged from lukewarm to frosty. Mostly the responses were glacial. Nelson Mandela spurned the new Party's members as 'subordinate henchmen of the ruling circles … of the Nationalist government'.[48]

Fighting Talk, the organ of the Congress Alliance, ridiculed Liberals for 'Speaking for the Natives', and claimed that the Party's black members were there to 'lend colour to the theory' that the Liberals were the 'group of Europeans [to] speak "for" this unspeaking, unthinking mass'.[49]

Yusuf Dadoo, of the South African Indian Congress, scorned the Party as 'half-baked and compromising'. He warned: 'The non-European people can no longer be deceived by any sheep's clothing ... Our demand is for the full and equal franchise without discrimination or qualification.'[50] Ahmed Kathrada, of the Transvaal Indian Congress, dismissed the Liberals as a paternalistic throwback: 'What the Liberals fail to realise is that the non-White people are no longer leaderless. They refuse to be treated as children.'[51] When Ballinger and Paton shared a platform in Durban with two Natal Indian Congress (NIC) leaders, JN Singh and IC Meer, they were accused of 'dividing the people'.[52] The Dundee branch of the Natal Indian Congress was far more forthright: it issued a colourful polemic setting out 'why we should wage a relentless war against the Liberal Party'.[53]

That particular call to arms was not heeded. In Natal, there were formal discussions and informal social gatherings with leaders of both the ANC and the Natal Indian Congress – many of them organised by Selby Msimang and Leo Kuper, respectively. One such meeting took place at the home of Chief Luthuli in Groutville on 14 October 1953. The ANC was represented by Luthuli, and by its Provincial Secretary, MB Yengwa, its Provincial Treasurer, MM Mtolo and Jordan Ngubane, who, along with Anton Lembede, had drafted the ANC's 1949 Programme of Action. The Liberal delegation comprised Brown, Paton and Msimang.

Contact recorded that the 'meeting was held in a very friendly spirit and provided the members of the two organisations with a very necessary opportunity of getting to know one another'.[54] At the outset, however, the ANC representatives identified 'a fundamental difference' between the two organisations in their approach to the franchise. The ANC, they said, would not encourage its members to join the Liberal Party, although they would not be barred from doing so. Nor would the ANC support a Liberal Party candidate for election to the Native Representative Council. The differences between the two were summed up as follows: while the Liberal Party was committed to constitutional means of change, the ANC supported non-constitutional, albeit non-violent, methods. Nevertheless, it was agreed that the two organisations might co-operate on specific issues, principally in opposing the Bantu Education Act and the Group Areas Act. Pursuant to this, the Liberals organised a series of protest meetings. On 18 November, for example, Paton shared a stage with Jordan Ngubane and prominent Natal Indian Congress member Ismail Meer.[55] They called upon the government to repeal the Bantu Education Act.

Relations between Liberals and the ANC varied from province to province. In the Cape, the ANC's Provincial Chairman, Thomas Ngwenya, and his ex-communist colleague, Joseph Nkatlo, attended the Liberals' 1954 Provincial Congress as observers. The Congress passed a resolution to 'co-operate with the ANC in its struggle for the removal of all discrimination against the African people'.[56] Ngwenya and Nkatlo were both vigorously opposed to communism and they resented the ascendancy of the far left in the ANC. This was often the clincher. As Brown remarked to a correspondent in 1955, there were two factions within the ANC: one inclined to communism which 'won't have anything to do with [the Party] at any cost', and another more liberal grouping, which would welcome closer collaboration with the Liberals.[57]

In later years, Brown would recall that senior figures from the Natal ANC, like Mtolo and Yengwa, 'didn't much like us, although … later on relations, individually … became much better'.[58] This was helped both by the relative weakness of the COD in Natal – and, more broadly, the feeble appeal of communism there – and individual friendships between senior ANC figures and Liberals. According to Janet Robertson, a historian of South African liberalism: 'In Natal there had been comparatively little dispute over involvement with the Congress Alliance. The COD was less active there than in the Transvaal and relations between leading Liberals, like Leo Kuper … and the Natal Indians were excellent.'[59]

Paton became good friends with prominent figures in the Natal Indian Congress, particularly Monty Naicker, and Ismail Meer and

his wife, Fatima. Brown described Suttie Mungal, who was involved
with the NIC in Pietermaritzburg, as a 'close friend'.[60] Brown also
got on very well with Mungal's colleague, Mahomed 'Chota' Motala,
who chaired the Pietermaritzburg branch of the NIC. He would be
invited to their family gatherings, and his visits were always warmly
received.[61]

As for the ANC, Paton and Luthuli struck up a close acquaintance. Luthuli often stayed at Paton's house, and Paton's thinking
seems to have influenced Luthuli's public utterances: on several
occasions the author wrote speeches for the Chief.[62] Brown himself became close to Archie Gumede, who was to be one of his
most enduring friends. Gumede had joined the ANC in 1949,
and rose from Assistant Secretary of the Pietermaritzburg Branch
to Assistant Secretary for the whole province in 1951. He joined
the Liberal Party soon after its formation, since he saw no incon-
sistency between its policies and those of the ANC. Like him,
Msimang and Njisane continued as card-carrying members of the
ANC, despite the organisation's reluctance to endorse dual membership.

In their early years, then, Liberals faced several difficulties: a
certain distance from the Congress movement, an initially sluggish
response from potential black supporters and, of course, the
Nationalists' nascent Draconianism. Brown was to recollect that
the Party had '[n]o conception – at that early stage – either of
how determined and ruthless the Nats were going to turn out to
be, or … of how difficult it was going to be to make big inroads into
the various black communities'.[63]

Then, too, the Party's identity was ambiguous: it was neither
black fish nor white fowl. And for all their professed non-racialism,
the Liberal Party's members were divided over what the role of a
non-racial Party should be. Should it be to win over white voters to
the idea of a non-racial, common society by a steady process of persuasion, in the hope that they might one day defeat the Nationalists through the ballot box? If so, the Party's energies should be
geared towards orthodox political activity, like fighting elections.
But there was another school of thought which held that while
some sort of electoral engagement might be necessary, it was by

no means a priority, for it was costly, time-consuming and resource-intensive. Would money, time and people not be better directed at increasing black membership and co-operating with black individuals and organisations on specific issues? In that way, the Liberal Party could make non-racialism a living reality.

Those arguments were to be refined as the Party matured. In 1954, however, the Liberals decided that they should contest the provincial elections. In fact, the Party had made its first foray into the electoral field at the end of 1953. In November, Leslie Cooper, a young architect and former student politician, campaigned for a seat on the Johannesburg City Council. He stood in Ward 9, which spanned the middle-class suburbs of Killarney, Saxonwold, Parkview and Greenside. He polled 809 votes to the UP's 1955.[64] To Paton, the result was 'encouragement of a high magnitude', since it meant that 'a considerable number of white people, even if they may sometimes think in terms of colour and race, reject apartheid as an all-important guiding principle'.[65] Beforehand, however, Natal Liberals had been under few illusions about their chances of electoral success. In its submission to the Election Commission Report, tabled at the first National Conference in 1953, the Natal division noted that the Union Federal Party was a 'complication' and that the white electorate was 'on the whole not very liberal'.[66]

Perhaps Cooper's fair showing served as a morale-booster, for in the 1954 provincial elections, Natal fielded three candidates: Ronald Morris and Violaine Junod in Durban and Brown in the Pietermaritzburg South constituency. Paton had written to Brown in March, ahead of nominations, expressing the hope that he would 'reach a wise decision about Maritzburg South'.[67] If he chose not to stand, Paton suggested involvement in 'some other Branch activity', and recommended '1) Editorship of *Contact*; 2) Writing for *Contact*; 3) Investigating Group Area proposals in Maritzburg; 4) Training young men and women of all races as public speakers'. Paton was a bit behind the times, since Brown had in fact been editing *Contact* since it appeared for the first time in its revised form, as a national Party newsletter, in January. In the event, Brown made himself available for nomination, and on 29 March, at a combined meeting of the Edendale and Pietermaritzburg branches, he was chosen to contest Pietermaritzburg South.[68]

For two months before the election, Brown campaigned solidly, canvassing door to door, addressing meetings and spreading the Liberal message to the apathetic and sometimes hostile voters of Pietermaritzburg. One of Brown's most ardent helpers was Sam Chetty, who walked the streets putting his candidate's manifesto into postboxes.[69] Archie Gumede spoke in favour of Brown's candidacy, arguing that his time as a 'Social Worker among our people at Edendale' had made Brown 'more acutely aware of the sorry plight in which people find themselves when they are unrepresented or even inadequately represented in Town Councils, Provincial Councils or Parliament'.[70]

Brown's opponents were PWJ Groenewald from the United Party and Major General AR Selby from the Union Federal Party. Selby, a rather crusty Briton, had served as a senior staff officer and commander in the Middle East during the Second World War, and came to South Africa afterwards to farm. A founder member and later National Vice-President of the Torch Commando, Selby helped found the UFP when it 'became clear that the Torch Commando was no longer an effective means of opposing Nationalist ambitions'.[71]

His party had come into existence on 10 May 1953, just twenty-four hours after the Liberal Party was born, and drew the support of some of those, like Geoffrey Durrant and Arthur Keppel-Jones, who had dabbled in the Liberal groups that eventually affiliated to the South African Liberal Association. In fact, in the press, Keppel-Jones had urged the two parties to join forces, arguing that: '[I]f the people of Natal ... would accept a Liberal racial policy in conjunction with the Federal programme, they would perhaps save the Whites of Africa from being driven into the sea.'[72] But the Federals weren't particularly interested in the Liberals' policy of non-racialism, preferring instead to punt what Selby, in his manifesto, vaguely referred to as a 'constructive and practical non-European policy' based on 'co-operation and friendship with the non-Europeans'.[73]

In later years Brown summed up the Federals' racial policy as

'we'll be nice to the Blacks, and perhaps have some sort of qualified franchise, and so on'.[74] At the time, he told his election audiences their policy was discriminatory since it set certain standards
for Africans to qualify for the common roll, but imposed none for
whites. Indians didn't seem to be able to qualify at all. Moreover,
the Federals' policy of communal representation for Africans and
Indians in the Provincial Council amounted to a 'zero-sum-game of
group interests'.[75]

The Federals' real appeal to Natalian voters lay not in their
'constructive and practical non-European policy', however, but
rather in their support for 'the Natal Stand against the Republic,
in defence of UNION UNDER THE CROWN', as Selby's manifesto barked. In a province where, into the following century,
drivers would still have bumper stickers affixed to their vehicles
proclaiming 'Natal – Last Outpost of the British Empire', this
thinly disguised jingoism might resonate with the electorate. For
that reason, Brown asked a gathering of voters to second their
provincial loyalties to a broader South Africanism. He told them:
'I am a Natalian and my people have been Natalians for as long
as anyone – nevertheless I am much more of a South African
than I am a Natalian and I am not interested in saving Natal in
particular from the dangers that beset it but the Union as a
whole.'[76]

As for the United Party, it tried to chart a middle course between
the extremes of English and Afrikaner nationalism. That was all well
and good, said Brown, but there were 'only two extremes which we
really have to fear and they are the policy of white supremacy ... and
the reverse policy of black supremacy'. He elaborated:

> It is quite clear ... that the UP wants to get all the White
> people together so that they can deal more effectively or
> bargain more effectively or oppose more effectively the
> non-Whites. The United Party ... has come to the conclu-
> sion that some sort of conflict between the interests of white
> and non-white in this country is inevitable and that it had
> better try and get all the whites on to one side. It is an
> admission of failure. The problem is too big. I believe that

the philosophy of white unity is a hopeless and barren policy in [South Africa] in 1954 and I believe that if pursued
any longer that it will lead to disaster.

Throughout its spells in government since Union, the UP's policies
of white unity and white leadership with justice had achieved only
a 'steady deprivation of rights of Africans, increased restrictions
placed upon Indians, and no single constructive and imaginative
attempt to present *all* the people ... with one common ideal to
which all of them could subscribe'.

In a speech entitled 'Liberalism is Realism', Brown reiterated
this message. The widening gulf between blacks and whites was far
more serious an issue than republicanism or federation or Union
under the Crown because, 'in the end, no matter what system of
Government you may have you will, unless you heal the rift between Black and White, have nothing'.[77]

This was remarkably forward-looking for the 1950s, when the
British Commonwealth, the monarchy and the constitutional
nature of the British connection were the chief issues in white politics. And so it seemed to the voters, who, more often than not, as
Brown was to recall, told him: 'You're long before your time.'[78]
However, the Pietermaritzburg electorate wasn't about to be
dragged into the future, and, come election day on 16 June,
Brown ran a distant third to Groenewald and Selby, polling only
154 votes. Even so, it was more than either Junod or Morris managed to muster.

At a National Committee meeting the following month, an
important letter was tabled – one that would have repercussions
for the Party and its relationship with the Congress movement. It
was dated 6 July 1954, and came from the National Action Council
of the Congress of the People (COP). The letter was signed by the
ANC Secretary-General, Walter Sisulu, Rica Hodgson of the COD,
Yusuf Cachalia of the SAIC and Stanley Lollan of SACPO. It
invited the Liberal Party to 'participate in the Congress of the
People to be called by the African National Congress and other
organisations'.[79]

The COP had a long genesis. First mooted by the ANC Cape

President, ZK Matthews, at a provincial congress in 1953, it was then taken up by the ANC nationally. At its annual conference in Queenstown in December 1953, the ANC resolved to prepare for 'the organisation of a "Congress of the People of South Africa", whose task shall be to work out a "Freedom Charter" for all the peoples and groups in the country'.[80] The resolution stated further that, in addition to the members of the COD, SAIC and SACPO, 'any other democratic organisations' should be invited.

The Liberal Party's National Committee first got wind of the resolution in February the following year, and decided that, if requested, it would participate if it could do so 'without danger to the Party'.[81] So, when the formal invitation arrived in July, the National Committee decided to accept it.[82] Over the next six months, the Liberal Party met with the National Action Council to discuss plans for the Congress of the People, and to nail down the terms of the Liberals' involvement and, possibly, co-sponsorship. By and large, the Liberals were initially enthusiastic about co-sponsoring the event: the idea of a large multiracial national convention appealed; co-sponsorship could help to improve relations with the Congress movement; and it might attract further black support.

There were some reservations too, though: the way in which the Freedom Charter was to be drawn up – by going out and asking people about their grievances and demands, and getting a drafting committee to assemble these into a document – seemed impractical. So too did the proposed aim of staging elections throughout the country, in which people of all races would elect representatives to speak and vote on their behalf at the COP. And, of particular concern to the Liberals, the initiative seemed to be largely planned and driven by communists. Joe Slovo acted as a spokesperson for the Congresses when their representatives met with Ballinger, Junod, Unterhalter and the prominent Johannesburg Liberal, Marion Friedmann, in July. And it was Pieter Beyleveld, the National Chairman of the COD, who addressed the Liberals on the COP at their National Committee meeting in October.

Before that meeting, Brown had told Junod that he was anxious to get a representative sample of members' views in Natal on co-sponsoring the COP.[83] He had attended a meeting in Kokstad to gauge public opinion, which was evenly divided, and hoped to attend meetings in Ladysmith and the Midlands in due course. He advised Junod to organise a similar meeting of the Coastal Regional branch.

On 12 October, Ismail Meer of the Natal Indian Congress addressed a combined meeting of the Liberal Party's Edendale and Pietermaritzburg branches on the COP. After he had finished, Hans Meidner moved that 'this branch of the Liberal Party recommends that the Party accept the invitation to co-sponsor the Congress of the People'.[84] His motion was carried by 33 votes to 5.

Nationally, there was by no means consensus within the Party. At the National Committee meeting held between 30 and 31 October, members resolved not to co-sponsor the Congress of the People 'without qualification'. What this meant was that the Party would be willing to 'co-sponsor the calling of a Congress *of representatives of organisations* of all races for the purpose of framing a Freedom Charter for South Africa'.[85]

The National Action Council was unwilling to modify its plans, and it did not respond to the National Committee's resolution. Yet despite not hearing back from the Congresses, the Liberal Party still envisaged that, regardless of co-sponsorship, it would participate in proceedings. After all, both the National Committee and the National Congress had resolved to participate, and those resolutions had not been amended or overturned. Early in 1955, Brown and other Liberals attended a COP meeting in Pietermaritzburg. But for the next few months, there was no news from the National Action Committee and only sporadic talk of the COP. On 6 June 1955, the Transvaal division learnt that the Congress of the People was to take place at Kliptown between 25 and 26 June. On 10 June, it received an invitation to send observers and a message to the COP.

Such haste caught the Liberals off guard. Unterhalter wrote to Wollheim at the national office that same day, seeking guidance. The National Executive Committee held an emergency meeting, which because it took place at short notice included only Cape members. Jimmy Gibson, who despite his radicalism was an implacable opponent of the COD (at whose hands he had twice been drubbed in the Cape Native Representative elections), urged them to dissociate the Party from the COP. The Executive was persuaded by his argument – that there should be no participation without co-sponsorship on terms acceptable to the Party – and Leslie Rubin telephoned Unterhalter to relay the decision. The Cape had been approached for direction, and it seemed to offer a *diktat* in response. The Transvaal division was justifiably incensed.

On 22 June, Unterhalter informed the national office by wire that the Transvaal Executive refused to accept the National Executive's decision, and that it proposed sending observers and a message in the name of the Transvaal alone.

It was Ballinger's turn to be outraged. High-handed at the best of times, she telephoned Unterhalter and laid down the law: '… the COP was now in the hands of Communist elements' and 'independent action [would] embarrass the general political field and cause new, internal strains'.[86] Her message was reinforced in a wire from Gibson, and, under extreme pressure, the Transvaal relented. The Natal division was kept out of the loop entirely: it knew nothing of the National Executive's decision. In the end, the Liberal Party sent no observers and no message of support to the COP.

Brown was to argue, some ten years on, that the Liberal Party's misgivings about the Congress of the People were well founded:

> The proposal for holding national elections, for marchers to converge from all corners of the country on a central point where they would discuss the draft of the Freedom Charter, which would contain a synthesis of their grievances and demands – both ideas were abandoned. Proper elections, even on a minor scale, were never held. A thorough canvas to collect grievances was never conducted. The triumphal marches from places throughout South Africa were never attempted.[87]

He could not predict then the fabulous status the COP would attain in the public imagination, nor the durability of the Freedom Charter as a *vade mecum* in the struggle for democracy. For years to come, Liberals would argue among themselves whether their absence was justified or not. Many viewed it as a 'missed opportunity'.[88] It is impossible to know whether Brown would have dissented from the National Executive's verdict. He had reported to the National Committee in October that Natal, in general, favoured co-sponsorship.[89] His personal opinion he did not elaborate. Paton, in his autobiography, claimed that 'Peter Brown, Hans Meidner, Violaine Junod, and others in Natal, were not enthusiastic' about participation or co-sponsorship.[90] Yet Junod personally endorsed co-sponsorship at the National Committee meeting in October, arguing that it could lead to closer cooperation with the Congress movement. And Meidner put forward the motion supporting co-sponsorship at a joint meeting of the Party's Edendale and Pietermaritzburg branches earlier in the month.

It seems unlikely that Brown would have had qualms about those Congress leaders who were pulling the strings of the COP in Natal – unlike Gibson in the Cape, for example. Once Gibson's friend Thomas Ngwenya was banned and could not steer local preparations, Gibson felt himself 'frozen out' of the Congress of the People by the COD.[91] In Natal, two of Brown's closest and most trusted associates from the ANC and the NIC – Archie Gumede and Chota Motala – were intimately involved with arrangements for the COP. Gumede led the ANC's Natal delegation to Kliptown and Motala chaired the Natal Midlands Committee of the Congress of the People. In June 1955, Motala made a speech on behalf of Luthuli, who was banned from the farewell function for the Durban delegates going to Kliptown.

Even so, by February 1955, Brown *had* become less enthusiastic about co-sponsorship. He told a correspondent:

> Although I supported co-sponsorship without any strings attached [at the National Committee meeting] in Johannesburg, I now think we were wise to stay out. I have attended several of these people's meetings, the last in Pietermaritz-

burg in December. At this meeting the main speaker spent two-thirds of his time talking about the American aggressors in Korea, the 'criminal' Chiang-Kai-Shek, Jomo Kenyatta and a lot of other rubbish calculated to put off, rather than draw in, potential support for the movement. It is a pity because the idea was a good one. Although an attempt is being made to keep the thing going I think it is now more or less moribund.[92]

It seems that Brown had changed his mind about co-sponsoring the COP, in part because he had heard very little about it between December 1954 and February 1955. But the idea of the COP itself seemed to him 'a good one', and he gave no indication prior to June 1955 that he was unwilling for the Liberal Party to participate in – as opposed to co-sponsor – the event.

The communist rhetoric of some of those who spoke in support of the COP may have put Brown on his guard, as his letter suggests. Paton notes in his autobiography that in 1955 the Liberal Party in Natal had just recruited Jordan Ngubane: 'He was an unequivocal anti-communist, and warned the party to have nothing to do with the [Congress of] Democrats, who in his view were turning the African National Congress towards communism.'[93] It is possible that Ngubane's caution prompted Brown's own, although it is equally true that Brown never shared Ngubane's visceral dislike of the communist left. He was certainly never attracted to communism – in fact he didn't much like it – but this was 'not as a result of any great intellectual rejection'.[94] He disliked the 'old [Marxist] jargon' employed by a large number of the Congresses' leaders, and abhorred 'the whole Bandung foreign policy line' which would be punted on platforms – where both members of the Liberal Party and the Congress movement were present – which had nothing to do with international matters.[95] But Brown was not one of those Liberals who sought to outflank or outmanoeuvre the communists in the sense of excluding them from combined action against apartheid. Jimmy Gibson and the student leader John Didcott, by contrast, wanted the ANC to abandon the COP because of the COD's machinations, and stage a national convention in conjunction with the Liberal Party instead. To this end, they brokered a meeting between Ngwenya, who was sympathetic to their cause, and Luthuli and ZK Matthews. It went ahead, but a banning order abruptly imposed on Ngwenya put paid to their plans.[96]

Perhaps Brown's unwillingness to become involved in such a power play revealed a lack of political instinct at this stage in his public career. (In 1963, the left-leaning writer, Ronald Segal, would describe Brown as a 'figure of considerable political intelligence and realism [who is] substantially responsible for swerving the Liberal Party towards a recognition of the changing demands of political resistance in South Africa'.[97]) At any rate, if Brown had been present at the National Executive meeting, and if he *had* refused to participate in the COP, it seems improbable that his decision would have been ideologically motivated. In other words, it seems unlikely that he would have eschewed participation because he declined, on principle, to cooperate with communists for ideological reasons. He was not an 'ideological' person in the general sense of the word. Years later, Brown would tell the Black Consciousness poet, Mafika Gwala, that it was necessary to 'forego the luxury of ideological argument ... to oppose a common foe'.[98]

Indeed, Brown acknowledged in an interview in the 1990s that communists had been engaged in 'constructive work' against apartheid: 'It wasn't what they were doing, it was the language they tended to speak which was the problem.'[99] Certainly, he found communist dogma tedious, and he was by no means oblivious to its undertones of totalitarian violence, but he got on well personally with various communists and he was prepared to work with them in fighting a shared enemy. Catherine Shallis, who served first as Secretary to the Natal provincial office and, later, to the national office in the late 1950s, recounts an anecdote which illustrates Brown's position. His friend from the NIC, Suttie Mungal, who often sported a red tie as a marker of his political affiliation, used to tell the following joke about the Freedom Charter:

The masses are being told:

– You will have land!
– You will have rights!
– You will have freedom!
– You will have money!
– You will live in a land of milk and honey!

And then some lone voice shouts out that the masses don't
want milk and honey. Back comes the reply:

– Then we'll ram it down your throats!

Brown enjoyed this joke heartily and Shallis suggests that although
'some Liberals, including Peter, regretted that they hadn't attended
[the COP] ... it [the anecdote] does show that Peter could relax
with those who went to Kliptown and at the same time question the
doctrinaire aspects of the speeches and document'.[100]

We simply do not know whether Brown would have rebuffed
the consensus view of the National Executive and made the case
for official Liberal attendance at the COP. He is said to have felt in
retrospect that the Liberals should have taken part.[101] What we do
know is that the Liberal Party's absence from the Congress of the
People had two major consequences.

Firstly, it alienated them from the Congress movement – not
irretrievably, but at the time profoundly. Luthuli believed, as he
formulated it years later, that 'Africans will judge you by what you
do for them, not by your ideologies'.[102] In the circumstances, the
Liberals had been found wanting. Paton himself thought that the
Party's action 'displeased' Luthuli, and surmised – perhaps pre-
dictably – that Luthuli 'felt that our action pushed him further into
the arms of the left'.[103]

Secondly, the way in which the Party's non-attendance had
been decided – by decree of the Cape members of the National
Executive alone – inflamed tensions between the Transvaal and
the Cape divisions, and irked Natal. In Brown's view, it 'widened
the gulf which already existed in the Party between its conservative
and radical wings'.[104] Clearly, the breach could not be healed from

the national office in the Cape. The Natal division, with its reputation for centrist sensibleness, not to mention its growth, its
dynamism and its evident success in winning over black support,
seemed the natural mediator. So it came to pass that, in 1956, the
national office moved to Natal, and Brown stepped onto the
national stage.

9

ONTO THE NATIONAL STAGE
1956-1960

B rown had entered politics as a novice in 1953. His political
education, his awakening to the deep injustices of apartheid
and his growing conviction that South Africans could only prevent a
racial showdown by working together towards a non-racial society –
all of this had been shaped by his social work at Edendale. He was
a stranger to the parliamentary domain of white politics, and despite having met and befriended members of the Congress movement, black politics, too, was a foreign land. Of the internal world
of liberal politics – its staid Cape torchbearers, its emphasis on
'constitutional' activity through public institutions and its insula-
tion from black political organisations – he knew very little. There
were many issues that divided Liberals: universal franchise, extra-
parliamentary activity, and cooperation with the Congresses, for
instance. The pros and cons, and the sense of urgency with which
they were argued – those too were largely uncharted waters for
Brown. He had a cool and open-minded, but cautious, approach to
contentious matters, and, in his mind, the creation of a common
society was the priority. Healing the breach between black and
white, and presenting them with a shared ideal to which they could
both subscribe, as he told his constituents in 1954 – that was where
his political interest lay. And because he was a practical man, he
went out and *acted*. As Natal Provincial Secretary, he put organisational structures in place in the province, and he went out of his
way to recruit a multiracial membership. By 1956, Natal had the
most members of all the provincial divisions, and the most racially

diverse membership. As he became immersed in politics – unlike most other Liberal office-bearers, this was his full-time occupation – and more attuned to its undercurrents, Brown found his political voice. Already by 1953 he had met Luthuli, and made contact with senior leaders from the Natal Indian Congress. In anti-apartheid circles, he was beginning to be taken seriously as a man of substance. And within the Liberal Party, through his editorial columns for *Contact* and his contributions to the National Committee, Brown's was soon recognised as a voice of sanity, a voice of reason. By 1956, he was ready to step onto the national stage.

* * *

Margaret Ballinger was displeased with the Party's overture to the voteless masses at its 1954 National Congress. Herself committed to the qualified franchise, she saw no reason for the Party to stake a claim to universal suffrage on behalf of blacks, and she took its decision to do so as a personal affront and a personal betrayal. The Liberal Party had joined her, after all, not vice versa, and her views should be the Party's views. At the time, Ballinger threatened to stand down as leader, but was dissuaded from doing so. She also found it onerous to combine her stewardship of the Party with her duties as leader of the Native Representative Council in Parliament. It was even harder, she remarked to the current National Chairman, Leo Marquard, in 1954, 'without the active support of a group of people of my own type, in whose judgment and integrity I can have confidence'.[1]

Marquard himself resigned the chair due to ill health, and in 1955 the Party redefined the National Chairman's post so as to lighten Ballinger's load. The Cape conservatives, Oscar Wollheim and Leslie Rubin, both took on the role for a spell, but neither was able to devote himself to it wholeheartedly. In any event, the fiasco surrounding the Liberals' absence from the Congress of the People had disenchanted the Transvaal and Natal divisions with Cape control. What was needed, in Brown's words, was 'a Chairman who would be able to hold office for some time ... [and] who could command the loyalty of all sections of the Party and not [as] a representative of either its Right or Left wings'.[2] It became all the more pressing to find a conciliatory commander after Ballinger eventually resigned the leadership in November 1955. At the time, she moaned bitterly: 'I don't owe the Party anything except a lot of personal discouragement and belittlement.'[3]

At the Transvaal's behest, Paton, who was away in America, was to be approached to assume the chairmanship on his return. In the meantime, at a National Committee meeting in January 1956, Leo Kuper was elected Acting National Chairman with Brown as his deputy. EV Mahomed was chosen to take over as Treasurer, and it was decided to move the national office to Pietermaritzburg. The balance of power had shifted decisively to Natal. Brown's impression from this meeting was that the Cape members of the National Committee were quite happy to see the headquarters move. 'They started off with the feeling that the Party was something which was almost a personal Cape possession,' he commented wryly, 'but somehow … it seemed to have got out of their control.'[4]

The following month, Michael O'Dowd congratulated Brown on his appointment, telling him that 'everyone in the Transvaal is very pleased'. He felt that the Party was 'now receiving the guidance from the national level which it so badly needs, and it is already making a difference'.[5] Patrick Duncan, the ruddy-faced political entrepreneur whose career would take him from supporting the United Party to joining the Pan Africanist Congress, with a Liberal interlude in between, had joined the Liberal Party after attending the Natal Provincial Congress in 1955.[6] Afterwards, he had gone to a *braaivleis* at Brown's home, Shinglewood, where the multiracial complexion of those present had made an impression on him. Nobody there seemed to give any thought to his or her race, Duncan wrote in *Contact*, and, from listening to the Congress speeches, he was persuaded that the Natal Liberals had 'set sail irrevocably towards a new society where the injustices of modern South Africa will be checked at source, by the grant of the vote, and full and equal status to all'.[7] The former Governor General's son now wrote to Brown, expressing his delight that the Party's centre of gravity had moved to Natal. This, he told Brown, was 'a compliment to Alan [Paton] but also … a recognition of the hard routine job of organisation that you have done'.[8] To Paton's wife, Dorrie, Duncan confided that the only hope the Party had of growing was under the novelist's chairmanship. 'The only alternative,' he postulated, 'would be Peter Brown, who ... would be quite excellent in every way – but he hasn't written *Cry, The Beloved Country*. And that does matter so much.'[9]

Duncan's throwaway comment was spot-on. Brown did the grunt work of building up the Party; he also, no doubt, possessed the personal qualities – the even-temperedness, the steadiness, the firmness and the gravitas – to unite and lead the organisation. But in 1956, as a young man, he was still in Paton's shadow. Paton, who had confided to Ballinger in 1954 that politics was not his calling, was hardly a natural *political* leader; he was certainly no political strategist, but his bestselling novel had conferred on him international fame and status and moral authority. He was the Liberals' prize asset, and the obvious choice to lead the Party. Of course, he had other attributes, too: he was a dazzling speaker, his speeches crafted in his beautiful, lyrical prose, and delivered in the clipped, powerful cadences of his distinctive Natalian accent. Brown, by contrast, was not a great orator: he had a habit of clearing his throat regularly when he spoke, and his speeches were always laconic, seldom rousing.[10] Catherine Shallis, the Party's National Secretary in the late 1950s, sums up the difference thus: 'Peter tended to speak about the practical consequences of the injustice he had personally witnessed in Natal and beyond, and Paton gave really inspiring and motivating speeches about what could and should be.'[11]

Yet, in some ways, Brown was much more politically minded than Paton. The latter had entered politics as a detribalised writer, hoping to end a period of creative stagnation, and he was probably more at home in the world of letters. The tension between his writing life and his political life eventually caused him to resign the Party chair in 1958. When Brown stepped into his shoes, between 1958 and 1964, the Party made its most significant contribution to fighting apartheid, although there were other factors, apart from Brown's banning, which caused the Party to wither and die between 1964 and 1968.

Brown's style of leadership is clearly illustrated by David Evans, who became Secretary of the Natal division in the 1960s, and who was a friend and research assistant to Paton. He remembers the 'calmness' which Brown brought to coping with 'often stormy disagreements in the party':

> He was, I thought, an excellent chairman of the party with its diversity of race, class and ideology. Tolerant without being soft, he understood both right and left of the party rather better than they understood each other, dealing with us all with good humour and a nice dry wit, the latter qualities undoubtedly helping him through detention and banning.[12]

Paton and Brown complemented one another, and their friendship was at once personal and political. Together, they were the public face of a particular strand of South African liberalism in the 1950s and 1960s, one which Albert Luthuli, in his autobiography, said took its stand on 'principles and not on expediency – a new thing indeed in white politics'.[13] And the way that strand was woven had as much to do with their personal chemistry as it did their political like-mindedness.

John Mitchell, a young schoolmaster who Brown had met when the Liberal Party started and who subsequently became a staunch friend, thought Paton and Brown had 'rather a sort of father-son relationship … although, in a sense, Brown was the dominant character in the relationship'.[14] Liz Pitman, who served as the Party's National Secretary in the early 1960s, drove around the country with Paton and Brown on Party business. She remembered that their rapport was forged through a good deal of banter and teasing. Both men were keen bird-watchers; on their trips, Paton would see a yellow-billed kite, for instance, and say to Brown: 'What bird is that?' Later on he would see another, repeat the same question and elicit the same answer. Eventually he would snort derisively, 'Brown, every damn bird you see is a yellow-billed kite!' Brown responded in kind, but Paton could sometimes be testy: 'I'm not in the mood for badinage today,' he would snap.[15]

Paton was struck by Brown, and, with his writerly incisiveness and keen sense of intuition, was insightful about the younger man. In a column penned during Brown's 1958 election campaign, entitled 'Crusader on a Polo Pony', Paton wrote that it was 'quite difficult to explain Brown's character, not because it is enigmatic, but because it isn't'.

> He is a zealot who doesn't look zealous. He is a crusader who rides a polo pony. His fairy godmother gave him intensity without intenseness, depth without heaviness, passion without fanaticism. He hates injustice neither hotly or coldly; he just hates it, and neither doctrine nor passion will take him off the course. His determination also has this strange natural quality. It is not fierce, or inexorable, or consuming, or steely. It just stays on this incredibly natural course. It is accompanied by an easy humour, in which teasing plays an important role. He teases people to surpass themselves. He teases himself too, and pokes fun at the Party's earnestness. He might be a cynic, only he can't be cold. He might be cynical about human beings, but he can't, because he has so many friends (or vice versa, one doesn't know which) … The longer one knows Brown, the more one thinks of him. The more one looks at these modestly displayed goods, the more one realises their quality. Generous of nature, he has virtually given his life to the Party. That gives him an authority surpassed by none.[16]

In 1956, it was Paton whose literal authority over the Liberal Party was unsurpassed; the national chairmanship still lay ahead of Brown. And now Brown's immediate objective as Deputy Chairman was to boost the Party's profile, to extend its sphere of influence and to garner for it greater credibility as a serious player in non-racial anti-apartheid politics. The most effective way of doing that, he soon realised, was by campaigning on issues directly relevant to disenfranchised South Africans.

One of the first things Brown did was to hire Patrick Duncan as the Party's National Organiser. It was the beginning of a productive relationship for the Party, albeit one that was often fraught and which would later sour. Brown would say of Duncan: 'Nobody more likeable or charming you could find'; he was a 'great person, but impossible to work with ... totally unpredictable'.[17] Needless to say, with his mercurial reputation, Duncan did not endear himself to the Cape old guard. Brown canvassed their views on his becoming National Organiser, and Walter Stanford reported back that they were mostly strongly opposed, with the exception of Leo Marquard. Always a wise counsel, Marquard thought that Duncan 'had a lot of courage and character ... that he was energetic, and that he could not do much harm as National Organiser'.[18] Margaret Ballinger informed Brown that she was 'strongly opposed' to Duncan's appointment, since he was, in her view, 'completely unstable and undependable'. She accurately predicted that 'he will constantly be at loggerheads with us on one issue or another and ... ultimately he will leave us'.[19]

In part, Ballinger's sentiments about Duncan were coloured by a previous run-in. In mid-1953, Duncan announced that in the forthcoming Senate elections he would oppose William Ballinger, Margaret's husband, who held the Transvaal and Orange Free State seat on the Native Representative Council. Although Duncan subsequently abandoned his plan, his actions caused a rift with the Ballingers. Then, too, he had poured cold water on the Liberal Party shortly after its formation. In May 1953, Duncan had published a pamphlet entitled *The Road through the Wilderness,* which encouraged voters to support the United Party and accused the founders of the Liberal Party of being 'without an adequate appreciation of the part that political power plays in politics'.[20] Despite Duncan's chequered political past, Brown thought his appointment would 'mark a new chapter in our story' and 'provide vigour and imagination and create a new spate of Party activity in all spheres and amongst all sections of the community'.[21] And indeed it did.

Brown, for his part, sought closer cooperation with the Congresses. In May 1956, he attended an All-in Conference in Durban, hosted by the Natal Indian Congress, to explore ways of resisting the Group Areas Act. The Liberal delegation comprised Brown, Paton, Ken Hill and three of the Party's most active Indian members –

EV Mahomed, Rajen Naidoo and Pat Poovalingam.[22] Brown remarked to Duncan on the Liberals' warm reception: there was
much applause whenever one of them got up to say something.
Brown took this as a 'good sign', although he was unable to explain
it. He joked with Duncan: 'It may, of course, just be that the new
Moscow line has reached Durban.' But Brown wasn't too fazed
about the Congress motives: '[T]here seems to be a fair prospect
of our working closely with the NIC and ANC in a campaign
against Group Areas and other removal plans. That can do nothing but good.'[23]

Brown reported back to the Natal Provincial Executive Committee that the meeting had taken place in a 'friendly atmosphere',
and he remarked upon 'the unanimity of the views expressed'.[24]
Out of the conference was born the Group Areas Vigilance Committee, consisting of both Liberal and NIC members. They travelled the length and breadth of Natal, addressing audiences and
raising awareness. Brown would later recall that:

> Too often the occasions were used by the Congress speakers
> not to attack the Group Areas Act alone but to win support
> for their views and to make the kind of doctrinaire anti-
> imperialist, anti-capitalist, communist-oriented speeches
> which achieved nothing except to antagonise people who
> were anxious to fight Group Areas without becoming in-
> volved in ideological wrangles.[25]

Whatever his personal views on the Congress movement, particularly whether it might be in thrall to the Reds, Brown held his
tongue in public, preferring instead to seek consensus and build
relationships in opposing apartheid. Although privately he could
be critical, publicly his attitude to the Congress of Democrats was
similar to that of Luthuli, which Paton vividly described in his autobiography: 'South Africa was on fire, and he found it impossible to
say to his fellow fire-fighters, "Where does your water come from,
and what kind of bucket are you carrying it in?"'[26]

To Jordan Ngubane, the buckets mattered. He wrote a series of
articles for Manilal Gandhi's *Indian Opinion* in 1956, claiming that

the ANC (of which he remained a member) had become awash
with communists, and that Luthuli had done nothing to stem the
tide. Brown found these public attacks embarrassing: although he
conceded that 'much of what Ngubane said was probably true', he
thought it wise that 'Luthuli and other liberal members of the
Congress should be kept as close to the Party as possible'.[27] When
Luthuli's banning orders – imposed for two years in terms of the
Suppression of Communism Act of 1950 – were lifted in the winter
of 1956, Brown attended his presidential address to the ANC on the
subject 'The struggle must go on, bans or no bans'. Luthuli himself took this as evidence of 'cooperation across the race barrier',
noting in his autobiography that 'Dr Motala represented the Indian
Congress, and Mr Peter Brown came for the Liberal Party'.[28]

Cooperation between Liberals and the Congresses was soon to
acquire another dimension. On 5 December 1956, after police
investigations arising from the Congress of the People, 156 members of the Congress movement were arrested and charged with
treason – among them, Luthuli, ZK Matthews, then ANC Secretary-
General Oliver Tambo, Nelson Mandela and Walter Sisulu. Liberals mobilised rapidly to express their support and raise funds for
those standing trial. That same day, Brown, Paton, Leo Kuper and
Violaine Junod set up the Civil Liberties Defence Committee in
Natal, and discussed creating a specially dedicated fund for the
accused. The fund was launched the following day, at the Gandhi
Library hall in Durban, and it soon amalgamated with similar
funds run by Bishop Ambrose Reeves in Johannesburg and Archbishop Geoffrey Clayton in Cape Town, into the Treason Trial
Defence Fund.

This was the start of the International Defence and Aid Fund,
which channelled money from the British, Scandinavian and other
foreign governments through a London-based organisation run by
Canon John Collins.[29] From Natal, Paton and Kuper were most
closely associated with the local Fund. In fact, when they made their
appeal for funds in Durban on 6 December, they were arrested
under a by-law for taking part in 'an assembly of natives'. As a personal friend of Collins, Paton was also the South African point-
person for the Defence and Aid Fund, which continued to make

clandestine disbursements to the Congresses even after they were banned in 1960 and after the so-called Treason Trials collapsed, with no convictions, in 1961. The Liberal Party in general served as a vital conduit for these payments, but saw very little of the money come their way, since Collins, in Paton's words, 'to a large extent ignored liberals'.[30]

Brown liaised with Collins, sometimes sending an 'urgent appeal' for funds,[31] but the two men appear not to have met. This may have had to do with a minor altercation occasioned by something Brown wrote in *Contact* in 1954, when he repeated the accusation that Collins had failed to keep an appointment with the Chairman of the Non-European Affairs Committee while on a visit to Johannesburg. Brown was berated by Margaret du Manoir for this, who informed him that Collins was 'very hurt by your reference in *Contact*'. 'He is one of our most interested and active supporters over here,' she chided him, 'and you shouldn't alienate one of the very few people who understands us and wish [sic] us well.'[32] Du Manoir proposed that Brown issue an apology to Collins, but he stuck to his guns, telling her that 'no apology is due to Canon Collins'.[33] Diana Collins, the canon's wife and a great admirer of Brown's, stayed at Shinglewood when she toured South Africa undercover on a fact-finding mission in 1966.

Throughout 1956, Brown travelled extensively in the rural areas, signing up new members. He made his first foray into the Transkei, along with Paton and Mlahleni Njisane, and signed up new members at the Holy Cross Mission in East Pondoland.[34] He also became increasingly involved in what would be one of the Liberal Party's most notable campaigns against apartheid – the struggle to oppose black spot removals in Natal.

In terms of the 1913 Natives' Land Act, Africans were not allowed to own land outside of the 'reserves'. Consequently, the pockets of African- and mission-owned land held in freehold title outside the reserves were termed 'black spots'. When the Nationalists came to power, they decided that these black spots should be eliminated through a policy of removal and resettlement. This uprooted communities, broke down networks of kinship and caused untold misery for people whose homes were destroyed and livelihoods imperilled.

In 1954, Selby Msimang discovered that the African residents of Charlestown, a black spot on the Natal border with the Transvaal, were to be evicted and resettled without freehold rights in an inhospitable area called Buffalo Flats, 60 kilometres to the south. Those who worked in Charlestown could stay, but their houses would be demolished, and they would have to live in a location attached to a white town.

In August that year, the matter was discussed at a meeting of the Natal Provincial Committee.[35] At the Natal Provincial Congress in December, Brown tabled a motion recording the Party's 'emphatic disapproval of the proposal' to remove Charlestown residents.[36] Another resolution, proposed by Richard Robinow, called upon the Party to publicise the residents' stories of personal hardship. This eventually culminated in the publication of *The Charlestown Story*, written by Alan Paton, which recounted a 'miserable story of meanness, incompetence, delay and heartbreak'.[37]

In the meantime, together with Paton and Msimang, Brown had visited Charlestown and met with members of the community to find out more about the proposed removal. Peter Mtimkulu, a young medical student, had spent part of his vacation conducting research in Charlestown and other black spots in northern Natal. The following year, he, Brown and Ngubane spent several days visiting a number of black spots in the area, alerting residents to their plight, and giving thought to how the removals might be stopped or delayed. Brown told Walter Stanford after his visit that 'the most dangerous feature of the whole business ... is that this process is going along slowly while nobody knows about it. Even if we can only give it publicity it will be something.'[38]

Brown was to write of his trip with Mtimkulu and Ngubane that it was 'really the beginning of the campaign which the Party later launched against Blackspot [sic] removals'.[39] Indeed, in 1956, the Natal Provincial Committee appointed Brown, Msimang and Ngubane to a subcommittee, tasked with planning the campaign. Brown visited Charlestown, Khumalosville and Newcastle, and he met with Luthuli to determine whether the ANC would welcome a joint campaign to oppose and publicise the removals. He reported back to the Natal Provincial Committee that Luthuli 'was pleased with the idea'.[40] Brown also consulted with Gabriel Nyembe, the ANC's leading light in northern Natal. In December, Brown informed the Committee that Elliot Mngadi, the court messenger whom he had met at Walter and Adelaine Hain's house in Ladysmith, was 'quite prepared to accept the position of organiser' for the campaign against black spot removals.[41]

Mngadi himself had grown up in a black spot called Roosboom, outside Ladysmith, where his father had bought a plot for £11 and built a house. Mngadi senior was a sickly man, an asthmatic, and, because he was rarely in work, Elliot had helped to pay his own way through school by performing domestic work in Ladysmith during the holidays. He continued his education at St Hilda's College for Girls, which accepted a number of local boys as day scholars, and this was where he mastered the English language. Later, Mngadi would cultivate the air of an English gentleman. While working in Johannesburg to put his younger brothers and sisters through school – alternately as a deliveryman and storeman – he saved enough money to buy his own plot at Roosboom. Now that, too, was under threat from the government, which signalled its intention to move his community to a proposed village, Vulandondo. Mngadi was approached to be the Town Clerk of Vulandondo, but turned it down rather than compromise himself by collaborating with the system.[42] Instead, he accepted – at a lower salary – the Liberal Party's offer of the post of campaign organiser against black spot removals.

Brown worked closely with Mngadi, and together they trudged through black spots in northern Natal, raising awareness among landowners and tenants threatened with removal, and discussing ways to resist. The information they gathered was compiled by Mngadi into detailed monthly reports. Brown's individual efforts were greatly valued by those faced with eviction. In one of many such letters written to Brown, a Charlestown resident, Jeremiah Mkhwanazi, thanked him for his help: 'I greatly appreciate the services you are prepared to render me and thank you for all the trouble you have taken on my behalf.'[43]

In 1958, Mngadi estimated that between 100 000 and 250 000 people in northern Natal stood to be displaced by the government's policy on black spots.[44] The number of black spots were eventually pegged at 350 nationally, 250 of which were in Natal.[45] By mid-1958, Mngadi had mobilised 40 black spot communities to join a proposed organisation which would oppose their impending removal. This was launched later in the year as the Northern Natal African Landowners' Association (NNALA), with the consent of both the ANC and the Liberal Party, and Mngadi became its Secretary.[46] In October, Mngadi was also appointed the Party's organiser in northern Natal. Brown wrote to Luthuli before Mngadi's appointment, lest the Chief think there might be a conflict of interest between Mngadi's work for the Association and his work for the Party. Luthuli had no objections, either to Mngadi's appointment as Party Organiser or the establishment of the NNALA, but he expressed a reservation that forming 'parochial and isolated political groups ... would weaken united African political progress'. He feared that unless the NNALA was 'properly guided from the start it may come to regard itself, to the exclusion of the Liberal Party, the ANC or any other major political party, as solely responsible ... in political matters'. He preferred African communities to align themselves with 'national or major political body or bodies of their choice'.[47] Unlike Luthuli, Brown was confident that the NNALA would not become a political loose cannon. Partly this was because he trusted Mngadi implicitly, and partly because the Association's committee members were all either staunch Liberals or Congressites.[48]

For the next six years, the association waged a relentless campaign against black spot removals, until the government started imposing banning orders on its key workers – Mngadi, Michael Ndlovu and Christopher Shabalala – and its most ardent advocates, like Brown and Msimang. The NNALA achieved some success in delaying removals: for example, it took over twenty years to complete the relocation of Charlestown freeholders to Buffalo Flats, and tenants to Duck Ponds. Of course, the wheels of bureaucracy turned inexorably, heedless of all obstacles in their path. However, through their involvement with the campaign, Liberals managed to express solidarity with dispossessed rural Africans and identify with their issues in a way that no other political organisation did at the time. In so doing, they made a unique contribution to the struggle against apartheid in the 1950s and 1960s. They also broadened the scope of South African liberalism, whose welfarist impulses, historically, had been directed at the amelioration of African living conditions in urban areas. The result was increased support for the Liberal Party among rural Africans. New branches were formed in black spots like Charlestown and Khumalosville, and Brown played a vital part in recruiting members. His fluency in Zulu and his 'unequalled dedication', in Mlahleni Njisane's words, enabled him to communicate in such a fashion that racial distinctions seemed to blur.[49] Paton noted that Brown 'certainly had the gift of communicating with black people'.[50]

In her report to the 1958 Natal Provincial Congress, which was opened by Luthuli, Catherine Shallis reported on the Party's expansion in inland country areas such as Cedarville, Ladysmith, Winterton, Bergville, Charlestown and the Midlands. Provincial membership now stood at 860, and, Shallis noted: '[T]he Party in Natal owes much of its strength and stability to the ceaseless energy of Mr. Peter Brown.'[51]

Brown's work against black spot removals, and its impact on the Party, made him realise that extra-parliamentary activity was vital if the Liberals were to attract black support, breathe life into the idea of non-racialism, and shape liberalism as a dynamic political force. His conviction was reinforced by Liberal successes in the rest of the country: in the Transvaal, membership had trebled by 1957 thanks to the Party's active opposition to the Resettlement Board in Sophiatown and its support for those involved in the Alexandra and Lady Selborne bus boycotts.[52] The Cape conservatives, meanwhile, looked upon this spate of extra-parliamentary activity with foreboding. They wanted the Party to affirm its commitment to the 'constitutional means' clause in its founding principles. As early as February 1956, Brown wrote to Duncan about the clause: 'I would now be quite ready to see it go and had, in fact, intended raising the whole question at July's National Congress.'[53] His views were subsequently tempered after a chat with Leo Kuper, who thought that forcing the issue would rock 'the Party to its foundations'. Brown told Duncan that he had 'a great respect for Leo's opinions and would not lightly go against them'.[54]

At the Natal Provincial Congress in October, the majority of delegates resolved to remove the clauses that restricted political action to a narrowly defined constitutionalism.[55] Although Brown supported the resolution, he was anxious that it should not split the Party nationally. When Jordan Ngubane, who had long argued the merits of extra-parliamentarianism, submitted an article to *Contact* on the subject, Brown rejected it. He did not want to pre-empt matters before the next National Congress, 'the whole success' of which, he wrote to Ngubane, depended 'on everyone coming there with open minds, and completely trusting one another'. He added: 'They *might* (the conservatives) just feel that we had taken advantage of them by means of this publicity.'[56]

Brown would recall of the Natal resolution: 'We were on the edge of the brink again and stepped back from it only by referring these resolutions to the National Committee.'[57] There, the Cape members accepted that extra-parliamentary activity should be *complementary* rather than *ancillary* and *secondary* to electoral work. Accordingly, the Natal resolution was withdrawn and did not go to Congress.

Despite his newfound enthusiasm for extra-parliamentary initiatives, Brown still thought it was necessary to participate in elections, since he was 'averse to … giving up opportunities of hammering the whites', and he regarded 'elections as one of the best opportunities for doing that'.[58] To Bunny Curran, the Party's headstrong representative in the Cape Provincial Council, he wrote:

My view is that, when an election comes along, one takes part in it, not with any particular thoughts of success but simply to prepare White minds for change. During the rest of the time one's main pre-occupation is with extra-parliamentary work … My fear is that, by neglecting to sow the seeds of doubt in White minds, i.e. by contesting elections etc., they will sink into a rigid inflexibility which will make it impossible for them to bring themselves to give anything away unless it is won from them by force.[59]

In fact, both Curran and Patrick Duncan opposed contesting the 1958 general election. Their arguments failed to sway the Party, which fielded three candidates: Jimmy Dey in Orange Grove, Johannesburg; Gerald Gordon in Sea Point, Cape Town; and Brown in Pietermaritzburg District.

Trying to shift the allegiance of Pietermaritzburg's voters from the United Party to the Liberals was an uphill battle. One of Brown's constituents asked him to reconsider standing against the UP's candidate, Bertram Henwood, who had been returned to Parliament unopposed since 1948, and suggested a seat in Durban instead. 'In a modern city like Durban,' HM D'Ommett wrote preciously, 'Liberal idealogy [sic] must appeal more than to a quiet and, it must be said of our beloved city, old-fashioned [one], like Pietermaritzburg.'[60]

Not all voters were as diffident as HM D'Ommett. Derick Marsh, a young lecturer in the English Department at the University of Natal, who would come to be detained with Brown, volunteered to help in the campaign. He later recalled some of the perils of canvassing:

> For the most part they [those being canvassed] looked embarrassed, but some laughed at us, and some spat on us, or threatened to shoot us or set the dogs on us. Everyone hated canvassing. Even Harold Strachan, who could usually derive some perverse satisfaction from the most unpromising of situations, preferred travelling the streets at midnight with Sam Chetty in Harold's battered Morris Minor, putting up our posters in places where they would cause maximum annoyance the next day, to knocking on doors and trying to persuade by rational argument.[61]

Even so, Brown's campaign did not shy away from the hard questions. Regarding universal suffrage, he told an audience: 'Africa is moving towards it and there is no reason why South Africa should be immune to the trends which are active in the rest of the world.'[62]

His manifesto proposed the entrenchment of a Bill of Rights in the Constitution; the abolition of all racial legislation; the extension of freehold ownership of land to all races in 'town and country'; a dedicated ministry to deal with housing backlogs; and a campaign for free and compulsory education for all children up to Standard Six.[63] Another pamphlet, aimed at allaying voters' fears that they would be splitting the opposition by voting Liberal, carried endorsements from an African, E Khumalo; a Coloured, S Pietter-sen; and an Indian, Sam Chetty.[64]

One of Brown's most successful campaign meetings was held in Howick, which, unlike most of the other towns in his constituency, permitted blacks into the local hall. *Contact* reported that 'there was a mass attendance of Indian and African factory workers … Dozens were left outside and … Jordan Ngubane had to go and hold a second meeting on the verandah'.[65]

However, Brown's appeals to non-racialism failed to strike a chord, and in a two-cornered contest, Brown polled 604 votes to his opponent's 6 000-odd.[66] Even so, Brown told a correspondent, this was 'a good many more votes than I had anticipated'.[67] And it was marginally better than the seven percent Dey polled in Orange Grove.

* * *

By mid-1958, Paton was growing restless with his chairmanship of the Party. He had still not finished writing the biography of his friend, Jan Hofmeyr, which had been years in the making and whose completion had been held up by the obstructiveness of Hofmeyr's domineering mother. It was time to focus on his writing and hand over the baton of leadership. In his autobiography, Paton describes the circumstances of Brown's succession half-jokingly. Referring to Brown as 'Sir Galahad', a man knightly in every way 'except for his sardonic wit', Paton recollects:

> Now it so happened that Peter Brown wanted the national chairmanship for himself, and he came to me and said, not sardonically but very winningly, 'You know, Paton, you'll never write that life of Hofmeyr while you are National Chairman, and it is very important that this life should be

written, really extremely important, and no one can write it
better than you, so I think you ought to give up the national
chairmanship, and we'll create a new post of National
President, and you can take that.' So I took the post of
National President, and who do you think was the new
National Chairman? Sir Galahad, of course.[68]

Paton conceded that there was 'another version of this story', one
in which Brown could see that the Liberal Party was damaging
Paton's writing career, and so he volunteered his services. 'I must
say that Peter prefers the second version to the first, and I must
have half believed it myself,' Paton continues, 'because when I had
finished *Hofmeyr* I dedicated it to him.'

The second version may have been more accurate than the
first. It is true that Brown thought Paton was the best person to
write Hofmeyr's biography. He also felt that Paton 'should put his
writing first', as he would tell Leslie Cooper in 1961. But, equally,
Brown had 'doubts about the value of the Hofmeyr biography from
our [Party] point of view'. He remarked to Cooper: 'I think it will
probably be an excellent biography but I am afraid that the ideas
for which he [Hofmeyr] stood have been left so far behind by
events that they will not mean a great deal today.'[69]

At the time of Paton's resignation, Brown was hardly eager to
replace him. In May 1958, he told Bunny Curran: 'The news about
the Chairmanship is still a bit vague ... I am certainly no keen
starter.'[70] At the National Committee meeting later that month,
Paton stood down and Brown was the only person nominated to
succeed him. He was elected unanimously.[71]

Brown inherited the chairmanship ahead of a period of considerable flux in both black and white politics. After JG Strijdom's
death in September, Hendrik Verwoerd would become Prime
Minister, ushering in an era of unprecedented ideological rigidity
and brutality. There were ructions in the ANC, which eventually
led to the breakaway of an Africanist faction and the formation of
the Pan Africanist Congress (PAC) in 1959. In the United Party,
too, there were murmurings of dissent about the Party's new
conservative leader, Sir de Villiers Graaff, from some of the more

liberal Members of Parliament. They would eventually hive off into a new party, the Progressive Party, also launched in 1959.

In accepting his nomination, Brown stressed that the Party's function was largely an extra-parliamentary one. This was because he had come to set little store by Parliament as an institution. In 1959, Brown would write that South Africa had never had true parliamentary government. Since 1910, both the UP and the Nationalists had made 'Parliament more and more one-sidedly representative of purely white interests'. The abolition of Native Representatives in 1960 would be the final nail in the coffin. Parliament was not a 'democratic institution for all South Africans', and democracy had died in 1948, according to Brown:

> The Parliamentary system in South Africa is dead, and it is dead because the Nationalists have killed it. They continue to go through the democratic motions because it gives the stamp of respectability to their policies and deludes a diminishing number of their opponents, at home and abroad, into thinking that democracy functions here.[72]

In the absence of a legitimate Parliament, Brown, as National Chairman, redoubled the Party's efforts in the extra-parliamentary sphere. From 1959 to 1960, for example, Liberals played an important role in organising an overseas boycott of South African goods. This led to cooperation with the Congress movement once more.

The idea of a consumer boycott – of products from companies linked to the National Party – was first mooted at the ANC's National Congress in 1958. The ANC Executive approached the Liberal Party to become involved, and a group of Transvaal Liberals (Leslie Cooper, Jock Isacowitz, Jack Unterhalter, Patrick van Rensburg and Ernie Wentzel) met with ANC leaders (Duma Nokwe, Robert Resha, Walter Sisulu and Oliver Tambo) to discuss the matter. But discussions broke down after it became clear that the Liberals would be reluctant participants – their lack of enthusiasm occasioned by the usual fear of manipulation by the COD.

Other Liberals, particularly the Cape conservatives, frowned upon the notion of a boycott altogether. Oscar Wollheim wrote smugly to Brown: 'I have not bought Rembrandt cigarettes or Veka clothing or patronised any of the shops in the Cape Town Groote Kerk Gebou for many years but have not made a song about it.' Liberal participation in the boycott would show that 'we [have] become less and less a political party and more and more a pressure group'. If the Liberal Party must conduct campaigns, Wollheim urged, they should be geared towards 'converting Afrikaners and voters to our way of thinking'. 'We have never made a serious attempt at this,' he lamented, 'but we keep on going miles out of our way to attain a mass black following.' The Liberals should have full sympathy with the ANC in its attempt to boycott Nationalist products, but 'without necessarily involving the Party, or without the Party proclaiming the fact that it supports the boycott movement.[73] In sum, the Party should stick to parliamentary politics.

Wollheim's letter betrayed a profound misapprehension of how South African politics had developed by the late 1950s. He continued to labour under the illusion that Parliament could drive meaningful reform; that white voters might eventually be persuaded to reject a policy of racial overlordship (when, in fact, it suited most of them just fine); and that black political organisations were either a sideshow or an irrelevance to the process of political change. His liberalism was an atavism, but it was shared by many, and it would paralyse the general body of liberal thought in South Africa for years to come.

Brown's liberalism was shaped by a keener perception of the political forces at work and a more nuanced understanding of the politics of non-racialism. The latter wasn't going to be achieved, in his view, by campaigning among Afrikaners in the *platteland*. He responded to Wollheim that if the Liberals did not cooperate with the ANC on the boycott, the ANC might 'decide to throw us over once and for all'. As regards the parliamentary and extra-parliamentary roles of the Party, one need not preclude the other. But at this time the Party should be going all out to increase its African support: 'African politics have been thrown into a new state of fluidity by the emergence of the PAC and it seems to me to be of the greatest importance that we should win Africans to support

Liberalism before they are persuaded that their only hope lies in extreme nationalism.'[74]

Wollheim was unmoved. The liberal wing of the UP was restless, he said; he was 'more than ever convinced that a grand re-shuffle of power is due very soon', and if the Liberals continued to intensify their extra-parliamentary activities, they would alienate their white support base for good. For that reason he was concerned that the Party should get back to a firm and clear statement that it stood for political change through 'constitutional means', and supported a qualified franchise. He was even more anxious to 'play down the role of gaining mass support of semi-literate and ignorant and unenfranchised people', and told Brown: 'I feel that we must leave the "black Nationalist" movement to their own devices.'[75]

In the end, Brown issued a statement in clear support of the boycott, which was published in the COD-aligned *New Age* on 23 July 1959. In *Contact*, the Liberal news magazine started by Patrick Duncan in 1958, and which borrowed its name from the Party newsletter that Brown had edited, Brown wrote that 'not to boycott is to surrender' to the status quo.[76] He also threw his weight behind an overseas boycott of South African goods, orchestrated by the Transvaal Liberal Party organiser, Patrick van Rensburg, now based in London. Brown signed a statement, along with Luthuli on behalf of the ANC, and Monty Naicker on behalf of the NIC, that was published in the British press, which appealed to Britons to 'strike a blow for those whom the state would keep in continual subjection in South Africa'.[77] On 20 February 1960, Brown and Luthuli jointly issued a press statement announcing the overseas boycott as 'yet another phase in our struggle to liberate non-whites from the intolerable bondage of apartheid and to create in South Africa a non-racial democratic state'.[78]

Again, Brown took flak from the Cape conservatives, Wollheim and Walter Stanford, with Stanford writing a dissenting letter to *The Times* in London.[79] Wollheim decried Van Rensburg's activities overseas as 'political suicide for the Liberal Party among potential voting support here'.[80] Brown defended himself to Stanford by pointing out that every single African member of the Party he had spoken to was in favour of the boycott. The boycott also showed

Africans for the first time that the world was on their side, and that it identified emotionally with them in their struggle. 'I do not think one should underestimate the importance of this emotional identification,' he remarked.[81]

The overseas boycott precipitated Bunny Curran's resignation, although he had been at odds with the Party for some time; after seeing Curran in Umtata the previous year, Brown had told David Lang, the Chairman of the Port Elizabeth branch: 'I think we must expect an explosion there – he is certainly going off at a tangent.'[82] Several more resignations of white members followed. Brown told Hjul that those resigning were 'white South Africans more than they [were] Liberals and time was bound to find them out'.[83]

Despite the fallout, the Liberals' official endorsement of the boycott – and indeed their pivotal part in it – bolstered their standing in the eyes of the Congress movement, and signalled a commitment to extra-parliamentary activity from which there was no turning back. Liberals subsequently backed a series of sports boycotts, many of which were initiated by Paton's friend, Dennis Brutus.

In opposing the internal boycott, Wollheim had reiterated his call for the Party to repudiate universal suffrage and recommit itself to the qualified franchise. Brown rejected this, noting that it would 'be the end of any hope for "liberalism" as a long-term hope for South Africa and would be regarded by non-White South Africa as the final sell-out'. In prescient terms, he elaborated:

> It seems to me that the one fact above all others which we must all face is that we live in Africa, that there is no possibility of White, Asian or any other groups continuing to do so on any basis of privilege and that, sooner or later, we are going to have majority rule based on universal suffrage.[84]

Brown explained his transition from advocate of the qualified franchise to proponent of universal suffrage to another Cape conservative, Jack Causton:

> I started off as a strong advocate of a franchise on a high basis of qualification. The last few years have persuaded me

that it is impossible to lay down a franchise qualification which will guarantee a responsible electorate. White South Africa enjoys compulsory, free education up to a high standard, its income level is high, its members own property on a substantial scale, yet politically it is quite irresponsible. I have canvassed many voters who knew virtually nothing about what was happening in South Africa and who voted almost entirely by habit. On the other hand, I have attended Liberal Party meetings where nobody could speak a word of English but where the degree of responsibility shown in discussion has been remarkable.[85]

Causton dismissed Brown's views as 'sentimental' claptrap, and remarked that by adopting a policy of universal suffrage the Party would throw away 'our chance of influencing white opinion', and 'risk losing such people as the Ballingers, Oscar Wollheim, Gerald Gordon ... and *many* more'.[86]

Peter Hjul, for the Cape Provincial Committee, confirmed this: Wollheim was 'determined to go out on the franchise issue'. The province would not follow him, but it risked losing at least 100 members and about half its monthly income.[87] What was more serious, from Hjul's point of view, was the possibility of the Cape conservatives forming an alliance with the large group of Cape liberals that stood between the Liberal Party and the United Party: 'Such a group led by Mrs Ballinger, Stanford, Wollheim, Marquard, and perhaps even Molteno might be well supported in Cape Town.'[88] Brown trusted Hjul's instincts. He told Jack Unterhalter in the Transvaal: 'I know that Jock [Isacowitz] feels that Wollheim and Co. won't leave. I think he is wrong.'[89] And, indeed, the conservatives' exit was about to be made that much easier.

In August 1959, just two months before the provincial elections, twelve liberal-leaning United Party public representatives broke away to form the Progressive Party. Among them were the Progressives' future leader, Dr Jan Steytler, as well as Colin Eglin, Helen Suzman and Ray Swart. Their departure was triggered by a resolution adopted at the UP's congress in Bloemfontein, in terms of which the Party undertook *not* to acquire more land for African reserves. The dissenting members believed, rightly, that this was a breach of faith, since additional land had been promised under the 1936 Hertzog Bills.[90]

Randolph Vigne, the Liberal activist who later wrote the history of the Liberal Party, remarks of the dissidents:

> [H]aving gained the inestimable advantage of financial support from their former parliamentary colleague, Harry Oppenheimer, [they] launched their new party, occupying almost the identical ground that the Liberals had taken up six and a half years earlier. They lacked the initial non-racial composition of the Liberal Party and it was plain they were not seeking it.[91]

At the time, Brown tentatively welcomed the Progressives as 'a new element [in] our political situation which could have an important influence on the future shape of South African politics'. The new party had yet to enunciate its policies, but they were unlikely to be as progressive as the Liberals', according to Brown: 'For the time being they may find Liberal policies a bit much to swallow but they represent the destiny to which South Africa must move if there is to be any real hope for the establishment and survival of authentic democratic institutions in South Africa.'[92]

Tensions within the broader liberal movement over 'constitutional means' and the franchise, alongside competition for electoral support, meant that relations between the Liberals and the Progressives were always going to be slightly uneasy. Even so, in the October 1959 provincial elections, the Liberals decided not to contest seats against the Progressives. In fact, the Liberal Party withdrew its candidate from the Pinetown constituency, Guinevere Ventress (who fought Ixopo instead), so as not to oppose the Progressives there. It had done so, Brown explained, not because of Progressive policy, which remained undefined, 'but because they [the Progressives] have taken a stand on an important matter of principle and should be supported in that stand'.[93]

In the event, neither the Progressives nor the Liberals made much of a showing in the provincial elections. Still, the new party's arrival on the scene was a threat to the Liberals, and Brown confided to Unterhalter that the Progressives 'are going to stop many if not all White sympathisers from coming to us'. They would contest the same seats as Liberals, and do so with greater resources. They would try to enhance their respectability by assuring white voters that 'they are nothing so irresponsible as *Liberals*'. In the event of that happening, Brown believed 'our own respectability in white eyes may diminish and we may find ourselves driven towards the COD position where we really have no influence over white opinion whatsoever'. He concluded his analysis:

> Are we to become more active in the Non-White field and, if so, how? ... Do we go all-out to re-establish our former relations with them [the Congresses] or do we go all-out to build up our own membership and face the fact that we are rivals of theirs in this field and that the more members we get the less they will like us? ... You may be able to destroy my feelings of apprehension but I am strongly of the view that we face a very important turning-point in the Party's history and that we must tread very warily if we are not going to make serious mis-judgements and mistakes.[94]

It is noteworthy that the two alternatives Brown put forward – restoring relations with the Congresses or embarking on a membership drive that would pit the Party against them – both involved the Party in the 'non-white field'. Nowhere in his letter did Brown ask, 'Are we to become more active in the white field?' That was not an option.

Even so, the potential loss of white support was clearly playing on Brown's mind, and he became more critical of the Progressives. His point of attack was the Party's all-white membership, which seemed to him a glaring contradiction of its professed non-racialism. In his Chairman's Report for September to November 1959, he noted that the Progressives' was 'an all-white launching and the policy decisions were all-white decisions'. It would be a 'long step backwards' for Liberals to join the Progressives: 'We [the Liberals] are and always have been essentially a non-racial Party and that has had

tremendous influence on every one of us. The indications are that
the Progressive Party will not be a non-racial Party but a white Party
with some non-white members.'[95] He relayed the same message to
a broader audience in *Contact* the following month: if Liberals
defected to the Progs they would be 'stepping out of a non-racial
organisation into a white political party'. By the time the Progressive Party was 'prepared to accept non-white members it will already have assumed the character of a white political party and it
will be too late to change'.[96] In *The Star* he was even more forthright: the Progressives' qualified franchise policy represented a
'compromise with the electorate' that would fool no one. Moreover, it was 'nonsense in contemporary Africa' for whites to arrive
at decisions and 'demand non-white acceptance'. He concluded
that the Progressive Party had 'still to rid itself of white supremacy
overtones'.[97]

For his part, Wollheim believed that the Progressives were 'elec-
torally viable', and that the Liberals had 'no possible chance' as a
political party in the near future – or even the next ten years. The
Liberal Party seemed likely to 'atrophy as far as electoral or Parliamentary significance' was concerned, and the only direction it
could follow in that case was to 'become a more militant body to
mobilise and organise non-white opinion and activity'. It would
then compete with the ANC, the COD and the PAC. Wollheim felt
that the Liberal Party should cease operating as a political party
and revert to its original status as an association dedicated to developing 'liberal thought and opinion in Southern Africa'.[98]

In March 1960, a number of Cape members unhappy with the
direction being taken by the Liberal Party met at Wollheim's house
to discuss their position. Among those in attendance were the
Ballingers, Leo Marquard, Gerald Gordon, Rodney Davenport and
Jack Causton. After the meeting, Wollheim wrote to Brown, seeking assurances that the Party would in future concentrate on 'the
normal work of a political party' and that it had no aspirations of
'any kind towards initiating a mass movement'. He hoped the Party
would revert to the qualified franchise, or at least insist that a universal franchise could only be based on universal education 'after
such education has had enough time to work through the whole

population'. And with a veiled threat, Wollheim promised to 'welcome any gestures from the National Committee which would make it possible for us to remain with [the Party]'.[99]

Brown, who had been requested by Wollheim to respond to Ballinger as he was away, offered no grand gestures. He undertook to do what he could to have the franchise policy left intact, but he 'could not possibly support' any retreat from existing policy, which would make the Party 'more or less indistinguishable from the Progressives'.[100] A small flurry of resignations and defections to the Progressives ensued – most notably Jack Causton, Gerald Gordon and, in September 1960, Wollheim himself. Donald Molteno and Walter Stanford had already crossed over. Wollheim told Ballinger that he was 'genuinely sorry to leave a Party with which people like Alan Paton, Peter Brown and Leo Marquard are associated'.[101] After receiving Stanford's resignation, Brown wrote to Unterhalter and asked him to probe Ballinger. 'It is possible that she might leave the Party,' he told Unterhalter, 'although not necessarily *for* the Progs.'[102] In the event, Ballinger held firm, as did Leo Marquard; both rendered valuable service to the Party to the end of its days. Brown would write of Ballinger: 'I was more often in disagreement with her than I was in agreement, but I take off my hat to her. Once committed, however reluctantly, she stayed with us to the very end.'[103]

The conservatives' secession freed the Party to strike out as a radical organisation. At their National Congress in Cape Town in May 1960, the Liberals at last decided to embrace universal franchise without any provisos or interim qualifications or 'interpretations', as they had had to do in 1954. A moving speech by Elias Tabethe, a black member from northern Natal, helped to seal the decision. During the 1960s, the Party would proceed to adopt policies that signalled a departure from the traditional liberalism of the Cape conservatives, thereby giving the organisation a non-racial, social-democratic edge.

Shorn of most of its vocal and influential traditionalists, the Party could now become 'more active in the Non-White field', as Brown had mooted it to Unterhalter shortly after the formation of the Progressives. One way of doing this was by strengthening the

Party's links with black political organisations. Actually, on the weekend of the National Congress in Johannesburg in April 1959, Robert Resha, the Treason Trialist who would shortly launch the ANC's boycott campaign, had approached Brown and Jordan Ngubane with two suggestions for future cooperation. He proposed either a direct link between the ANC and the Liberal Party or, alternatively, a seat for the Party on the National Consultative Committee of the Congress movement. Resha had preferred the second option and the Liberals had favoured the first. The matter was to have been discussed further at a meeting between eight Liberal leaders and an ANC delegation on Monday, but, as it transpired, only one ANC representative arrived. Oliver Tambo later sent a letter of apology, but offered no explanation for the no-show. Resha's offer was not repeated.

Why had Resha made his proposal to Brown and Ngubane? Brown would later write that it might have been because 'he, and those who felt like he did, wished to tip the balance away from the COD and its supporters on the [National Consultative] Committee'.[104] Another possible reason was that the PAC had been holding its inaugural conference in Orlando at the same time as the Liberals' National Congress, and Ngubane had attended it as an observer. The ANC had sought out cooperation on political campaigns with Liberals in the past, and it is not unreasonable to imagine that the organisation did not want the Liberal Party to give its official sanction to, or collaborate with, the PAC, which, after all, was an ANC splinter group. Despite the Africanists' racial exclusivity and a strong element of anti-white sentiment in their ranks, future cooperation between them and the Liberals would prove this theory less outlandish than it may seem.

Ngubane's presence at the PAC conference, revealed by Benjamin Pogrund in the *Rand Daily Mail* on 6 April, upset many Liberals, who saw it as an act of disloyalty to the Party and a snub to the ANC. Ngubane defended himself by arguing that he had attended in order to support those PAC leaders who were not 'racialists', and to try to swing support behind non-racialists like Robert Sobukwe. Sobukwe's election as PAC President had vindicated his position. Brown felt there was 'another reason for

Ngubane's support of the PAC', namely, that 'he regarded it as a counter to the Communist-dominated (as he would have had it) Congress Movement'.[105]

Indeed, Brown's analysis was correct. Peter Hjul wrote to him after the National Congress in 1959 that:

> Jordan's participation in the Africanist Congress had a good effect on this movement in the Western Province, and we have now made contact with some of its leading members ... The [PAC] has most of the former ANC leaders, and, in discussion, we find they share our strong anti-communist and anti-COD views; and, here at least, they seem more interested in working towards a non-racial society than in the pursuit of an exclusive black nationalist goal.[106]

Brown replied that he was 'rather perturbed' by Hjul's suggestion that the Party in the Western Cape was 'moving towards identifying itself with the Africanists as opposed to the ANC':

> I hope this is not so. I think it most important that we continue to maintain a position of 'positive neutrality' in this matter [because] ... any indication from us that we were taking sides in this affair could completely undermine what good relations we have established with the ANC. If, as you suggest, the ANC is in decline, this may not matter in the long run but I have serious doubts as to whether it is in decline. There is no doubt that it completely stole the show over Africa Day celebrations in Natal. As far as I know the Africanists never even showed their faces.[107]

To Unterhalter, Brown summed up his views: 'My attitude towards the Africanists is that we should treat them courteously but cautiously until we see what they are going to develop into.'[108]

Brown's prudence can partly be ascribed, as he did himself, to the fact that in the 'non-white field' power still lay with the Congress movement, and he was keen to keep the Party's oar in with it. In June 1959 the Liberals held a successful meeting with the ANC

and NIC in the Pietermaritzburg City Hall. Brown told Unterhalter: 'It was certainly the biggest meeting of an inter-racial nature
ever held in Maritzburg and according to the City Hall caretaker,
"the best meeting since the Torch Commando".'[109]

A number of Hjul's fellow Cape radicals, like Collingwood
August, Timothy Holmes, Randolph Vigne and Tom Walters shared
his interest in the PAC, and, in varying degrees, his hostility to communism in general and the COD in particular. Patrick Duncan,
who, since launching *Contact* in 1958, now lived in Cape Town, was
another. In fact, August, Holmes, Hjul and Vigne all served on the
editorial board of *Contact*. Duncan's attacks on the COD in *Contact*,
and his often-repeated claim that the COD had a stranglehold over
the ANC, irked Brown, who was anxious not to estrange the Congress movement. Although *Contact* was entirely independent of the
Liberal Party, it was read by many as the Party's unofficial mouth-
piece, and Brown's own position was complicated by the fact that
he contributed a fortnightly column to it, entitled 'The Long View'.
Paton had penned the first of these columns in January 1958, while
attending an All-African Church Conference in Nigeria.[110] At Duncan's prompting, Brown took over the column in February 1959, so
that Paton could concentrate on his biography of Hofmeyr.[111]

Even before Brown started writing 'The Long View', Duncan's
editorship of *Contact* had given him cause for concern. In 1958,
Duncan had refused to run advertisements for COD meetings in
his newspaper. Brown gradually came to believe that Duncan was
'conducting a one-man guerrilla war against the COD'; 'something
which in my mind,' he told Wollheim, 'he has no right to do.' Personally, Brown held 'no brief for Communists', but they had been
close allies of the ANC before the Liberal Party had come into existence, and he felt that 'to hope for any public repudiation of
people who have been as close as this to the ANC is ridiculous'.[112]

Before Duncan flew with Jordan Ngubane to Ghana in December 1958, where they represented the Liberal Party at the All-Africa
People's Conference in Accra, Brown had written to him and stipulated various conditions for Liberal participation. Two of these
were that there could be no attacks on any individuals or organisations in South Africa committed to a non-racial future for the

country, and there could be no identification with Pan-Africanism 'at this stage'.[113] Duncan informed Brown that he had stuck to these terms,[114] but back in South Africa he felt beholden to no such considerations. On 2 May 1959, he published 'An Open Letter to Chief Luthuli' in *Contact*, responding to Luthuli's call in *New Age* for the Liberal Party to 'drop its anti-communist plank'.[115] Duncan maintained that Luthuli could not 'expect Liberals to give up their opposition to Communism, for Liberals never can love oppressors, and Communists are the worst oppressors of the modern age'. And he accused the communists of using the ANC as a front, asking: 'How many times has the ANC followed a line during the last five years which would displease the Kremlin – surely not once.'[116]

Luthuli was deeply offended by Duncan's attack. Many Liberals, too, were angry with Duncan, and wanted him expelled from the Party. Some threatened to resign at a meeting chaired by Brown, who managed to lighten the atmosphere by stating gruffly: 'I'm taking resignations later.'[117] In truth, Brown was put out by Duncan's open letter, and told him that his attack was ill-conceived and ill-timed. Luthuli had tremendous moral standing and prestige, and to direct an open letter to him was a 'great mistake'. Brown fired a series of questions at Duncan, a rapid volley of irritability unusual in his correspondence:

> Should this sort of charge be made while the Treason Trial is on and while many of us are trying to collect money for it? I don't think so ... What do members say when they are asked whether they support your article? What do I say, as a contributor to *Contact*, if somebody writes a letter to the paper asking if the Party agrees with the views expressed in the article? You yourself in the article say that you hope the Party will support them. It seems to me inevitable that somebody will ask whether it does. What do I then answer? I do not agree with the article but can I say so without appearing to support communist influence in the Congress movement? And if I do say so, what hope is there of future co-operation with the Congresses? What of personal relationships between Luthuli and his supporters and leading

members of the Party? In many instances these are now good
but it has taken some pretty hard work to make them so.[118]

Having had time to ponder it, Brown thought it best to dissociate
the Party from Duncan's diatribe in one of his 'Long View'
columns. He submitted his copy to Duncan at the end of May,
telling him that he was 'not at all happy' about his tie-up with
Contact.[119] If Duncan felt the need to reply in public to his column,
Brown said, then he should spike the article and Brown
would discontinue his contributions to the newspaper altogether.
Duncan relented and carried, without comment, Brown's column
on 13 June.

In it, Brown credited communists with being 'in the forefront
of those who have put up the most spirited defence there has been
of fundamental democratic rights' in South Africa. He contrasted
their role with that of most whites who, despite being 'ostensible
upholders of all that is good in western democratic values', had sat
on the sidelines, 'not raising a finger to help'. And he pleaded for
the enemies of apartheid to sink their ideological differences and
'get on with the job of disposing of the devil we know', rather than
'dissipate our energies in boxing a [communist] shadow which
may never develop into anything more substantial'.[120]

To Duncan, this feel-good, softly-softly approach to communism was naïve and short-sighted. He surveyed the political scene
and found the PAC, with its resolute rejection of communist influence, increasingly attractive. It is true, as his biographer points out,
that Duncan's attraction to the Pan-Africanists was complex; that it
stemmed neither from his anti-communism alone, nor even from
his sympathy for Kwame Nkrumah's Pan-Africanism. He was only
really drawn into the movement, to which he eventually defected
from the Liberal Party, once it actively demonstrated two qualities
he prized most highly in politics: the ability to win a mass following, and the ability to practise non-violence in the face of intense
provocation.[121] That took place in March 1960.

In March, the Liberal Party's National Committee discussed a
letter from the PAC Secretary-General, Potlako Leballo. He asked the
Party to assist the dependants of people who might be imprisoned

in an anti-pass campaign planned by the PAC, under the slogan 'no bail, no defence, no fine!' The Committee agreed to offer whatever assistance the Party could afford, and Brown was asked to communicate its decision to the PAC. On 21 March, the PAC launched its campaign. Only a month previously, the British Prime Minister, Harold Macmillan, had remarked in the South African Parliament that 'the wind of change is blowing through this continent'. His words were prophetic.

On the morning of 21 March, between 5 000 and 7 000 protestors converged on the local police station in Sharpeville, near Johannesburg. By midday, police would claim, there were nearly 20 000 of them. Without their pass books they were contravening the law, and they offered themselves up for arrest. Confronted with such a large crowd, albeit a peaceful one, the police were jumpy. Eventually they panicked, and started firing at random. They shot wildly, indiscriminately, mowing down men, women and young children as they fled. Of the 69 people who were killed, many of them were shot in the back. Over 180 were injured.

In Cape Town, that same morning, large crowds of protestors gathered in Langa and Nyanga townships. A small group of Liberals – principally those associated with *Contact*, like Duncan, Hjul, Holmes and Vigne – had already forged ties with local PAC leaders such as Christopher Mlokothi, Chairman of the PAC's Langa branch, and were kept apprised of developments. Indeed, the PAC had met in the Liberal Party office, the Duncans' house and the *Contact* boardroom to organise and plan its campaign. At Langa alone there were over 10 000 marchers by late afternoon, when news of the Sharpeville massacre began to trickle through. Remarkably, the 23-year-old Philip Kgosana, the PAC Western Cape Regional Secretary and a *Contact* sales agent, managed to restrain the crowd with his powerful reiteration of his leader Sobukwe's plea for non-violence. The police, however, were nervous. Their demands for the protestors to disperse were inaudible. They became agitated. They charged into the crowd with batons. And, like their counterparts at Sharpeville, they panicked. In the ensuing chaos, three civilians were killed and 47 were injured.

The events of 21 March drew Patrick Duncan closer towards

the PAC. Other Liberals, in the immediate aftermath of the massacres, helped in various ways: Liberal lawyers took statements from the injured at hospitals; the Party faithful drove lorry-loads of food into the townships as part of the relief effort; and members collected funds to help the dependants of those who had been killed, wounded or imprisoned.

The national mood was charged. Brown would later write that the Party's Transvaal Provincial Congress met between 26 and 27 March in 'an atmosphere of the greatest tenseness'. He remembered 'leaving it to be taken to a dingy upstairs room in downtown Johannesburg to confer with the official PAC spokesman'.[122] The ANC, which had planned its own anti-pass campaign for 31 March, called for a national stay-away and day of mourning on Monday 28 March. At lunchtime on Saturday 26 March, news filtered through to the Transvaal Congress that the pass laws had been suspended. 'There were scenes of incredible jubilation', according to Brown. That night, Luthuli was photographed by a *Sunday Times* journalist burning his pass at the home of John and Meg Brink, two leading Liberals from Pretoria. Brown, who witnessed the event, thought that it 'was an attempt by the ANC leadership to recapture the initiative which the PAC had so dramatically seized from them on 21 March'.[123]

On Monday morning, an elated Brown, feeling that 'the end of apartheid was hardly a day away', drove out of Johannesburg. On the way home, he stopped to visit Party branches in northern Natal, and as he went he flung handfuls of stay-away leaflets out of his car window to startled road-workers. 'I spent the first part of that night in my bed in Pietermaritzburg,' he would later write, 'and the second half on the floor of the Pietermaritzburg gaol.'[124]

THE STATE OF EMERGENCY
30 March-31 August 1960

The massacre at Sharpeville and the shootings in Langa signalled a turning point in South African history. On Wednesday 30 March, the government proclaimed a State of Emergency. A ruthless clampdown ensued. There were mass detentions. Heavily armed police swarmed into the townships, brutally assaulting residents. In Cape Town, army and naval reinforcements threw 'steel cordons' around Langa, Nyanga and Gugulethu, thwarting entry and exit between dawn and dusk. This was the beginning of a new phase of apartheid. On 7 April, the pass laws were reimposed. On 8 April, the ANC and PAC were banned.

How suddenly the atmosphere had changed. On Monday 28 March, Brown had left Johannesburg in a state of near euphoria. He had seen Luthuli dramatically burning his pass. 'Anything seemed possible', he had thought, with the government 'giving the impression that it had suddenly lost its bearings and self-confidence'.[1] Early the next morning, he was lying on the floor of the Pietermaritzburg prison.

Shortly after 2.00 am on Tuesday 29 March, Brown was woken by thunderous knocking at his front door. As he passed his entrance hall window, he caught a glimpse of three thickset white men outside: one in police uniform, the other two in plain clothes. When he opened the door, Lieutenant Christoffel Andries Lategan identified himself and asked Brown to do the same. He was immediately placed under arrest.

Brown asked Lategan to produce an arrest warrant, but was told that none was needed. Lategan then ordered him to fetch a change of clothes and followed him into his bedroom. By this time, Phoebe and the children were awake. Still clammy-eyed with sleep, the sight of three burly men, one of them in uniform, was a shock

to Chris and Vanessa, then aged eight, and Anton, only five years
old. Brown refused to leave them alone without a friend, and so, at
Brown's request, Lategan instructed his colleague, Detective Constable Du Preez to telephone Simon Roberts, Brown's close schoolmate and also, fortuitously, his lawyer.

In the meantime, Lategan conducted a search of the house.
Again, Brown asked for a search warrant, but Lategan claimed not
to require one in terms of what he called the 'Emergency Regulations'. When Brown asked what these were, he got a blank stare
in return. Later, in an affidavit, Brown would recollect his 'impression that [Lategan] did not know what these regulations were any
more than I did'.[2] Lategan and Du Preez then searched Brown's
study while the armed uniformed constable stood guard. His letters, diaries and papers were sorted out and confiscated.

At about 2.30 am, Roberts arrived and joined the men in the
study. Brown's bedroom was then searched but nothing was removed from it. As the police moved to leave the house, with Brown
in tow, they searched his car, and took a stash of Party documents,
including 125 signed application forms for membership.

As they drove into town, Brown still had no idea where they
were going or why he had been arrested. Only when Lategan told
Du Preez to head towards '*Burgerstraat*', did he know that the
Pietermaritzburg prison was their destination.

At the prison, Brown was led into the office of Captain Smidt,
head of the Pietermaritzburg Special Branch, and a familiar face to
local Liberals. His name and address were recorded, and his personal effects removed, but there was still no explanation for his
arrest. As he was gruffly commanded into his cell – 'In there!' –
Brown motioned to the officer, 'After you.' To the occupant of the
cell next door, this 'well-known voice ... which in its combination
of instinctive natural courtesy and refusal to be daunted could only
belong to Peter McKenzie Brown'.[3]

Derick Marsh, a 32-year-old English lecturer and former chairman of the Liberals' Pietermaritzburg branch, was still heavy-headed
from his birthday celebrations which had ended only a few hours
before. He must have been mightily relieved to hear the voice of
the man he considered his 'closest friend', his squash partner and

the godfather of his son, Nicholas. He shouted out to Brown to let him know he was there.

Just as it was getting lighter, there was a tramping of feet outside Brown and Marsh's cells: '*Links, regs, links, regs*. Halt!' This was not the arrival of more prisoners, but the entrance of well-drilled officers, and Marsh half convinced himself that he and Brown were about to face a firing squad.

It was merely the day shift taking over from the night shift, however, and the two men were able to return to their straw mattresses, in futile pursuit of sleep. The next morning, they were kept apart. Separately they were led to breakfast, then to ablutions, and then to a lunch of watery stew, watery pumpkin and watery potatoes substituted for the breakfast porridge.

At some stage in the early afternoon, a voice growled: '*Oefening!* Exercise!' Being unsure what was about to happen, Marsh asked the officer if he should take his jacket with him. The officer considered the question seriously for a moment, and then, without a hint of irony, said in his heavily accented English: 'Better take it. There's a hell of a lot of criminal types around here.'

It was during the exercise session that Marsh and Brown were finally able to talk and swap notes. They were soon joined by Hans Meidner, of whose arrival at the prison they had been unaware. All of them were oblivious of the reasons for their arrest, and their confusion was about to grow. For just after 5.30 pm, their cells were unlocked again, and the three of them were marched up to the front office, where the Deputy Commissioner of Police for Natal informed them of their release. What had happened was that their lawyers had sought and obtained a court order for their discharge; the three had been arrested before the Emergency Regulations had been promulgated in the *Government Gazette*, and so their arrests had been unlawful. Before they could start congratulating each other, Captain Smidt pointed out that as the regulations had now been published, he proposed to have his men re-arrest them as soon as they stepped onto the street. The two Liberal lawyers who were present, Simon Roberts (acting for Brown) and Leslie Weinberg (acting for Marsh and Meidner), argued hard and fast: the judge who had granted the order for their release might feel his authority had been slighted if Brown, Marsh and Meidner were re-arrested immediately. If they were allowed out overnight, the men would voluntarily surrender themselves at 8.00 am, Thursday 31 March. And so, to the consternation of their families, the men went home for one night, only to return to prison the following day.

Back in the *tronk*, as they dubbed it, on 1 April, Brown, Marsh and Meidner were moved into a communal cell, and so began their months of shared detention: Marsh was released after two months, Brown and Meidner after three. The men forged a close bond; both Marsh and Meidner would remain lifelong friends and correspondents of Brown even after they went on to pursue distinguished academic careers in exile – Marsh as Professor and Head of the English Department at the University of Western Australia and Meidner as Professor and Head of the Biology Department at the University of Stirling in Scotland. On his trips to visit Vanessa in England in the 1980s, Brown would always make a point of seeing Meidner and his wife, Olga, in Scotland. In the 1990s, Marsh spent three weeks travelling around South Africa with Brown, and the two men revisited the site of their earlier imprisonment.

During their detention, the three were not allowed contact with other prisoners, nor to work or attend chapel, though they could see a clergyman of their own religious denomination. As they were all largely agnostic, none of them took up the offer. When Marsh mentioned his agnosticism to an officer, he looked mystified. 'I don't think they come here,' he said.[4] In time, they were allowed two visits a month – one from a family member and one from a friend, or both from a family member.

They had each been allowed to bring a book with them, and this initially gave them something to talk about during their long hours of inactivity. Brown read Saul Bellow's *Henderson the Rain King*, which, according to Marsh, he 'stoutly maintained to be the worst novel ever written'.[5] They quickly fell into a routine. In the mornings, each would occupy himself with work of some kind. Marsh wrote what became his PhD thesis on William Shakespeare's last plays. Brown attempted to write a short story.[6] In the afternoons, they would play cards, at which Marsh – an accomplished gambler since his student days at Rhodes University – excelled. Alternatively, Marsh and Brown would compete against each other in a game of Marsh's devising while Meidner looked on disapprovingly. The game required the opponents to stand facing each other, about three or four metres apart, legs apart, while each tried by strength or guile to get a ball through the other's legs, without allowing him to catch it. Meidner, with what Marsh remembers as his 'Slavic tendency to glumness' never quite took to this diversion. In the early days of detention, when the three met only during exercise time, Meidner was given to saying things like: 'They're bound to shoot us, you know.'[7]

But by the evening Meidner would have recovered his humour sufficiently to participate in what became known as the 'adult education programme'. Brown would teach Zulu; Marsh would offer an introduction to English poetry, for by this time they had been allowed a few more books; and Meidner would instruct his cellmates in the rudiments of botany.

Visits from family and friends helped ease the tedium. One regular visitor was Edgar Brookes, the former liberal Senator and current Professor of History at the University of Natal, who had helped to set Brown on his career path. Brookes was yet to join the Liberal Party, but he knew Marsh and Meidner as colleagues from the university, and Brown he had known for a long time. Brookes's visits were always eagerly anticipated. He would update Brown on the latest rugby and cricket scores,[8] and inform Marsh of recent political developments 'under the cloak of the state of a totally fictitious ancient Rome'.[9]

On 21 May, Brown was summoned to an office in the prison, where he was later joined by Simon Roberts and Kenneth Johnson, the man who Phoebe's mother remarried. Without Brown's knowledge, Johnson had asked Harry Lawrence, Smuts's former Minister of Justice, to approach the current Minister, FC Erasmus, with a view to releasing Brown on certain conditions. Brown refused. As he subsequently wrote in his affidavit:

> ... [B]ecause I was and am convinced that the Liberal Party had done nothing whatsoever to justify the arrests of

members, including myself, I considered that I could not accept a conditional release whilst ordinary members were still detained for political beliefs similar to mine. Furthermore, I was and am convinced that I had done nothing to justify my arrest, and I considered that if I accepted a release subject to purported conditions, I would be condoning the actions of the Police in arresting and detaining me in a manner not normally lawful. I therefore did not accept the offer.[10]

On 20 June, Brown was asked by Captain Smidt whether he had changed his mind. He again refused a conditional release. On 4 July, he was told to pack his effects in anticipation of his discharge. This time he was not requested to accept any conditions; they were simply imposed. He was given an opportunity to acknowledge them in writing, which he declined. In terms of his release certificate, Brown was not allowed to participate in the activities of any organisation, or attend any meetings without the prior approval of a magistrate; he could not visit or communicate with people who were still in detention; he was forbidden to publish anything about his detention; he was confined to the magisterial district of Pietermaritzburg; and he had to report weekly to the local police station.[11] Brown attempted to have the conditions overturned, but they remained in force until the State of Emergency was lifted on 31 August 1960.

Brown, Marsh and Meidner were not the only Liberals to be detained during the State of Emergency. Many detainees came from Bergville and Ladysmith in northern Natal, where the Party was active in opposing black spot removals. Elliot Mngadi was detained, as were Franklin Bhengu, Albert Cebekulu, J Gangai, Peter Khumalo, Jacob Mbongwe, Robert Zondi and Zephaniah Zuma. In the Transvaal, Liberals and COD communists were detained together in Pretoria Central Prison: Ernie Wentzel and John Lang, the two Liberal attorneys who had taken statements at Baragwanath Hospital from those wounded at Sharpeville, spent a great deal of time getting to know Rusty Bernstein, Joe Slovo and Harold Wolpe. However, their shared tribulations produced no political meeting of the minds.

The Liberal Party's standing was greatly enhanced at this time by its comportment in the period leading up to the Emergency, and by the detention of so many of its members and leaders, who were evidently ready to suffer for their beliefs. With the Black Sash, Liberals set up an Emergency Relief Fund on 31 March, to help the families of detainees. They had the unofficial support of the Progressives, and the 'thorough ill-will' of the United Party who wanted nothing to do with the fund, according to the National Secretary, Sue Spence.[12] *Contact* was the only newspaper to provide full details of what had happened at Sharpeville, of the Emergency itself, and of the appalling prison conditions in which many detainees were kept; most other publications had been scared into silence by the ban placed on such news by the Emergency Regulations.

Jordan Ngubane believed that Brown's incarceration 'showed the Africans that the white liberal was determined to destroy white supremacy', especially Brown's refusal to be set free unless 'his colleagues on both sides of the colour line were also released'.[13] The impact of the detentions on the Party was enormous; it galvanised supporters and fortified them for the struggle ahead. Jack Spence, who was the Chairman of the Pietermaritzburg branch at the time, and led a march to protest against the detention of Brown, Marsh and Meidner, recalled: 'There was a real mobilisation of opinion against the arrest of three perfectly decent, respectable men who had never done anything of a subversive nature against the state.'[14] In later years, Brown would describe the detentions as 'painful' but 'quite important' and 'good' for the Party.[15]

What of the personal impact on Brown and his family? Punch and Cynthia feared for the safety of their daughter and grandchildren, and wanted Phoebe to leave Peter.[16] Of Phoebe's reaction to the political activity which had led to his detention, Brown was to say: '… [I]t wasn't an issue because she never made it an issue. I'm sure she wasn't happy about … the possible spin-offs, but she certainly never made an issue of it.'[17] Indeed, it never occurred to Phoebe that Peter's detention should divert him from his political course, or that she, as the mother of his young children, should prevail upon him to hang back after the Emergency was lifted.[18]

Nearly fifty years on, Vanessa had only 'vague impressions' of her father's arrest and detention.[19] She knew from an early age that he ran the risk of being arrested, so for her, at an intellectual level, it wasn't something difficult to grasp. Chris and Anton, too, even at that young age, knew that their father's politics set him apart from most of their peers' parents, and that his activities were likely to cause him difficulties with the authorities.[20] Brown himself thought that his detention 'almost certainly had an effect' on his children's political outlook.[21] He believed 'having parents out of the [political] mainstream' was 'probably a problem' for his children. However, in later life, none of Brown's children begrudged their father his political views.

Vanessa, more than her brothers, shared something of her father's political idealism and anti-authoritarianism. As a teenager and young adult, while her brothers were socially and politically more conservative, Vanessa was, in her own words, a 'hippie'. When she left South Africa at the end of 1973 to do a teacher training course at the University of Durham, she spent a good deal of time with Walter and Adelaine Hain and their family in the London suburb of Putney. By this time, Peter Hain's political star was on the rise in British anti-apartheid circles. He had led the campaign to 'Stop the Seventy Tour' of the South African national cricket team – the Springboks – to Britain in 1970. The campaign had gained much international publicity for coordinating mass demonstrations against, and disruptions of, the tour, and had been preceded by a similar series of protests against the touring Springbok rugby side. Hain was also active in the Young Liberals in the 1970s, and Vanessa supported both the Liberals and left-liberal causes more broadly. In a letter to Hans Meidner in 1974, Brown reported that his daughter had been 'frantically involved in the election for the Liberals in Putney'.[22]

Immediately after his release from detention, Brown came home to find his family 'in good spirits'.[23] He set about contacting friends and other Party members who had been detained and was glad to find them cheerful and 'not especially dismayed by their experience'.[24] In fact, Brown thought the Party had managed to handle the detentions and the Emergency very well, and had been strengthened by the experience. Paton had provided crucial leadership as Acting National Chairman during Brown's imprisonment. Brown told Leslie Rubin of a meeting in Pietermaritzburg in June, addressed by Paton and Ngubane, which drew over 1 000 people. In Cape Town, especially, he thought the Party had 'strengthened itself quite remarkably' during the Emergency – adding impishly, 'I don't know whether that has got anything to do with the fact that Rubin is in Ghana or not.'[25] The limitations on his movements did weigh on him, however. He explained to Peter Hjul that he was in a 'state of suspended animation, fenced in by these damn conditions'.[26]

Among other things, Brown could not return to writing his 'Long View' column immediately. When eventually he was able to, in September, he asked why Liberal Party members had been imprisoned but not charged – singling out by name Hannah Stanton, the only female Liberal to be detained, and Colyn van Reenen, a student at the University of Pretoria. Van Reenen had burned the word 'Uhuru' into the hallowed grass of Church Square – the concourse dominated by the statue of Paul Kruger, which made it a central shrine of Afrikaner nationalism.

Brown believed that intimidation was the answer: the government had thought that by arresting Liberals it would 'persuade those it did arrest to give up opposing its policies, it would frighten those it did not arrest into silence and it would frighten away from the Party other people who might be thinking of supporting it'.[27] But these tactics had not worked, and Brown wanted to assure the government, in case 'it should be under any illusions ... that it has succeeded in none of these purposes'. Instead, their imprisonment alongside individuals of other races had strengthened the detainees' commitment to non-racialism, non-racial political organisation and action on non-racial lines.

Brown's defiance was echoed in a media statement that he issued when the Emergency was lifted. He pointed out that during the Emergency the Party held its 'most successful' National Congress ever – in Cape Town – and that membership was on the rise. Moreover, he insisted, 'those of us who were arrested have not been deflected from our purpose by this experience. We will continue to strive to replace apartheid by a democratic system of government in which rights and responsibilities will be shared by all.'[28]

With the lifting of the Emergency, Brown was free to leave Pietermaritzburg. He embarked on a series of nationwide visits in September. With Elliot Mngadi, Hans Meidner and Roy Coventry, he addressed a post-Emergency meeting in a Ladysmith cinema, attended by at least 400 people. Later that month he spoke at a meeting of the Parktown North branch of the Liberal Party in the Vrede Hall, where he presented the Party's 'prison graduates' to the public.[29] He went twice to the eastern Cape, first to speak at a meeting in Port Elizabeth, to protest against the deportation of Bishop Reeves, and later, with Jordan Ngubane, to meet with students from the University of Fort Hare.[30] Brown was undeterred. If anything, the Emergency and its aftermath had strengthened his belief in the Liberal cause. And he was soon to pay dearly for that conviction.

TOWARDS THE BAN
1960-1964

The banning of the ANC and PAC left a political vacuum which the Liberals realised they could not fill on their own. In September 1960, Brown, John Lang and Alan Paton met Luthuli to discuss the formation of a new organisation, whose initial aim would be to fight the pass laws. Brown reported back to Hjul that they had had an amiable discussion, but 'the Chief was non-committal, as one would have expected him to be'.[1] Brown was tasked with drafting a set of principles for the proposed organisation, but they elicited no response from the underground ANC leadership after they were sent. In point of fact, the ANC was planning its own initiative.

Later in the year, invitations were sent to various African notables, asking them to attend an African Leaders' Consultative Conference, to be held in Orlando between 16 and 17 December. Several Liberals received invitations signed, *inter alia*, by Luthuli, ZK Matthews and Duma Nokwe, the Secretary-General of the ANC. Bill Bhengu, a member of the Party's National Executive; Julius Malie, the Liberals' Transvaal organiser; and Joseph Nkatlo, the Party's Vice-Chairman in the Cape, all attended. However, Jordan Ngubane failed to turn up, despite having agreed to go after he was urged to, in person, by Luthuli. Brown was annoyed by this, and told Ernie Wentzel that, as National Chairman, he would have to write letters of apology to the conference sponsors.[2]

The Orlando gathering resolved to stage an 'all-in conference representative of African people', which would call for a 'National

Convention representing all the people of South Africa'.[3] A Continuation Committee was elected to organise the conference, with Ngubane as its chairman. Malie was chosen to chair the steering committee, and Bhengu was entrusted with the resolutions committee. Brown saw their 'main task', as he described it to Wentzel, as ensuring that 'the whole affair does not fall into the hands of the Commies at its next stage'.[4] He would later regret that Ngubane had 'failed to take a firm grip on the Orlando Continuation Committee'.[5]

By the following year, the ANC had captured the initiative and the PAC had pulled out; its spokesman, ZB Molete, claimed that the ANC was using the conference as a vehicle to 'build their own political movements'.[6] Bhengu and Ngubane resigned from the Continuation Committee. Ngubane complained that while he was 'most anxious to do all I can to consolidate African unity … it has to be genuine unity, in which people are not forced into the position where they have to carry out predetermined and immutable plans'.[7]

The All-in African Conference took place at Edendale in March 1961. Neither the Liberals nor the underground PAC sent any official representation, and the conference had the air of an ANC rally, replete with Congress songs, copies of *New Age* and COD pamphlets. The star of the show was Nelson Mandela, whose presence was made possible by the fact that his banning orders had just lapsed, and had not yet been renewed. He had been appointed Secretary of the Continuation Committee shortly before the conference was held. As the main speaker at the conference, he dominated proceedings. However, Creina Bond, a young journalist reporting on the conference for the *Daily News* (she was later to marry Neil Alcock, a central figure in Brown's post-Liberal Party operations) told Brown that Mandela 'said nothing of any importance'.[8] After his speech, resolutions were adopted rejecting the establishment of the republic, calling for a national convention and promising a nationwide stay-away.

Brown noted the 'considerable disenchantment amongst Liberals and others who, in spite of their earlier experiences, might still have been sympathetic to the results of the Conference, if there

had been any real [attempt] to achieve unity'.[9] In the circumstances, Liberals were disinclined to support the proposed stay-away,
which was to start on 29 May and culminate on the day of the
republic's proclamation, 31 May. The PAC was fiercely opposed to
the so-called 'stay-at-home', and distributed pamphlets on the Witwatersrand urging blacks not to strike.

Apart from Johannesburg, where half the workforce went on
strike, the stay-away flopped. In the other major urban centres –
Durban, Port Elizabeth and Cape Town – the response was sluggish. Brown wrote to Hjul that the campaign had backfired because it 'didn't touch people's lives or emotions in the way that
passes did in the first instance and Sharpeville did in the second'.
The republican constitution, he felt, was not something that black
South Africans could get worked up about. In most parts of the
country people hadn't been effectively organised into a movement
in which they felt they belonged and had confidence. Moreover,
plans for the stay-away had been announced too far in advance,
and, as a result, the government 'was able to lay all its plans with
time to spare'. Police intimidation and violence had undoubtedly
served as a deterrent. To Brown, the lesson was that 'the potential
of a non-racial organisation is the only hope for the future', and
the Party's 'target now must be the National Convention'.[10]

As part of its national convention strategy, the Liberals had
organised a meeting in the Pietermaritzburg City Hall on 1 November 1960, billed as an 'Anti-Verwoerd Rally' and advertised under
the banner, 'A Natal Convention?' They hoped to channel anti-
republican sentiment into support for a non-racial national convention. For many white Natalians, given their acute sense of ethno-
linguistic distinctiveness (in short, Englishness), their attachment to
the Commonwealth connection and their reverence for all things
British, republicanism was a subject to rouse the passions. Coming
shortly after Verwoerd's referendum on the republican constitution
in October, which the Nationalists had narrowly won in the rest of
the country but resoundingly lost in Natal, the meeting was well
timed.

Despite his traditional Natalian upbringing, Brown had no
truck with the parochial politics of 'the Natal Stand'. As he had

explained to his constituents in his 1954 provincial election campaign, he was a Natalian and his family had been Natalians 'for as
long as anyone'. Still, he was 'much more of a South African' than
he was a Natalian, and he was 'not interested in saving Natal in particular from the dangers that beset it but the Union as a whole'.[11]
After the referendum, he had written in his 'Long View' column
that: 'If one values the Commonwealth connection for sentimental
reasons only, or for economic reasons alone, then there is no
moral basis for our continued membership.'[12] The only moral basis
was for South Africa to embrace the Commonwealth's respect for
the individual rights of all men and women, regardless of their
race. Brown's anti-republicanism and allegiance to the Commonwealth were founded not on sentiment, but on a moral appeal to
rights-based non-racialism.

The Party was careful not to associate itself officially with the
'Anti-Verwoerd Rally', lest the call for a Natal Convention – which
the meeting's organisers hoped to contrive – be construed as a par-
tisan gambit. Even so, the meeting was chaired by Jack Spence, a
lecturer in politics and history at the University of Natal and the
Chairman of the Liberals' Pietermaritzburg branch, and the main
speakers were Brown, Meidner and Mngadi. The turnout was excellent – over a thousand people of all races – and the convention
idea gathered steam during proceedings. Proposals to that end
were made from both the platform and the floor by non-Liberals,
primed to do so beforehand, and were enthusiastically endorsed.
At the end, a multiracial planning committee was elected to organise the Natal Convention. No Liberals accepted nomination to the
committee, although it was chaired by Spence's university colleague, Edgar Brookes, who had visited Brown, Marsh and Meidner in prison, and who would join the Party the following year.
Brown was subsequently persuaded to take on the role of Organising Secretary to the convention.

The Natal Convention was held from 17 to 19 April 1961 at the
University of Natal, and was attended by some 220 delegates from
67 organisations.[13] In his opening address, Brookes dissociated the
convention from the 'Natal stand of the old type', and argued instead for a stand in favour of a non-racial society in which 'we and

our children after us shall share the future as friends and fellow-citizens'.[14] Fact papers were presented on the political, social and economic aspects of apartheid;[15] and the 'general feeling of the Convention [was] in favour of a non-racial franchise on the common roll'.[16] The proceedings of the convention were ultimately published in a booklet.[17]

Brown viewed the convention as a 'tremendous success', and remarked on the 'extraordinary equanimity achieved by a large number of people of widely differing backgrounds on a wide range of subjects'. The convention had rejected racial restrictions on land ownership and accepted school integration, and its report was a 'startlingly "radical" document'. What emerged most clearly 'out of Maritzburg was the craziness of apartheid, that the *only* way out of our difficulties *is the way we go together*,' Brown wrote in his column. And he took comfort from the fact that Natalians had been so receptive: 'If Natal, for so long the home of active anti-Indian and anti-Afrikaner sentiment and of passive acceptance of apartheid, can come out with a document like this Convention Report, there is hope for all of us.'[18]

There were other spin-offs. Brown commented to Patrick Duncan that it was 'quite extraordinary how, since the Natal Convention, the Party here has managed to gain an entrée into the Coloured community. Really good members too.' In September, he and Tony Mathews (subsequently an authority on state security laws) visited Raisethorpe, just outside Pietermaritzburg, and held a meeting in the house of a Coloured member. 'The result', enthused Brown, 'a new Branch of the Party'; '[q]uite a number of young Coloured people joined and this is something they would never have done even a year ago.'[19]

A few days before the Natal Convention had assembled, Brown had told Hjul about a plan 'hatched these last two days, with which we hope to put across something positive on an inter-racial basis, come the Republic'. This involved 'canvassing support for the idea of a National Convention, bigger and better than the [1957 Inter-denominational African Ministers' Federation] Multi-Racial Conference, either to be launched on or actually to be held on Republic Day'. Given his own experience organising the Natal Convention,

Brown had thought the timeframe to be unrealistic. What he had
believed might be possible was to hold a series of meetings on
Republic Day, 31 May, at which representatives from as many platforms as possible would call for a national convention. Brown hadn't
expected 'any miracles from this', but had hoped that backing
could be obtained from the Progressives, the churches, big business and the trade unions. This might serve to 'a) get white non-
Nationalist opinion moving and b) do something to check the drift
to anti-whiteism'.[20]

In the event, the Natal Convention elected a continuation committee, whose brief was to summon together political operators
from across the spectrum and gather momentum for the idea of
what was to become known as the National Consultation. From
Natal, Brown liaised closely with the Johannesburg Liberal, John
Lang, whose efforts in the Transvaal had given birth to a non-
aligned steering committee, which was also working towards a Convention. Despite its professed non-partisanship, the steering committee had several Liberal members: its secretary, Mary Walker,
belonged to the Party, as did Leslie Cooper. The committee chairman was Henri Kuiper, who chaired Standard Bank and was a
director of South African Associated Newspapers. Several other
representatives were drawn from the world of commerce. Their
presence, Brown would write, was an 'attempt to capitalise on the
post-Republican anxieties of big business and to draw them into
the Convention movement'.[21] The businesspeople inclined to
gradualism, however; they demonstrated no particular sense of
urgency to hold a national convention, and their political motives
and outlook stood in contrast to those of the Liberals. Nevertheless, Brown managed to obtain Luthuli's endorsement for the Transvaal committee's work. Other sponsors whom he approached successfully were Chief Justices HA Fagan and A van de S Centlivres;
Paton; Jan Steytler from the Progressives; and Richard van der
Ross, who at the time was involved in the movement for a Coloured
Convention.

Several factors conspired to take the wind out of the National
Consultation's sails in 1961, one of which was the fact that John
Lang disappeared suddenly and mysteriously overnight, into exile

overseas, leaving both the Party and his steering committee to face certain financial difficulties.[22] Efforts were made by Liberals to revive the movement later in the year, and in October Brown was invited both by leaders of the Coloured Convention and the Liberal Party to address a conference in Cape Town. He spoke on the Natal Convention. Brown shared the platform with Dennis Brutus, pioneer of anti-apartheid sports campaigning, who had held a convention meeting in Port Elizabeth in July, and the ANC Western Cape Chairman, Thomas Ngwenya, who delivered ZK Matthews's speech in his absence.

By the end of the year, the impetus for a national convention had fizzled out. In Brown's view, this was partly due to Verwoerd having called an early election in October. He believed that the election dampened enthusiasm for the Convention Movement at a crucial moment, and that 'drive was lost which was never to be recovered again'.[23] The movement's collapse was also caused, in part, by the sheer difficulty of political organisation across party and racial lines in the early 1960s. Granted, the Liberal Party was beginning to have some success in cooperating with Coloured South Africans. But the banning of the ANC and the PAC, leaving aside the paralysing effect of the rivalry between the two organisations, made it virtually impossible for Liberals to work effectively with Africans outside their own Party. How then could Liberals, beyond the immediate bounds of their Party, give practical expression to the politics of non-racialism? With whom could they forge alliances to promote the common society?

Cooperation with the Progressive Party was hampered by its predominantly white membership. In 1960, an internal Progressive commission, chaired by the former Liberal, Donald Molteno, filed its interim report. The so-called Molteno Commission recommended the adoption of a Bill of Rights, a long-standing plank in the Liberal platform, and a qualified franchise. Both Luthuli and Ngubane had tried to convince the Commission to come out in favour of universal suffrage, and all three of the Commission's black members – Dr S Cooppan, Selby Ngcobo and Richard van der Ross – opposed a qualification. Nevertheless, Molteno advocated a set of restrictions on the franchise, and at the Progressives'

Congress in 1960, the Party actually adopted higher qualifications than those recommended by the Commission. In 'The Long View', Brown asked: 'Why *should* the Progressives have reacted in this way?' He proceeded to answer:

> The fact is that, although they have travelled a long way since they parted from the United Party, they remain a White party with White views, convinced that a White-orientated policy holds the answer for South Africa and that White people can still produce a policy which non-White people will gratefully accept. This is a delusion. Those days are past if, in fact, they ever existed and, if the Progressives had an effective non-White membership effectively represented at their congress, they would have known it.[24]

Two weeks later, also in *Contact*, Patrick Duncan savaged the Progressives in a four-page spread entitled 'How Progressives weaken struggle for democracy'. He described the Molteno Report as a 'pretentious and ambiguous document'; a 'sickening document', in fact, which had 'proved that the slogan "merit, not colour", was a lie'. He concluded that 'the Molteno plan is just another of these tortuous devices for maintaining, behind a democratic-looking mask, the substance of White privilege, White wealth and White power'.[25]

Brown was taken aback by Duncan's blistering attack, and he told him that 'the four page indictment goes beyond the "friendly but critical" attitude [to the Progressives] adopted by the National Committee'.[26] He felt compelled publicly to distance himself and the Party from Duncan's diatribe in a letter subsequently published in *Contact*.[27] Duncan's imprudence had embarrassed Brown once more, as had a number of his previous editorial decisions. For example, Duncan had earlier published a 'Freedom Calendar' with photographs of anti-apartheid leaders including Sobukwe and Paton, but he had pointedly omitted Luthuli. An accumulation of such incidents led Brown to suggest that any official link between the Party and *Contact* 'should go', and the 'best way in which to do this,' he said, 'is through my stopping writing the Long View.'[28]

TOP LEFT: Dr Archibald McKenzie and his wife, Peter Brown's maternal grandparents. (*Phoebe Brown*)

TOP RIGHT: 'Monaltrie', the home in which Peter Brown grew up on Musgrave Road. (*Phoebe Brown*)

LEFT: Helen Mary 'Maisie' Brown, Peter Brown's mother. (*Phoebe Brown*)

TOP LEFT: Peter Brown, on the right, with his schoolmate and lifelong friend, Simon Roberts, early 1930s. (*Phoebe Brown*)

TOP RIGHT: At the polo grounds in Durban with his cousins and sister. *From left to right:* Archie McKenzie, Peter Brown, Christianne McKenzie (later Carlisle) and Bet Brown, early 1930s. (*Christianne Carlisle*)

LEFT: Peter Brown as a young soldier, c. 1942. (*Christianne Carlisle*)

Alan Paton addresses a crowd in Fordsburg on the Group Areas Act, 1957. (*Africa Media Online*)

Jordan Ngubane (standing) campaigns for Peter Brown in the 1958 general election. *From left to right:* Alan Paton, Ngubane, Derick Marsh, Brown. (*Alan Paton Centre and Struggle Archive, University of KwaZulu-Natal*)

LEFT: Chief Albert Luthuli burns his pass in Pretoria, 1960. (*PictureNet*)

CENTRE: Chief Albert Luthuli recieves the Nobel Peace Prize in Oslo, 10 December 1961. (*PictureNet*)

BELOW: Peter Brown with Pius Zondi (*extreme left*) and Selby Msimang at a Liberal Party public meeting, c. 1962.
(*Alan Paton Centre and Struggle Archive, University of KwaZulu-Natal*)

TOP: Roosboom Prayer Meeting, 1 September 1963. *Right to left:* Elliot Mngadi, Rev I Nyembezi, Rev R Fallowes, Bishop J Gwala, Selby Msimang. (*Alan Paton Centre and Struggle Archive, University of KwaZulu-Natal*)

LEFT: 'Remember Sharpeville': Peter Brown, early 1960s. (*Alan Paton Centre and Struggle Archive, University of KwaZulu-Natal*)

Peter Brown, 1960s. (*Phoebe Brown*)

Patrick Duncan with his wife Cynthia, 1960s. (*PictureNet*)

Margaret Ballinger, 1960s. (*PictureNet*)

Edgar Brookes, 1960s. (*PictureNet*)

Oscar Wollheim, 1970s. (*PictureNet*)

Peter Brown with his wife Phoebe after his banning orders lapsed, 1974.
(*Alan Paton Centre and Struggle Archive, University of KwaZulu-Natal*)

Peter Brown, late 1970s. (*Phoebe Brown*)

Alan Paton in the Valley of a Thousand Hills, 1983. (*Africa Media Online*)

Alan Paton with Beyers Naude *(left)*. (*Africa Media Online*)

Archie Gumede, President of the United Democratic Front, addresses a rally, 1980s. (*Gallo Images*)

Peter Bown with Ian Wyllie, editor of *Reality*, 1991. (*Alan Paton Centre and Struggle Archive, University of KwaZulu-Natal*)

Sir Raymond 'Bill' Hoffenberg after receiving his honorary doctorate from the University of Cape Town, 1993. (*PictureNet*)

After another tangle with Duncan, this time because Duncan criticised Ngubane's resignation from the Orlando Continuation Committee, Brown stopped writing his column after the issue of 4 May 1961. He didn't resume it until 19 April 1963, by which time Duncan had left both the Party and *Contact.*

Liberal–Progressive relations were on the agenda at the National Committee meeting in Grahamstown between 21 and 22 October 1961. It was agreed that Brown should meet with the Progressive leader, Steytler, and try to 'establish the principle that the Party should contest certain seats without being opposed by Progressives'.[29] Duncan, whose disdain for the Progressives was no secret, allowed himself to be nominated for the Party's deputy presidency at the meeting. He lost, and Jack Unterhalter, Selby Msimang and the Orange Free State stalwart, Jean van Riet, were installed as Paton's deputies. Privately, Brown was relieved. He told Jock Isacowitz that Duncan 'would or could be a great embarrassment to us as an office-bearer'.[30]

Brown's meeting with Steytler did not take place – the record does not reflect why – but in 1962 he wrote to Ernie Wentzel that 'it was a good thing that we didn't see them [the Progressives] late last year'.[31] After the National Committee meeting in October, Brown set out his views to Wolf Hamm, the Johannesburg Liberal who had gone into exile the day his passport expired in March 1960. Hamm became a good friend of Brown's; he was a prolific letter-writer, and the two men kept up an almost unbroken correspondence from 1960 until Brown's death in 2004.[32] To Hamm, Brown opined that the Progressives would 'just draw unnecessary enthusiasm and effort off into the purely electoral struggle while the main job remains to be done outside it'.[33]

He worked up this theme in the December 1961 issue of *Liberal Opinion,* the Party journal that had first appeared in September:

> Wherever the real opposition to Dr. Verwoerd's threatened attempt to make apartheid work comes from in the immediate future, it is not going to come from Parliament. That is certain. Parliament, over the years, has become more and more of a rubber stamp, useful to the Government only

because it gives to its decisions a respectable democratic
veneer. It is certainly not the place where Nationalists are
persuaded to change their ideas, and it is certainly not
Parliamentary debates which have made some white South
Africans start thinking. They have started thinking, to the
tune of 70 000 Progressive and Liberal votes, but the reasons for their doing so are to be found outside, not inside
Parliament – in the Defiance Campaign, in the activities of
the Liberal Party and the Black Sash, in the events leading
up to last year's emergency and the emergency itself, and in
South Africa's isolation from the Commonwealth and the
world.[34]

Brown's differentiation of extra-parliamentary from parliamentary
liberalism underscored the Progressives' own contrast between
'extremist' and moderate liberalism. In 1962, Brown informed
Michael Nuttall, the chairman of the Party's Grahamstown branch
(and the bishop who would later preside over his funeral), that the
Progressives had issued a 'fact paper' in Durban on the Southern
Rhodesian franchise proposals. The document castigated 'extreme
white liberals' for opposing the proposals and, under a section
entitled 'Who are *our* enemies?', identified, among others, the self-
same 'extreme white liberals'.[35]

The Liberals' own 'friendly but critical' approach to the Progs
should not extend, in Brown's view, to unnecessary displays of
amity. He counselled another Grahamstown member, Terence
Beard, not to appear on the platform of his local Progressive candidate in the 1962 election, telling him: 'I think it would be a mistake. I don't think a senior member of the Party should appear on
somebody else's platform.'[36]

However, for all their differences, and they were real enough,
the Liberals and the Progressives shared a similar conception of
what their long-term role would be, namely, as intermediaries and
bridge-builders between Afrikaner nationalists and African nationalists. Geoff Luffingham, a straight-talking Liberal farmer from
Winterton and, with Margaret Ballinger, a member of the National
Maize Board in UP days, wrote to Brown to 'blow off some steam'

and explain his reasons for wanting to emigrate. He felt that Liberals would never come to power through the ballot box, and even if they did they would be hemmed in by a hostile police force, army and civil service. He suggested to Brown that it might be better to 'go back to your Edendale days of social work'.[37] Brown's response illuminates his analysis of the contemporary political situation and his prognosis for Liberals:

> We won't get rid of the Nats through the ballot box. The implication is, then, that things will either get worse economically, or get worse politically between the races, or both, until there is such a deterioration that white voters won't stand for apartheid any longer. I very much doubt if, even at that stage, the Nats will be voted out of power. It seems to me to be more likely that they will prefer to negotiate. They will have to get together with people opposed to them and bargain. The bargaining will be tough but the balance of power is such that there will have to be an accommodation. The blacks have the numbers and the labour. The whites have the armed power, the skills and they have been clever to ensure that it is only they who know how to run the apparatus of state … At this stage of negotiation we would, I hope, have a vital role to play, provided we have built ourselves up enough in the interim and had managed to maintain a reputation for integrity on both sides of the colour-line.[38]

So much for the Liberals' future role; what of their strategy in the meantime? The wheels of a national convention had been put in motion, but by November 1961 they had all but spluttered to a halt. The government's attitude to the Liberal Party was becoming more menacing: in January, Verwoerd had accused the Party of inviting 'foreign allies to use force to break the Government', and one of his ministers, MDC de Wet Nel, had told Parliament that 'trouble is created by a small, organised group of white communists and members of the Liberal Party who get financial assistance from Russia'.[39] Police intimidation at Party meetings, constant

harassment of members at their workplaces and homes and, ultimately, individual banning orders were soon to follow.

The Party could continue to engage in broad extra-parliamentary activity, as Brown insisted it should. But this work did not
always yield tangible political results. In 1961, the Transvaal division got closely involved with the Johannesburg Rents campaign.
In the Cape, Party members did relief work in the Cape Flats
shanties of Windermere, and in Natal the campaign against black
spot removals proceeded apace. This was all important work, and
it boosted the Party's membership among blacks, but it did not
constitute a direct political challenge to the government, nor did
it attract the kind of international attention that might embarrass
the Nationalist regime. At the time, the Nationalists were trying to
enhance their international profile. They had helped to set up a
body called the South Africa Foundation, with funds from big business, to bolster the country's image overseas. Among its original
trustees were the business moguls, Harry Oppenheimer and Anton
Rupert[40] and its executive committee included Punch Barlow,
Brown's father-in-law, and Eric Gallo the doyen of the South
African music recording industry (and the father of Brown's future
daughter-in-law).[41] Brown would later call for the Liberal Party to
publicise that the foundation 'was not, and never could be, anything but an apologist for apartheid'.[42]

With the national convention idea on the backburner, what the
Liberals were grappling towards in 1961 was some kind of a campaign that could bring them into a close working relationship with
black allies outside of the Party, assault the ideological basis of
apartheid through a direct political challenge and hopefully draw
international notice in the process. The prospects seemed bleak,
however. In November 1961, Brown maintained to Duncan that
there was neither a 'miraculous way out of our situation here', nor
'any spectacular campaign which could be successfully mounted
against the Government at present'. There was no organisation to
back up such a campaign, in his view, and the government was
very much stronger than it had been before the events at Sharpeville. 'So, for myself,' Brown ended, 'I see the immediate future as
mostly sweat, and perhaps a few tears.'[43]

In a letter sent to Wolf Hamm at the end of the month, Brown argued that it was time 'we really got down to building the *organisation* which can conduct a long-drawn-out and disciplined campaign which will build up an effective opposition to apartheid, instead of going from one grandiose failure to another as the Congress Movement has done for so long'.[44] Evidently, he did not think the Liberal Party could, on its own, be the vehicle for such an organisation. Yet, with the ANC and the PAC banned, and the Progressives wedded to parliamentary politics, the Liberal Party would have to implement the 'long-drawn-out and disciplined campaign' under its own auspices. It found its opportunity in the Transkei.

Brown had first gone to the Transkei on Party business in 1956, when he, Paton and Mlahleni Njisane enrolled new members at the Holy Cross Mission in East Pondoland. Since then, branches had been formed at Cedarville, Kokstad and Matatiele in the Mount Currie district, which was not subject to the provisions of the Bantu Authorities Act of 1951. These branches kept in close contact with the Natal division, and Brown often visited them. In 1961, he was charged and found guilty of holding an illegal meeting in Kokstad (a 'legal' meeting was one attended by not more than ten Africans).[45] The really important link with the Transkei – the one that foreshadowed the Party's future involvement in the area – had been made in 1960. Hammington Majija, a Transkeian living in Cape Town, had organised for Patrick Duncan to address a group on the Mbashe River bank in August. There, Duncan had appealed to his 200-strong audience to resist the Bantu Authorities Act and establish an 'Anti-Bantu Authorities Committee'. They did, and this was the beginning of Liberal efforts to oppose Bantu Authorities and, in due course, 'self-rule', in the Transkei.

The story of Liberals and the Transkei, ably related by Randolph Vigne in his history of the Liberal Party, is not directly Brown's own.[46] In 1962, Verwoerd announced his intention to grant self-rule to the Transkei, thereby seeking, for the benefit of the outside world, a patina of legitimacy for his homeland, or 'Bantustan', policy. It was the Cape Liberals, Duncan, Hjul, Majija, Cromwell Nododile and Vigne, who then seized the initiative. They mobilised opposition to the façade of self-government, and made the

Party's Transkei campaign an integral prong of its broader strategic work for a common society, with all that it implied – common
citizenship in a common territory. Vigne acted as an adviser to the
Thembuland Paramount Chief, Sabata Dalindyebo, who believed
that by giving up their birthright as South Africans in exchange for
bogus Bantustan self-rule, Transkeians would be foregoing 'a cattle-
kraal for a fowl-run'.[47] It seemed to the Liberals that Sabata, and
another paramount chief, Victor Poto Ndamase, of West Pondoland, were the men to take on the apartheid government's stooge,
Chief Kaiser Matanzima, who chaired the Transkei Transitional
Authority (TTA). The *Contact* Liberals met regularly with Sabata,
Victor Poto and other chiefs in an attempt to shore up resistance
to the Transkei Constitution Act, the law that would establish the
first homeland legislative assembly. After Duncan, Hjul and Vigne
were all banned between 1962 and 1963, Grahamstown Liberals
like Terence Beard, Eric Harber and Clement Goodfellow resumed
their efforts. They too were banned for their troubles, and Brown
wrote: 'The implication was clear – Keep away from the Transkei.'[48]

Brown was never as active in the campaign against Transkeian
independence as he was in the campaign against black spot removals in northern Natal. But he deplored the homelands policy,
describing it in 'The Long View' as 'a policy which offends against
the dignity of every thinking African on the continent'.[49] He quickly
grasped the importance of the campaign, encouraged it, and was
briefed regularly by those involved. Between 1962 and 1963, he
wrote and spoke about it as one of the Party's main priorities. In a
Chairman's report, penned at the time, Brown said of the Transkei:

> This is one of the areas where our impact has been very
> great and I think we can claim with justification that it is
> largely through our efforts that a coherent opposition has
> developed there. For the moment the Government and
> Kaiser Matanzima are in the saddle but the commitment to
> non-racialism of Paramount Chief Sabata and the Party's
> very close relations with him are of incalculable importance
> for the future.[50]

After the Party opened an office in Umtata, which was constantly raided by the Security Police, Brown paid frequent visits, explaining to Jack Unterhalter before one such trip: 'I think it important that we should show them [the government] that we are not going to be frightened out of the Transkei and I think this brief visit is one way of doing so.'[51] He also met on several occasions with Victor Poto.

Despite the Liberals' best efforts, the Transkei Constitution Act was rammed through the TTA by Matanzima and his supporters. Brown warned in 'The Long View': 'African supporters of apartheid and Bantustans should know that they are condemning over six million of their fellows to perpetual serfdom.'[52] The results of the first Transkei Assembly elections on 20 November 1963 were more positive. Of the 45 seats contested, only seven were won by Matanzima's allies. Brown reported that '[t]he result of the election was a vindication of everything we [the Liberals] had done and a great credit to those of our members who had helped develop the spirit of opposition in the Transkei over the past few years.'[53] Alas, heavy-handed tactics by the South African security forces, and threats to the salaried chiefs, eventually saw Matanzima sworn in as Chief Minister in December 1963, in charge of a cabinet stacked with his acolytes. Brown lamented that in 1964 'ordinary Transkeians [could] look forward to having ... their affairs administered by a Chief Minister they didn't want supported by a "Cabinet" which does not represent them'.[54] Nevertheless, in the legislative election, the people of Transkei had sent a clear signal that they rejected Matanzima and all he represented. As Vigne justly notes: 'The government ... could never claim that the Transkeians had accepted "Bantu self-rule" and the loss of their South African citizenship. The great trophy for which the game had been played – international acceptance of "separate development" – had been lost forever.'[55]

The Liberal Party's crusade in the Transkei was an attempt to conduct the 'disciplined campaign which [would] build up an effective opposition to apartheid' that Brown had contemplated in his letter to Wolf Hamm. By creating alliances with local chiefs opposed to separate development, the Liberals had been able, with some measure of success, to discredit one of the cornerstones of apartheid – indeed, *the* cornerstone of 'grand' apartheid. Moreover, they achieved this in an area that, as Vigne remarks, had long been a 'political wasteland', overlooked by the ANC as part of its 'general political neglect of rural South Africa'.[56] In 1962, Brown still hoped to co-operate with the underground ANC in common-front campaigns against apartheid. His aspirations were shared by Luthuli, who, in writing to thank Brown for the gift Liberals had given him before going to Oslo to receive his Nobel Peace Prize, affirmed: 'Notwithstanding differences of opinion on tactics in our common fight for freedom, I trust our co-operation will continue and grow.'[57]

The ANC had altered its strategy and adopted armed struggle in 1961. In December that year, its military wing, Umkhonto we Sizwe (MK) – 'Spear of the Nation' – bombed electric power stations and government offices in Johannesburg, Port Elizabeth and Durban. At the time of the explosions, MK distributed pamphlets announcing its existence and claiming responsibility for the attacks. The pamphlets expressed the hope that the organisation would 'bring the government and its supporters to their senses before it is too late, so that both the government and its policies can be changed before matters reach the desperate stage of civil war ...'[58]

In the meantime, the underground PAC had begun organising cells along military lines. In December 1961, pamphlets were circulated in the Cape township of Nyanga, stating: 'The white people shall suffer, the black people will rule. Freedom comes after bloodshed. Poqo has started.'[59] The following year, members of Poqo (translated from Xhosa as 'We stand alone') rioted in Paarl, killing a man and a woman. On 5 February 1963, two white road engineers, one of their wives and two young girls, were murdered as they slept by the roadside of the Mbashe River Bridge in Transkei. Poqo was implicated in the attack, and Kaiser Matanzima blamed the killings on incitement by Patrick Duncan. The Nationalist minister, De Wet Nel, made similar claims in Parliament.

These events shocked white South Africa. Brown dismissed any suggestion of a link between the Liberal Party, Poqo and the

Mbashe Bridge murders, and stated in his column that 'Liberals have no connection and never have had any with Poqo'. Poqo was 'narrow, exclusive and violent, [and] as far removed from the Liberal Party as it could possibly be'.[60] In Brown's view, attempts by the government to associate the Liberal Party with Poqo were aimed at discrediting the Party, justifying the banning of people like Hjul and Vigne, intimidating Liberals out of the Transkei and masking the failure of its own policies, which had led to the creation of Poqo.

The turn to violence was to pose a predicament for many younger Liberals. Most of them instinctively recoiled from the use of armed force, which ran counter to their core liberal belief in a society based on the rule of law. But they felt frustrated by a repressive government whose own chronic abuse of its security apparatus seemed to render peaceful opposition to apartheid futile. In 1962, the so-called 'Sabotage Bill' – or 'Vorster's law', named after its instigator, the Minister of Justice, BJ Vorster – gave the government wide-ranging powers to crush opposition. It provided for the house arrest of anti-apartheid activists and instituted the death penalty for any number of crimes loosely and inaccurately termed 'sabotage'. It constituted, in short, a profoundly evil assault on civil liberties, and was condemned by the International Commission of Jurists, which deemed the Bill unworthy of civilised jurisprudence.

Helen Suzman fought the Bill roundly and bravely and alone in Parliament, though Ernie Wentzel told her he was disappointed by the 'attitude of the Johannesburg Progressives over this bill'; he was 'frankly dismayed by the coyness of the Progressives, their fear of sullying their fair reputations by association with Liberals, let alone communists'. It made Wentzel's blood boil, but luckily, he told Suzman: 'Your husband [Dr Mosie Suzman] is treating my blood pressure.'[61]

During the second reading debate, the Nationalists launched a scathing and portentous attack on the Liberal Party. Its campaign in the Transkei was singled out for mention; one MP, Blaar Coetzee, accused the Party of causing 'riots, arson and murder' and 'inciting the people to commit sabotage, in an attempt to paralyse the Government and force the policy of one man one vote on us'.

Whether Liberals were 'wittingly or unwittingly Communists', their
actions in the Transkei and their efforts to bring about universal
suffrage through extra-parliamentary activity amounted to 'high
treason', and, Coetzee concluded with a flourish, 'this law is intended for them'.[62]

The gauntlet had been thrown down, and Liberals were soon
to pay dearly with a barrage of banning orders that severely debili-
tated the Party. Alas, the Sabotage Bill was eventually enacted in
June 1962, and the Liberal Party marked its passing with wreath-
laying ceremonies outside the Supreme Court in Grahamstown,
Pietermaritzburg, Port Elizabeth and Pretoria; the wreaths bore
the inscription, 'We mourn the death of the Rule of Law in our
country.'[63] This was the culmination of a prodigious campaign
waged by the Party against the Bill, which had included mass protest meetings around the country. Brown thought the campaign
had been 'widespread [and] broadly based' and 'probably drew
wider support than any earlier anti-Nationalist campaign'.[64]

In 1963, Vorster introduced new legislation with the express
intention of destroying MK and Poqo. The General Law Amendment Act, or so-called Ninety-Day Act, authorised any commissioned police officer to detain a suspect without a warrant for his
arrest, and to hold him – without access to a lawyer – for a period
of up to 90 days for interrogation. Again, outside of Parliament,
the Liberal Party contested the Bill as it made its way through the
parliamentary process. Brown was the keynote speaker at a public
meeting in Pietermaritzburg called for this purpose, and he shared
the stage with members of the banned Congress movement,
including Archie Gumede, and the Black Sash. Afterwards, Brown
wrote to MB Yengwa, a loyal lieutenant of Chief Luthuli, to tell him
about the event and to assure him that the Party would submit rep-
resentations on the Bill as suggested by Luthuli.[65]

Students from the English-speaking university campuses had
been drawn into these campaigns; in Cape Town, the presidents of
their Student Representatives Councils (SRCs) had handed a memorandum of protest against the Sabotage Bill to Vorster. Many of
these students were active in the National Union of South African
Students (NUSAS) and had joined the Liberal Party. John Didcott,

a one-time President of both NUSAS and the University of Cape Town SRC, had been present at some of the Liberal Party's early meetings, as had another student leader, Irene Manderstam.[66] Other NUSAS presidents, from Ernie Wentzel, John Shingler and Neville Rubin to Adrian Leftwich and Jonty Driver, were all active Liberals, as were student leaders like Magnus Gunther and Hugh Lewin. Many of their names were soon to become well known to the South African public.

These students viewed themselves as radical Liberals, and, in the face of mounting state repression, they felt the need for the Party to identify with their radical proclivities. The Party's policies were, by the liberal South African standards of the day – indeed by the standards of classical liberalism anywhere – already radical. They went beyond the traditional liberal concern with civil rights and liberties, a concern which in itself was too progressive for Progressive liberals, who still denied black South Africans the most fundamental civil right of all – the unqualified right to vote. The Party supplemented its focus on civil rights with an emphasis on socio-economic rights. Brown himself was especially interested in the right to work – adequately remunerated work – and he threw his weight behind Bunny Curran's living wage campaign in 1959. More than once he returned to the theme in 'The Long View'.[67] He argued that poverty eradication would be central to any post-apartheid settlement. Referring to recent riots in Cato Manor, Brown remarked: 'The poverty of South Africa's African working population is one of the most pressing and explosive elements in the whole of the Union's highly-charged situation. Fail to get to grips with it and you fail to get to grips with the future.'[68]

In fact, the Party conceived of itself as radical. It did not subscribe to the classical liberal view of a non-interventionist state. State-led redistribution of land, for example, was central to its land policy. In a retrospective piece on the Liberals' tenth anniversary, Brown made both these observations, on the Party's radicalism and its conception of the role of the state, and noted how far the Party had moved from its origins as a rather staid, parliamentary party in the Cape liberal tradition:

From being a predominantly White Party it [the Liberal
Party] has become a predominantly African Party. From
being a 'reform' Party it has become a radical Party. From
being a Party believing in the abolition of all colour-bars and
in equal opportunities for all it has, while still believing pas-
sionately in these things, become a Party which accepts that,
in post-apartheid South Africa the state is going to have an
important task to perform in ironing out the racial disabili-
ties which will be a legacy of 300 years of White privilege.[69]

This was all well and good, but the younger Liberals wanted the
Party explicitly to identify itself as a social-democratic organisation.
Neville Rubin put the case for affiliating to the Socialist International.[70] Brown would have preferred the Party to join the Liberal International,[71] but members were divided on the matter and
the National Committee decided not to pursue it.[72]

Ernie Wentzel, the ebullient lawyer and former NUSAS President, sympathised with the Young Turks' desire for the Party to
reflect, in name, its social-democratic bent. Wentzel was a larger-
than-life character; he was fiercely intelligent, warm and voluble,
and he became another of Brown's close friends. When they travelled to Johannesburg on Party business, Peter and Phoebe would
invariably stay with either Jack and Beryl Unterhalter, or Ernie and
his wife, Jill – as Jill White, secretary of the Transvaal division.[73] To
Brown, Wentzel and Unterhalter provided the Party with a 'balance
between outgoing brilliance and steady, solid responsibility'.[74]
Although Wentzel thought Brown was 'a dreary public speaker'
and '[n]ot a forceful chairman at an Executive meeting', he perceived in him 'a keen intelligence, great courage and common
sense and considerable diligence'. To Wentzel, Brown 'was the
party in the real sense'; for he was a man of action, and he had 'a
compassionate nature and keen sense of humour which made him
respected by all sections of the Party'.[75] Paton, by contrast, was neither a political activist nor a strategist; according to Wentzel, '[i]n
essence this was Paton's limitation as a leader – he spoke magnifi-
cently but it signified nothing in the sense of action'.[76]

In 1961, Wentzel's supporters managed to have him replace

Jock Isacowitz as Transvaal Provincial Chairman. Isacowitz, himself a radical Liberal, resented the manner in which this was done – Wentzel's allies had organised a large bloc of African members' votes – and from time to time he expressed to Brown his dissatisfaction with Wentzel's leadership. Brown acknowledged that Wentzel had organisational deficiencies, but believed that he, 'more than anyone else', had been responsible for the Party 'really coming to mean something to Africans in the Transvaal'.[77] Indeed, it was largely through Wentzel's endeavours that the Party had managed to recruit African members in Rustenburg.

At a National Committee meeting in Grahamstown in July 1962, Wentzel mooted the idea of the Party changing its name. The minutes do not indicate what name he had in mind, but for some time Wentzel had thought the Party's name should reflect its social-democratic character.[78] The possibility of the Party renaming itself the 'Socialist Party of South Africa' had been bandied about. Brown disagreed with the proposal, though he did not voice his opposition during the meeting. Afterwards, he told Wentzel that he was 'against the change'. He believed that the Party's policies had already 'moved in that direction'; that was 'fair enough', but a name change would bring 'little gain and considerable loss in terms of membership and cohesion'.[79] He amplified these views in a follow-up letter to Wentzel, noting: 'Many Liberals are not socialists. They will accept a welfare state programme of the kind we now have but will walk out of the Party if it calls itself SOCIALIST. We cannot afford to lose these people now.'[80] Nor, in Brown's view, was the Liberal Party likely to recruit any Congress members by rebranding itself. Wentzel, for his part, had mistaken Brown's reticence in Grahamstown for consent, and now found himself in a quandary: 'I would not like to cause a huge and unnecessary split,' he confided in Brown, 'when as it is we are all so miserably weak.'[81]

Nevertheless, Wentzel pressed ahead with the idea, and at the National Congress in Cape Town the following year, he and Drake Koka proposed that Liberal policy be reconsidered 'with a view to its restatement in a form which will indicate clearly the Party's social democratic character'.[82] Some of the student politicians found this motion too tame. Leftwich called for a 'planned socialist economy in which the present inordinate inequalities can be removed and in which the social and economic welfare of citizens will be the responsibility of the state'.[83] He and Bill Hoffenberg, who was a trusted adviser to NUSAS,[84] moved that the Liberal Party should be renamed the Socialist Party of South Africa.[85]

The ensuing debate was heated, with some of the classical liberals threatening to resign. Brown argued that the Liberal Party had been formed primarily to fight racial discrimination and that matters of 'economic theory' should not cause it to split. In the end, Paton saved the day with a resolution, providing for the appointment of a Commission to reconsider Party policies, with a view to:

> ... [their] restatement in a form which will indicate clearly the Party's social democratic character and that the Party sees its role in the new South Africa as taking the lead in the building of a non-racial democracy, opposed to authoritarianism, in which one of the prime concerns of the state will be the economic and social welfare of its citizens.[86]

Both Brown and Paton might be described as social-democratic Liberals, but they were Liberals (and indeed 'small-l' liberals) before they were social democrats. Brown's allegiance remained with the liberal tradition, although he and the Liberal Party had broadened the scope of that tradition so that it now reflected, in part, a 'social-democratic character'. Not long after Wentzel had first put his proposal to the National Committee, Brown acknowledged to Duncan that the term '"liberal" has unfortunate connotations in certain respects in our country'. However, he thought the Liberal Party had 'done a good deal to overcome that and [that] it would be bad tactics, quite apart from anything else, to change now, with the Vorster Act behind us'.[87] Duncan, for this part, 'could not go along with a socialist party' and rejected a name change.[88]

By the time Brown and Duncan exchanged this correspondence, Duncan had already been served with a second banning order, on 18 April 1962. He made a public statement signalling that he would defy the ban, which confined him to the magisterial district of Cape Town for five years. Brown understood this to mean that Duncan would contravene his ban *inside* South Africa, and suffer the consequences accordingly – most likely a prison sentence.[89] Instead, Duncan chose to disregard the ban by going into exile in Basutoland. On 3 May, with the help of Hjul and Vigne, Duncan left Cape Town by car and quietly slipped over the border that evening. To his biographer, Jonty Driver, this was a calculated decision: Duncan could achieve more from a position of freedom in Basutoland than from captivity in the Cape. As such, 'he was not running away; he was making a fresh assault from a new position'.[90]

Duncan sent Brown a letter setting out his reasons for the move. The letter, Brown told Duncan in his reply, had shocked him. He had not expected Duncan's defection in the light of his public statement. He would wait to speak to Hjul before jumping to any conclusions, but for the moment, he said, 'I am worried.'[91] Brown saw Hjul and Vigne on a trip to Cape Town the following week and reported back to Duncan: 'I still think you made a mistake but I don't now think, as I once did, that it is going to be a serious one.' Even so, Brown did not believe Duncan could achieve much of use for the Party outside South Africa. Indeed, he remarked: 'I don't myself think that anyone who has left the country has so far had any influence on events [inside the country].'[92]

Already before his move to Basutoland, Duncan had revised his opposition to violence. From the time of the Emergency in 1960, he also felt increasingly drawn to the PAC. In December 1962, he wrote to Brown and made oblique references to the fact that his 'thinking' was 'moving' and that he had 'joined an organisation which shares much of this point of view'.[93] Not prepared to associate Liberals with violence or to countenance an ideology so seemingly at odds with non-racialism, Brown told Duncan matter-of-factly that he 'should now slip quietly out of the Party'. Brown was disappointed: both at the manner in which Duncan had chosen to defy his ban and at his abandonment, in Brown's view, of the Liberal cause. Yet he gave no indication of his displeasure, congenially ending his letter with the hope that the store run by Duncan in Basutoland 'is getting on to its feet slowly & not killing you in the process!'[94]

Duncan responded by formally tendering his resignation. However, he felt unable 'just [to] slide out without saying anything', and so he asked Brown to announce, at the appropriate time and in the following terms, that "'Patrick Duncan has resigned from the Liberal Party because he is no longer able to accept the party's policy of non-violence'". Duncan was naïve to think that Brown would accede to his request, but in fact he made a far graver error of judgment in his letter. Explaining the reasons for his resignation, he wrote:

> The circumstances are that I understand that the party has set its face against any of its members playing any part in a forceful attack on apartheid. I think that it might have been better not to present our members now with the need to choose – i.e. that a wiser path might have been to have let it ride, knowing that many of our best members have in fact joined other organisations whose sole aim is a violent assault on apartheid.[95]

Brown was justifiably furious, and he responded sternly:

> I cannot understand why you should have written a letter to me in those terms and to this address, especially as we had taken some trouble to arrange a code when I last saw you …
> I think it is a safe assumption that a photostat copy of your letter is filed away by people who will be glad to make use of it at a time suitable to themselves. It will confirm in writing accusations which have been made these past months. If there are, as you say, people here who share your views, I think you should warn them at once of this fact. I do not myself know of people who do share those views. However, if I did know of them, I would have to ask them to make up their minds between continuing to work within the limits of our policy and leaving us. Apart from anything else there is an obligation to those people who have joined us believing that our policies say what they mean.[96]

Duncan was aggrieved by Brown's reply, and wrote back expressing his regret that 'after eight years, and after all we have done together for the cause, your valedictory letter to me should have contained not one generous word, and ... no reference whatsoever to [his wife] Cynthia's resignation'.[97] Separately, he told Paton that he was upset with Brown since 'his letter accepting my resignation contain[ed] nothing except rather querulous reprimands'.[98] Paton defended Brown, and asked if Duncan had been 'ruthless and dishonourable or just unbelievably careless' in sending his original letter through the open post.[99]

There is no record of Brown's response to Duncan's letter. The day after Duncan wrote his angry missive, and presumably before Brown had received it, Brown sent Duncan a letter, enclosing a statement on his resignation: 'Patrick Duncan has informed the Liberal Party that he is no longer able to subscribe to the Party's policies ... His membership of the Party has therefore terminated.' Brown urged Duncan that if he considered it necessary to make a statement, he should avoid embarrassing the Party and its members since 'some of them ... are extremely vulnerable'.[100] Although Brown would remember Duncan fondly in later life, the circumstances of his resignation precipitated a falling-out between the two, and their fences remained unmended at the time of Duncan's death in England in 1967.

What was all this talk of 'vulnerable' members, and what did Duncan mean by saying that 'many of our best members have in fact joined other organisations whose sole aim is a violent assault on apartheid'? He was in fact referring to the National Committee for Liberation (NCL), whose origins could be traced back to the State of Emergency in 1960. Then, it will be recalled, several Transvaal Liberals were detained in the Pretoria Central Prison. One of them, John Lang, befriended a former Communist Party member, Monty Berman, and they discussed the possibility of using armed force, principally by sabotaging government installations. From their discussion the NCL was born.

The NCL soon established a countrywide presence, bringing together volunteer saboteurs from various anti-apartheid organisations. Between 1961 and 1964 it executed roughly twelve successful

sabotage attacks and numerous botched ones. In comparison with
Umkhonto we Sizwe, the NCL was small: it had about 65 members,
of whom 19 were Liberals.[101] In this way, the NCL was by no means
an offshoot of the Liberal Party; it was an underground organisation of whose existence the Party remained unaware until the fate-
ful events of 1964.

The NCL mounted its first sabotage operations in October
1961. Brown would later record that '... power lines were sabo-
taged near Johannesburg by the National Committee of [sic]
Liberation. We didn't know it, but that was some of us.'[102] In fact,
there were suggestions of Liberal involvement at the time. Jock
Isacowitz wrote to Brown on 10 November 1961, and mentioned in
a postscript: 'Ernie [Wentzel] will be phoning you today about official allegations that we are mixed up with sabotage.'[103] Whether
Wentzel contacted Brown about the allegations or not is unknown.
But a few days after Isacowitz sent his letter, Brown wrote to Wentzel, responding to a suggestion that he, Brown, should meet with
Vorster and tackle him about the government's campaign of harassment and intimidation against the Liberal Party. Brown dismissed
the possibility; whether from 'an overdose of pride or just plain
stubbornness' he had 'strong personal views against talking to any
representative of the present establishment'. But there was another
reason for his refusal:

> If we tell him we hate the commies & abjure violence and
> sabotage all he will do is shrug his shoulders and say 'Well,
> that's what *you* say!' There is another complication which
> cannot be widely discussed and that is the fact that I still
> don't know why your partner [at law, John Lang] left – and
> perhaps Vorster does ... If we thought it unwise to make a
> public protest at the time I am afraid there is nothing else
> we can do now.[104]

Ever since Lang's hasty retreat into exile, senior Party leaders had
harboured suspicions that some Liberal members might, in their
individual capacities, be involved in underground activities. At
some stage in 1961, Paton visited Cape Town for a National

Executive meeting, and he heard Leftwich make 'an impassioned and ambiguous speech' condemning conventional methods of opposing apartheid and urging the Party to 'break new ground'. Paton would recall in his autobiography: 'To me it could only mean one thing, that we should turn to violence.'[105] He subsequently asked Leftwich whether he was busy 'organising an underground', and Leftwich denied it.

Brown could certainly understand the rationale behind violence, and even empathise, as subsequent events would show, with its perpetrators. In January 1961, he asked in 'The Long View':

> If non-violence provokes violent reactions from the Government, what is the point in being non-violent? This is the question which many a South African of colour must be asking himself. There is violence in Pondoland. Where will it appear next? What is the effective alternative to it? This is the question to which the Liberal Party and all who hate violence must find some answer in 1961.[106]

Yet, as his column clearly indicated, he personally abhorred violence. In December 1961, he wrote to his old university friend, Antoinette Swart, noting that there was currently 'considerable excitement' about the sabotage attempts. He had 'no inclination towards this sort of thing', he told her, adding bluntly: 'I don't like it.'[107]

Brown also believed that it was the Liberal Party's duty to make a practical and intellectual case against the resort to violence. In an article for *Liberal Opinion* in March 1962, he stated that the Liberal Party remained committed 'to the principle of bringing change to South Africa by non-violent means'. There were 'good reasons, practical, expedient and moral, for this stand'. The South African Defence Force could easily suppress any armed uprising. Sabotage had been tried and had 'not yet raised a ripple on the placid surface of the South African economy'. In sum, the turn to violence signalled by the emergence of MK, the PAC's armed wing, Poqo, and the NCL (whose existence had not been publicly declared) would not provide a shortcut to liberation. Brown contended: 'It may instead be the beginning of a long detour which will keep the end of apartheid out of sight for years and ensure that when it comes, one racialism will be succeeded by another.'[108]

How much did Brown know about the involvement of Liberals in sabotage? The NCL had a presence in Natal, where two of its foremost operatives, David Evans and John Laredo, were Liberals. At some point between 1961 and 1962, Laredo tried, and failed, to recruit Brown's cousin, Pat McKenzie, into the NCL.[109] Around the same time, Evans unsuccessfully attempted to recruit a prominent Coloured Liberal, Dempsey Noel, who, according to Evans, might have given Brown to understand that such an attempt had been made.[110] While on a visit to Natal from Cape Town, either in 1962 or 1963, Bill Hoffenberg told Brown that Peter Hjul suspected some Party members of being involved in sabotage, or of planning to become involved.[111]

Paton had his suspicions about Randolph Vigne, who was banned in February 1963. Before a meeting specially called to protest against his ban, Paton tackled Vigne, who gave him an equivocal answer which Paton construed – misconstrued, in Vigne's view – as a denial.[112] At the last National Committee meeting attended by Vigne at Kloof in January 1963, Paton made a strong statement that any member who had any connection with the use of armed force should resign from the Party at once. Vigne realised this would attract attention to the resigner, so he wrote a brief letter of resignation while the meeting was under way and gave it to Brown as he was getting into his car. Vigne said: 'Put this in a safe place and don't read it until it's clear to you that you must do so.'[113] When Vigne was banned in February 1963, his membership of the Party automatically lapsed – since his banning orders forbade it – and no resignation was necessary. It is not known whether Brown read the letter in 1963. Vigne asked him about the letter years later, and Brown claimed to have forgotten all about it. In an interview with Norman Bromberger in 1995, Brown would recall:

At some stage I certainly got a hint from Randolph [Vigne] that he was involved. Now I'm not a great one for psychology, but, from my point of view I find it interesting that I had absolutely no recollection of his ever having given me that hint until he reminded me not so long ago … Whether this was some sort of defence mechanism set in motion I don't know, but when he told me *then* I could remember, but until then I had somehow completely got it out of my mind.[114]

When the NCL was active, Bromberger, who was recruited into it by Rubin,[115] got the impression from Rubin that a doctor was 'on call' in case of a medical emergency, such as if someone accidentally severed a hand. Bromberger wondered whether it might be Bill Hoffenberg. On hearing this in later years, Brown discounted the possibility, joking: 'Hoffenberg would have fainted if he had seen that … We once tried to suggest he might help with a cow which was having a calving problem and all he did was get well out of earshot of its bellows. I'm pretty sure he wasn't involved.'[116] Bromberger was later able to assure Brown that Hoffenberg was not, in fact, involved.

It is possible that Brown had an inkling that a few Liberals were involved in clandestine activities of some sort, though his recollection of how much he knew at the time was hazy in later life. Like all the other executive leaders of the Party, he would have known nothing of the NCL as an organisation, or of its plans. But his own political career was about to be brought to an abrupt halt, never to be resumed in the way of active politics, and the activities of the NCL (renamed the African Resistance Movement, or ARM, after its last operation) provided the catalyst for the government to act against him.

Early in the morning of 4 July 1964, the Security Police raided the homes of more than sixty Liberals around the country, including Adrian Leftwich's flat in Cape Town. At random, an officer removed a book from Leftwich's bookcase, and found in it a document identifying targets for sabotage. Leftwich was placed under arrest and taken to the Caledon Square police station; within 96 hours, by Paton's reckoning, he had agreed to talk.[117] He had also agreed to give evidence for the state – damning evidence, in fact, which would put many of his colleagues in the ARM behind bars for a very long time.

In Natal, Brown was the only Liberal whose home was raided on 4 July; both his house and garden were searched for two hours. Party material was confiscated, along with a number of Brown's books, among them Mary Turok's *Lift the Ban*.[118] He had been fortunate to elude banning orders up until then. After Duncan in April 1962, and Hjul and Vigne in February 1963, nine more key Liberals were banned over a fourteen-month period. Five of them came from Natal: Jordan Ngubane (May 1963), EV Mahomed (July 1963), David Evans (August 1963), Bill Bhengu (November 1963) and Elliot Mngadi (March 1964). After Mngadi was banned, he wrote heart-rendingly to Brown: 'To separate me from the Party and its work is just like separating a mother from her child … My whole life was completely intertwined with its work … Peter I am happy because you are still fine, and I know that you will keep up the good work of nursing our baby …'[119]

But the state would not allow Brown to go on holding the baby for much longer. He was, after all, the Party's principal financial support, caregiver, motivator, role model and champion. His success in attracting black membership, his personal contacts across the colour bar, his readiness to work with the underground Congresses, his determined campaigning against black spot removals, his visible support for the Party's work in the Transkei and, ultimately, his prominence – all this was reason enough for him to have been banned long before any other Liberal. Why, then, did the state wait until 29 July 1964 to serve him with his banning orders?

Brown's movements had been monitored by the Security Police for some time. The first detailed report on record, motivating for his proscription, is dated 10 June 1964, and was sent from the Commissioner of Police to the Secretary of Justice. The Commissioner's covering letter drew attention to Brown's 'frequent visits to the Transkei', in particular his meetings with Victor Poto, and noted that there was 'every reason' to believe that Brown was helping Poto's Democratic Party in 'word and deed'.[120] The Commissioner recommended that Brown should be banned under the Suppression of Communism Act; that he should be prohibited from attending 'any gathering'; and that he should be precluded from entering any 'Bantu, Coloured or Indian residential area'. The

Commissioner concluded dismissively: 'Abovementioned [Brown] belongs to the Anglican Church, but is not a regular churchgoer. However, he is a keen polo player.' The attached memorandum on Brown's activities emphasised his links with the Congress movement, and catalogued his appearance on joint platforms, as well as various meetings he had had – and, mistakenly, some he had not – with senior leaders of the ANC and the SAIC. Bizarrely, a claim was made that, on 13 May 1954, Brown, Meidner and Moses Kotane, the Secretary-General of the South African Communist Party, had visited Cape Town to meet with the Soviet *chargé d'affaires*. 'The visit to Cape Town would also have been used to collect funds from the banned Communist Party, which contributed more than R8 000,' the report asserted confidently – and utterly erroneously.[121] Indeed, Brown had never even met Kotane. For the rest, the document stressed his role in the campaign against black spot removals, his various visits to the Transkei in 1963 and his promotion of the liberal cause through his writings in *Contact* and *Liberal Opinion*. It also recognised that due to Brown's 'dedication to liberal ideology, several branches of the Party have been formed; not only in the white areas but also in the black areas [*bantoe woongebiede*] and homelands'. An internal memorandum produced by the Department of Justice, and signed by the Minister on 22 July, made the additional observation that Brown's ban would hopefully contribute to *Contact*'s demise ('… *sal bydra om daardie publikasie te smoor*').[122]

Brown was never given the official reasons for his proscription. If he was to ask why he had been banned, however, the official response was to be as follows: 'Since 1953 you actively associated yourself with certain organisations and so-called liberation and peace movements which aim at bringing about political, industrial, social or economic change within the Republic by the promotion of disturbance or disorder, by unlawful acts or omissions or by the threat of such acts or omissions.' Personally, Brown believed that, 'on the whole, they [the state] banned people who had strong cross-colour links'.[123]

Although Brown's ban had been in the offing since at least June 1964, the eventual timing may well have had to do with Leftwich's arrest and his implication of several Liberals in acts of sabotage.

Brown's banning orders, signed by Vorster, were dated 22 July.[124] But if the government was looking for some trigger to justify the imposition of the ban – though, to be sure, it was not in the habit of justifying itself – then the events of 24 July must have come as a perverse godsend. That morning, John Harris, a member of the Transvaal Provincial Committee who had been banned in February, placed a time bomb in the main concourse of Johannesburg's Park Station. He telephoned the police to tip them off, expecting that they would arrive in time to defuse the bomb, since it was strictly against NCL policy to take human life. The police, for whatever reason, stalled. The bomb exploded at 4.30 pm, severely injuring a 12-year-old girl and her 77-year-old grandmother, who died 27 days later.

That evening Brown vehemently condemned the incident. In a press statement, he said: 'Action of this kind can only solidify group attitudes in South Africa and make violence on straight racial lines an increasing possibility for the future … This latest explosion may mark a turning point in our history.'[125] Indeed, it marked a turning point in the Party's history, the country's history and his personal history. A few days later, on 29 July, Brown was served with the banning orders that would banish him from public life for five years in the first instance, and then another five after they were renewed in 1969. Their imposition did not take him unawares; he remarked to Leo Marquard: 'I can't say the ban surprised me,' adding, 'It is a tragic commentary on the state in which we find ourselves that I almost felt relief when they presented the banning orders & didn't whisk me away for 90-Days or more.'[126]

In terms of his banning orders, Brown was prevented from attending any social, political or educational 'gathering', defined thus:

(i) any social gathering, that is to say, any gathering at which the persons present also have social intercourse with one another;
(ii) any political gathering, that is to say, any gathering at which any form of State or any principle or policy of the Government of a State is propagated, defended, attacked, criticised or discussed;

(iii) any gathering of pupils or students assembled for the purpose of being instructed, trained or addressed by you.[127]

Furthermore, he could not leave the district of Pietermaritzburg without the permission of a magistrate. This was onerous, and it discouraged him from visiting friends and family members outside the city precincts. His farms, too, which he had regularly inspected in the past, could now only be checked upon once or twice a year, and even then after drawn-out correspondence with a magistrate. Brown also had to report to the officer in charge of Town Hill police station every Monday at some point between 7.00 am and 5.00 pm.[128] Within Pietermaritzburg, Brown's movements were heavily curtailed: he could not visit any 'location, native hostel or native village as defined in the Natives (Urban Areas) Consolidation Act, 1945'.[129] Finally, his public voice was muted: the platforms, both written and spoken, from which he had lucidly articulated the liberal message of non-racialism for over ten years, were closed to him. These proscriptions were a serious setback both to the Liberal Party and to the cause of common-society liberalism, which Brown had done so much to promote.

PART
THREE

THE BANNED YEARS
1964-1974

The coincidence of Harris's bomb and Brown's ban dealt the Liberal Party a body blow from which it never recovered. Edgar Brookes, who had joined the Party somewhat belatedly in 1962, now took over as acting National Chairman. He and Paton immediately distanced both the Party and Brown from the sabotage activities carried out by Party members, affirming: 'At a time when the temptation to use extreme violence against authority is strongly felt by desperate and frustrated people, [Brown] is utterly opposed to the use of violence.'[1] In an internal memorandum, the two acknowledged that Brown's ban had been 'a heavy blow to the Party' as had 'the bannings of other members, the raids and detentions'. They added ruefully: '[T]he [Justice] Minister – and others – will … claim that his attacks on the Party were justified from the beginning.' They ended their message:

> [A]lthough we lack many of the gifts and advantages enjoyed by our banned National Chairman, [we] will endeavour to give the same kind of leadership. And we ask you to hold to the course you have always thought right and give us your encouragement and support … [so as] to show our appreciation of what our National Chairman was, and is, to us …[2]

The sentiments expressed by Brookes and Paton conveyed the esteem in which Brown's leadership was held by the Party. A contributor to *Contact* expanded on his 'gifts and advantages': he was self-disciplined, lucid in both the written and spoken word and possessed 'the ability to organise and lead'. His 'gifts of character' were his honesty, his strength of purpose, and his ability 'to inspire and sustain others when things were bad'.[3] Having resumed 'The Long View' column in *Contact,* Paton wrote that the Party would 'greatly miss the steady hand of Peter Brown'. At a time of confusion and despair, in the wake of the Park Station bomb, he would have inspired confidence with his 'extraordinary sanity'. He would have condemned the use of violence, Paton claimed, not only as wrong but as senseless. However, he would also, 'in that astonishing way of his', have made it clear that ordinary decent people did not turn to violence until they had reached some point of despair.[4]

Without Brown's hand on the tiller, the Liberal Party became a much less effective political force. But by 1964 the Party had been so badly weakened anyway, by the cumulative effect of banning orders, the persecution of its most committed activists and the sheer difficulty of operating in a political space that was rapidly being closed down by the state. By 1968, the closure would be complete. In June 1965, Vorster gave notice of his intention to proceed with a Bill that he had already threatened, whose aim would be to prevent 'interference' by whites in non-white politics. In 1968, the Prohibition of Political Interference Act put the Liberal Party out of business, outlawing, as it did, non-racial political organisations. The result was that non-racial liberalism in South Africa ceased to have a political home. The Progressive Party continued to propound parliamentary liberalism, but, as far as many Liberals were concerned, its racially exclusive membership and advocacy of a qualified franchise cast a shadow over its commitment to the common society.

It is doubtful whether, had he remained active in public life between 1964 and 1968, Brown's leadership could have reversed the Liberal Party's declining fortunes. During that time, however, he worked quietly behind the scenes, and took a vigorous interest in Party affairs. Of equal significance, as Randolph Vigne observes, he became to Liberals 'a symbol of the just leader held captive by an unjust State, and to some non-Liberals, and certainly to all who knew him, of the cynicism and moral rottenness of those who had banned him'.[5]

* * *

The first six months of Brown's ban were dominated by John Harris's trial, and those of Party members implicated by Leftwich in the ARM. John Lloyd had planned the Park Station attack with Harris, but, by his own account, had changed his mind shortly beforehand and had tried to dissuade Harris from proceeding. Suspecting that he might know something about the incident, the police, who had arrested him in the raids of 4 July, took him to the station. On surveying the scene of destruction, he had apparently cried out, 'My God, what has Harris done now?'[6] Lloyd subsequently turned state witness against Harris. His evidence substantiated the prosecution's case that Harris had committed premeditated murder, as opposed to manslaughter; the penalty for the former was the death sentence. During the trial, Brown wrote to Marion Friedmann, one of the founding Liberals who had gone into exile in England, and commented on both Harris's trial and its repercussions for the Party:

> There seems little hope for Harris unless it is established that he is insane. What a terrible thing for everyone who is in any way connected with it. One gets the impression that they [the members of the NCL/ARM] thought they were involved in a game of adult cops and robbers without ever realising that the cops were the Gestapo. The implications for the Party are, of course, very serious ... [T]he ammunition which they can use to destroy the Party adds up by the day and will, one suspects, go on adding up each day one of these trials lasts.[7]

Brown pitied Lloyd as he pitied Harris: 'Poor Harris, but poor Lloyd too,' he remarked to Hans Meidner, now in exile.[8] Of Lloyd, he said to Wolf Hamm: 'All one does know is that he is going to have a problem living with himself for the rest of his life.'[9]

Lloyd's testimony sank Harris, despite the best efforts of Harris's attorney, Ruth Hayman, a leading and dedicated Transvaal Liberal. Harris was given the death sentence, and some Liberals – Walter Hain, Maritz van den Berg and Ernie Wentzel – visited him the night before his execution. Hain later remarked on his fortitude in the face of death.[10] Walter and his wife, Adelaine, both banned by the time Harris was hanged – Adelaine in October 1963, Walter in September 1964 – had taken a special interest in Harris's case. They had cared for Harris's wife, Ann, and the couple's young son, David, throughout the trial. Walter had visited Harris in prison, providing him with invaluable solace and moral support in the wake of vicious beatings by his interrogators. Although they were both banned, the Hains were given special dispensation to attend Harris's funeral. Their fifteen-year-old son, Peter, read texts from Shakespeare and John Donne in a non-religious service.

Walter and Adelaine Hain were a down-to-earth couple. In his autobiography, Paton describes their attitude to Harris as 'noble'.[11] It is a wholly inappropriate word. Their actions stemmed from genuine compassion. They found it difficult to sympathise with Lloyd, however, on whose evidence Harris had been sent to the gallows. In December 1964, Walter Hain wrote a long, impassioned letter, and sent it to Phoebe Brown; as both he and Peter Brown were banned, they could not, in terms of their banning orders, correspond with one another. He told her that he was distressed 'to hear that John Lloyd is likely to be welcomed back in 'Maritzburg if not with open arms, then with no more than a few polite expressions of regret'. Through his testimony, which he had given to save his own hide, he had betrayed a friend, and this showed 'a lack of loyalty and moral fibre that cannot be ignored'. He continued:

> To accept them [the state witnesses] back with a few shakes of the head, as though they'd been caught cribbing at school is, to me, unthinkable. I want to urge that they are left in no doubt that they are no longer welcome at their old haunts and in their old circles, and that the general consensus of opinion is that the sooner they clear out, the better. The fact is that they have shown themselves to be

thoroughly untrustworthy when the going gets tough and quite unscrupulous of the effects of their actions on others; they can never really be trusted again, and we shouldn't have them around.

Hain did not want to seem 'vindictive about this or fundamentalist', and he was not suggesting that anyone should be abusive towards Lloyd, but he felt strongly that Lloyd should be 'politely but firmly ostracised'. For Hain, the issue had segued from the personal into the political: in the current climate of state repression, opponents of apartheid could ill afford to treat 'informers or traitors' with kid gloves, and if they did they would be 'betraying the Elliot Mngadis and the P. Browns – not to mention the Hugh Lewins & John Harris' [sic]'.[12]

There is no record of a reply to Hain's letter, and in any event, rather than settle in Pietermaritzburg, John Lloyd soon fled to England. Many years later, in 1995, he sought to contest the Labour seat for Exeter, and some of the exiled South African Liberals brought his past to the attention of the press. One of his stoutest defenders during the campaign was Maritz van den Berg, who had visited Harris in prison.[13]

What would Brown's attitude have been had Lloyd gone back to his 'old haunts' and attempted to re-integrate himself into his 'old circles'? In his correspondence from the time, Brown never showed the slightest impulse to pass judgment on those who had turned state witness. In October, he told Marion Friedmann: 'Nor do I think that one can blame the people who give the evidence. Who knows whether [one] can stand up to 90-days [detention without trial] and its refinements?'[14] The following month, he reiterated to her: 'Nobody can blame anyone for turning state witness under 90-days …'[15]

Leftwich gave evidence for the state both in Cape Town and Johannesburg. Brown found him 'tragically pathetic', 'pour[ing] forth everything [he] know[s], like a Moral Rearmer confessing his sins'.[16] But he sympathised with him, too, and mused to Meidner: '… who knows whether [under the strain of 90 days' detention] a similar state of affairs would not be induced in his mind.'[17]

Leftwich's testimony resulted in long prison sentences for a number of Liberals involved in the ARM: Eddie Daniels, a one-time National Committee member and former chair of the Maitland branch, received fifteen years; David de Keller, who had Swiss nationality, got ten years (of which he served two before being released early); Hugh Lewin was given seven years; and David Evans and John Laredo were each sentenced to five years. Patricia Evans and Ursula Laredo stayed at Shinglewood while their husbands' case was heard. After the verdict was passed, Brown told Ruth Hayman that they were both 'delighted' with the result: 'It is a sign of the times in which we live but there is really no better word than "delighted" to describe how they were when they came home in the evening.'[18]

Brown's beef was not with the state witnesses or with the trialists. In fact, he thought the 'only people who come out of it [the tragedy] with any credit are those in the dock, Hugh Lewin particularly, who refused to go and leave others behind'.[19] He reserved his disapproval for those who had managed to leave the country before they could be arrested. He explained to Derick Marsh:

> The terrible tragedy is that the people in the dock are many
> of them comparatively small fry. The bigger fish were either
> out of the country or got out fast. Lang seems to have been
> an instigator and Neville Rubin and Randolph Vigne two of
> the leading lights.[20]

Rubin had been imprisoned in Mozambique after Leftwich's arrest and subsequent disclosures. The holder of a British passport, he was deported to Britain, however, and never stood trial. Vigne made a dramatic, eleventh-hour escape, and boarded a ship to Canada, travelling as his publisher friend, James Currey.

Brown bore no grudges against those who had got out in time, though, and he and Vigne kept up a close friendship to the end of his days. On Brown's suggestion, Vigne wrote a history of the Liberal Party, and dedicated it to Peter and Phoebe. It was not in Brown's nature to condemn or pontificate, unless he was denouncing apartheid and its functionaries. In this way, he was quite unlike

Paton, who, in his autobiography, relived in excruciating detail his revulsion at the ARM episode and its aftermath. Of Harris he said:

> If he had ever sent any message to me asking for my forgiveness, I would have forgiven him with my lips but not with my heart. I was totally revolted by what he had done. They say that to understand is to forgive. That is not true. I understood the twisted and tragic reasons that led him to do what he did, but I was never able to forgive him.[21]

Paton took it upon himself to extend the hand of forgiveness to Leftwich, however, telling him that 'those against whom he had sinned had now forgiven him ... [t]herefore, he must forgive himself'.[22] 'I forgave him,' Paton wrote, 'because I thought he had suffered enough.'[23] Brown did not see it as his role to forgive, or to parade whatever he felt in a litany of hand-wringing self-righteousness. After he had read the chapters in Paton's memoirs dealing with the ARM, Brown reflected to Derick Marsh: '... Paton takes a strong, Victorian view of what happened and I don't think has ever understood the turmoil going on inside those people at that time.'[24]

In Brown's view, the Liberal Party had managed to endure the ARM trials 'remarkably well'. He thought Brookes had passed through his baptism of fire as National Chairman 'extremely well', while the rank-and-file Party membership had been 'absolutely solid'.[25] Brown kept up to date with what was happening in the Party. He informed Bill Hoffenberg in March 1965 that Selby Msimang had started liaising with African trade unions in Durban and gained a foothold in a number of factories; the Party's Youth Group had visited almost all the African rural branches in the previous six weeks; and enthusiasm and activity were running high in Natal, despite two recent bannings and three warnings.[26] Yet, with many of its leaders and most dynamic members banned, there was no escaping the fact that the Party was in decline. In 1965, the Cape Chairman, Barney Zackon, was banned, as were two Natal stalwarts, Selby Msimang and John Aitchison. Bill Hoffenberg reported back to Brown on a Liberal public meeting in Cape Town where the platform was 'loaded with grey, bald & rather fragile old people, who gave an image of respectability ... but who failed completely to present the party as a virile, forceful entity'.[27]

Brown tried to keep up his links with political associates across party lines. He wrote to Thomas Ngwenya, one-time Chairman of the ANC in the Western Cape, who replied: 'How nice we feel to know that even people in your predicament still remember us, when everything seems lost to those fighters for freedom and liberty. However, we must all keep the faith.'[28] However, his main line of contact was with his former colleagues, and much of his knowledge of Party activities was gleaned during visits from Liberals like Paton, Edgar Brookes, Tony Mathews and, before she was banned herself, Heather Morkill. In later years, Brown would recall to Norman Bromberger that 'Alan [Paton] used to come ... quite regularly, so obviously that was the main point of contact'.[29] In fact, the Patons – Alan and his sons, David and Jonathan, and their wives – dropped in at Shinglewood over the Christmas holidays in 1964. In recounting their visit to Derick Marsh, Brown revealed that he retained his wry sense of humour. 'They run to fat those Patons,' he noted; '[p]aunch-wise they've got something to show for themselves. As the younger ones' wives are usually pregnant it's not always easy to know who you're talking to.'[30] Peter and Phoebe also saw their friend Mary Corrigal (known as Maimie), a local Liberal stalwart, for a drink at her house once a week.

This ongoing contact with Liberals irked the Security Police. In January 1966, security policemen came to see Brown; 'the clear implication of which,' he told Jack Unterhalter afterwards, 'was that they were considering putting me under house-arrest.'[31] In February, the Commissioner of Police wrote to the Secretary of Justice, protesting that in spite of the restrictions on him, Brown was still playing a 'leading role in the Liberal Party' and maintaining regular contact with Party members.[32] The Commissioner's letter drew attention to a visit paid by Brown to Corrigal on 12 January, on which occasion John Aitchison, now banned, and Pat McKenzie, Brown's cousin and the Party's Executive Secretary, were apparently both present. The subject of their discussion was unknown, the Commissioner remarked, and Brown was not followed since, had this been done, the Security Police's source of information would have been unmasked. Nevertheless, in the light of Brown's 'sustained activities', the Commissioner proposed that he be placed under house arrest, by preventing him from leaving Shinglewood during the evenings, weekends and public holidays. The only visitors permitted to see him at home, the Commissioner recommended, should be a medical practitioner, his mother, his parents-in-law, his siblings, his siblings-in-law and his farm manager, Matthew Taylor. Other proposed amendments to his banning orders would prohibit him from 'being within any Bantu residential area' and 'any area set apart under any law for the occupation of Coloured or Asiatic persons'. The Department of Justice supported the Police Commissioner's recommendations, but for undisclosed reasons, both the Secretary and Minister of Justice rejected the option of house arrest. They consented to amend Brown's banning orders only insofar as the provisions on entering black, Coloured and Indian areas were concerned.[33] This prohibition was a particular hardship for Brown, since it prevented him from going to Edendale, the township in which his commitment to non-racialism had taken root and where some of his closest friends, like Sam Chetty, still lived. The revised banning orders were dated 25 April 1966 and delivered to Brown on 9 May.[34]

Throughout his banned years, Brown was subject to ongoing surveillance. Shinglewood is situated just off the Old Howick Road between Pietermaritzburg and Hilton, a route which steeply winds its way up past an area of dense forest known as 'World's View'. At an elevation of 1 083 metres, World's View offers a spectacular panorama over Pietermaritzburg, and it remains a popular tourist destination, partly, too, because the original Voortrekker wagon tracks can still be seen leading down from the ridge. During the years of his ban, members of the Security Police would station themselves atop World's View and peer through their binoculars directly onto Brown's house below. They followed him around town, too. A report from September 1966 noted: 'He is currently being closely watched with a view to entrapping him, because according to intelligence he has been in contact with another banned individual, John Aitchison, at Mary Corrigal's house.'

According to his widow, Brown was scrupulous about not contravening his banning orders – more out of concern for the trouble
this might cause fellow Liberals with the Security Police than out of
deference to the Suppression of Communism Act – so such intelligence was, in all likelihood, false.[35] Brown's letters were also inter-
cepted. The same report remarked that in a letter to Wolf Hamm,
Brown had said of his amended banning orders, 'None of these
things worry me a great deal.'[36] His telephone was tapped too: 'He
still calls well-known leftists like Marie Dyer, Tony Mathews and
others,' the report ended.

In 1966, Brown's mother, Maisie, took ill, and he visited her, initially at the Musgrave Road house in Durban now occupied by his
sister Bet, and later at the Berea Nursing Home on Ridge Road.
Every time he wanted to leave Pietermaritzburg, however, Brown
would have to apply in writing for permission to the local magistrate. This was time-consuming and onerous, and often the magistrate would leave it to the last minute to respond to his applications. For example, on 26 March 1966, Brown sought permission
from the magistrate to visit Maisie on either 4 or 5 April.[37] The
magistrate granted the request, but his letter was dated 4 April.[38]
Even then, Brown could not leave Pietermaritzburg earlier than
9.00 am; he had to announce his departure from Pietermaritzburg
and his arrival in Durban at their respective central police stations;
and he could not leave Durban later than 5.00 pm. On 1 October,
Brown's mother died, and he had to seek permission to attend her
funeral in Durban on 6 October.[39] The fact that he had to obtain the
go-ahead from a magistrate to be present at his mother's funeral
was given prominence in the Bloemfontein newspaper, *The Friend.*[40]
On the eve of his re-banning in May 1969, the Commissioner of
Police would hold this publicity against him, sniffing to the Department of Justice that, 'It is clear that he does not even flinch
from exploiting his own mother's death for political capital.'[41]

During the first few years of his ban, Brown occupied himself
by writing a chronological history of the Liberal Party. Because he
was not allowed to publish anything, he did not want the Security
Police to spy him working on the manuscript, and so he compiled
his 386-page tome at the home of his friend and fellow Liberal,

Leslie Weinberg (who had been Marsh and Meidner's lawyer during their detention in 1960) and his wife, Pessa.[42] The work took him about two years to complete, and he went to the Weinbergs' home most weekdays. The research for his manuscript, which is housed at the Alan Paton Centre at the University of KwaZulu-Natal and remains unpublished,[43] kept him in touch with a number of Liberals. He sent them requests for information, documents and personal reminiscences about the Party's early days.[44]

Brown undertook this work not merely to pass the time, but also to take stock of the role of Liberals (and liberals) in South African political history. This was a subject much on his mind at the time. Towards the end of 1964, Paton's biography of Jan Hofmeyr was published.[45] Brown read the book, which was dedicated to him, with avid interest. Marion Friedmann told him that she was glad that the book had been 'dedicated to you who have made something fine out of an insubstantial liberal heritage'.[46] To Wolf Hamm, Brown expressed the opinion:

> As regards liberal history we could have done some more homework ... Pre-war one's impression is that it was based very largely on wishful thinking ... If we had done our homework better we might have become more radical sooner and that would have been a good thing ...[47]

Brown was more interested in what *Hofmeyr* had to say about liberalism in its subject's lifetime than the subject himself. While Paton was still working on the book, Brown had confided his doubts about the project to Leslie Cooper, whom, it will be recalled, he had told: '... the ideas for which he [Hofmeyr] stood have been left so far behind by events that they will not mean a great deal today.'[48] Having read the book, Brown was better placed to understand the significance of those ideas in their historical context. However, he still felt that they had been 'based very largely on wishful thinking' and surpassed by the radical, extra-parliamentary, left-leaning, genuinely non-racial liberalism of the Liberal Party. In that sense, *Hofmeyr* confirmed for Brown his own conviction that the Liberal Party marked a rupture with the South African liberal tradition.

Hofmeyr remains perhaps the finest history of Union politics yet published. As a political biography of a South African liberal, it is unrivalled. Yet Brown did not identify closely with Hofmeyr's liberalism, and he felt it was important to record the distinctive contribution made by Liberals in offering an alternative to competing racial nationalisms. For that reason he approached Leo Marquard, who, as Paton's friend and editor at Oxford University Press in Cape Town, had in fact edited *Hofmeyr*,[49] to write an autobiography.

Marquard was in some ways a curious choice. He was himself a close, though not uncritical, political associate of Hofmeyr's. During the Second World War, Marquard had served under EG Malherbe as the second-in-command of the Army Education Services (AES), a vehicle which sought to inculcate a shared sense of Anglo-Afrikaner nationhood among white troops, while opening them up to liberal political ideas about non-racial, common citizenship.[50] As a niggardly Finance Minister, Hofmeyr had more than once tried to prevent increased spending on the AES, and, in spite of Marquard's petitions, he was unconvinced about its prospects as a mobilising force for postwar political change. At one point during the war, Marquard had written half-jokingly to his wife that he would like to write a book called *JH Hofmeyr – A Study in Liberalism*: 'I'm sure it will sell like hot cakes. Hoffie's friends will buy it and won't be able to get their money back when they find out what's in it; and all his enemies will buy it as soon as they hear what's in it. Liberalism indeed!'[51]

Marquard's liberalism is not easy to pigeonhole. In 1943, under the pseudonym of Jan Burger, he published *The Black Man's Burden*, which advocated a kind of 'socialist liberalism'. The book made a great impression on Brown, who read it while he was on active service. Although Marquard was keenly attuned to the possibilities for a radicalised postwar liberalism – hence his decision to co-found the Liberal Party in 1953 rather than support the liberal wing of the United Party – he became a Liberal in the traditional Cape mould. Politically, he probably had more in common with Margaret Ballinger and Oscar Wollheim than Brown and Paton. He believed in the pre-eminence of parliamentary politics, and was never quite at home with the Liberal Party's focus on extra-parliamentary activity. Like Ballinger, and unlike Wollheim, however, he never left the Liberals for the Progressives, and he remained with the Party to its end. In November 1966, along with Marie Grant, David Welsh and Jack Unterhalter, he appeared before a Commission to protest against the Bill that would effectively shut down the Liberal Party. The four of them argued that for thirteen years the Liberal Party had shown that it was 'possible for whites and non-whites to work together harmoniously in interracial political organisations'. They claimed that by preventing blacks and whites from cooperating in the same political party, the 'Improper Interference Bill' 'would be doing the cause of race relations in South Africa a grave and dangerous disservice'.[52] Their pleas fell on deaf ears, however, and the Bill was enacted as the Prohibition of Political Interference Act on 9 May 1968.

Rather than conform with the Act's requirement that membership of political organisations should be racially exclusive, the Liberal Party went into voluntary liquidation. So ended its short, but brave, life; a visionary Party whose advocacy of non-racial liberal democracy combined with a commitment to social justice had failed to win over the white electorate, but whose ideas would pave the way for a negotiated constitutional settlement years later. It must have been a double knock-back to Brown to see the Party he had done so much to build up precipitately demolished, and then, too, not to be able to pay his last respects publicly. Without Brown in the driving seat, the Liberal Party might well have become a pale imitation of the Progressives, sans their parliamentary representation. It was largely thanks to his efforts on the ground – in recruiting African members in rural Natal and driving campaigns like the one against black spot removals – that the Liberals managed to achieve what no other liberal party in South Africa had done before it (or would do for years after it): attract a significant black membership and demonstrate a tangible commitment to non-racialism. That was Brown's single-most important contribution to the history of South African liberalism, and it was no mean feat.

In 1968, Brown wrote to Marquard, suggesting that he pen his memoirs:

It seems to me that this is something South Africa very
much needs – a Liberal account of the time since Union. I
suppose white racialists wouldn't want to read it now, and
Black racialists won't want to read it in the future. That
can't be helped. What seems important to me is that the
experiences of your life should be on record, not only as
evidence of the existence & achievements of Liberals during this time but also as an inspiration for them and other
non-racialists in the future.[53]

A self-effacing man, Marquard did not wish to write an account of
his own life, which is a great pity since he made an immense contribution to the liberal tradition in South Africa. He did this both
as a political agent, in institutional contexts as diverse as the
National Union of South African Students (which he had founded
in 1924) and the Liberal Party, and as an historian, as the author
of books such as *The Peoples and Policies of South Africa* and *The Story
of South Africa*.[54] It was a mark of Brown's admiration for Marquard
that he believed his life history should be recorded for the benefit
of future generations of liberals and non-racialists. Brown and
Marquard kept up a sporadic correspondence until Marquard's
death in 1974. Subsequently, *Reality*, the magazine edited by Brown
after his banning orders lapsed, paid Marquard a well-deserved
tribute.[55]

Another of Brown's main occupations during his ban, apart
from writing his history of the Liberal Party, was working in the
Pietermaritzburg branch of his family's wholesale business, WG
Brown & Co. Although this was not strictly permissible in terms of
his ban, the state took no action against him. In 1968, David Carlisle, who was married to Brown's cousin Christianne and who
served as the company's Managing Director, approached Brown to
help run the newly established Pietermaritzburg showroom.[56] The
job provided Brown with a much needed social outlet; its 'main
redeeming feature', he would tell Hans Meidner in 1973, was 'that
a large number of its customers are black',[57] and he accepted the
position with that in mind, rather than with a view to mastering the
wholesale trade. As he told Marquard: 'I continue to grace the

wholesale trade – & vice versa! I wouldn't say I have acquired many of its arts, but at least I haven't got the sack yet. Of course, being one of the family helps a good deal in that direction.'[58]

Brown took the job on two conditions. He described them to another employee, Jack Clouston, the following year: 'that the firm should feel free to ask me to go if at any time it was felt that I wasn't doing the job as it should be done', and that he would do the job for a year.[59] After his year was up, he asked to stay on, regardless of whether his banning orders were re-imposed or not in July 1969. If the ban was allowed to expire, however, he felt it necessary to stress that he had no intention of abandoning his public opposition to apartheid, 'or of letting the political and personal relationships amongst all races, which derived from it, wither away'. This meant that he might make public statements that could embarrass the firm, and that he would need to be able to get away from work, to visit Edendale, for example, more easily than he presently could.

In the event, Brown was served with new banning orders at the end of the month, extending his quarantine from public life for another five years, until they were allowed to expire in July 1974. The new orders were substantially the same as the original ones, as modified by the amendments of 1966. As early as April 1969, the Commissioner of Police had recommended that Brown's banning orders be re-imposed, and the new Minister of Justice, Peet Pelser, signed the orders on 14 May.[60] In making his recommendation, the Commissioner declared dramatically that if a man of Brown's 'calibre and means and current political vision' was unbanned, he would 'leave no stone unturned in enthusiastically fanning the slumbering leftist fires under the Bantu' ['*geen steen onaangeroerd sal laat om die sluimerende linkse vuur onder die Bantoes kragdadig aan te blaas nie*'].[61]

Gatherings were held around the country to protest against the second set of banning orders. Two public meetings, attended by between 150 and 200 people, were held in Pietermaritzburg and Durban on 8 and 13 August, respectively, both of them organised by the Black Sash.[62] In Pietermaritzburg, Edgar Brookes and Marie Dyer spoke. In Durban, Tony Mathews and Pat Poovalingam shared the platform. Paton addressed both meetings. Although he

claimed to be 'more intimately associated with [Brown] in politics
than anyone else', he was perplexed by the reasons for the renewal
of Brown's banning orders: 'He never took any action that caused
me any disquiet. He never concealed any action from me. He
never lied. He never intrigued. Any kind of underground dealing
was foreign – and is foreign – to his nature. Whey then has he been
banned again?' Paton answered:

> It is because Mr Peter Brown does not give a slavish obedi-
> ence to authority, and because he does not respect an order
> that permits injustice, that he has again been silenced and
> restricted ... He doesn't see why he should refrain from
> making common cause with any South African who believes
> in the same things that he believes in.[63]

It is true that Brown's commitment to fighting apartheid was undi-
minished, and that he saw no reason not to make 'common cause'
with his fellow South Africans in pursuing that goal. This was one
of the reasons why he never contemplated leaving South Africa. He
told Leo Marquard: 'On the whole I am opposed to people leaving,
but when they can no longer make a living, like the Hains, or can't
do their job, like Bill [Hoffenberg], there may not be much choice
for them.'[64] The Hains had gone into exile in England in April
1966, and Hoffenberg had followed in April 1968.[65] Hoffenberg
had been banned in July 1967, partly in an attempt to sever his ties
to student leaders – who regarded him highly as an adviser – at the
University of Cape Town (UCT) and in NUSAS. A popular medical
scientist at Groote Schuur Hospital and UCT, his ban provoked a
huge public outcry, with poster demonstrations, protest meetings
and petitions from university staff and students. UCT sent a delegation comprising its Chancellor, Harry Oppenheimer, Vice-Chancellor
JP Duminy, Council Chairman Clive Corder and the head of the
medical school, Professor JF Brock, to lobby Pelser. Oppenheimer
was reported in the press as saying that the delegation had been
cordially received, which caused Brown to comment to Marquard
(like Brown, a great friend of Hoffenberg's): 'Sounds ominous! I
hope he [Oppenheimer] wasn't taken in. I have a profound dis-

trust of Corder & Duminy but some hope that the other two are not too gullible.'[66]

As it transpired, Oppenheimer's faith was misplaced: Hoffenberg's ban was enforced, and he and his wife, Margaret, were left with little choice but to leave the country so that he could pursue his career as a specialist endocrinologist. Brown had found the campaign against Hoffenberg's ban 'very good', but he joked with Marquard:

> I must say I can't go all the way with a fellow who buys advertising space to push his case. You would think, too, if he was going to plaster the papers with pages of names of purported protestors, he would at least think up names that *looked* real. As I said to David Welsh ... [t]he whole thing was an obvious fake.[67]

But there was no bitter edge to Brown's wit; Hoffenberg was a kindred spirit, an intimate and long-standing friend from student days, and Brown was genuinely dismayed by his ban. When the Hoffenbergs left South Africa on an exit permit, they were given a rousing send-off by hundreds of students and staff at the airport. Brown remarked to Marquard: 'Bill's send-off, sad as it was, could hardly have been better, could it? That marvellous photograph at the airport in Cape Town.'[68] After his own banning orders were renewed, Brown heard that Hoffenberg might 'have a crisis of conscience over the re-ban', and he asked Marquard 'to persuade him that he needn't'.[69]

Brown's friendship with Hoffenberg endured, and he was one of several exiled Liberals – along with David Craighead, the Hains, Wolf Hamm, Derick Marsh, Hans Meidner and Randolph Vigne – who Brown would make a point of seeing once he started travelling again internationally in 1986. (He refused to re-apply for a passport, which the state had confiscated during his ban, until then.) Brown regretted not being able to maintain these friendships through more frequent contact, both by virtue of his ban and the geographical distance that separated him from his exiled friends. But even local friendships were hard to keep up, and new ones

were almost impossible to cultivate. One of his social outlets remained the polo field, and he defied his ban by continuing to play
at Otto's Bluff.

Despite his reserve, Brown was a sociable person; he enjoyed
the company of others, and he liked making new acquaintances.
Writing for the *Sunday Tribune* in 1979 on the impact of his ban, he
observed: 'In the normal course of events, one goes through life
picking up new acquaintances along the way, making new friends
out of those you really come to like.' However, '[i]n this respect
1964 to 1974 reflects a total blank in our lives'.[70] The ban made
him suspicious of new people; his immediate reaction to 'anyone
new who tried to be friendly was that he must be a plant'.

Communication with other banned people, among whom num-
bered several of his friends and former colleagues like Dempsey
Noel, was forbidden. Other friendships faded away through lack of
contact. And for Brown, face-to-face contact was important.
Banned people, he said, 'need contact with as much of the world
around them as they can get' since it was easy even for someone in
partial isolation 'to get out of tune with the moods of society'.

Brown's ten years of enforced isolation took their toll, both privately and publicly. He was not forgotten, of course. The Progressive MP, Helen Suzman, tried repeatedly to have certain provisions
of his banning orders relaxed. On numerous occasions, she either
wrote to, or went to see, the Minister of Justice, and petitioned him
to ease two conditions in particular. Firstly, Brown had to apply in
writing every time he needed to visit his farming operations. When
his mother died, he inherited her farm 'Brownstones' at Mooi
River. Although he had attempted to run the farm in conjunction
with her farm manager, Matt Taylor, through occasional consulta-
tions at Shinglewood, this had proved to be extremely difficult. In
addition, he owned the farms 'Stanley' and 'Groote Mielietuin' in
the Weenen District, 'Tigerfontein' in Mooi River, and 'Snowflake'
near the Giant's Castle Game Reserve, and was required to inspect
them regularly. Once his ban expired, he also purchased a farm at
Nottingham Road, where he farmed prize-winning Hereford cattle –
the breed to which he had taken a liking while at Cambridge.

The magistrate's approach to processing Brown's applications was often dilatory.[71] When permission was eventually granted, there was the added encumbrance of Brown having to report to various police stations en route between his farms. After driving from Brownstones to Snowflake, for example, he would have to clock out at the Mooi River police station and clock in at the Ntabamhlope police station in the Drakensberg. As Ntabamhlope was 25km off the direct route of his farm, he would take the opportunity to visit ex-Liberal Party members along the way – clearly, something the Security Police had not considered.[72]

Secondly, Brown's ban prohibited him from visiting educational institutions, so he was unable to see the twins at boarding school (Christopher at Michaelhouse, Vanessa at St Anne's) or to attend school functions. In 1969, Suzman asked for both of these restrictions to be eased.[73] Brown thanked her for her efforts, though he didn't relish the thought of 'those ghastly Speech Days'.[74] In any event, the Minister was unbending, and he declined Suzman's requests, both at the time[75] and on subsequent occasions.[76]

The privation Brown felt most acutely was not being able to visit any African, Indian or Coloured area, which kept him out of Edendale. When he returned there at the end of his ban, Brown hardly recognised it; 'a whole new generation of people had grown up', he noted ruefully, who probably only recognised him 'as just another "whitey"'. This was sad not just for him personally, he believed, but for South Africa, too; '[f]or in Edendale in 1964 there was still a reasonable prospect of building support for a non-racial movement committed to working amongst all races for a shared future'. In fact, at the time, the movement was established and growing. What the prospects were for rebuilding it by the end of the 1970s, Brown was uncertain. One of the reasons for this was that his forced disengagement from public life between 1964 and 1974 served to de-familiarise the political landscape. As it was, the terrain shifted perceptibly during that decade – perhaps more ideologically, with the growth of the Black Consciousness Movement, than politically, since a period of intensified state repression led to a lull in protest politics.

After 1966, the Nationalists entrenched their power, taking 21 seats from the parliamentary opposition in the election of that year –

their biggest gain since 1953 – which left them with 126 out of the 170 seats in the House of Assembly. In September 1966, Verwoerd was assassinated, and was succeeded by Vorster, the man who, as Justice Minister from 1961, had given vast new powers to the Security Police and presided over an era of intense state repression. Along with the head of the Security Police at the time, Hendrik van den Bergh (who subsequently became Secretary for State Intelligence when Vorster acceded to the premiership), Vorster had effectively turned South Africa into a police state.

On 11 July 1963, acting on the advice of one of Van den Bergh's protégés, Johan Coetzee, the Security Police had raided Liliesleaf Farm in Rivonia, and arrested almost the entire leadership of Umkhonto we Sizwe, including Govan Mbeki and Walter Sisulu. The ensuing trial, dubbed the 'Rivonia Trial', culminated in life imprisonment for the organisation's leaders, among them Nelson Mandela. As they were also the senior figures in the underground ANC, the banned liberation movement was left directionless, without a local stewardship to guide it. Underground, the PAC had all but ceased to function in South Africa. The combined effect of its dormancy, the move into exile by many of its activists and those from the ANC, the outcome of the Rivonia Trial and the dissolution of the Liberal Party, was political quietude in the extra-parliamentary political opposition between 1964 and 1976.

While the state had managed to immobilise opposition to apartheid – partly through detentions and bannings and house arrests, which took key individuals out of circulation and fractured political cohesion – it still found itself confronted by hostile ideological opponents. And the course of ideological resistance was changing, charged by a new current: Black Consciousness. In 1969, a group of African students disaffiliated from the white-dominated National Union of South African Students (NUSAS) and formed the all-black South African Students' Organisation (SASO) with Steve Biko as its president. The breakaway symbolised the growing isolation of liberals from mainstream black politics. In fact, NUSAS had long been a microcosm of national politics. Founded by Marquard to foster a sense of civic patriotism among white students, NUSAS soon came to adopt a liberal approach to the so-called

'native question'. This led dissenting Afrikaans universities to
secede from the organisation between 1933 and 1936, and, ultimately, to the affiliation of the (black) University of Fort Hare in
1945.[77] By the end of the 1960s, NUSAS's message of colour-blind
non-racialism was failing to resonate with a new generation of
black students radicalised by Sharpeville – hence the creation of
SASO.

Biko developed a sophisticated critique of white liberals in various essays, most notably 'Black Souls in White Skins?' and 'White
Racism and Black Consciousness'. In Biko's view, liberals' political
gradualism and paternalism, combined with their emphasis on
colour-blind integration as the only route to non-racialism, blunted
black consciousness and stunted revolutionary change. In particular, he denounced liberal concepts of integration and inter-racial
political collaboration, arguing that:

> The myth of integration as propounded under the banner
> of liberal ideology must be cracked and killed because it
> makes people believe that something is being done when in
> actual fact the artificial integrated circles are a soporific on
> the blacks and provide a vague satisfaction for the guilt-
> stricken whites. It works on a false premise that because it is
> difficult to bring people from different races together in
> this country, therefore achievement of this is in itself a step
> forward towards the total liberation of the blacks. Nothing
> could be more irrelevant and therefore misleading. Those
> who believe it are living in a fool's paradise.[78]

Biko opposed the sort of integration that, in his view, masked the
'assimilation and acceptance of blacks into an already established
set of norms and code of behaviour set up by and maintained by
whites'. Such integration produced a 'superior-inferior white-black
stratification that makes the white a perpetual teacher and the
black a perpetual pupil ...'[79]

The withdrawal of SASO from NUSAS, and the rejection by
the Black Consciousness Movement of the liberal 'myth of integration', encouraged black South Africans to withdraw from liberal

organisations and institutions in other fields. In 1971, the Black
People's Convention (BPC) was established as an umbrella political body for various Black Consciousness organisations. Although
the BPC never attracted a large membership, the ideas for which it
stood gained momentum during the second phase of Brown's ban –
especially the notion that blacks should liberate themselves psycho-
logically from perceived white trusteeship. Black Consciousness
was as much about conscientisation and the affirmation of identity –
helping black people 'not [to] regard themselves as appendages to
white society'[80] – as it was about political activism. In fact, psychological liberation was seen as a necessary precursor to effective
political action.

Once Brown's ban came to an end, he would write regretfully
of the Black Consciousness Movement that 'it was a new force to be
reckoned with in South Africa, [and] I hardly knew anything about
it at all'.[81] In later years Brown was to say: '[T]he Biko influence was
obviously strong, and a good thing, I think, in general.'[82] At the
time of its growth and development, however, Brown was unsure
what to make of the Black Consciousness Movement. Partly this was
because his isolation left him ill-equipped to fully understand it;
nor was he able to forge relationships with its leaders in the way
that the liberal editor of the *Daily Dispatch*, Donald Woods, did with
Steve Biko.

Although the state had managed to neutralise Brown politically,
the Security Police continued to view him as a threat. In 1972,
GC Tomlinson, a partner in Simon Roberts's law firm, approached
the Minister of Justice to remove the restrictions placed on
Brown.[83] The police notified the Department of Justice that it
'would oppose the matter on the grounds that he is certain to turn
to active participation in leftist politics again'.[84] The Minister con-
curred, and the head of ministerial services informed Tomlinson
that '[t]he Minister is not prepared to withdraw or relax the restrictions in force against Mr Brown'.[85]

Between 1972 and 1974, if the dearth of material in the Security Police files is taken as a guide, state surveillance of Brown sub-
sided. Perhaps that coincided with a growing weariness on Brown's
part, as the psychological effects of his ban wore away at him and

he retreated further into himself. By 1974, the Justice Ministry's attitude to Brown had softened, and an internal memorandum dated 27 June 1974 and signed by the Private Secretary to new Minister, Jimmy Kruger, noted: 'The Minister has decided to grant an interview to [Brown] in our Cape Town office in the Hendrik Verwoerd Building at 3.00 pm on Wednesday, 17 July 1974.'[86] The meeting had been set up by Helen Suzman and agreed to by Brown. The requested briefing document from the Security Police was unusually concise, and ended thus: 'During the second term of restriction, as far as is known, the activities of the abovementioned [Brown] were not such that this Department can recommend further restrictions after 31.7.1974.'[87]

In the course of their meeting, while thumbing through Brown's dossier, Kruger accused him of being the 'arch-inciter' in the East Pondoland uprising of 1960-61 – a charge earlier levelled by Vorster in internal government correspondence.[88] Brown had never heard the claim before, and dismissed it out of hand, as he did Kruger's insistence that he should undertake to remain politically disengaged should his restrictions be removed. Despite Brown's unwillingness to give any such guarantees, the meeting with Kruger bore fruit, and, on 18 July, the Secretary of Justice notified the Commissioner of Police that Brown's banning orders would not be re-imposed.[89] At midnight on 31 July 1974, Brown became a free man again.

An editorial in the *Rand Daily Mail* celebrated Brown's regained freedom but lamented that he had 'lost ten years through an odious, frightening process of secret trial by faceless officials'.[90] A feature article in the same newspaper said of Brown:

> Today, he is a much more rugged man than he was in his heyday of politics. He is still a simple man and still resolute in his beliefs. He has aged somewhat, the telltale wrinkles around his piercing blue eyes marking his advancing years. He is a 'free' man at a time when the term 'liberal' has become a swear word in Black politics. Peter Brown, however, has the strength and fortitude to accept this and still propound his innate belief in a multiracial society for South Africa as a liberal.

How, though, did Brown intend to go about propounding his beliefs after ten years of public silence and immobilisation? At some
stage in 1974, before his ban expired, he set out his views in a long
letter to Wolf Hamm.

In January, Hamm had spent a week in Johannesburg for his sister's wedding. He flew non-stop across Africa during the day, and
reported back to Brown that this had given him a sense of the
wholeness of the continent. This pleased Brown, who believed
'that feeling of the entity of the continent ... *must* set the tone for
what one thinks about the future here'.[91] Brown believed that white
South Africans *were* Africans. Whites were neither temporary sojour-
ners in Africa, nor were they entitled to a special status on the continent by virtue of their race. He asked Hamm: 'If it was clear to us
in the LP that the idea of a privileged position for white South
Africans in the future was crazy, how much clearer has it not become in the past ten years?'

For Brown, the goal he fought for as National Chairman of the
Liberal Party remained unchanged: 'a non-racial, one-man one-
vote democracy with, hopefully, individual liberties sustained by a
Bill of Rights acceptable to all'. In Brown's view, the means where-
by the end should be pursued – non-racial political activity – were
no longer available with the Prohibition of Political Interference
Act in force. How, then, should one work for change?

> [O]ne continues to do what one can as an individual, say-
> ing the same old things whenever the opportunity presents
> itself, trying to fight issues as they arise, often at a very local
> level, perhaps even a petty level – better wages and working
> conditions where one can do something about them; try
> not to do anything more than the minimum which involves
> one in keeping the system going; support, where one can,
> anyone or any group which is fundamentally opposed to
> the present system and in general committed to producing
> a non-racial society.

'The question', he continued, was, 'who ... *in general* [is] committed to a non-racial society of the kind I want?' The current

generation of students was more radical than liberal, and although they had 'plenty of guts' and said 'most of the right things', for them the cause was more important than the individuals that promoted it. Brown understood the argument that Black Consciousness was a temporary phenomenon, 'a device, appropriate to the moment, to establish black confidence and a sense of identity which will provide the powerbase from which to change the system'. Yet he feared that it was bound to turn into 'another, fiercer racial tiger'.

As for the homelands, some of their leaders struck Brown as genuine non-racialists. Despite the fact that he did not regard the homelands policy as irreversible, Brown believed it would be in force for some time yet, and so, he asked Hamm rhetorically: 'Should one not, therefore, in the meantime, give what support one can to its non-racial leaders in trying to build non-racial enclaves within the country?' At the same time, in 'white' South Africa, liberals should carry on the battle for a non-racial society as best they could, although this was made difficult by two factors: firstly, such efforts were, for the most part, restricted to individual actions, and secondly, white access to the new cohort of black leaders was limited. In Brown's case, his ban was partly responsible for that, because, as he told Hamm, 'from the moment you are banned, you virtually make no new friends ... [s]o one doesn't meet new black people and it is quite possible that, black consciousness being what it is, even if one were free to do so, they wouldn't want to talk to you'. In spite of this, Brown believed it was vital to maintain his cross-colour-line contacts in 'white' South Africa and to keep open the lines of communication with non-racialists in the homelands.

Brown summarised what the role of a former Liberal should be:

i) continue to proclaim the ideal of a common society publicly and privately ... In private argue the case wherever you can and try to keep your own life as 'non-racial' as it can be: ii) Keep alive whatever cross colour-line contacts one has, and try to find some new ones (damned hard!): iii) Make as much stink as possible about the continuing injustices of the system and every new encroachment on individual

freedoms … : (iv) accept that the Bantustans are there as a
fact of life, even if only temporarily, and try to work with
those people in them who share the ideal of a common society. Keep pointing out that as a solution to our problems
the whole scheme is a fraud – not enough land, development, towns, factories, harbours, roads, and that it has been
foisted on to people without their consent, that it can only
be justified on the basis of a fair distribution of resources
accepted by black people – and if one is going to have to go
to those lengths wouldn't it just be easier to aim at a non-
racial society, federal at least initially, instead?

The task that Brown described would be made more difficult for
him by the lack of a political home in the Liberal Party's absence.
Furthermore, his return to public life would see Brown trying to
rediscover his political voice at a time when South Africans, black
and white, seemed even less willing to hear it than before. These,
then, were two of the biggest challenges facing Brown as he
attempted to carve a role for himself once his banning orders had
lapsed. For want of an institutional base, the kind of radical, social-
democratic, non-racial liberalism he had espoused as leader of the
Liberal Party never quite regained a foothold in South African politics over the next twenty years – not, to be sure, that it had left
much of an imprint on the white electorate. As a result, Brown
channelled his energies into various enterprises that were not
strictly of a political nature, although his overriding goal was always
to promote the common society. One way of doing this was by picking up the pen that his ban had forced him to put down, and articulating the Liberal message with the clarity and simplicity which he
had mastered while writing for *Contact* and various Party publications. He found his medium in a magazine called *Reality*.

THE DEPENDANTS' CONFERENCE AND *REALITY*
1974-1984

From the late 1960s to the mid-1970s, at the very time Brown was banned, there was a sea change in anti-apartheid politics. The Black Consciousness Movement, which gathered momentum from 1969, scorned the role of white liberals and rejected their core belief in colour-blind non-racialism. Within the broad liberal fold, there was a sense of directionlessness. The demise of the Liberal Party in 1968 meant that common-society liberals were now politically homeless. To be sure, Helen Suzman continued to fly the liberal flag on her own in Parliament, and a swing to the Progressive Party in the 1974 election meant that others would soon be there to help her. But many Liberals – and Brown was certainly one of them – were ambivalent about the Progressives. The reasons were partly historical. Firstly, the defection of prominent Liberals to the Progressives between 1959 and 1960 had caused the LP some momentary awkwardness. Secondly, Liberals were generally sceptical about the prospects of change being driven from Parliament: the institution was all white; it was dominated by the Nationalists; and it was run by executive decree. In the 1960s, these Liberals had preferred to channel their energies into extra-parliamentary initiatives, such as boycotts, and the campaigns against sham 'self-rule' in the Transkei and black spot removals in Natal.

But what really hindered complete Liberal identification with the Progressives was the latter's refusal to support universal suffrage. By this time more than merely a historical relic, the qualified franchise symbolised the Progressives' alienation from black aspirations. There were other stumbling blocks, too, of course: by the mid-1960s, the mainstream of the Liberal Party accepted as given the need for benevolent state intervention in the economy – hence the Party's support for land redistribution. The Progressives, by contrast, emphasised the primacy of free markets, and their economics were distinctly laissez-faire. This incompatibility of economic aims was a lesser consideration in the grander scheme of things, however. For Brown, whose liberalism was synonymous with non-racialism, the Progressives' outmoded attachment to the qualified franchise and their racially exclusive membership (necessitated by law) prevented his joining them and wholeheartedly supporting them. So although he had the greatest respect for Helen Suzman, whose efforts on his own behalf during his ban were tireless, he kept his distance from her party.

In the absence of a congenial political home, why did Brown not build his own? There were several reasons. Many of those who could help with the construction were banned or exiled or had moved onto other things. And the market for new political homes was pretty saturated in his view. So what was to be done? As he had told Wolf Hamm in 1974: '[O]ne continues to do what one can as an individual, saying the same old things whenever the opportunity presents itself, trying to fight issues as they arise … support[ing], where one can, anyone or any group which is fundamentally opposed to the present system and … committed to producing a non-racial society.'[1] When his banning orders were lifted in July, those were the tasks to which he applied himself. He began to say 'the same old things' through *Reality*, the journal founded by former Liberals in 1969. He fought, through the Dependants' Conference, against penury and deprivation among those families whose breadwinners were detained and imprisoned in the mass detentions after 1975. And he supported the rural upliftment work of Neil Alcock, which in its own way undermined the apartheid system, through the Church Agricultural Project. In all of these endeavours, he collaborated with a close-knit group of friends, most of whom had been formerly active in the Liberal Party. These friendships were a source of sustenance, and, in a significant way, the overlaps between his social life and his political life help contextualise his choices and his actions in publicly opposing apartheid again, once he could.

* * *

Freed beyond the bounds of Pietermaritzburg, Brown celebrated the expiry of his banning orders by travelling around the country, first to Johannesburg then to Cape Town, and renewing old acquaintances. This, he reported to Wolf Hamm, involved 'seeing people here and there, drinking a good deal more beer than I should, trying not to be too much overwhelmed by the superficialities of the material progress there is around'.[2] In Johannesburg, he and Phoebe stayed with Jack and Beryl Unterhalter, who threw a party for them which was attended by former Liberals. His decade-long isolation had taken its toll, though: he found that most of the people he had known 'weren't there any more', and he had some 'nasty moments trying to attach names to half-forgotten faces'.

On the drive back they passed through Duck Ponds, the slum to which tenants from Charlestown were eventually removed, twenty years on, despite the Liberal Party's valiant efforts in the 1950s. In Pietermaritzburg, the Natal Liberals laid on a party – a 'marvellous event', he informed Hamm, which 'started at 11.00 am and ended at 5.00 pm when the last beer had been drunk'. About 100 people were there, including Sam Chetty, Elliot Mngadi and EV Mahomed.

One of the joys of his regained freedom was being able to revive the social rituals of old. Among these was an annual weekend party at his cottage in the Drakensberg – a tradition started in the mid-1950s, which continued until the year before his death in 2004.[3] On the weekend closest to 16 December, Brown and a small group of male friends would make their way to the mountains for a bout of walking, talking, fishing, and, chiefly, drinking. In its own way, the excursion was a political statement: 16 December had been declared a public holiday to commemorate the Boer victory over the Zulus at Blood River in 1838, and Brown preferred to cock

a snook at this annual orgy of white triumphalism by heading for
the hills.

Before Brown's banning orders were imposed, the core troupe
comprised Sam Chetty, Alan Paton, his university friend Bill Hoffenberg (who was himself banned in 1967, left the country later
that year, and went on to pursue a distinguished career in medical
science in England, where he served as President of the Royal
College of Physicians in the 1980s) and John Carlyle Mitchell, a
young teacher who Brown had met through the Liberal Party. Mitchell became a great friend. Totally committed to non-racialism, in
1977 he opened the doors of King's School in Nottingham Road,
where he was headmaster, to black pupils. This led to the school
losing its government subsidy. When hard times hit, Brown bailed
out the school and became chair of its board of trustees.[4] He was
a generous benefactor to King's, often making his contributions
anonymously.[5]

From the late 1970s, the usual suspects would be joined, on
occasion, by other ex-Liberals, like Colin Gardner and Brown's
cousin, Pat McKenzie. David Welsh, the prominent liberal academic who was appointed Professor of Politics at the University of
Cape Town in 1980, attended the gathering in 1976. Welsh had
joined the Liberal Party in 1958, and got to know Brown better
during the latter part of the 1960s, while doing research at the
archives in Pietermaritzburg for his PhD on 'native policy' in colonial Natal. Brown, on discovering that Welsh was lodging at a local
hotel, said to him: 'Pack your bags.'[6] From that point on he was to
stay at Shinglewood on his trips to Pietermaritzburg. Brown was
banned at the time, and, to avoid the attentions of the Security
Police, Welsh would park his car next door and cut through the
hedge in order to access the Brown home. When his PhD was published in 1971, he co-dedicated it to Brown and Jack Simons, the
communist intellectual who had lectured both Brown and Welsh
at UCT.[7]

In Welsh's recollection, the weekend was typically a bibulous
affair, with lots of robust banter between the men. The cottage itself was pretty rudimentary: for one thing, it had no running
water, and ablutions had to be performed in a stream that crossed

the property. One morning, Welsh and a ragged-looking Paton – the effect of the previous night's whiskies now evident – slowly made their way down to the stream. As they approached, a bird fluttered past Paton, singing. Like Brown a great bird-lover, Paton looked intently at Welsh, and said earnestly: 'David, I think I must be like St Francis of Assisi, because I can talk to these birds and they respond.'[8] Welsh, momentarily speechless, retorted wittily: 'I don't think that's it. I think they come to you because you look so seedy this morning.' Paton, whose sensibilities regarding religion and his own reputation could sometimes be delicate, was not amused.

Another ex-Liberal who became a regular fixture was Harold 'Jock' Strachan, whose mother Brown had visited regularly during Strachan's incarceration in Pretoria Central Prison in the 1960s. In paying tribute to Brown after his death, the irreverent writer and artist recalled that 'joining [this] gaggle of decrepit old fifties political coelacanths for the annual loaf and beerswill in the Dronkensberg eventually became the high point of geriatric fun'.[9] On the Spartan conditions at the cottage:

> The long-drop cottage was pretty geriatric too … held in place by steel-tie rods like some old bloke's failing limbs with titanium bolts. Devoid of luxury, minimal, ascetic. For passing German tourists and Japanese aesthetes on their way to the cave paintings at Giant's Castle the first introduction to God's own Wilderness was clapped-out old pensioners standing naked in a trout stream next to the road, covered in soap.

Brown enjoyed his return to the Berg in 1974. He commented to Derick Marsh that Paton, then seventy, was 'too decrepit to get up the hills these days'. Chetty, who ran his own transport business until the Pietermaritzburg Corporation took it over at the end of the decade, was surprisingly sprightly given that 'he never does anything more energetic than lie under a bus'.[10]

Paton's annual birthday bash was another highlight on the social calendar for the Liberal network. Like the December jaunts

to the Drakensberg, these parties started in the mid-1950s when
Paton was living at Kloof. Paton's biographer, Peter Alexander,
notes that they soon began to follow a formula: one of the writer's
friends would propose a toast; then a poem, specially written for
the occasion would be read out; and finally Paton would deliver a
humorous speech, reflecting on the state of the nation, in response. His first wife, Dorrie, would make sure that the guests,
whose number swelled as the years passed, were well fed and
watered. During the 1960s, the festivities served a greater purpose: according to Alexander, as prominent Liberals were
harassed, detained and banned, 'these parties were a way of rallying and encouraging the remnants of the Party, and reaffirming
the worth of what it stood for'.[11] Brown looked forward to Paton's
gathering, but chose not to attend while his banning orders were
in force.[12] So it gave Brown real pleasure to make the trip up to
Botha's Hill, where Paton had moved with his new wife, Anne, in
January 1975.

Brown had enjoyed a warm relationship with Dorrie, although
he saw less of her immediately before her death, when he was
banned and she was ill. 'One in a million' is the way she apparently
described him to Sam Chetty.[13] But he found Anne cold and awk-
ward, overly protective of Alan's time, and somewhat out of synch –
both politically, with her conservative views, and personally – with
the Liberal crowd. When Paton asked him his advice about marry-
ing Anne, Brown is alleged to have said, gently but decisively: 'She
won't do.'[14]

Anne, for her part, found her husband's birthday get-togethers
burdensome: too many people, too much preparation. So it seemed
to Brown, who reported back to Derick Marsh after Paton's party
in 1975: 'Alan's new wife is quite incapable of making anyone feel
she's glad to see them.'[15] Nevertheless, chatting to old friends and
associates from his time in active politics compensated for Anne's
froideur. Brown was particularly glad to see Mangosuthu Buthelezi,
the Chief Minister of the KwaZulu homeland, who would go on to
revive Inkatha later that year; Ismail and Fatima Meer, together
with Monty Naicker, all of whom had been prominent in the Natal
Indian Congress; and his friend, Archbishop Denis Hurley, whom

he had first met in 1950. Brown proposed the toast to Paton, and just as he was starting to drink his way 'into a reasonable state of mind after the speech-making', he informed Marsh, Selby Msimang, whom he and Phoebe had given a lift, said it was time to go home.

Of course, his closest friends had continued to visit him during his ban, but for Brown, being able to see them when and where he chose, and re-establishing his familiar social routines, was a source of great fulfilment after ten long years of enforced seclusion. And because his political life and his social life were so entwined, it seemed inevitable, now that he was able to raise the liberal banner in public once more, that his route to the flagstaff would be through his Liberal friends.

One such friend was Colin Gardner, who had chaired the Liberal Party's final National Committee meeting in March 1968. He had taken up a position as a lecturer in the English Department of the University of Natal in Pietermaritzburg in 1959 – the same department where Brown's fellow detainee, Derick Marsh had taught before his departure overseas – and by the 1970s he was a Professor. After the Party's demise, Gardner combined his career as an academic with an active involvement in liberal bodies like the South African Institute of Race Relations (SAIRR) and progressive quasi-political bodies like the Christian Institute (CI), on whose national board of management he served as the Natal representative.[16] Founded by English and Afrikaans clergy in 1963 under the prophetic leadership of Beyers Naudé, the CI soon turned from what Gardner remembered as 'a rather staid constellation of biblical discussion groups' into 'a movement actively dedicated to the complete liberation of South Africa'.[17]

Brown went to a meeting of the Christian Institute early in 1975 and met Naudé for the first time. He found the meeting 'very good'; there was 'a very large black turn-out for one thing', he told Wolf Hamm, and he was 'impressed by Naudé's toughness in the face of great pressures'. 'Maybe I should join the church?' he joked.[18]

Unlike Paton, or Gardner, whose Catholic faith nurtured his sense of social justice and shaped his political activism, Brown's

Anglicanism was ancillary to his liberalism. ('Not a regular church-goer', but 'a keen polo player', as the Security Police had reported.)[19] His Christianity was 'of a general kind', said Gardner of Brown in his eulogy at the Cathedral of the Holy Nativity.[20] John Mitchell thought Brown would have smiled at the fact that his funeral service was conducted by a former bishop.[21]

Perhaps Brown might have been described as a 'Christian agnostic',[22] the term used by former Progressive Party MP and deputy chair of the Truth and Reconciliation Commission, Alex Boraine, to identify his own theology later in life. At any rate, Brown's attitude to religion might explain his disinclination to join those ecumenical associations, like the CI, that served to rally liberal (and, predominantly, left) opinion in Pietermaritzburg in the 1970s. Another was the Pietermaritzburg Agency for Christian Social Awareness (PACSA). Founded in 1979 by a committed Anglican, Peter Kerchhoff, PACSA aimed to continue some of the work done by the CI after that organisation was banned in 1977.

It was more due to contingency and circumstance than religious conviction that the three main institutions or projects with which Brown *did* become involved in the 1970s were somehow connected to the church. The informal committee started by Brown and the Quaker Liberal, Bunty Biggs, to help the families of political detainees in 1976 only came to be taken over by the Dependants' Conference (DC) of the South African Council of Churches (SACC) at a later stage. Neil Alcock's Church Agricultural Project involved the clergy because it was initially run on mission-owned land. Alcock himself had a rather tempestuous relationship with the men of the cloth, as, in fairness, he did with most people with whom he worked. And although the Association for Rural Advancement, founded in 1979 and chaired by Brown throughout the 1980s, was funded by the SACC, he insisted that it should retain a 'secular image'.[23]

What of Brown's dealings with those quasi-political bodies, like the Black Sash and the South African Institute of Race Relations, whose welfare work and empirical research had shaped the liberal tradition in twentieth-century South Africa? He certainly kept up his contacts. When Jean Sinclair was elected President of the Black Sash in 1975, Brown wrote to congratulate her. She responded graciously: 'It was the courage & suffering of people like yourself which gave us the strength & determination to carry on.'[24]

As for the SAIRR, Brown was a lifelong member, and, along with Colin Gardner and Leslie Weinberg, he served on its local committee for a period in the mid-1970s.[25] By then, according to an eminent scholar of South African politics, the Institute had emerged as 'the most significant and almost sole representative of traditional liberalism in South Africa'.[26] Certainly, the Institute was the voice of mainstream liberalism, and a number of its members had been Liberals, but it also comprised a deeply conservative strain. The conservatives viewed with caution, and sometimes outright hostility, the radical liberalism espoused by NUSAS at the time. They were also ideologically estranged from the social-democratic thrust of the Liberal Party's later policies.

In 1972, Brown's old schoolfriend, Duchesne Grice, then a prominent lawyer in Durban, was appointed President of the SAIRR. In some ways, Grice and Brown mirrored each other. Both scions of distinguished Old Natal Families (ONFs, in local parlance), they came from privileged stock. They shared similar upbringings as part of Durban's settler elite; they attended Michaelhouse together; and, temperamentally, they were alike – kind and courteous and understated. In the 1970s, they were both involved in the Church Agricultural Project. In 1975, Grice invited Brown to replace Edgar Brookes as a trustee of the Natal Native Welfare Trust.[27] Founded in 1937, the Trust disbursed funds to the SAIRR, Bunty Biggs's Relief Committee for Banished Africans, the Black Sash, the Regional Council of Churches in Durban and Pietermaritzburg, and deserving students.[28] Yet for all their similarities, although they both occupied the same broad liberal spectrum, politically they were different: Duchesne Grice was not the kind of man to spend his weekends deep in rural Natal, mobilising communities against black spot removals.

Grice sought to steer the SAIRR along the 'middle-of-theroad',[29] and he was anxious to deflect negative attention from the

government. For that reason, he agreed to testify before the
Schlebusch Commission of Inquiry in 1973. Appointed by Parliament under the chairmanship of Alwyn Schlebusch the previous
year, the Commission was tasked with investigating the CI, NUSAS,
the SAIRR and the University Christian Movement to determine
whether they were a threat to national security. The Commission's
preliminary report was used to justify the banning of eight NUSAS
leaders.

Grice's decision caused something of a rift within the Institute
and the liberal establishment as a whole. Four of the Institute's
younger members, including Paton's son, Jonathan, refused to give
evidence. Outraged by Grice's kowtowing to government, Paton
junior called for the Institute to be replaced by a new organisation.
The Progressives, to their credit, had opposed the appointment of
the Commission, describing it as a 'McCarthy-type witch hunt'.[30]
Helen Suzman was privately upset with the compliant stance adopted
by Grice and Ellen Hellmann – an Institute executive committee
member who agreed to bear witness.[31]

Brown explained to Wolf Hamm:

> The stand being taken is that the people concerned [those
> Institute members who refused to testify] have been con-
> vinced by the Commission's report on NUSAS that it is not
> an impartial body and that, while they wouldn't mind giving
> evidence before a judicial commission, they aren't prepared
> to give it before this one. It is a line one must approve and
> one which is likely to be taken by a number of Christian
> Institute members when the Commission moves on to
> inquire into it.[32]

It would be erroneous to interpret Brown's support for Paton and
company as a snub to Grice or a rejection of the political direction
in which the South African Institute of Race Relations seemed to
going under his Presidency. All the same, Brown chose to devote
most of his time to worthwhile liberal causes other than the SAIRR
in the second half of the 1970s.

One of these causes was assisting the families of activists who had been banned, detained or imprisoned for their political activities. In December 1975, the Security Police swooped on the ANC underground in Natal. Ten men were arrested and detained and eventually put on trial. The wives of two of the men approached Brown for financial assistance. Early the following year he wrote to Angela Pringle, the Director of the DC, telling her that he had managed to deal with their immediate needs. He wanted to know if the DC had a subsidiary organisation in Pietermaritzburg through which aid could be channelled.[33] In the meantime, Pringle had been given a list of the detainees' names by Phyllis Naidoo, the anti-apartheid campaigner who ran a law firm with Brown's friend, Archie Gumede. Pringle told Brown that she had sent the detainees' wives R60 each for January and February, and asked him, in the absence of a DC field worker in Pietermaritzburg, to act as a point of support.[34]

By March 1976, Brown had rallied a small group of ex-Liberals into action. Out of his own pocket, he helped detainees' families with money for school fees, rent and food. He visited them to ascertain their needs and learn more about their personal circumstances, and took careful note of their hire-purchase commitments.[35] He also liaised with Amnesty International's (AI) offices in Sweden and Germany to raise funds. For example, after visiting Truman Magubane's wife in August, Brown recounted her plight in a letter to the German AI officer, Marianne Knappstein. She had lost her teaching job at a farm school when the farm owner discovered her husband had been detained. She then found a job at a store, which the Security Police visited and where they pressured her employers to dismiss her.[36] In November Brown organised a fundraising evening at the university, with Paton giving readings from his most recent book, *Knocking on the Door.*[37]

In August the following year, Brown reported back to the AI officer in Sweden that the trial was over. One of the men, Joseph Mdluli, had died in detention at the hands of the Security Police. Moses Bhengu, whose family the Swedes had supported, was released after giving evidence for the state. All the accused, with the exception of William Khanyile, were found guilty. Life sentences were given to four of the men, one of whom was Harry Gwala.[38]

For two years, from the end of 1975 to the end of 1977, the DC's work in Pietermaritzburg was facilitated by Brown, who visited and cared for detainees' families and liaised with AI offices overseas. Norman Abraham dealt with financial and legal matters, and Bunty Biggs arranged for family members to visit Robben Island, where the Natal accused were incarcerated. Biggs was a social worker who had helped to found the Child Welfare section of the Edendale Welfare Society in 1958.[39] This *ad hoc* arrangement worked well enough at the time, but by 1978 the Pietermaritzburg Council of Churches (PCC) decided to play a more hands-on role.

In January, members of the Pietermaritzburg Council of Churches' Commission for Justice and Reconciliation met and agreed to act as the local committee for the Dependants' Conference.[40] The Reverend Bob Clarke was elected committee chairman with another former Liberal, a politics lecturer from the University of Natal, Douglas Irvine, as his deputy. Throughout the 1980s, Brown was called upon to act as chairman of the committee on-and-off, eventually resigning as a committee member in 1991.[41] He continued to visit the families of prisoners and detainees, and took a personal interest in Harry Gwala's family, often paying out of his own pocket for Gwala's wife, Elda, to visit him on Robben Island.[42] Brown also arranged with the *Natal Witness* to have newspapers sent to Harry on the island.[43] In the late 1980s he asked Helen Suzman to approach the Minister of Justice, Kobie Coetsee, to release Gwala on compassionate grounds since his health was poor.[44]

This social work appealed to Brown, but he was anxious to publicly communicate the Liberal message – the idea of a non-racial common society – as he had done in the 1950s and 1960s. As it happened, soon after the Party disbanded, a group of Pietermaritzburg Liberals decided to launch a journal of liberal opinion. They hoped to keep the Party's vision in the public imagination, its ideal of non-racialism in currency, and its spread-out former membership in contact.

Among the initiators were Alan Paton, Colin Gardner and Marie Dyer, all of whom were present at the Party's final National Committee meeting. Like Gardner, Dyer lectured in the English Department at the University of Natal, and maintained external political links. She was a founder member of the Midlands Branch of the Black Sash, and worked in the organisation's Pietermaritzburg Advice Office for many years.[45]

Suggested names for the planned publication included 'The Needle' (preferred by Paton), 'The Liberator', 'Anger' and 'New Society', but in the end 'Reality' was chosen, with 'A Journal of Liberal Opinion' as its subtitle.[46] This was a reference to the Liberal Party's in-house journal, *Liberal Opinion*, published between 1961 and 1968. In 1972, the subtitle was amended to 'A Journal of Liberal and Radical Opinion', in an attempt to broaden its appeal.[47]

Reality appeared for the first time in March 1969. To begin with, its editorial board comprised Paton (as chairman), Edgar Brookes, Gardner, Dyer, Alan Tonkyn, Maimie Corrigal and Sallie Lundie. Liberal stalwarts like Leo Marquard and Jack Unterhalter were co-opted in an advisory capacity soon thereafter. Selby Msimang joined the board in due course.

The editorial in the first edition promised that the magazine would portray 'the reality of our South African situation' and attack the moral indefensibility of apartheid.

Reality would 'defend human rights against all attempts at restriction' as the Liberal Party had done before it. Its chief duty would 'not be to preserve racial identity, nor to maintain the "traditional way of life", but to proclaim and pursue our ideal of a new South Africa, in which a citizen's worth and place and future will not be determined by his race and colour, but by his willingness to serve the country that belongs to us all'.

The editorial argued the merits of universal suffrage in terms notable for their emphasis on class. Without the vote, black South Africans would be doomed to remain 'migrant labourers, poorly paid workers, tools of the ruling class, servants of the ruling white society'.[48]

While his banning orders were still in force, Brown could not join the editorial board, but he was kept informed of developments by Paton, who used to spend the night at Shinglewood after board meetings. After his ban came to an end, Brown was unanimously elected to the board in November 1974.[49] He attended his first board meeting in January the following year.[50]

Late in 1974, Paton began work on what was to become the first volume of his autobiography, *Towards the Mountain*.[51] Assisted by Gardner, he was also preparing for publication some of his uncollected poems and shorter writings. These appeared in *Knocking on the Door*, published in 1975. Paton was therefore ready to pass on the editorial mantle at *Reality*, although he was to tell Brown later: 'I resigned the Chairmanship partly because of age, and partly because I wanted to see you back in public and political life.'[52] Brown, who seventeen years earlier had relieved him of his 'Long View' column in *Contact* so that he might complete his biography of Hofmeyr, stepped into the breach once more. In March 1975, he was elected chair of the editorial board, with Paton as his deputy.[53]

Reality involved other Brown family members too: Phoebe wrapped and posted the publication, and Pat McKenzie attended to banking matters.[54] Brown himself wrote most of the editorials[55] and proofread the mock-ups. In addition to his editorials, he consistently wrote reviews and feature articles for *Reality* during the twenty-seven years he was associated with it. He claimed not to 'enjoy writing anything at all': 'I have to force myself to sit down and thump out that sort of first draft ... and after that it's usually a bit better, but ... getting started is the usual problem,' he told Norman Bromberger when reminiscing about *Reality*.[56]

The magazine was financed partly by Paton, partly with money from the Defence and Aid Fund, and, when funds ran dry, from Brown's own pocket.[57] In March 1976, the cover price of *Reality* went up to 35c a copy. It cost roughly R310 to produce a single issue.[58] For a nine-month period ending in March 1976, the balance sheet reflected an income of R1 245,78 and expenditure of R1 585,67.[59] The financial position was always precarious. Minutes from a board meeting in May 1976 stated bluntly: 'The financial position is deteriorating.'[60] By August there was only R470 in the Trident, the building society used by *Reality*, and the financial situation was deemed 'serious'.[61] By September it had become 'critical'.[62] Sometimes there were unforeseen setbacks. For example, the July 1976 issue was printed and ready to be dispatched when it had to be returned to the printer so that quotations from a recently banned publication – 'Detentions and Détente in Southern Africa' – could be removed.[63] Norman Bromberger, who was detained in 1964 along with other young other Liberal activists, joined the editorial board in 1980,[64] by which time he was lecturing in economics at the University of Natal. He was to recall 'these somewhat embarrassing editorial board meetings where these accounts would be presented and there was some deficit and it was unclear what would happen to it'. 'Since none of the rest of us were apparently in a position to volunteer to carry it, we just kept silent.'[65] Often, old Liberal Party members would come to the rescue, as Ernie Wentzel did with a R250 donation in January 1977.[66]

Under Brown's editorship, *Reality* attempted to position liberals as potential intermediaries in what, by the mid-1970s, increasingly seemed like an inevitable showdown between rival racial nationalisms. As such, the magazine invited contributors to map various liberal models of political, economic and constitutional change. This was a debate that had been going on since the beginning of the decade, when the SACC and the CI conjointly founded the Study Project on Christianity in Apartheid Society (SPRO-CAS).

SPRO-CAS was directed by Peter Randall, a former Assistant Director of the South African Institute of Race Relations, who, when Grice and Hellmann testified before the Schlebusch Commission, accused the Institute of being a 'white-led, white-dominated, bourgeois organisation [that] stifles black initiative [and] is an obstacle to change'.[67] SPRO-CAS comprised six commissions, involving over 150 academics and researchers, and produced detailed reports on social, economic, political, educational and legal change.[68] Another commission focused exclusively on 'apartheid and the church'.[69]

The political commission's report, entitled *South Africa's
Political Alternatives*, advocated a dispensation based on liberal
principles like the rule of law, civil rights and equal opportunity.
Its real focus, however, was on constructing a model to devolve
political power away from the administrative centre of state in
such a way as to involve the disenfranchised majority. There was
by no means consensus on this consociational approach, and the
commission exposed broad cracks between those, like the conservative Denis Worrall, who favoured a group-based model of
change, and those classical liberals like Edgar Brookes who were
sceptical of a federal solution premised on group identities and
rights.

But even among common-society liberals like Brookes and
Paton there were differences of opinion. Paton contributed a
paper to the commission in which he suggested that 'one might
proceed by means of a federal constitution towards a common
society', although he hastened to add, 'SPRO-CAS could, or should
[not], provide any blueprints for any kind of society'.[70] When the
political commission's report was finalised, Brookes registered his
objections in a minority report. He believed SPRO-CAS had gone
too far in proposing a federal solution, and he reiterated these
views in *Reality*. In particular, he took issue with the idea that 'federation [could] solve the problems of the franchise in the context
of South Africa's racial composition'.[71]

The question of whether South Africa's political problems
should be solved within the context of a unitary state or a federal
state – and how this impacted on voting rights – surfaced repeatedly
in the pages of *Reality*, and in the meetings of the editorial board,
during the 1970s.

On a visit to the United States, Paton tried to persuade Cyrus
Vance, then Secretary of State under Jimmy Carter, that the American government should give South Africa more time to devise a
federal settlement. He argued his case in *Reality* in an article entitled 'The Americans and Us', published in 1977.[72] Brookes was upset by Paton's article. In particular, he objected to Paton's view that
federalism could serve as an alternative to universal suffrage. He
wrote to Paton, copied the letter to Brown, and lamented that:

'From you more than from any other person I learnt the gospel of universal suffrage leading to majority rule. Now you seem to have abandoned it ... and I find it difficult to unlearn the good lesson that I learned from you.'[73] He continued:

> There is something to be said for it [federation] in terms of principle – more real local government – but in the context of your article it seems ... a way out of the franchise issue. But it really cannot be a way out for the franchise issue. Divide the Republic up as you will, in every part of it, even in the Free State, when universal suffrage is granted the whites will be in a minority. I can quite see that we may have to accept something short of the ideal for some time to come. But if so, would it not be better to accept a qualified franchise on a common roll (the solution of the Progressive Party) than something like a variant of Mr Vorster's unholy trinity?

Paton replied that he realised South Africa would ultimately become a unitary state, with universal franchise and majority rule. The federal proposal was not 'a way out of the franchise issue', as Brookes had claimed, but 'an attempt to find a way out of desolation and the destruction of Afrikanerdom'.[74]

The previous year, Paton had in fact offered to resign from the editorial board over the same issue. He had written an article for the *Natal Witness* which he sent to Brown with a covering letter stating that, given *Reality*'s commitment to 'the unitary society, universal suffrage and majority rule ... I feel it only right to offer my resignation from the Editorial Board'.[75] He undertook not to attend the next meeting so that the board could discuss the matter without the embarrassment of his presence. Brown would not entertain any such notion, and, in the event, Paton's presence at the next editorial board meeting on 10 August 1976 was recorded in the minutes.[76]

In fact, Brown was non-committal about the virtues of the unitary state over the federal state, or vice versa. In his long letter to Wolf Hamm, written just before his banning orders were repealed,

and in which he set out his thoughts on the current role of former
Liberals, he had told Hamm:

> [A]ccept that the Bantustans are there as a fact of life, even
> if only temporarily, and try to work with those people in
> them who share the ideal of a common society. Keep point-
> ing out that as a solution to our problems the whole scheme
> is a fraud – not enough land, development, towns, factories,
> harbours, roads, and that it has been foisted on to people
> without their consent, that it can only be justified on the
> basis of a fair distribution of resources accepted by black
> people – and if one is going to have to go to those lengths
> wouldn't it just be easier to aim at a non-racial society, fed-
> eral at least initially, instead?[77]

As far as Brown was concerned, '… if we do get a non-racial society
I can't say it would worry me much whether it was unitary or federal
or a bastard relation of either'. And, reflecting on the spat between
Brookes and Paton three years later, he reaffirmed: '… I don't
much care any longer whether we end up with a unitary or a
federal or some other kind of state, the important thing is that it
should be worked out by all groups together.'[78]

What Brown would not countenance was any departure from
the Liberal Party's principled position on universal suffrage. That
is what stopped him from joining, but not from voting for, the
Progressive Party. During the 1974 election campaign, he told a
correspondent:

> Almost every time the Progressives open their mouths dur-
> ing an election it is to reassure white voters that their policy
> doesn't mean more blacks than whites voting for the next
> God knows how many years, that *they* won't force school
> integration, that *they* really won't make white South Africa
> face up to the facts of life at all. I suppose it is inevitable at
> an election that you try to frighten off as few voters as pos-
> sible, but I find the whole performance nauseating.[79]

When the Progressives made their gains in that election, adding five seats (Johannesburg North, Orange Grove, Parktown, Rondebosch, Sea Point and, later that year, another, after a by-election in Pinelands) to the one retained by Helen Suzman in Houghton, Brown jibed: 'Hardly the heart of the platteland, that lot, and their policies are no better than they ever were.' But he conceded that '... it is probably a good thing to have them there, hopefully making sensible suggestions, as ... the situation becomes more tense'.[80]

When the Progressives merged with Harry Schwartz's Reformists to form the Progressive Reform Party (PRP) in 1975, Brown wrote an editorial in *Reality* saying that the merger made sense, since '[w]hite South Africa certainly couldn't afford two parties whose views were so close to one another's'.[81] He welcomed the Party's commitment to a bill of rights, the rule of law, an independent judiciary, the removal of discriminatory legislation and free and compulsory education but expressed reservations about 'the proposed franchise requirements for voter qualification' in a federal state. 'It may be a difficult step for a new party seeking the support of White voters to take,' he wrote, 'but for our part we would have liked to see it come out boldly for universal suffrage in each constituent state of the federation.'

Even Brookes was prepared to accept a qualified franchise on a common roll in a unitary state rather than consenting to Paton's federal solution. In February 1976, he submitted a piece to Brown entitled 'False Dawns', which called for the formation of a Liberal Voters' League. 'By limiting ourselves to voters,' he argued, 'we shall in effect have an all-white association and so not be breaking the evil law which caused our dissolution.'[82]

Not only was Brookes willing to entertain the idea of a racially exclusive political outfit, but, sixteen years after the LP had finally rejected the qualified franchise, he was ready to revert to it as an intermediary step on the way to universal suffrage: 'We may have educational or property qualifications, but they will not be race qualification [sic] and in the end we must face the fact that within a foreseeable time every man and woman in South Africa may have the vote.'[83]

Brown dismissed the idea, stating that 'those of us who were regarded as leaders of the Liberal Party and who were associated with its decision to close down when it could no longer be non-racial, should, in our political lives, not belong to anything which is racial'.[84] He elaborated further:

> We can support the Progressives, or agree with the Labour Party, or understand how young black people should come to commit themselves to SASO [South African Students' Organisation], but I don't think we should belong to a racial organisation which, inevitably, a voters' association is bound to be. I think this is particularly important for those of us who are white and who, willy-nilly, because of colour, have some association with the group which has forced everyone into racial categories. It may not be a logical way of thinking but I can understand why Dempsey Noel [a prominent Coloured ex-Liberal] should get involved in the Labour Party, or Selby [Msimang] in Inkatha, and yet still feel that it would be wrong for me to be associated with a white voters [sic] group. My view is that, while we should attach ourselves to what non-racial organisations of real value there still are, in the *political* field we will have to go through the difficult period immediately ahead, acting as individuals, and pro-claiming, insofar as we are able to do so, the ideas for which the Party stood.

Brookes ultimately withdrew his article, finding himself 'very much in agreement' with Brown's argument.[85] It is much to Brown's credit that where other common-society liberals – and indeed, Liberals – wavered or obfuscated or reneged, he held the line, both person-ally and editorially in *Reality*.

Brookes's own judgment slackened as he aged. At times, his contributions to board meetings were injudicious: on one occa-sion, for example, he suggested a campaign to stick stamps upside down on letters. The board dismissed his idea, noting that unless it 'was widely supported it would be counter-productive'.[86] Brown confided in Hamm that he thought Brookes was 'past his best' and that his writing had become 'often rather embarrassing'.[87] When he moved to Gillitts, Brookes found it onerous to travel the extra distance to editorial meetings in Pietermaritzburg. This, together with his deteriorating hearing, led him to tender his resignation to Brown in March 1978.[88] Brown accepted it with reluctance,[89] but in the event the board persuaded Brookes to stay on as an advisory member.[90]

Brookes lacked Brown's clarity of vision. He was, in David Welsh's words, somewhat of a 'mushy' liberal.[91] When Welsh, along with Marie Grant, Leo Marquard and Jack Unterhalter, appeared before the commission that held public hearings into the so-called Improper Interference Bill, Brookes was unable to attend. But he submitted a memorandum on behalf of the Liberal Party asking for the 'abandonment of such provisions of the Bill as will make its [the Party's] legal position impossible'.[92] Of Brookes's unseemly plea, Brown was to state: 'Having taken so long to make up his mind to join it [the Liberal Party], did he feel he owed it to those who had started it to go to almost any lengths to save it when most of them would have preferred him to be telling Vorster to go to hell?'[93]

None of this is to detract from Brookes's place in the pantheon of South African liberals. Brown praised Brookes for his 'courage, his steadfastness, his flexibility of mind and his faith' when he delivered the Edgar Brookes Academic and Human Freedom Lecture in August 1979, after Brookes died in April that year.[94] Brown's esteem for Brookes went beyond collegial fealty, for Brookes had played an important role in both his personal and his professional development. They first met, it will be recalled, when Brown was a schoolboy at Michaelhouse and Brookes was the principal of Adams College. Brookes had initiated a programme of exchange visits between the two schools, and Brown's outing to Adams had had a dramatic effect on him. In his own words: 'It shattered the accumulated stereotypes about black people with which I had grown up.'[95] Brookes had also taken a close interest in Brown's career from the outset. It was to Brookes that Maisie Brown had written during the war, seeking advice on

Peter's future studies. It was on Brookes's recommendation that Brown took his degree in Native Affairs and Administration at UCT, and it was to Brookes that Brown first turned as a newly graduated work-seeker. The job at the Edendale Local Health Commission had followed as a result.

Then, too, Brookes had been assiduous about visiting Brown, Marsh and Hans Meidner during their detention in 1960. It was an act of kindness that Brown did not forget. As for Brookes, he was a great admirer of Brown. He wrote in his autobiography: 'I know of no man who lives so fully in the C Major of life (as Browning puts it) and yet is so utterly and with so much determination dedicated to his ideals.'[96] He was much taken with the young man 'born with a silver spoon in his mouth', who 'had everything in his favour – looks, personality, a private income, a good school and university record, finally noteworthy skill as a polo player'.

The language echoed Paton's own in his early *Contact* profile of Brown – 'The Crusader on a Polo Pony'. There was something about the young man who, for all his wealth, had a '"social conscience" about justice, equality and the rule of law',[97] in Paton's words, which charmed and drew in and impressed the two older men. Perhaps it was a paternal instinct. Perhaps it was the fact that, despite his affluence and his upbringing – so different from theirs, Paton the son of a shorthand-writer, Brookes the son of a grocer – Brown seemed to them to be completely without airs.

If Brookes expressed his political ideas less lucidly as he neared his death, what of Paton? In the 1970s it became something of a commonplace among certain Liberals that Paton was moving to the right. Occasionally he would upset them with public utterances that appeared to contradict what the Liberal Party had stood for. Brown was not immune from expressing such displeasure. After reading an interview with Paton in the press, Brown protested to Hamm: 'If you are feeling tired, shut up, for God's sake. Alan, of course, has this compunction to bare his soul. It is probably the source of many of his talents, so one must allow for it, I think. But still ...'[98]

In 1971, Paton was interviewed for *The Times* by John Clare, the former editor of *Contact*, who had gone into exile in London.[99]

Clare suggested that Paton's support for Chief Buthelezi meant that he was endorsing the government's policy of separate development, and thereby legitimising apartheid. Brown advised Hamm that he didn't 'regard John Clare very highly', and that it was 'a snide article, designed to put Alan in a bad light'.[100] However, he conceded: 'Unfortunately, it seems that he [Paton] has been saying at least some things which are very disturbing.'

Paton attempted to clarify his views in a right-of-reply. He wrote that the 'new instruments of power', the territorial authorities in the homelands, might be put to 'a use not entirely foreseen by their white creators'. He found apartheid 'wholly unacceptable' but hoped that 'separate development and the creation of territorial authorities may open doors that under apartheid would have remained closed forever'.[101]

Brown later summed up his views on the 'instruments of power' in an editorial on Inkatha: there was a danger of 'overrating their effectiveness as levers of change towards the open society'.[102] At the time, he regretted Paton's emphasis on the Bantustans, for he believed 'the task of a Liberal' was 'to make a non-racial society a possibility in the 87% "White South Africa" whatever may happen in the Bantustans'.[103] This probably wasn't good *politics*, Brown acknowledged, since the chances of achieving a non-racial democracy seemed so remote. But it was 'important that it should be known that there are still Liberals around whose ideas have not changed and who are still committed to the same old visions'.

Later in the decade, Paton said to an interviewer from the *Daily News* that 'one man, one vote in a unitary system would come only from the barrel of a gun'. He argued that to prevent violence, a constitutional settlement should be brokered in terms of which 'two or three regions would be governed by white majorities'. Realising that such views had begun to surprise and occasionally alienate former LP members, Paton insisted that he was not repudiating what he had stood for in the 1950s and 1960s. His ideals remained the same, but the idealism of the LP 'did not amount to a realistic political programme'. In the current context, it was important that 'policy should be pragmatic'.[104]

One of the Liberals who took strong exception to the sentiments expressed by Paton was John Aitchison, the LP activist
banned at the age of twenty, whom Brown was to describe as 'one
of the most fearless and indefatigable Liberals the Party ever
boasted'.[105] In an open letter to Paton, originally published in
Reality and later reprinted in the *Natal Witness*, Aitchison declared
that over a number of years he had become 'more and more disturbed' by Paton's statements, and that his agitation had since
turned to anger and disillusionment.[106]

To Aitchison, Paton's statements were 'flagrant contradictions'
of what both the LP and Paton himself, especially in his 'Long
View' columns, had espoused. He rejected Paton's self-styled pragmatism, which was a negation of the 'old (unreconstructed)'
Liberal belief that 'the only way out of the present mess was to
share power among all the people of this country'. Furthermore,
Paton had no right to preach his new views as the 'former
President of the Liberal Party'. And with a final thrust of the knife,
Aitchison suggested: 'I believe that if you had maintained your
present views in the days of the Liberal Party you would have been
summarily expelled.'

Paton was unrepentant in response. He told Aitchison that his
mind was in a 'straitjacket'; he clung to the 'policies and solutions
of the "sixties"' and confused them with ideals. Drawing his own
dagger, he added: 'Your courage I never doubted, but I have often
doubted your wisdom.'[107]

This was explosive stuff. Such a public airing of dirty laundry
was uncommon among Liberals, especially in a small, cohesive
community like Pietermaritzburg. The *Natal Witness* approached
Gardner and Brown for comment, but they either couldn't be
reached or wouldn't be drawn. The minutes from the editorial
board meeting immediately before and after the publication of the
Aitchison/Paton correspondence are curiously silent about the
fallout.[108] Brookes wrote to Brown, enclosing a letter for publication in *Reality* that expressed 'regret [at] the public disagreement
between two leading Liberals'. Why did Aitchison have to attack
Paton as a traitor, he asked: 'He is our chief asset in the outer
world: why must you besmirch him?' Significantly, however, Brookes

added: 'But in essence, John, I agree with you. I have stood and still stand for universal franchise in a unitary state and, like you, I learned this from Alan.'[109]

Brown declined to publish Brookes's letter. He hadn't been particularly happy about Aitchison and Paton's exchange in the first place, but thought the issues raised were 'sufficiently important for Aitchison to be given the opportunity to write about them and for Paton to be given the opportunity to reply'. Now that the storm had passed, it was better that 'their differences be allowed to die a quiet death'.[110]

By the mid-1980s, Brown would tell Dot Cleminshaw: 'There isn't much one can do about some of the things Alan says periodically.'[111] His feeling was that, while until about fifteen years previously Paton had seen blacks as the underdog, he now increasingly felt that Afrikaners would be the underdog of the future, 'unless he [the Afrikaner] can somehow be persuaded in time to see the madness of what he is doing'. As a result, Paton saw and hoped for signs of change which suggested that 'the Nats are slowly coming to their senses', but, as Brown noted, 'most of us are much more sceptical'.

Reality provided an opportunity for Liberals to rethink their role and credo – though Brown chose to stick to his – and to put forward liberal ideas for effecting political change. Yet it was also very much a journal – a record of current affairs – and from Brown's editorials it is possible to construct a narrative of South Africa's political transition from a liberal point of view. And in documenting that process, *Reality* sought to engage with the protagonists of the day.

Early issues gave much attention to the Black Consciousness Movement.[112] When its leader, Steve Biko, died in detention in 1977, Brown wrote that he felt a deep sense of despair: 'despair that a man of Steve Biko's calibre should be lost to us all, but particularly that he should be lost to us in this way. For this was a man to whom any sensible authority, trying to ensure a reasonable future for all people in South Africa, would have been talking – not driving him to his death.'[113]

Reality also devoted a good deal of coverage to Inkatha when it was resuscitated by Chief Buthelezi in 1975. An editorial made 'no apology for this', since Inkatha was 'new' and 'important'.[114] Brown invited Buthelezi to produce an 'authoritative' article on Inkatha for *Reality* – 'its origins, its revival, its make-up, and what it sets out to do for the Zulu people in particular and for South Africa as a whole'.[115] Buthelezi set the movement's Secretary-General, Sibusiso Bengu, to the task, and his piece appeared in the September issue.[116] *Reality* also ran Buthelezi's address to the Inkatha general conference later that year.[117] An article by David Welsh the following year concluded that 'the prospects for a democratic movement are not propitious, and the circumstances of Inkatha will test to the utmost the undoubted democratic instincts of its leaders'.[118]

At first, Brown was responsive to Buthelezi and Inkatha, but his enthusiasm gradually waned. In 1971, he had confided in Wolf Hamm that Buthelezi was a 'genuine non-racialist [who] fought against the application of the Bantu Authorities system to the Zulu people with great skill and tenacity for many years'.[119] Seven years on, he told Hamm that 'right now, the way he [Buthelezi] is taking Kwa-Zulu and the Inkatha movement certainly doesn't make me very happy'.[120] In 1979, to Adelaine and Walter Hain, he remarked of Inkatha: '[A]lthough I don't like it much [it] seems to have an irresistible attraction for almost any Zulu person over the age of 30.'[121] In the 1980s, his verdict became more damning. In 1984, he assured the celebrated poet of Black Consciousness, Mafika Gwala: 'I doubt if there is any fundamental difference between us in our view of Inkatha. I find it, in general, a sinister and potentially dangerous organisation.'[122]

Brown was to gain firsthand experience of Buthelezi's famed hypersensitivity when the Chief overreacted to an article Brown wrote in *Reality* reflecting on Robert Sobukwe's memorial service. Despite the many contacts between the Liberal Party and the PAC in the 1960s, Brown did not meet Sobukwe at the time. Their first and only meeting was arranged by Theo Kotze of the Christian Institute, and took place at Groote Schuur Hospital in Cape Town a few months before Sobukwe's death. Although the meeting lasted for just over a quarter of an hour, Brown found it 'a quite exceptional experience'.[123] Sobukwe gave the impression of immense strength. He seemed to be entirely free of bitterness or despair. And so, along with other white liberals like Helen Suzman and Sobukwe's great friend, Benjamin Pogrund, Brown went to pay his respects in Graaff-Reinet on 11 March 1978.

The atmosphere at the funeral was tense. The organisers of the service were pressured by militant youths to remove Suzman and Pogrund from the speakers' list. Buthelezi was jeered at and man-handled, and was eventually persuaded to leave by Desmond Tutu so that the funeral could proceed.[124] Brown reported matter-of-factly on what had transpired, but added that it did not serve any pur-pose to write of Buthelezi's detractors at the funeral as 'irresponsi-ble and impudent "puppies"':

> Some of them may well be that but most are nothing of the sort. They are tough, brave and committed and they repre-sent the new black mood which has been evident since Soweto. This is not a passing mood. It is here to stay until black aspirations are met and will become an increasingly powerful influence in shaping the future of our country. Nor is it correct to say that it was only a small group of young people who wanted Chief Buthelezi and the others to leave the funeral.

At the same time, Brown thought it would be misguided to write off Buthelezi, since he remained an 'extremely powerful figure in South Africa' and Inkatha was developing into a mass movement 'drawing into political activity a large body of people who have never been involved before'. He hoped that the disputes between black radicals and Inkatha could be resolved, because if they weren't, 'the future for all South Africans looks more ominous than ever'.

Buthelezi did not like Brown's account in 'Reflections on Graaff-Reinet', and wrote a heated letter to the editor of the *Daily News*, rebutting it.[125] Brown replied to the editor that he had 'no wish to enter into a public dispute with Chief Buthelezi', but that he stuck by his 'assessment of what happened on that day'. From

Buthelezi's reaction to his article one would think that it had been hostile to the Chief: 'As it so happens,' Brown continued, 'it was not.'[126]

Brown reflected to Hamm that it was 'impossible to say anything about [Buthelezi] in the least bit critical without him taking offence immediately, which is a great pity, because he has many good qualities'.[127] The two men eventually patched up their differences. Buthelezi was sorry that they had 'had to exchange hard words about the incident'.[128] But this was the first of several wrangles between Brown, in his capacity as editorial board chair, and Buthelezi or his minions about the way in which Inkatha and its leader were portrayed in *Reality*.

In 1980, Brown commissioned two articles independently of one another: one by Mafika Gwala on Black Consciousness and the other from the Secretary-General of Inkatha, Oscar Dhlomo. The two articles were to appear in the September issue, although this was not deliberately planned. Brown warned Dhlomo that Gwala's article consisted of 'a pretty robust attack on Inkatha and its philosophy and strategy'. However, he hoped that by printing them in the same issue, *Reality* 'might be able to provide a forum in which the differences between the two points of view could be discussed rationally and perhaps, to some extent, reconciled'.[129]

Dhlomo was willing to accept that the simultaneous appearance of the two articles was inadvertent, but was 'not prepared to accept that you [Brown] and your Board are being fair to me and Inkatha'.[130] Dhlomo recommended various steps Brown might take for 'the sake of black unity', which amounted to asking Gwala to amend his piece, or spiking it. In the end, Brown agreed that it would be unfair to Inkatha to run Gwala's piece as it stood, and he undertook to obtain a more 'positive' article from the author.[131] Gwala's original submission could then be used to generate a debate in future issues, with Inkatha being given a right-of-reply.

This solution must have been unpalatable to Gwala, for there is no sign of his article in *Reality* – either the original version or the proposed revision. Gwala kept up a lively correspondence with Brown on liberals, however. In 1983, he noted derisively to

Brown that the President of the SAIRR, Duchesne Grice, was 'Gatsha's [Buthelezi's] "paperwork man"'.[132] His presidency left much to be desired about the 'liberal sector in the eighties', according to Gwala, who went on to ask: '[H]ow many times has the liberal sector betrayed humanist ideals thru [sic] throwing in support for fascist-minded leaders like Gatsha, Mangope, others?'

Brown responded in terms that shed light on his attitude to ideological cleavages in the fight against apartheid:

> I am reminded over and over again, when I look at our sit-uation, of how the European Resistance of the Nazi era, *did* forego the luxury of ideological argument, while they came together to oppose a common foe, and I cannot see that it should be beyond the capacity of opponents of apartheid here to come to the same arrangement.[133]

The editorial board of *Reality* was by no means oblivious to the criticisms levelled at liberals in the 1970s and 1980s – both by adherents of Black Consciousness and from within the broader ranks of white democrats. Indeed, that is why *Reality* had altered its name to 'A Journal of Liberal and Radical Opinion' in 1972. At the time, this was deemed necessary to accommodate a younger generation of radicals who felt that traditional liberalism had too often been, 'like the policies of the Progressive Party, an expression of half-detached generosity on the part of the fairly privileged rather than a genuine expression of the *need* of the dispossessed or of those who are truly prepared to associate themselves with the dispossessed'.[134] What was needed, according to *Reality*'s editorial writer, who employed the vocabulary of the Marxist cultural critic, Raymond Williams, was a switch from the liberal idea of *service* to the radical idea of *solidarity*.

Paton resisted the name change, although when he was overruled by the rest of the board, he yielded good-naturedly enough, sending Gardner a poem about his conversion from 'trad Lib to rad Lib'.[135] *Reality* tried to reflect this accommodation with the radicals by occasionally carrying articles and book reviews which bore the stamp of neo-Marxist thought that was then pervading the academy. These contributions often made Paton bristle, and in 1983 he took particular exception to a review by David Maughan-Brown of the publisher David Philip's 'Africasouth' series. In his piece, Maughan-Brown claimed that the 'attitude towards the crowd' in Harry Bloom's *Transvaal Episode* derived from a 'clearly identifiable petit-bourgeois class position and finds an ideological home in liberalism ...'[136] Paton was incensed. He wrote to Brown, demanding to know: 'What is such an article doing in *Reality*?' Paton might agree, though not willingly, to a Liberal-Marxist dialogue in *Reality*, but 'this attack on liberalism is not part of a dialogue. It is a gratuitous insult in an article which purports to be about something quite different.'[137] The editorial board should have rejected such 'neo-Marxism masquerading as literary criticism', and he added sarcastically: 'Are we now going to make *Reality* a journal of liberal and radical and neo-Marxist opinion?'

The more Paton thought about it, the more worked up he became. He saw Gardner at King's School on Speech Day, and informed him that he was going to resign from the editorial board over the matter. Gardner passed this on information to Brown, who attempted to dissuade Paton from taking such action. Brown 'did not like the review' either, he told Paton, nor had he been in favour of *Reality*'s name-change when it occurred.[138] Under his own editorship he had 'made no attempt personally to get articles from "radicals"' and at one stage he had proposed reverting to 'A Journal of Liberal Opinion'. That had been resisted at the time by Norman Bromberger, who was trying to get radicals to contribute to a series of his on land reform. In retrospect, he regretted publishing Maughan-Brown's article, and he urged Paton not to resign. And, as it was December, he ended his letter: 'I'm enclosing your Berg shopping list. See you on Wednesday.'

Brown was to keep Paton informed of any neo-Marxist copy which he thought might ruffle the novelist. In 1984, he warned Paton of a review in the forthcoming issue which was critical of liberal historiography.[139] What did Brown's deference to Paton's feelings signify? Was it the respect of a younger man for a mentor in his dotage; evidence that Brown's own liberalism was strictured;

that he had failed to embrace the need for a dialogue between liberalism and radicalism that other board members thought vital? Most probably, it indicated his own distaste for any position which he considered to be 'ideological'. His own liberalism he viewed not as ideology, but as common sense. And then, too, his experiences in the Liberal Party had made him cautious of the far left, although, as he told Mafika Gwala, it was necessary to forego the luxury of ideological argument in order to oppose a common foe.

Through his other involvements in the 1970s and 1980s, most notably in AFRA, Brown would be called on to collaborate with people whose views ran the gamut of anti-apartheid politics. And because many of them were academics, their political outlook was often influenced by the neo-Marxist scholarship then in currency. By the mid-1980s, with the formation of the United Democratic Front (UDF) in 1983 and the Congress of South African Trade Unions (COSATU) in 1985, their activism was also sometimes shaped by the dual rise of civic radicalism and trade unionism. Brown therefore found himself having to straddle two worlds. On the one hand, he still inhabited the world of the 1950s and 1960s Liberal, whose adherence to the old precepts he found it important to reiterate, especially when others seemed to vacillate. On the other, he had to familiarise himself with a brave new world in which the demands of Black Consciousness required white democrats to refashion a role for themselves. This became even more urgent after the Soweto uprising of 1976. In Brown's case, the task was complicated by a hiatus in public life – an effect of his banning orders, which had removed him from society at the very time this process was initiated. Of course, once his banning orders lapsed and he resumed a public role, he was able to grope towards some kind of an understanding of how Liberals might position themselves among the advocates of Black Consciousness and a younger generation of radical liberals. But this was complicated by a host of other things, notably the absence of a non-racial political home that could enable Liberals to perform collectively as actors on the political stage. *Reality* did its job in keeping the Liberal message in the public domain, but it could never hope to have the same reach

or clout as a political party. Paton told Ernie Wentzel in 1984 that:
'I think it is quite impossible for an editorial board to have any
political importance. A paper such as *Reality* should stand for the
policies of a party or organisation, but it can hardly stand for
itself.'[140] In the circumstances, it seemed inevitable that pressure
would mount for the Liberal Party to be revived. That eventually
led to Brown forming the Liberal Democratic Association in 1986.
In the meantime, he busied himself with rural development and
welfare work, thus reprising an earlier theme in his political career.

14

BACK TO THE LAND: THE CHURCH AGRICULTURAL PROJECT
1974-1979

With his banning orders lifted and participation in public life now possible, Brown cast about for ways to resist apartheid and promote the common society. *Reality* provided one avenue, offering him a platform to articulate the defunct Liberal Party's message of non-racialism. As contributing editor, Brown's writing skills – honed by years of incisive commentary in *Contact*'s 'Long View' column – were put to the service of liberalism once more. *Reality* reached a small audience, however: a coterie of mostly urban professionals, clerics, academics and students, whose politics were, by the standards of the day, already well left of centre. In the absence of a non-racial political party to whose mast he could nail his colours, Brown sought involvement with individuals and institutional structures that shared his vision. Central to that vision was a belief that black South Africans, dispossessed of their land by conquest and territorial segregation, should have a sense of ownership over the soil. In the tradition of twentieth-century South African liberalism, which tended to prioritise welfare work among urban Africans, this attentiveness to rural concerns distinguished Brown from his contemporaries.

Two opportunities soon presented themselves via his old friend, Neil Alcock, namely, an agricultural development project in northern Natal, and an organisation opposed to the government's policy of forced removals. The first option interested Brown because he was a man of the soil himself, a farmer, and because he believed such work had ramifications beyond the modernisation of subsistence farming, land rehabilitation and soil conservation. If degraded farmland could be rehabilitated by African workers, and this could serve in turn as an example to residents of South Africa's badly denuded reserves, then both the material and spiritual legacy of rural dispossession might, in some way, begin to unravel. The second venture appealed to him because it provided a thread of continuity with his work against black spot removals in the 1950s and 1960s. And so, despite his wariness of Alcock – who was, by most accounts, a difficult man – Brown got involved with two of Alcock's initiatives: the Church Agricultural Project (CAP) and the Association for Rural Advancement (AFRA).

* * *

Born in 1919, Neil Alcock was a Midlands farmer with a passion for justice. He was also a force to be reckoned with, both physically, at six feet three inches, and temperamentally. Rian Malan recalls how Alcock once chased down a passing steam engine whose sparks had set fire to the grass on his property. Having caught up with the train, he parked his car across the railway tracks, got out and bellowed to the stunned driver that he was under arrest. 'This is an image of Neil Alcock we must hold in our minds,' writes Malan, 'a man with thunderbolts of anger in his eyes, facing down a train because that was the right thing to do.'[1]

As the 1950s wore on, and the pernicious consequences of the Nationalists' racial polices became clearer, Alcock's anger and righteousness were channelled into liberal politics. After a stint as United Party chairman in the Bulwer and Underberg region, he joined the Liberal Party during the first State of Emergency, when Brown was detained with Hans Meidner and Derick Marsh. He was inspired to do so, the story goes, after seeing a poster in the rear window of Olga Meidner's car, which she used to update daily and which read 'My husband has been in jail without trial for ... days.'[2]

Alcock was a man of action. 'Nothing that can't talk can beat me,' he is reported to have claimed.[3] In some ways, the Liberal Party – with its preponderance of intellectuals, its regard for the rituals of debate and the propensity of some of its members to split hairs over policy – was bound to beat Alcock. In a memorandum submitted in 1961, he urged the Party to abandon 'useless academic liberalism' and commit itself instead to 'practical liberalism'.[4] At meetings of the Natal Provincial Committee, Alcock consistently argued that the Party should engage in 'practical work' to improve the lives of rural Africans. Of course, by this time, the Liberal Party was closely involved with the campaign against black spot removals in Natal. Its practical work in the Transkei had not yet begun in earnest, but, even so, the Party's shift in attitude and emphasis since Sharpeville, its welfare work and its concern with land rights issues meant that Alcock's accusation of 'useless academic liberalism' was somewhat off beam.

For Alcock, one way of putting liberalism into practice was by promoting rural healthcare through sound nutrition. His own success as a farmer had been achieved through milk, which he sold at a subsidised price to the government Milk Board. In the late 1950s there was an oversupply of milk, and the government began dumping its surplus into the sea. Yet, shamefully, many rural Africans were malnourished.

In Pholela, the African homeland which bordered Alcock's farm, the signs of deprivation were in abundance. The infant mortality rate stood at 40 percent; those that made it to early childhood were often plagued by rickets; and their parents, themselves malnourished, frequently succumbed to infections such as phthisis (tuberculosis). To compound matters, the Nationalist regime took a policy decision to close down the Pholela Health Centre, one of several rural community health centres founded by the United Party government in the 1940s. In 1960, Alcock petitioned the government to reopen the centre, but to no avail. The result was a steady increase in diseases caused by malnutrition, such as kwashiorkor.

This amalgam of factors – the closure of the Pholela Heath Centre, the resurgence of malnutrition and the milk glut – prompted Alcock to action. He began selling his entire milk run to the people of Pholela at discounted prices. He bought his neighbouring farmers' surpluses and sold them too. At this point he decided to get the Liberal Party involved. At a National Committee meeting in Grahamstown in 1961, he suggested that the Party should spearhead a programme to make milk and other surplus agricultural produce available to poor Africans at cost. What he had in mind was a national distribution scheme.

The committee was sympathetic to the idea, but Alcock's reputation for refractoriness preceded him. At any rate, the Party decided to 'give what support it could ... without becoming completely involved'.[5] This took the form of a donation of 100 pounds,[6] a not inconsiderable sum for those days, which enabled Alcock to travel around the country raising awareness about his plans and garnering expertise, assistance and financial support. He managed to attract a good deal of publicity for the scheme in the English-language press, and he solicited donations from business and his network of liberal contacts. By the beginning of 1962, pilot projects of the distribution scheme were established in Pretoria, Johannesburg, Cape Town and Pholela.[7] In June, Brown expressed concern about the haphazard way in which the project was developing. He confided to a correspondent: 'I just hope this bloody thing isn't getting out of hand. The papers here are full of people making statements, each one different from the other.'[8]

Alcock's travails eventually bore fruit, and, in July 1962, Kupugani (Zulu for 'raise yourself') was launched as a national non-profit organisation with a board of directors. With Kupugani occupying most of his waking hours, and understandably eager to avoid banning orders, Alcock gradually withdrew from active involvement in the Liberal Party. He travelled around the country collecting surplus foodstuffs and setting up distribution outlets. He ploughed all his own resources into Kupugani. In his obsession with the enterprise, he lost his first wife to divorce, ran into debt and eventually lost his farm too. He became, in Malan's words, a 'monk penitent', 'a wandering ascetic, sleeping on roadsides, subsisting on milk and army-surplus biscuits'.[9]

Hearing that Alcock had taken to sleeping in his Peugeot station wagon in the plantations outside Pietermaritzburg, Brown insisted that he stay at Shinglewood. From Alcock's time there, one incident stood out for Brown. Since his detention in 1960, the Security Police had been paying close attention to the Liberal Party leader. One day, sometime in 1963, an officer raided his house. Alcock was no longer in residence, but Brown had given him a room in one of the outbuildings to store his belongings. Alcock had secured the doors to the room with copious amounts of wire, tied in complex knots. The officer fixed Brown with a suspicious look and drew a deep breath. He was onto something. Anticipation soon turned to disappointment, however. Through Kupugani, Alcock had begun purchasing the heads and skins of impala from officials at the Natal game reserves, whose parks were overstocked and subject to culls. Alcock bought and sold the surplus meat, and was trying to find a market for the heads and skins. The outbuilding at Shinglewood seemed like a good storage place. And, so, as the unwitting officer rammed into the door, he was overwhelmed by a foul smell as the heads and hides of Alcock's impala came tumbling down on him. Years later, Brown recalled gleefully how the officer 'staggered back and more or less gave up his search after that'.[10]

In time, Kupugani ran a variety of welfare projects with an agricultural and health-care slant, and employed staff to teach its customers about nutrition. Some of its more commercially minded directors were uneasy about these additional functions. They felt that Kupugani should revert to its core business, rely less on donor funding and cover its own operational costs. Alcock would have none of this. Often tetchy, frequently contrarian and usually convinced that no one else understood the unique significance of his work, he eventually fell out with the directors and left Kupugani in early 1965.

The parting of the ways was not altogether bitter. Before leaving Kupugani, Alcock persuaded some of the sympathetic directors to make him a grant so that he could start a small agricultural development project. He had become convinced of the need for such a scheme during his many travels to rural areas while working for Kupugani, and had hoped that Kupugani itself might branch out into development work.

In seeking a site for the project he concentrated on mission-owned land. This was for two reasons. Firstly, there was a history of agricultural development projects among Africans living on mission-owned farms. In the 1920s and 1930s, for example, Father Bernard Huss of Marianhill Mission had encouraged agricultural cooperation among the mission's African tenants through the establishment of cooperative credit societies.[11] At Marianhill College, he taught about rehabilitating land in the reserves and ways to modernise peasant farming. Secondly Alcock realised that he would have greater freedom of movement on mission-owned farms than on the reserves.

So, having lobbied church leaders in Natal, Alcock set up the Church Agricultural Project on five mission farms with the seed money he raised on leaving Kupugani. CAP was launched as a joint venture of the Catholic, Anglican and Lutheran churches. A board was appointed, with the Catholic Archbishop, Denis Hurley, as chairman. Soon, more donations came in, the most generous of which was a R10 000 grant from the World Council of Churches for 1965/66.

CAP was headquartered at a Catholic mission settlement called Maria Ratschitz, on a farm which nestled beneath the Hlatikulu Mountain near Wasbank in northern Natal. The farm itself was home to some 100 African tenant families. Alcock had recently married a new wife, Creina – a young journalist on Durban's *Daily News* – in a ceremony presided over by Alan Paton as guest of honour and Chief Mangosuthu Buthelezi as best man. The couple moved onto Maria Ratschitz, and Neil commenced his duties as farm manager. Immediately, he identified three priorities for CAP:

- To produce food for sale at low prices to the African market, especially in rural areas. The production of milk, meat, eggs etc is aimed at combating malnutrition.
- To develop co-operative farming among the tenants on the missions.
- To provide practical agricultural education for those Africans who want this type of training, which can be acquired nowhere else in South Africa.[12]

Using donor grants, CAP purchased cows and day-old chicks. It sold fowls, eggs and *amasi* (sour milk) to local African communities at cost. Together with the African tenants on the farm, Alcock set about repairing farm buildings, constructing fences and recovering grass in eroded areas. He gave training courses on veld management to Africans from other mission farms as well as the reserves. Creina was put in charge of 'home industries', which involved the female tenants in basket-weaving and bead-making.

Alcock's chief project was the cattle cooperative. He persuaded the mission tenants to pool their 700 head of cattle into one large herd. In this way, communal land could be fenced and the livestock could be moved around to graze, thus enabling the grass to recover. In effect, the tenants exchanged their tangible stock, cattle, for intangible stock, shares, in the cooperative. Their cows were valued and they were given credit accordingly. They could withdraw money, or stock to the appropriate value, by notifying an elected farm committee, which was given responsibility for the herd and which managed rotational grazing. As such, the cattle-owning tenants became shareholders of CAP. The idea was that, should the farm become viable, its profits would be distributed among the stockowners proportionally to their investment in CAP.

Although the grazing recovered well, the cattle cooperative was never an economic success. Funding was always a problem, although in 1969 the Chairman's Fund of the Anglo American Corporation and Misereor, a German charity, awarded generous grants to CAP. There were other difficulties, too: in 1968, as a result of the government's resettlement policy, about half of the African tenants on the farm – those not employed by the CAP or by the mission itself – were forced into resettlement villages. This compelled Alcock to reconsider CAP's priorities and functions.

By far the biggest problem was Alcock himself. He was an outspoken critic of the church; he was forever castigating the clergy in the most colourful of terms for its perceived lack of support for his initiative; and he seemed to go out of his way to antagonise the Franciscans at Maria Ratschitz. The priests, for their part, frowned upon his divorce, and resented his atheism which, with typical dryness, Brown noted 'wasn't the best kind of foundation' for good relations.[13]

The tensions between Alcock and the Franciscans, in particular the landlord of Maria Ratschitz, Monsignor Banks, boiled over in 1974. These developments were complicated by the emergence of factions among the farm's African tenants: a group opposed to CAP, headed by the former chairman of the farm committee who had been fired by Alcock, backed the Franciscans. As friction mounted on the farm, the atmosphere turned sinister. In August, a young Catholic boy started a fire which destroyed large sections of the farm.

Alcock kept Brown abreast of developments, and sought his advice. Brown told him that he should 'draw the teeth' of the Franciscans by giving 'them everything they want which [would] not affect your continued successful running of the farm'. Alcock needed their acquiescence even if he could not win their support. Brown concluded: 'The work itself seems to me to be so important that – from this safe distance! – I would strongly recommend one last try.'[14]

On a visit to Johannesburg the following month, Brown spoke to Paul Henwood of the Anglo American Chairman's Fund about the problems at Maria Ratschitz. He expressed his hope to Henwood that Anglo would be 'sympathetic to the idea of buying the place' once Alcock's lease, due to expire at the end of the year, was up.[15] Henwood responded that such a purchase did not fall within the remit of Anglo's Special Projects. Moreover, further financial support from Anglo would depend on the CAP board giving a clear indication about the future of Maria Ratschitz.[16]

In the meantime, Chief Buthelezi, who sat on the board, had caught wind of the conflicts at Maria Ratschitz and went to see the board's chair, Duchesne Grice. The latter had forged a close relationship with Buthelezi, and later advised him on the 'consolidation' of KwaZulu. He served on the Buthelezi Commission (1980-1982) as a member of its Central Working Group and convened the Constitutional Committee of Buthelezi's Indaba in 1986.

Buthelezi was due to visit to Europe at the end of the year, and he asked Grice whether a meeting with the Pope might help engineer a rapprochement between the Franciscans and Alcock. Grice thought this a good idea, and elaborated his views in a follow-up letter to Buthelezi:

> I think you might go … further and ask in view of the practical importance of Ratschitz that in the event of reconciliation proving impossible, the possibility of the transfer of responsibility for Ratschitz from the Franciscans to the OMI [Oblates of Mary Immaculate] (Hurley's Order) be contemplated, if it can be shown this will help. And, finally, if this is not possible, that CAP and its supporters be given the opportunity of say, one year, of finding someone … who could purchase Ratschitz with the object of leasing it to CAP.[17]

Grice hoped that the Catholic Church would retain ownership of the land, or at least continue its involvement, since this would give the directors of CAP the time and opportunity to improve the management of project. It would also allow Alcock, 'in conjunction with KwaZulu, to extend the educational services we believe CAP could provide'.

Douglas Blausten, a young Briton who had worked at Maria Ratschitz during his gap year, reported back to Brown on Buthelezi's trip. At a special meeting of the British Council of Churches, Buthelezi spoke strongly in favour of CAP and praised the role of the Chairman's Fund in funding the scheme. He conveyed the same message to audiences in Uppsala and Bonn. In Rome, Blausten dined with Buthelezi, whom he had met during his time at Maria Ratschitz, and the pair 'talked long into the night about CAP and Neil Alcock's value': 'The only white Zulu we can really trust,' Buthelezi is alleged to have said of Alcock, 'And yet the Europeans are intent on getting rid of him, or even breaking him.'[18] Buthelezi's reception by the Pope was friendly enough, but, Brown noted in reply to Blausten, it seemed 'highly unlikely that anything [would] be done about [Monsignor] Banks'.[19]

At any rate, the divides that had emerged between CAP's factions were to prove unbridgeable. Before the end of the year, the CAP board decided to terminate operations at Maria Ratschitz and appoint an advisory committee to plot the way forward. The committee was to consider the possibility of continuing CAP's operations at another locality, or, should that not prove feasible, to advise on the sale of assets, the reimbursement of donors and the

future provision for home industries dependent on CAP at Maria
Ratschitz.

Archbishop Hurley asked Brown to serve on the committee.
Brown had met Hurley back in 1950, aboard the *Stirling Castle*,
when both were making return trips to South Africa from England.
The young bishop's easy air of humanity made an impression on
Brown. They spent a good deal of time together on board, talking
and amusing themselves with rounds of quoits, and quickly struck
up a warm acquaintance. So when Brown agreed to serve on the
advisory committee, he joked with his old friend that 'the loyalties
forged in the red hot furnace of deck quoits competitions don't
break easily'.[20] The other committee members were Grice, Professor JD Scott (the Department of Agriculture's official in charge
of research stations in Natal who had praised CAP's reclamation
work at Maria Ratschitz), Elliot Mngadi and Roger Lamb (an
accountant who kept CAP's books).

Brown was genuinely impressed with what he viewed as the
'remarkable success achieved by Neil ... in inspiring people and
rehabilitating land' at Maria Ratschitz.[21] And, even after Hurley
had informed him of the board's decision to quit Maria Ratschitz,
Brown hoped that funds could be found to buy the land and continue CAP's work there. If that failed, he told Paul Henwood, 'we
must look around to find some derelict area near or in KwaZulu,
where the same thing can start again'.[22]

While the advisory committee was meeting on a Thursday morning in January 1975, Alcock phoned Brown to say that that he had
found just such an area. About 30km from the town of Weenen, on
the road to Tugela Ferry and adjoining the Msinga district of
KwaZulu, Alcock had seen three farms – Lorraine, the Spring and
Koornspruit – covering some 6 000 acres. They were owned by the
same farmer, whose condition of sale was that they should all be
bought together. The farms were badly eroded and chronically
overgrazed. In fact, they looked like semi-desert, prompting one
CAP staff member to refer to them as 'Mdukatshani' – the place of
vanished grasses.

Brown had his doubts about the site, in particular about rain-
fall, access to water and the quality of the soil. It was, moreover, 'in

a grim part of the world'; 'step over the boundary,' he told Blausten, 'and you're in hell, and it goes for miles.'[23] But he could recognise its advantages: it wasn't far from Maria Ratschitz, which would facilitate a smoother move; it was unoccupied; and because it was run-down it would be cheap. And so, he told Blausten: 'My present view is that if a place as awful as this one sounds to be can be turned into something that looks fairly good the impact on Black land use and social rehabilitation could be much greater than it could be from Maria Ratschitz.'[24]

A few weeks later Brown visited the farms, and surveyed them on foot with Alcock. He thought them fairly typical of the neglected thornveld areas surrounding Weenen which had been used as 'labour farms' by white farmers before the system of labour tenancy was abolished. They were badly run-down, but they provided an 'ideal opportunity' for CAP to tackle a land-reclamation challenge: 'If CAP can succeed in rehabilitating this land,' he wrote in a report after his visit, 'there is no telling what influence [it] might have on the rehabilitation of land and people in KwaZulu.'[25]

With Brown's backing, the board agreed to the farm's purchase. Alcock auctioned off some of CAP's chief assets – namely, some of its 800 head of cattle – to raise the necessary funds. At the end, CAP was left with 500 cattle, but, because the price of cattle declined sharply in early 1975, the sales did not yield as much income as expected. Alcock believed that it would be futile to sell the remaining herd, since running the cattle cooperative would still be CAP's chief occupation at the new site. Some members of the advisory committee, like Lamb, felt that Alcock should sell more cattle in order to get the enterprise on a sounder financial footing. As it was, after its lease at Maria Ratschitz expired, CAP owed the bank more than R51 000, including R33 800 for the purchase of the new farm. In due course, the Anglo American Chairman's Fund came to the rescue: it gave CAP a grant of R190 000 over a five-year period beginning in 1976.

Brown was excited by the potential of the new venture, both agriculturally, in terms of development, and politically, for he believed it could, in some small way, reverse the effects of rural dispossession wrought by the Nationalists' land policy. From early

1975, he began visiting Mdukatshani regularly. To Douglas Blausten, he described his activities with characteristic humour:

> I spent a day-and-a-half at the new site soon after I last wrote to you. I slept on a major ant highway. All night long they walked in at one end of my bed and out at the other. Next day I inspected the higher reaches of the farm, where the ticks have never tasted good, white meat before. They have now. The week after that I had tick-bite fever. Last week I was back there again. Today I was helping Neil sell cattle at the Elandslaagte sale. You can't say I'm not trying!'[26]

Having had time to brood on it, Alcock found the Elandslaagte sale galling. From telephone calls with Brown, he gained the impression that Brown wanted to sell more cows, calves and oxen – about 70 in total – on 18 March. Meanwhile, Alcock had made plans to be away from Mdukatshani between 10 and 20 March, since he had secured a meeting with Chief Matanzima in the Transkei. This also meant that he would miss a meeting of the farm committee, onto which Brown and Elliot Mngadi had been co-opted, on 19 March.

Alcock wrote to Brown, noting that the sale of stock in February had resulted in a loss of R9 000. 'Can we really afford to lose another R9 000 by selling a lot more stock at the current prices?' he asked.[27] He felt that it would be 'suicidal to sell our stock on a falling market'. In his experience, cattle prices tended to fall between December and April, then pick up again until November. As such, he was against an immediate sale.

Brown was irked by the tone and tenor of Alcock's letter, which had been preceded by an equally plaintive and accusatory missive to CAP's directors and farm committee members the previous day.[28] He told Alcock that such letters did not 'do anyone any good', and proceeded to justify his position.[29] It was necessary to sell the cattle at Elandslaagte in February to avoid the tax implications of selling them after the end of that month, and to guarantee the initial cash payment on Mdukatshani. Brown was not opposed to delaying the sale of further stock. He explained to Alcock: 'I am not opposed to postponement. I don't want to lose the farm; and when it seemed that we might have to find the money before the end of March, I was certainly opposed to it.'

This was the first of several run-ins with Alcock over CAP which dampened Brown's enthusiasm for the project. Early the following year, Blausten tried to convince Brown to make himself eligible for the chairmanship of CAP. He felt Brown would 'strike a balance between the "Anglo/Duchesne" [Grice] school and the bare foot tick bitten school of warriors [sic]'.[30] Brown dismissed the idea, stating that he was 'not a CAP fanatic' and that he found Neil 'very taxing to work with'.[31] Although he thought CAP was engaged in worthwhile work, his assessment of its importance in the wider political scheme of things had sobered.

He doubted whether CAP would 'have any influence on the immediate course of events'. Certainly, it had 'something new to offer our society', but it was too isolated to be meaningfully involved in a 'period of change', should one come. Brown believed his personal contribution would be made elsewhere: '[I]f there is to be change I just hope that I might be able to do something towards seeing that a reasonably decent non-racial society is what comes out of it.' In sum, he was prepared to continue to act from his position on the farm committee 'as some sort of intermediary between the tick-bitten brigade and the money-bags', but he was 'not prepared to do it as chairman'.

* * *

CAP itself was plagued by problems from the outset. In the first of their circular letters, Alcock and his wife, Creina, commented:

> If we had had the choice of land anywhere in KwaZulu to try out our ideas we would have chosen the worst bit of all, Msinga. Nowhere else is there such a population, such poverty, such staggering soil erosion. Msinga is a byword for destruction and hopelessness.[32]

The people of Msinga were not always welcoming. Because the pre-

vious owner had not lived on-site, Africans were used to crossing
over from the reserve to graze their cattle, goats and donkeys. All
this changed when CAP fenced off the farm. Even so, the fence was
regularly cut, and stock theft became rampant. Disease, too, took
its toll: in the first year at Mdukatshani, as many cattle were taken
away by heartwater, a tick-borne ailment, as they were by thieves. In
short, the cattle cooperative was a disaster, and CAP was forced to
reorder its priorities. It set up smaller projects, like vegetable gardens, and provided welfare services to the local community, such
as adult education classes and assistance with obtaining pensions.[33]

Anglo American, meanwhile, was concerned that its generous
stipend was not being used as intended. The basis of the agreement
between Alcock and the Chairman's Fund was that, over five years,
building on an initial cattle herd of about 480 head, the farm would
become self-supporting. After a stock count in May 1976, Anton
Hlongwane, who served as secretary to the farm committee, told
Brown that there were only 210 cattle in the beef herd and 30 in the
dairy.[34] In other words, CAP had lost half of its livestock. Alcock
argued that the only way to secure the livestock, and to find out
where they were going, was by establishing a relationship of trust
with the residents of Msinga. But, as Brown noted dryly to Blausten:
'The trouble is that by the time one does find out, there may not be
any left.'[35] In the meantime, CAP's main negotiable asset was drain-
ing away, and along with it the ability to pay out any members of the
cooperative who might want to withdraw their money.

According to Brown, these cattle losses aggravated a difference
of emphasis between Alcock and Roger Lamb on the financial side.
For his part, Brown wrote to Blausten in May, he found himself
'standing between Roger [Lamb] and Neil';[36] Lamb was too much
of a book-keeper for him, and Alcock, with his disdain for book-
keeping, was insufficiently attentive to the economic viability of the
project. Brown summed up his thoughts:

> I do not think Mdukatshani can be regarded as a bottomless
> pit into which white business concerns, or even overseas and
> local welfare concerns, should be expected to put money
> indefinitely. There must be at least some evidence that, 'wel-

fare' work apart, the farm can be rehabilitated and provide the people on it with a reasonable livelihood. Otherwise how the hell is it going to serve as an example to anywhere else? Vast parts of Southern Africa are in a worse state than Mdukatshani from the agricultural and conservation point of view, and something must be done to try to save them. Mdukatshani is surely intended to show that it can be done, by involving the local people in the rescue operation, convincing them in the process that, by succeeding, they will have shown the world that they are as capable as anyone of a doing a tough job effectively. Confidence in themselves will be restored and a new type of Black rural person will have emerged, independent and with his manhood vindicated.

Another problem at Mdukatshani was the constant threat of violence from Msinga next door. With its countless warring factions, Msinga was a bloody, hostile, hate-filled place, and its brutality often spilled over into Mdukatshani. Initially, CAP's black staff, rather than Alcock and his white assistants, were the targets of aggression. On their first Christmas at Mdukatshani, Neil and Creina woke to a burst of gunfire, which Creina described in one of her newsletters:

> Afraid of hut burnings women have evacuated, hiding their possessions in the bush and praying it won't rain … Children have scattered and disappeared … 'You needn't worry,' Black friends assured us. 'Whites are royal game. Nobody will touch you.'[37]

CAP's African workers feared for their lives much of the time. In 1976, the manager of the farm committee was held up and assaulted by gangsters from Msinga. He quit the project soon thereafter. Another African employee, who had served as CAP's book-keeper from Maria Ratschitz days, fled Mdukatshani in terror in 1978. Gradually, those members of the farm committee who had moved from Maria Ratschitz to Mdukatshani were replaced by local men from Msinga. But the spectre of bloodshed was always present.

It would be quite understandable had this state of affairs, in which CAP's black workers were more susceptible to attack than its white employees, bred a degree of racial resentment. Certainly, there were tensions between Alcock and his staff members, both black and white, but these arose principally from the difficulty of working with him. He could be dogmatic; he could be truculent; and at times he seemed accountable to no one but himself.

Lamb thought, somewhat unjustly in Brown's view, that the blacks on Mdukatshani were 'Neil's teaboys'.[38] Brown feared that Alcock steamrollered his views through the farm committee. Hlongwane, in Brown's view, was not a very forceful personality, and was unlikely to out-argue Neil on any point. The farm committee did manage to arrive at some sort of consensus most of the time, but this was possibly a 'consensus of exhaustion, everyone having been beaten to their knees by the interminability of Neil's rhetoric'.[39]

The members of the farm committee, who were predominantly black, also ended up carrying the can for CAP, since Alcock spent a great deal of time away from the farm, leaving Michael Mabaso to oversee the agricultural projects and other committee members to handle the stock problems. It was difficult for them to get the police to be proactive in following up charges of stock theft. In fact, Brown claimed, the difficulty for CAP's black farm committee members of dealing with the whole edifice of white authority was one reason why Alcock should spend more time at Mdukatshani.

There was another reason why Brown was sceptical about Alcock's absences, since many of them were occasioned by his desire to strike up direct links with the KwaZulu authorities in order to sell them his vision of land rehabilitation in the reserves. Brown wrote to Blausten that 'Neil's involvement with KwaZulu mystifies me'.[40] Although Brown supported Alcock's ideas in principle, he had 'reservations' about 'work[ing] with KwaZulu', and would only sanction it 'provided this involves no acceptance of the present dispensation as adequate'.[41] In fact, Brown's qualms about KwaZulu ran deeper. When Alcock suggested replacing Bill Bhengu (formerly Chief Albert Luthuli's attorney and LP National Vice-President, by now practising law in Durban) on the advisory committee with somebody from Msinga, Brown commented: 'This will just turn the whole thing into an adjunct of KwaZulu with no representative voice of the Black urban community to tell the local community and the board ... of what is going on where the real pressures for change are building up.'[42] With one foot in Mdukatshani and the other in Pietermaritzburg, Brown had a more balanced perspective than Alcock on the political relevance of KwaZulu to CAP's work.

In the meantime, disputes between Alcock and his staff at Mdukatshani continued to flare. In October 1976, Brown complained to Mngadi that there were 'more arguments and rows', and that he had been asked by Alcock to broker a peace.[43] The ill feeling persisted through the following year; in September 1977, Pat Macdonald, the white secretary and medical assistant at CAP, told Brown that '[d]espite things going well superficially, there is still a lot of tension on the farm'.[44] Stingingly, she suggested that Alcock appeared 'to have no discretion', nor did he 'understand the meaning of integrity'. Alcock, in contrast, felt that he bore the overwhelming responsibility for all tasks on the farm and that white workers in particular were not pulling their weight on the administrative side.[45]

As for CAP's actual work, the depletion of the herd and the collapse of the cattle cooperative mean that, for the remainder of the decade, Alcock focused on working with local communities in Msinga and Tugela Estates.[46] He instituted a weekly lecture series on farming methods for subsistence farmers. He allowed them to dip their cattle on the farm and graze them there, provided they helped him in exchange by building fences, making firebreaks and patrolling. They also cooperated on a number of schemes, such as the erection of a water wheel to pump water from the Tugela River and a community project to dig furrows and lay pipes which carried water to the gardens adjoining their homesteads. CAP also opened a school for local children.

Mdukatshani became less and less safe as gunmen from Msinga wandered freely across the farm, setting up ambushes on the crossroads. In 1979, Creina quoted the poet Roy Campbell in her newsletter: 'The hurricanes of chaos have begun to buzz like hornets in the shifting sands.'[47] Neil became increasingly involved in mediating between the rival factions responsible for this terror, which eventually cost him his life.

On 28 September 1983, he organised a ceasefire meeting in the Tugela Ferry courthouse for the parties involved in two wars – one between the residents of Mashunka and Ngubo in Msinga, and the other between the residents of Ndlela and Mhlangaan. Driving the Mashunka and Mhlangaan delegates back home in his microbus, Alcock was ambushed by Ndlela men who were lying in wait for their Mhlangaan enemies. He was felled by a single bullet from an automatic rifle.

After Alcock's death, Brown continued to play a central role in CAP by providing strategic direction both to the farm committee and the advisory committee over the next decade. He went on to chair the board of what became known as the CAP Farm Trust. Creina often turned to him for advice on matters both agricultural and domestic: Brown had a good rapport with the Alcock boys, Marc and Rauri, who spent time at Shinglewood in their school holidays. Creina's mother, Elsie Bond, told Brown that 'Creina trusts you [and] has a regard for you, as she has for none other of Neil's friends'.[48]

In due course, the farm committee would come to occupy itself not only with the running of the farm but also with engaging residents of Msinga on national and international affairs. In 1985, for example, Brown described a farm committee meeting to Marc (nicknamed 'GG' for the government garage trucks which arrived to carry out a forced removal the day he was born): '… [W]e had a long talk about current affairs, trying to get the Msinga people up-to-date on what was going on in the world and in South Africa.'[49]

In 1987, three members of the farm committee, caught up in the war between the Mthembu and Mchunu, were murdered. Several others, together with a number of CAP employees, were forced to abandon the farm and go into hiding. This severely hampered the project's operations, and, in a remarkably frank self-assessment penned that year, CAP's failures were acknowledged. CAP had failed to:

– establish independent small farmers able to live off the land
– establish the minimum size necessary for a garden to keep a local family self-sufficient in food

> – [and] make agriculture an attractive alternative to the
> city, especially for the young men.[50]

The causes of these failures were many and varied. Had Alcock
been alive, he might have lain part of the blame at the door of what
he called the 'liberal establishment'.

In an angry letter to Brown in 1976, less than two years after
CAP had relocated to Mdukatshani, Alcock set out his stall.
Through CAP he aimed to show that 'cooperation with the masses
was simple', even in 'the most inflammable rural area in SA'.[51] He
believed this had been 'proved as far as the blacks are concerned',
but that 'getting the white [liberal] establishment to see any worth
in the experiment' had been a 'dismal failure'. The latter, he
claimed somewhat misleadingly, was unwilling to 'offer time, research or money'. He ascribed white liberals' alleged lack of interest, and that of some black liberals too, to their misdiagnosis of the
political situation. 'As you know,' he told Brown, 'I have been out of
step with practically all opinion in white SA,' explaining further:

> You, Paton, Grice, Bhengu, Mngadi & the rest of our gener-
> ation are hoping for non-violent ordered change through
> negotiations with the upper bracket blacks of SA – the so
> called leader class people who can be reached through the
> Urban Foundation[,] [the Institute of] Race Relations[,]
> SA Foundation & such like bodies. A potential upper black
> middle class is in this way being promoted by giving them
> fringe benefits in the laager.[52]

Such efforts were misdirected. They flowed from a 'doomed policy'
which was likely to cause the 'neglected mob' to rise up against
privilege, both white and black.

Alcock continued, thundering:

> Because we don't want our privilege destroyed we have the
> petty gestures that we don't want discrimination. Churches
> fighting to have a few wealthy blacks admitted to private
> schools & other evasive gestures. To sum up I have tried to

explain to you how frustrated I am by the part time [sic] dabbling that the liberal section of our white population indulge in [which] is worse than useless.

Was the accusation of 'part-time dabbling' a veiled reproach to Brown? It is true that Brown's commitment to CAP wavered at times. This had less to with halting support for its core work, which he thought important, than with his ambivalence towards Alcock, from whom he preferred to keep a 'safe distance'.[53] In terms of character, Brown and Alcock were poles apart. Where Alcock was emotional and given to histrionic outbursts, lashing out against those he thought had let him down, Brown was rational and measured. While Alcock was abrasive, Brown could be blunt, but he was never uncivil. Where Alcock was single-minded in pursuing his vision, maniacally pouring all his energy into a single cause, Brown preferred to channel his efforts against apartheid in a variety of directions.

For all his cautiousness around Alcock, Brown respected him. In his post-mortem tribute to Alcock, published in *Reality*, Brown called him 'a man of ideas, a great innovator'; his death would be mourned by friends, 'not least [because] while he was alive, whatever you were doing in your own particular area of opposition to apartheid, you always felt that ... Neil was doing more'.[54]

Before one visit to Mdukatshani, Brown told his old cellmate, Hans Meidner, that he didn't relish the idea of going, 'partly because Alcock leads a life of poverty & makes me feel that I should be doing the same'.[55] Did Brown's circumspection stem from the feeling that, as a white person opposed to apartheid, Alcock spoke and acted with greater authority for having renounced the privileges of whiteness? Perhaps there was an element of that. On returning from one visit to Mdukatshani, Elliot Mngadi reported back to Brown, roaring with laughter, 'Oh, how Neil hates us all!' Reflecting on this, Brown acknowledged to Bunty Biggs, the Quaker social worker who had been part of the Pietermaritzburg Liberal network before settling abroad, that 'we haven't made the sacrifices [Neil] has'.[56]

However, Brown was under no illusions about the broader political significance of CAP, unlike Alcock, who seemed to believe that CAP was at the coalface of change.

In one of his several broadsides against the directors of CAP, delivered at the height of the troubles at Maria Ratschitz, Alcock charged:

> Our Directors are all men who recognize the need for change in South Africa. Won't you then face up to what change really means [?] It is not just the polishing of a corner here, an improvement there. It is an upheaval that leaves things different from the way they were before. Those who have criticized us have made the basis of their complaints the fact that things are not what they were. Of course not. We are involved in change. Those with privilege fear change. The trivial details of the petty squabbling at Ratschitz are simply outward signs of the trauma of change.[57]

Alcock's letter was a rather self-serving gloss on the melée at Maria Ratschitz. His analysis of what the 'white liberal establishment' was trying to do – that is, promote a black middle class whose members might serve as negotiating partners in peace talks down the line – was correct. However, he was quite incorrect to include Brown, and indeed several other former Liberals, among those establishment figures. Rather, he should have identified the likes of Anglo American mining magnate, Harry Oppenheimer, whose liberalism, along with that of other English-speaking industrialists seeking to effect reform through the Urban Foundation, was more in the mould of the Progressive Party than the Liberal Party. Be that as it may, Alcock misunderstood the macrocosmic nature of the changes to come, how they would come about and how former Liberals like Brown would be placed to influence them when they did. Brown, partly perhaps because he had been the leader of a national political party, with the 'long view' this afforded him, did comprehend, even if he was unsure of what his own political role would be in the circumstances.

So if the transition away from apartheid was to occur not through an agrarian revolution but rather through a brokered settlement at the level of 'high' politics, why was Brown doing nothing to reoccupy the political space he was forced to desert in the mid-1960s? That was the question on Alcock's mind in 1979 when he wrote to Brown and accused him of 'helping to create a leadership vacuum in South Africa' by 'baulking at the sort of action [in which] you indulged in the 1960s'.[58] The time was ripe, Alcock argued, for Brown to revive the Liberal Party in some form. Was he 'baulking' because he feared another ban? '[I]t must be awful to invite a repeat dose [of banning orders] by continuing to fight,' Alcock ventured, 'but I do not think you have it in you to give up forever.' He ended by imploring Brown to use his 'talents & experience to pull together a small determined group of know-ledgeable people' to have talks with the Prime Minister, PW Botha, and 'try to stop the suicide train'.

Even by Alcock's standards, the tone of his letter was provoca-tive. In part, he was aggrieved by Brown's decision not to make himself available for the chairmanship of AFRA, the organisation formed by ex-Liberals in October 1979 to halt the eviction of farm labour tenants in Weenen. Alcock witnessed the effects of these removals first-hand from his vantage point at Mdukatshani, and it was through him that the initiative was kick-started. In fact, Brown assumed the chairmanship in January the following year, but, battle-weary from his dealings with Alcock through CAP, he was ini-tially reluctant to play a leading role.

Despite the provocation, Brown responded thoughtfully and at length. The questions raised by Alcock, Brown assured him, had 'been very much on my mind since my ban ended, and perhaps particularly during the past six months or year'.[59] His disinclination to restart the Liberal Party, or to form a similar body, wasn't be-cause he feared being re-banned: 'Of course I don't want to be banned again, but I don't think the possibility of that happening would put me off doing something which I thought would be *effec-tive* in ensuring our ideas a reasonable chance of surviving here.'

Still, the two banning orders had taken their toll. From his own experience, Brown believed that 'a ban *does* have an effect on any-one who is not a fanatic, whether their fanaticism is religious, nationalist or communist'. Somebody like him, 'lacking the same fervour, and whose ideas, or so [I] like to think, are based more-or-less on reason, begins to wonder what the hell to do'. In his case, the questioning was reinforced by 'what might be regarded as a rather sentimental attachment to my recollections of the Liberal Party'. He found it difficult to get enthusiastic about any other political party opposed to apartheid, since they all seemed 'very much a second-best'. The revival of the LP was a non-starter, at least in present circumstances. This was partly because the law prevented it, and Brown was unwilling to compromise on non-racial membership, but largely because the political terrain had changed so much since the LP closed down:

> In the public political arena you now have a PRP [Progressive Reform Party] which ... might be getting somewhere, Inkatha, the Black Consciousness Movement, the Labour Party, the pro- and anti-SA Indian Council groups. In all of them, probably, you would find people who were members of the Liberal Party or who might have been by now. I very much doubt, however, whether you would persuade many such people, at this stage, to leave whichever of those organisations they might belong to, to join another political *party* ... Most of them would, I think, argue that the political scene is sufficiently cluttered up with political organisations at present and that they feel they are more likely to achieve something through working through the existing organisations to which they already belong ... For these reasons I doubt if this is the right moment to try to start a new political organisation which would be competing for support in the public field, in spite of the fact that one has real reservations about all the others which are doing so.

One possibility that Brown had discussed with Ernie and Jill Wentzel when he was in Johannesburg the previous December was the formation of a non-racial pressure group for democratic change. Unfortunately the history of open pressure groups in South Africa wasn't promising: the Torch Commando, the Anti-Republican League and the Covenant Movement, for example, were all short-lived, and none of them 'achieved what they were supposed to achieve'.

Forging consensus over economic policy would also pose problems:

> I was discussing a possible new LP with Jack and Beryl
> [Unterhalter] in Johannesburg late last year and this was
> the first thing we talked about. We all agreed that the capi-
> talist system had been a miserable failure in giving everyone
> in South Africa a reasonable slice of the cake, and that a
> policy much more radical than the old Liberal Party policy
> was now needed – much higher taxes, redistribution of
> land, a programme designed to effect a massive transfer of
> wealth from rich to poor, which means, more or less, from
> white to black. How much potential 'liberal' support in
> other organisations would a policy statement as radical as
> that frighten off? After all, both Inkatha and the PRP are
> committed to a free enterprise system.

The following factors then, were, in Brown's view, stumbling blocks
to the re-institutionalisation of the Liberal Party in some guise: the
law against non-racial political organisations; the proliferation of
new political organisations over the preceding decade, some of
which had absorbed Liberal support; the difficulties associated with
starting a pressure group; and the broad range of opinion within
the liberal fold on how to effect socio-economic transformation.

What was to be done instead? Liberals should continue to push
their ideas through 'whatever organisations are around and reasonably sympathetic', like the SAIRR and the SACC. For Alcock the
visionary, the maverick who believed in grand not 'petty gestures',
the practical liberal who equated change with 'upheaval', this
Fabianism did not hold much appeal.

In the end, personal issues locked on to a difference of opinion
between Brown and Alcock on the role of liberals in promoting
change, and produced a gradual parting of the ways. However,
Brown went on to devote a great deal of time and energy to
Alcock's brainchild – AFRA – which became, after the Liberal
Party, the most important institutional involvement of his career.

BACK TO THE LAND: THE ASSOCIATION FOR RURAL ADVANCEMENT
1979-1990

Brown supported Neil Alcock's ideas about agricultural development, which he thought would help to modernise African farming and rehabilitate land in the reserves, thus making both people and land more productive. In his correspondence Brown indicated that, were these ideas to be replicated throughout the countryside, they might engender a greater sense of independence among rural Africans. Of the political impact of this development work, whether it might be used to mobilise communities, promote a culture of assertiveness about land rights and agrarian reform, and thereby serve to influence change, Brown was less persuaded. He believed CAP was 'too isolated'; he mistrusted Alcock's overtures to Buthelezi, fearing they would turn the project into an accessory of the administrative apparatus of apartheid; and he was convinced that pressure for change would come primarily from the urban areas.

This was a fair assessment. Not since the 1920s, when the Industrial and Commercial Workers' Union transformed itself into a strong rural resistance movement, garnering support from both the reserves and African labour tenants and workers on white-owned farms, had rural Africans united in a nationwide organisation. For their part, the national political organisations had failed to tap into rural discontent. As Nelson Mandela later conceded in his autobiography, 'In general, we did not penetrate the countryside, a historical weakness of the ANC.'[1]

Furthermore, after a decade of muted protest between 1964

and 1974, there were tremors in the urban areas by the mid-1970s. Militant strike action by black workers signalled the turbulence to come. In 1976, Soweto erupted over the use of Afrikaans as a medium of instruction in schools. Townships became a locus of rebellion against apartheid, while new community and civic organisations were formed to channel urban dissent.

The growth of black trade unionism, the rise of civic radicalism, and the escalation of urban protest in the 1970s and 1980s meant that broad-based movements opposed to apartheid, such as the United Democratic Front (UDF), formed in 1983, found their natural constituency in the urban areas. As a result, they tended to neglect rural concerns. During the period of tentative political and economic reform initiated by Prime Minister PW Botha between 1979 and 1984, mainstream liberals – what Alcock called the 'white liberal establishment' – were equally focused on urban issues. They channelled their energies into bodies like the Urban Foundation. Founded by Progressive-minded liberal businesspeople in 1976, it sought to promote a black middle class and improve living conditions in the townships.

For all this activity on the urban front, rural South Africa was in crisis, and most political opponents of apartheid, be they liberal or leftist, were looking the other way. The implementation of separate development, and the imposition of homeland citizenship on all Africans in 1970, unleashed forced removals on an unprecedented scale. Between 1960 and 1983, some 3.5 million people were relocated in accordance with the battery of laws governing removal and resettlement.[2] In the countryside, African labour tenants on white farms, freeholders living in black spots and black squatters in 'white' rural areas were all required, by law, to move out of 'white' South Africa.

* * *

For Brown, the policy of forced removals and resettlements was 'one of the worst aspects of apartheid'.[3] Once his ban was lifted, he got in touch with some of the communities that he and Elliot Mngadi had assisted during the Liberal Party's campaign against black spot removals in the 1950s and 1960s. In *Reality*, he told readers what had become of those residents forcibly removed from Charlestown, whose experiences had been movingly related by Alan Paton in *The Charlestown Story*.[4]

The inhabitants of Mngadi's own community, Roosboom, where the Northern Natal African Landowners' Association (NNALA) held its famous prayer meeting in 1963, were eventually moved to Ezakheni between 1975 and 1977. Brown visited Mngadi in mid-1976. Ordinarily, he would have gone straight to Roosboom and met Mngadi there, but, on this occasion, before Brown's visit, Mngadi wrote to him on the back of a telegraph form: 'I am writing this letter at the Post Office because I have no home. It is a strange experience to be without a home. But please don't worry, I will pull through.'[5] The two eventually met at the Ladysmith Post Office, where Brown tried to persuade Mngadi to write an account of his removal. Mngadi was reluctant: 'Peter,' he said, 'what is the point in my writing about this? There is nothing new for me to say. This removal has been just as terrible as we always said a removal must be. It is just terrible – and that is all there is to it.' So 'the sharp prick of [his] friend's experience' having reawakened him to 'the awful implications' of removals, Brown wrote about it himself in *Reality*.[6]

Ezakheni was 24 kilometres to the north of Ladysmith, twice as far from the town as Roosboom. Mngadi was given a plot 15 by 20 metres in size. On it stood a 'flatcraft' hut (3 by 7 metres). There was no floor, just bare earth. The wind whistled underneath the ridging. It was an icebox in winter, Brown noted, and would probably be an oven in summer. In the corner of the plot furthest away from the flatcraft was a sentry-box size building, inside which were a lavatory and a shower. The water supply had been cut off since Mngadi moved in.

At Roosboom, the residents had lived on half-acre plots. They built wattle-and-daub houses, but at Ezakheni the soil was not suitable for wattle-and-daub. There were no schools at Ezakheni. The cost of transport into Ladysmith was double what it had been at Roosboom. Livestock were not allowed: Mngadi was forced to sell the nine head of cattle which had provided his family with milk. Brown concluded:

Roosboom was a small, intimate and cosy community where everyone knew everyone else. Ezakheni is a soulless human dump, spreading over the countryside like a sore, destined to house undisclosed thousands of Black people whose breadwinners will either commute or migrate to work for White South Africa.

Mngadi was someone Brown truly admired. He had worked indefatigably for the Party in opposing black spot removals in the 1950s and 1960s, firstly as the Liberals' own black spot campaign organiser, and then as Secretary of the Party-sponsored NNALA, founded in 1958. Like Brown, Mngadi had been detained in 1960 and had later served two five-year bans. Mngadi was 'a man of generous spirit', 'enterprising' and 'industrious'; and 'for exhibiting these great qualities,' Brown wrote ruefully, 'apartheid, in his late middle-age, has rewarded him with that flatcraft hut, that 15 m x 20 m plot, and that sentry box.'

The injustice done to Elliot Mngadi and his family brought home to Brown the iniquity of forced removals. It reminded him of the pioneering work done by the NNALA, and convinced him of the need to continue its legacy. As it happened, through his involvement with CAP, Brown's attention had been alerted to another equally miserable facet of the state's policy on resettlement. When he took CAP to Mdukatshani, Neil Alcock had to deal with the consequences of the Labour Control Board's 'five-family edict'. In those magisterial districts where they operated, Labour Control Boards could impose an arbitrary quota on the number of African labour tenant families allowed to live on white farms. In Weenen, the number was set at five families.

It was difficult for the evictees to take with them their one substantial asset, cattle, when they were evicted. Those parts of the KwaZulu homeland adjoining Weenen, where they resettled, were overgrazed, and their cattle often wandered back to where they had come from. As a result, the cattle were impounded, and this led to clashes with white farmers.

On one of his visits to Mdukatshani, Brown was told by Alcock about the evictions and the abuses to which African farm labourers were subjected by their white employers. Alcock proposed the establishment of an organisation to protect the workers' rights, and Brown approached the Progressive MP, Ray Swart, for advice.[7]

In the meantime, Alcock alerted his old liberal network in Pietermaritzburg to these problems, and called for a meeting to consider what could be done. On 4 October, a group of 36 people met in the hall of the Bantu Presbyterian Church in Loop Street. Billed as a 'meeting of concerned people dealing with the Natal rural situation', the gathering included former Liberal Party members like Brown, John Aitchison and Colin Gardner.[8] There was also a strong church presence: the meeting was chaired by the Anglican Bishop of Natal, Philip Russell, and attended by Bishop Ken Hallowes, who had served on the board of CAP. Two Natal-based ecumenical organisations, Diakonia and the Pietermaritzburg Agency for Christian Social Awareness (PACSA), hosted the event.

PACSA, it will be recalled, was formed earlier in 1979 by Peter Kerchhoff, as a sort of legatee to the banned Christian Institute (CI). The CI had been run locally by Cosmas Desmond, the fiery PAC-supporting priest who was in residence at Maria Ratschitz when black landowners from the area were forcibly removed to Limehill in 1968. His 1971 study of African resettlement, *The Discarded People*, was a seminal work.[9] Like Desmond, Kerchhoff was appalled by the suffering inflicted on communities by forced removals. With his wife, Joan, he made contact with people living in resettlement villages in the Ladysmith area.[10]

Several labour tenants from Weenen addressed the Loop Street meeting. They gave background information on the evictions and described the abysmal conditions in their resettlement villages. Cherryl Walker, a young academic employed by CAP – later the first Land Commissioner for KwaZulu-Natal in the post-apartheid order – analysed the labour tenancy system and its impact on rural life. Suggestions were made for possible action. These included a publicity campaign, legal assistance to evictees, the resurrection of the Natal Citizens' Association (formed in 1968 to oppose the Limehill removals) and the creation of a farm workers' union. In the end, a decision was taken to form an action committee under the stewardship of Kerchhoff, with a view to launching a new organisation.

Kerchhoff held a follow-up meeting on 24 November, chaired by a local lawyer, Peter Rutsch. Both Brown and Colin Gardner, who were unable to attend, had been approached to chair the action committee, and both had declined. In Brown's case, this was due to his reluctance to be involved with any project in which Alcock had a guiding hand.[11] Rutsch agreed to fill the position temporarily. Marie Dyer, the former Liberal who lectured in English at the University of Natal and served on the editorial board of *Reality*, was elected vice-chair. Kerchhoff was elected interim secretary and treasurer.[12]

The action committee moved for the formation of a new organisation, which it called the Association for Rural Advancement (AFRA). In its constitution, adopted at this meeting, AFRA undertook to 'monitor, enquire into, record and publicise the social and economic position of rural people of Natal, and ... take action to alleviate hardships, discrimination and oppression suffered by them and to encourage their social and economic advancement'.[13] In this way, AFRA sought to broaden its scope beyond resisting removals; it hinted at an activist role in lobbying for the socio-economic rights of Natal's rural population.

Brown was again asked to become chairman of the action committee at its next meeting in December. He promised to reconsider the request and report back.[14] In the meantime, Dyer had asked Brown's friend, Maimie Corrigal, to convince him that he was the only person who might be able to control Alcock.[15] His experiences of Alcock through CAP had given Brown ample reason to doubt this, but he relented. In January the following year, he accepted the chairmanship. As it turned out, Alcock's involvement with AFRA was only sporadic; his energies were consumed by his work at Mdukatshani.

Why did members of the committee pursue Brown for the chairmanship with such persistence? Firstly, because of the predominance on the committee of former Liberal Party members and liberal sympathisers who held him and his leadership abilities in high esteem; and secondly, because of his intimate knowledge of the history of forced removals in Natal.

On assuming the chairmanship, Brown set out what he viewed as the aims of organisation. AFRA should draw attention to impending forced removals and try to halt them. If such efforts failed, 'every attempt at ensuring full rights for uprooted people should be made'.[16] Brown's ambitions for AFRA were much narrower than those set out it its constitution. In some respects, this was because he saw the organisation as an heir to the NNALA.[17] What he could not foretell at this stage was how AFRA's work would come to be shaped by the dominance of Inkatha in Natal's rural communities on the one hand, and, on the other, the involvement of white field workers and researchers, whose politics owed less to the liberalism of the 1950s and 1960s than to the leftist civic radicalism of the 1980s.

AFRA was initially funded by the SACC, which donated R2 420.[18] Unlike many of his peers in Pietermaritzburg, Christianity was incidental to Brown's liberalism. He was determined that AFRA should not become linked with the SACC and that it should retain a 'secular image'.[19] PACSA gave the Association use of a room in its Loop Street offices, and in June AFRA employed Cherryl Walker as its field worker. She was later joined by Jean Ngubane. Their job was to gather information about communities threatened with removal, as well as resettlement areas, and to report back to the committee.

Between 23 June and 3 July, the two of them embarked on a field trip through northern Natal along with Laurine Platzky, national coordinator of the Surplus People Project (SPP), an organisation formed in Cape Town in 1980 to publicise and resist forced removals. The three went to find out more about the plight of African labour tenants on white farms, to assess the impact of the prevailing drought and to speak with community leaders.[20] They travelled from Ezakheni through Nkandla to Paulpietersburg, gleaning information on 65 resettlement areas, 26 areas threatened with removals and 15 areas from which people had already been moved. They also visited black spots in the Bergville district, where the Liberal Party had garnered a strong following three decades earlier.

AFRA initially concentrated on exposing and opposing the

eviction of labour tenants on farms in Weenen. It procured legal
assistance for tenants, which was aimed at delaying evictions,
prosecuting abuses by farm-owners, and contesting the dispro-
portionate fees levied on African stock-owners at the local pound.
In these endeavours, it was substantially helped by Ray Swart.
Brown sent Swart material compiled by AFRA, and in return
Swart used the parliamentary mechanisms at his disposal to elicit
more information about the evictions.[21] Through Swart, Brown
lobbied the Minister of Cooperation and Development, Piet
Koornhof, to halt the eviction of African families in Weenen,
pending the outcome of the Van der Walt Commission, which was
appointed by the government in 1979 to advise on the 'consolidation' of KwaZulu.[22]

Brown wrote to Chief Buthelezi, calling for his government to
institute a commission of inquiry into the activities of the Labour
Control Board in Weenen and the adjoining parts of Msinga.[23]
He asked that such a commission should also investigate the tensions on the Weenen–Msinga boundary, which Alcock had
brought to his attention. Buthelezi responded by fully endorsing
the objectives of AFRA and congratulating Brown for his initiative,
but he rejected the idea of a special commission for Weenen.[24]
The Buthelezi Commission and its terms of reference, which
were to examine the 'requirements for stability and development
in KwaZulu and Natal', had already been established, he noted.[25]
Moreover, a Select Committee had been appointed to investigate
living conditions in KwaZulu, and it would visit Weenen in due
course.

There may have been another reason for Buthelezi's rebuff: a
fear that his own government would be tainted by association. He
told Brown that although he didn't object to drawing public attention to the iniquities of forced resettlements, 'there has been a negative type of publicising, where because we are what is called a
KwaZulu government, certain people have tried to put us in [a]
bad light as if we do not do anything even where we are not responsible for the removals at all, and where there is nothing we can do
about it except to raise the matter with the Republican government'.[26] This was an early indication of the uneasy relationship

AFRA would come to have with Buthelezi's organisation, Inkatha, over the next decade.

* * *

At the end of its first year of existence, Brown reported that 'AFRA was equally involved in the overwhelming problem of removals and resettlements from "black spots"'.[27] As far as labour tenants on farms were concerned, AFRA had only been able to delay eviction through legal aid. Brown commented that this was time-consuming and expensive and placed a burden on Pat Stilwell, the lawyer who offered his assistance. He wanted to know whether AFRA should persevere with legal action or concentrate exclusively on black spot removals, since its financial and staff resources were limited.

In the end, it was agreed that AFRA should continue its legal aid work for farm workers, but that this should be seen as part of a wider strategy to lobby organisations like the Natal Agricultural Union (NAU) so as to publicise the inhumanity of evictions. At this point, Walker advocated that AFRA should encourage rural Africans to organise themselves in resistance to removals and evictions. In Weenen, contacts with the Church Agricultural Project and local leaders might make this possible. A sub-committee comprising Brown, Walker and Rutsch was appointed to talk about an appropriate strategy.

The sub-committee met in January the following year.[28] Again, Walker argued that AFRA should help to mobilise rural communities. She suggested, for example, that someone be employed in Weenen to focus on evictions and stock impoundments and to build up a group to represent farm workers in negotiations with farmers about their future. Brown countered that such a person would be extremely vulnerable, and might be subject to victimisation. In the end, his argument prevailed, and the sub-committee resolved that:

> [I]t was premature for AFRA to embark on a programme of local organisation. Instead it should first research similar programme[s] in other parts of the world and in SA to gain

a clearer understanding of methods, prospects and pitfalls which could be balanced against the resources AFRA has. Possible groups to look at include peasant movements in South America, farm worker organisations among Chicanos in the USA, the ICU [Industrial and Commercial Workers' Union] in SA.[29]

Brown was convinced that AFRA should prioritise opposition to black spot removals, since it was in a 'stronger position to intervene positively', and once black spots were eliminated they were irretrievably lost. Rutsch agreed with him that AFRA was more likely to 'embarrass the government' by lobbying against black spot removals. But Walker, whose intellectual formation and political trajectory were different to those of Brown and Rutsch, was concerned that in focusing on black spots, AFRA tended to deal with landlords who were the elite and the power group in their communities. AFRA needed to decide what its long-term goal was, she insisted; was it to stop removals or to politicise rural people? The latter never having been seriously discussed before, nor having been part of AFRA's founding objects, it was clear where Walker's sympathies lay.

Two days later, Brown convened the same group to revisit the matter, along with Dyer and Kerchhoff. Brown again stressed that AFRA's first priority should be to campaign against black spot removals, and its second priority should be to research and publicise information on resettlement areas.[30] He did not believe that AFRA should concern itself with agricultural development work, for example, since other organisations were better resourced to offer practical assistance in this regard.

In the ensuing discussion, Brown's narrow emphasis on black spot removals came under fire. Walker argued that any success AFRA achieved in helping communities living in freehold to resist removal would be limited. Black spot removals were merely one type of removal, and they had to be seen in the broader context of various state policies that undermined blacks' land rights. By delaying removals through legal loopholes, by winning minor victories, AFRA might serve to raise false hopes. Moreover, merely stopping removals in particular areas would not solve many of the problems facing those communities, such as overcrowding and conflicts between landlords and tenants. Stopping removals was only the first step and not an end in itself. What, then, should that end be? She made a case for AFRA's work to be 'geared towards building up progressive organisation within rural areas and that it have a politicising input, even while recognising that AFRA's role in these areas will necessarily be limited by its size and the nature of its over-whelmingly white membership'.

Walker's argument was not altogether foreign to Brown. After all, the NNALA had been set up by the Liberal Party in 1958 in consultation with the ANC; it had mobilised communities to resist government action; and its work had been self-consciously political. In fact, at the time, it was the ANC, not the Liberal Party, that was concerned the Association might flex too much independent political muscle. The Association conducted its work in a political milieu familiar to Brown. Twenty-three years on, Brown found the political environment – both nationally, and locally, in KwaZulu and Natal – less familiar, more ambiguous and trickier to navigate. Of course, apartheid was still the enemy, but apartheid's own enemies were more ideologically diverse than before, and more fragmented.

In some measure, this was due to the rise of Inkatha, to whose revival in 1975 Brown had given much coverage in *Reality*. The more AFRA was drawn into working with Natal's rural committees, the more it encountered Inkatha as a political force, and the less Brown and his colleagues liked it. In 1981, when the discussion group met to discuss AFRA's priorities, and Walker lobbied for the organisation to have a 'politicising input', Brown's unease about Inkatha had not quite crystallised. He was uneasy nonetheless. And part of that disquiet, although Brown was by no means a hostage to political ideology, must have stemmed from a realisation that Walker's politics were not his own.

These unresolved tensions notwithstanding, Brown threw himself into AFRA. He was determined that it should oppose black spot removals as part of its core work, and, towards the end of 1980, he became personally involved in resisting the removal of residents of KwaPitela, near Himeville.

KwaPitela had been bought in 1900 by Pitela Hlophe. In 1969, the Bantu Affairs Commissioner informed one of his descendants, Ezekiel Hlophe, that: 'Owing to its situation, the above mentioned property is a black spot which in terms of Departmental policy will have to be eliminated in due course.'[31] There were no further developments until September 1979, when a magistrate from Himeville told residents that the state was going to buy the land and relocate the community. They were instructed not to plough or plant crops. The following winter, while struggling through the resultant food shortage, tenants from KwaPitela were taken to see their proposed resettlement village, Compensation, in the Impendle district some 70km away. The magistrate apparently persuaded them to agree to move.

Hlophe then contacted AFRA to complain about the conditions at Compensation: there was no water, fields or grazing land, and the prospects for gainful employment were bleak. In October 1980, Walker and Ngubane met with KwaPitela residents to find out whether they wanted to move or were being pressurised to do so. Their feeling was that the community did not want to go to Compensation, but that they were too disorganised and fearful to resist the move.

Through AFRA, pressure mounted on Minister Koornhof to prevent the removal. In May 1981, Brown approached Hlophe and the resident headmistress at KwaPitela, a Miss Mncwabe, to sign affidavits stating their unwillingness to move.[32] Hlophe and Mncwabe were both landowners. A meeting was scheduled at which tenants would sign similar affidavits, but two days before it was due to take place, in the middle of July, government trucks arrived, houses were demolished and the community was relocated to Compensation.

AFRA's failure to halt the removal from KwaPitela – which in fact was the only black spot removed in Natal after AFRA was formed – prompted a bout of introspection, and it was reviewed at length at a committee meeting in July. Some members felt that the intervention had been unsuccessful because AFRA failed to establish any meaningful relationship with the tenants, and 'inadvertently found itself associated on the landlord side of a tenant/-

landlord conflict'.[33] It was extremely difficult, when going into a community for the first time, not to get entangled in local politics. This, some committee members felt, made it imperative for AFRA's workers not to compromise their position before becoming fully conversant with the local situation, which required caution, sensitivity, regular follow-up and communication. Furthermore, AFRA should in future work with committees and groups, not individuals, 'even if those individuals are strong, respected local leaders'.

Was this an attack on Brown's way of doing things? He had, after all, struck the link with the two freeholders, Hlophe and Mncwabe, and attempted to liaise with the tenants through them. Was there an insinuation that his approach, while it may have borne fruit in the 1950s and 1960s, was ill suited to the current environment? If there was, Brown took it on board. He conveyed to Bishop Russell that KwaPitela was 'a weak community'; 'ignorant and ... isolated and [unable] ... to take a stand against authority'.[34] Part of the problem, however, he acknowledged, was that his line of contact to the community was through the landlords; AFRA 'had no real relationship with the tenants'.

Brown continued to visit KwaPitela after the removal. On 28 September, he accompanied a professional valuator, George Forder, to determine the value of the land and buildings remaining and to hazard a guess at the pre-removal value of some of the homes already destroyed.[35] A year down the line, AFRA conducted a survey to discover how the community had been affected by the move. It found that half the people had been unable to build normal-size homesteads. About 90 percent of them had lost their livestock. Because job opportunities in Impendle were few and far between, unlike in Himeville, the number of migrant labourers had doubled, leading to a breakdown of family structures.

Despite his reluctance to engage in 'politicising' work in the rural areas, Brown did, on occasion, attempt to broker a political solution to factional feuds. He kept abreast of what was happening in Weenen and Msinga via Neil Alcock, both in terms of removals and the community's seemingly intractable politics. In March, he sent a memorandum to Bishop Russell and Ray Swart, recording a clash between two groups of hostel-dwellers in Johannesburg the previous year, which was sparked by a dancing competition. The fight resumed and intensified when the workers returned home to Msinga, resulting in several deaths.[36] Brown hoped that Minister Koornhof might arrange for some 'dramatic gesture', such as a joint visit by Buthelezi and the Commissioner-General of Bantu Affairs to defuse tensions. He also proposed a commission of inquiry into the various faction fights in Msinga. Russell forwarded the report to Frank Mdlalose, who noted that the KwaZulu government had conducted numerous investigations into the problems at Msinga, but conceded that 'we are not anywhere near a solution'. Indeed, he felt that 'our Msinga problems may develop to be as insoluble as the Irish Catholic/Protestant conflict'.[37]

Alcock sought AFRA's help with another of his bugbears. Towards the end of the 1970s, the South African government fenced off various routes which the residents of Msinga had traditionally used to travel into Weenen and down to the Tugela River. These rights-of-way crossed white-owned farmland, and the farmers feared that, should they be reopened, Africans would be allowed to drive their cattle onto the land and water them where the routes crossed a watercourse. Alcock took the matter to court and, without too much thought as to how he would pay for it, hired senior counsel.

In July, Brown wrote to Bishop Desmond Tutu, at the time General Secretary of the SACC. The SACC was AFRA's principal donor. Now, Brown requested a R12 000 donation towards the case. He informed Tutu that that the 'closing of traditional routes [was] likely to increase' with the establishment of homelands, and that the case '*might*, therefore, be of significance to people living along the black/white boundaries throughout the Republic'.[38] Tutu was sympathetic to Brown's request but notified him that the Council's funds were exhausted. Even so, he felt compelled to add that, in future, he would 'be very reluctant to have any dealings with any project in which Mr Alcock is involved'.[39] Alcock had apparently given the SACC 'very unfavourable publicity' about Devcraft, an employment agency set up by the Council in 1974.

It wasn't only the 'rabble-rouser for peace'[40] who Alcock upset at the time. According to Rian Malan, in 1981 Alcock wrote a series of letters to old friends from the Liberal Party, asking why they had abandoned him to his 'fatigue, inefficiency and failure': 'Why me alone?' he pleaded.[41] Apparently, no replies came. Brown was undoubtedly one of those alienated by Alcock's letter. In September, he told Bunty Biggs:

> I got sick of being slated for not doing anything, or not doing enough, by Neil, and wrote and told him, about six months ago, that I would, from then on, decide myself what I would do and what I wouldn't and, if he didn't like it, he could lump it – or words to that effect! Well, he didn't like it, and since then I have enjoyed a marvellous reign of peace – not without some prickings of conscience, I must confess!'

At any rate, Alcock was preoccupied with the faction fighting in Msinga and keeping CAP afloat at Mdukatshani. Despite the fact that AFRA was, to some degree, originally his idea, his involvement with it was marginal. The course adopted by the Association was guided far more by Brown than Alcock.

* * *

In the early 1980s, AFRA focused on fieldwork in rural communities. Its field workers, Ngubane and Walker, visited black spots in and around Ladysmith and Estcourt, as well as resettlement villages in Nkandla, Nongoma and Hlabisa. They went on fact-finding missions to the northeastern coastal region, covering Richards Bay to Kosi Bay in Maputaland, and to the Nqutu and Lower Tugela districts.

The data they gathered was channelled back to the AFRA committee, and documented and filed at the AFRA resource centre. Additional information was sourced through parliamentary questions, and on occasion Brown drafted statements for Progressive MPs to read out in the House of Assembly, condemning removals and the consolidation of homeland territories. In 1982, for example, he scripted a statement for Pierre Cronje, describing the government's decision to hand over the land and people of Ingwavuma and Kangwane to Swaziland as 'breathtaking' and 'cynical'.[42]

AFRA publicised the stories of various communities in its newsletters. By mid-1982, it had published 17 reports which were dispatched to over 1 200 addresses on its mailing list.[43] Much of this material was made available to the press. From 1981 onwards, reports were published in both English and Zulu. AFRA also produced bilingual factsheets for rural communities on practical matters such as accessing pensions and the legal aspects of removals.

Walker and Ngubane's findings provided an archival treasuretrove for the Surplus People Project, which at the time was compiling a multi-volume report on forced removals in South Africa. Walker played a key role in writing the overarching report, and she authored the fourth volume, which dealt with Natal.[44]

AFRA started hosting workshops for communities threatened with resettlement. In November 1981, Brown opened a workshop in Ladysmith on 'removals and the law'. It provided information on the Land Acts, expropriation, compensation and the legal status of tenants.[45] It was attended by about 80 people from 12 communities.[46]

On 26 March 1983, Sam Mkhize attended one such workshop. He represented the residents of Driefontein, a community living in freehold in the southeastern Transvaal. A week after the seminar, the people of Driefontein gathered to discuss their threatened removal. The police stormed into the meeting and declared it illegal. An altercation ensued, shots were fired, and Mkhize was left lying in a pool of blood. For Brown, Mkhize's death could not be laid solely at the door of the policeman who shot him, but 'more firmly at the doors of Dr Piet Koornhof [the Minister of Cooperation and Development] and Mr PW Botha, whose lunatic policy it continues to be to destroy settled communities'.[47]

At its annual general meeting in 1983, Brown identified AFRA's achievements in the preceding year: the research into resettlements in Natal which had been incorporated into the SPP's report on forced removals; the establishment of an advice office at Wembezi near Estcourt, run by Jean Ngubane, which advised residents on issues such as pensions, maintenance grants and workman's compensation; and the contact made with threatened and relocated people in Natal and beyond.[48] He thanked Cherryl Walker, who was about to leave AFRA for the United States, for her work, which had 'created the scope and direction of its [AFRA's] practical activities'. Walker's departure was a big loss for the organisation she had toiled tirelessly to build. In later years, Brown would simply say: '[W]e were lucky with Cherryl.'[49]

As for the year ahead, AFRA would have to keep abreast of official actions and policies, and inform and assist the people affected by them. Brown thought it should give 'extra emphasis' to advising poor and threatened communities on agricultural development, since removals could be better resisted 'by people who had plans to regenerate their lands and could not be accused of degrading the environment'.[50] One such development project AFRA had sponsored was run by an organisation called Phakamani Mzimhlophe, which administered a revolving loan fund in the resettlement village of Mzimhlophe in Nkandla. AFRA donated the initial capital – R1 000 – for the revolving fund, which was used to buy seeds, day-old chicks, fertiliser and fencing for the community.[51]

Meanwhile, growing conflict between Inkatha and UDF supporters in Natal was becoming a serious obstacle to AFRA's work in the rural areas. An AFRA field worker remarked in 1984: 'Although AFRA remains neutral in the conflict between different political groupings, it will be increasingly difficult for AFRA to work with varied groups with different political inclinations and yet to be seen as neutral.'[52] Many of the former Liberals on the AFRA committee – Brown, Dyer and Lundie, for example – believed that the organisation should remain non-aligned. However, several new and younger members, whose outlook had been shaped by the radical campus politics of the early 1980s, supported the UDF and saw no reason to cloak their sympathies.

The Surplus People Project attracted many leftists. In 1984, Laurine Platzky wrote to Brown, proposing that the SPP be reformed with an expanded mandate. She noted that while the Grahamstown Rural Committee (GRC) in the Eastern Cape and the Transvaal Rural Action Committee (TRAC) were doing work complementary to that of AFRA, similar groups did not exist in the rest of the country. In the Western Cape, the SPP acted on an *ad hoc* basis. What Platzky had in mind was a nationwide umbrella organisation that, like AFRA, could deal with broader issues of socio-economic welfare in the rural areas. She suggested a seminar early the following year 'to assess the national removals scene'.[53]

Brown responded that the AFRA committee was unenthusiastic about 'becoming involved in another organisation at another level'.[54] In his view, if the SPP was revived, it should serve as a clearing-house for information collected in different areas and as a convenor of occasional national get-togethers at which problems and experiences could be shared.

Quite probably, Brown's lukewarm response was occasioned by ideological misgivings. Interviewed a decade later, he said that antagonism between the left and some former Liberals 'didn't bother me in AFRA', but 'it did bother me when the ... umbrella organisation was set up'. 'Then I was rather on the defensive with regard to those people.'[55]

The meeting proposed by Platzky went ahead in May 1985, and was attended by members of GRC, TRAC, SPP and AFRA. Out of it was born the National Committee Against Removals (NCAR). SPP was represented by two activists from the left, Alan Hirsch and Willie Hofmeyr. That year, Hofmeyr was elected to the Western Cape executive of the UDF. (He, Hirsch and Platzky would all go on to enjoy high-profile careers in post-apartheid ANC governments: Hofmeyr as Deputy National Director of Public Prosecutions; Hirsch as Chief Director of Economic Policy in the Office of President Thabo Mbeki; and Platzky as Deputy Director-General of Economic Development and Tourism in the Western Cape provincial government.) AFRA's delegates were Mini Shembe and Patti Henderson.

One issue that came up for discussion was the rivalry between Inkatha and the UDF; although endemic in Natal, the rivalry was unknown in the rest of country since Inkatha was a regional force. AFRA worked with people who did not want to move, rather than with political organisations, its representatives said. This was not as straightforward as it sounded, however, because when field workers encouraged people to unite, the people asked, 'how, under Inkatha, [or] UDF?'[56]

At the annual general meeting in 1986, Brown reinforced the need for political neutrality in the ongoing battle between Inkatha and the UDF. On AFRA's relationship with NCAR, he noted that AFRA committee members had a wider range of political views than those who served on NCAR. It was useful for AFRA to be affiliated to NCAR because of the mutual benefit of sharing experience and research, but, he warned, AFRA's incoming committee should insist that any proposals from NCAR be treated purely as recommendations. He said: 'AFRA shouldn't be compromised by committing us to anything without the approval of the committee … [A]ny statement should come from AFRA not NCAR.'[57]

Brown elaborated his views on the conflict between Inkatha and the UDF in a letter to Cherryl Walker that same year. AFRA had just lost two of its staff members: Mini Shembe resigned and took up a position with the SACC, and Jean Ngubane went back to study at university. Having heard that Walker might be returning to South Africa from the United States, Brown wrote offering her a job. He wanted her as a director, but because other committee members thought this might upset the rest of the staff, he was only in a position to offer her a post as 'a sort of researcher cum keeping-an-eye on the office sort of person'.[58] He was careful not to underplay the new set of challenges attendant upon such a job. One of these would be the 'inter-black conflict in Natal'. Although Brown's perception was that 'most violence comes from Inkatha', he felt 'sure that elements supporting the UDF don't hesitate to use it on occasions'. What was AFRA to do in the circumstances? Brown contended:

Although most AFRA committee members are probably UDF sympathisers this conflict is one I am convinced AFRA must avoid any involvement at all in. In most of the threatened areas of rural Natal Inkatha is the only organisation of any significance and to be suspected of being hostile to it would I think be disastrous for our prospects of influencing any organised campaign against removals in those areas.

In sum 'AFRA should be seen to be non-partisan', and if it managed to maintain that position, hopefully one day it might be able to 'play some kind of reconciliatory role'.

In years to come, Brown would attempt to broker a ceasefire by bringing together Buthelezi and Archie Gumede, the founding President of the UDF. Gumede and Brown went back a long way. A confidant of Chief Luthuli, in 1955 Gumede led the ANC's Natal delegation to the Congress of the People. He also joined the Liberal Party in the 1950s, and took part in the campaigns against black spot removals from Charlestown and Roosboom. He and Brown kept in touch, despite the fact that they were both banned during the 1960s. When Brown's ban was lifted in 1974, he would often visit Gumede at his legal practice in Pinetown, and Gumede would turn to him for personal advice. For example, in 1978, Brown told a correspondent: 'I had a very sad meeting with Archie the other day, having been asked by Chota Motala, former president of the local NIC [Natal Indian Congress], after a visit from Archie's wife, to go and talk to him about family problems.'[59] Brown's counsel was sometimes of a political nature: when Gumede was asked to brief a parliamentary committee on the possibility of black participation in the President's Council, Brown set out his doubts.[60]

At one point, Gumede was assaulted by Inkatha supporters, and he wrote in protest to Buthelezi about the incident. Buthelezi's reply, which Gumede passed on to Brown, was unsympathetic: he found it 'difficult to believe' that Gumede was the victim of 'an unprovoked assault', but he did extend his 'hand ... in brotherhood' and request Gumede to meet with him and 'talk about these matters'.[61] Brown reported back to Gumede that although he didn't like the tone of Buthelezi's letter, he thought a private meeting between the two of them might 'defuse a very threatening situation', and he advised Gumede to accept the invitation.[62] Such an arrangement, on Buthelezi's terms, was, of course, impossible for Gumede to agree to in the seething atmosphere of the mid-1980s; he would have lost all credibility among his UDF followers. Still, Brown persisted. After Alan Paton's funeral in 1988, Phoebe arranged a wake at Shinglewood. Gumede attended, and Brown invited Buthelezi too, in the hope that the two leaders might have an amicable chat. But Buthelezi couldn't make it, and Brown regretted the missed opportunity to 'get going some reconciliation momentum'.[63]

Brown's insistence that AFRA remain politically impartial, and his hope that it might, in time, mediate between Inkatha and the UDF, were viewed alternately as fence-sitting and wishful thinking by some of the younger and more radical committee members and staffers who joined AFRA in the mid-1980s. For some of them, their reservations about AFRA's political disengagement dovetailed with concerns about its organisational structure. They were keen, as one of them suggested, for AFRA to be 'a political pressure group, concentrating on the political aspects of removals as examples of a larger system of oppression of poor rural people'.[64] In their view, Inkatha was part of that oppressive system.

Among the Young Turks were Patti Henderson, who had been appointed as an organiser, and David Walwyn, who did research work for AFRA and shot several films of resettled communities. Walwyn was eager for AFRA to position itself in such a way that its 'legitimacy [was] not swept away'. The time was ripe, he argued at a committee meeting in 1985, because '[t]he state is in crisis with widespread resistance and unrest; and capitalist interests are applying pressures'.[65]

Another committee member who pursued a line to the left was Sheila Meintjies. In later years Professor and Head of the Politics Department at Wits University, at the time Meintjies was researching her PhD thesis on the history of Edendale and African land purchase in nineteenth-century Natal. In 1985, she and John Aitchison were tasked by the committee with drawing up a report on administration. They suggested a number of changes to the way AFRA was administered, pointing out that, 'We are no longer a small, amateur, do-gooder organisation.'[66] The accusation of do-goodery made their subtext clear enough: interventions by a group of well-meaning white volunteers on behalf of black, dispossessed, rural folk smacked of paternalism. It was time for AFRA to shed its liberal mantle.

Left–liberal tensions were never far from the surface in AFRA during these years, and they welled up between March and April 1987. In March, Brown penned a document reflecting on the strife between Inkatha and the UDF, its impact on AFRA and his personal position with regard to the antagonists. He noted that the AFRA committee was home to a wide range of political views. No one on it supported Inkatha, but it did have members who were 'committed supporters' of the UDF and COSATU. Others might not want to be closely identified with either side in the current conflict, 'particularly insofar as their work in AFRA is concerned', and that, Brown said, 'is the position in which I find myself'.[67]

The question of political neutrality went to the heart of AFRA's relationship with NCAR, and Brown summed up his thoughts on the matter:

> I think AFRA has to preserve its non-partisan position in rural Natal, but I sense that the NCAR may feel that this involves an unacceptable compromise with the forces of darkness, that AFRA is a bit of a maverick in the organisation, not entirely in tune with the prevailing view. And that may well be true, and may continue to be so, for I think AFRA has to try to pursue its objects, for the foreseeable future, within a very difficult and complex situation in rural Natal, not like that anywhere else, and not fully understood anywhere else.

The commitment to Inkatha in rural areas might be no more than a nominal one. It might even be based on convenience. Nevertheless, it was there and AFRA had to accept it. Brown thought it was 'pure fantasy' to think that AFRA could go into such areas and try to build up an alternative organisation to Inkatha. Nor should it try to do so. Instead, AFRA should 'reaffirm [its] independent and non-partisan position in the UDF/Inkatha conflict'.

At the end of the month, AFRA's secretary, Susan Mathieson, resigned from her post. Partly this was because she found her secretarial work unchallenging, and because she had been overlooked for the research and field-worker vacancies. However, in her resignation letter, which she copied to all committee members, she gave as her ostensible reason for resigning her unhappiness with AFRA's 'policy of political neutrality'.[68]

She claimed that two of AFRA's major development schemes were run in an undemocratic manner by Inkatha members who were 'involved in vigilante activities'. The projects referred to were most likely those at Matiwane's Kop and Steincoalspruit, two black spots in the Klipriver district, where clean-water facilities had been installed and community gardens cultivated. In fact, the previous year, the AFRA committee had agreed to cease its involvement with the leadership at Matiwane's Kop for this very reason.

At any rate, to Mathieson, AFRA's dealings with Inkatha, solicited or not, 'displayed the weakness of having such a wide range of political views represented' in the organisation. For this broad range of opinion rendered AFRA 'paralysed in the face of [a] swing to the right in the rural areas'. It hampered AFRA from 'looking clearly at the issues', and working out 'some way to move forward'.

Furthermore, Mathieson claimed that she had been up against 'a very deep rooted distrust of the work of other organisations, particularly of our affiliates'. In what must have been a reference to NCAR, and the other groups belonging to it, she remonstrated:

> They are not dangerous ultra-leftist radicals as they are sometimes portrayed … They are not affiliated to the UDF and do not intend to be, although they are broadly committed to the struggle for a non-racial democratic future for South Africa … I do not see where we have reason to wish to distance ourselves from them. If AFRA has that attitude to the affiliates it must have a similar attitude towards me, because I don't have any problems with them.

Mathieson's letter encapsulated some of the frustrations of the pro-UDF grouping within AFRA. Significantly, however, Brown was able to contain that discontent, and he managed to retain the broader support of committee members, many of whom admired him for his even-handedness and pragmatism. At the end of March, he was re-elected as chairman. But in what may have been a sign that he was weighed down by the internal wrangling, Brown stated that he would be unavailable for re-election the following year.[69]

Apart from navigating the stormy waters of politics, both provincial and institutional, Brown continued with hands-on work in the rural areas. Between 1984 and 1987, he made regular visits to Clermont, where residents were resisting incorporation into KwaZulu.[70] With Elliot Mngadi, he visited residents displaced from Charlestown to Osizweni, to discuss setting up a crèche.[71] He helped oversee the development of a tree nursery and community gardens at Matiwane's Kop.[72] He accompanied field workers to meet communities threatened with eviction from Weenen in terms of the Conservation Act because of overgrazing.[73] He met with the Steincoalspruit community to discuss drawing up a development plan for the area,[74] and he sorted out the problem of rotting potatoes at Phakamani Mzimhlophe.[75]

Brown had always seen AFRA's primary occupation as helping communities to resist removals. For some time – since the early 1980s, even – the government had been promising to end forced removals. In 1981, Minister Koornhof promised there would be no more forced removals.[76] That same year the residents of KwaPitela were moved to Compensation. Moreover, several locations, including Driefontein near Ladysmith, were designated 'white areas' and excised from KwaZulu.[77] Not for nothing was the Minister's sobriquet 'Piet Promises'. In 1982, a government circular instructed officials to engage with communities targeted for removal 'on a persuasion basis'.[78] Finally, in 1985, Koornhof's successor as Minister of Cooperation and Development, Gerrit Viljoen, announced that the government would put a halt to forced removals pending a review of its consolidation proposals.

In his opening remarks to the AFRA annual general meeting in May that year, Brown noted that the thirty-year struggle against removals was 'at last having some results'.[79] The government was 'confused'; it had 'lost the rigidity of Verwoerd and his policies'. In particular, the granting of a 99-year leasehold to township residents in the western Cape and Natal was viewed as a major shift. Ninety-nine years was the equivalent of freehold, he argued, since apartheid could not last another 99 years. And in a call to arms, he ended: 'We hope that the suspension of removals by Viljoen will lead to their abandonment, but this will not happen without continuing pressure.'

In early 1985, a commission set up by the Department for Cooperation and Development submitted to Viljoen its final set of proposals for the consolidation of Natal and KwaZulu. It overturned previous proposals, with the result that several parts of KwaZulu would continue to be dotted across white Natal. The commission also recommended that resettlements and new land purchases should be curtailed, while 810 000 hectares should be added to KwaZulu.[80]

The communities affected by these proposals were invited to air their views at public hearings held by the commission. In December 1985, Brown contacted the secretary of the commission and arranged for AFRA to make an oral submission to it the following month.[81] On 16 January 1986, AFRA testified before the commission. It was agreed beforehand that Brown would give background information on AFRA and discuss the allocation of land. Mike Cowling (a Law lecturer at the University of Natal and current AFRA vice-chairman) would introduce and lead AFRA's evidence, and offer legal and practical solutions. Patti Henderson would give evidence on specific communities (Reserve Four and Hlanganani) and on areas that had not appeared before the commission but which had given AFRA affidavits granting permission to speak on their behalf (Matiwane's Kop, Steincoalspruit, Mbulwane and Hopewell). Sheila Meintjies would talk about the general historical background to, and effects of, removals. David Walwyn would pay attention to the plight of squatters and farm workers, and address development and conservation issues with reference to AFRA's work at Hopewell (where it had helped to install a water scheme) and Matiwane's Kop.[82]

AFRA's appearance before the commission was not a great success. Several of the commissioners were openly hostile, and bombarded AFRA's witnesses with questions about the racial composition of the AFRA committee; how the organisation was funded; and its links with political organisations and non-governmental organisations like the Legal Resources Centre. In a written post-mortem on the hearing, one of the witnesses remarked that they were 'impressed by the accuracy with which Peter [Brown] had anticipated [these] questions' and that he 'successfully evaded revealing both the identity of our donors and the full extent of their funds'.[83] The commission challenged AFRA on the source, accuracy and representativeness of its evidence, especially as it related to the community of Reserve Four, threatened with re-settlement to facilitate the expansion of Richards Bay. The commissioners were confrontational in their cross-examination of AFRA's evidence and quarrelsome in their questioning. For example, when AFRA asked for more land for blacks, they interpreted this as an argument for the forced removal of white farmers. Ultimately, to AFRA's surprise, the commission seemed to accept without fuss the organisation's fundamental argument: that the policy of forced removals should be scrapped.

Brown found the whole experience 'very gruelling', but it did force him to re-evaluate AFRA's role and ponder the future of land policy in South Africa.[84] An exchange between Brown and Graham McIntosh illuminates the direction in which Brown's thoughts were moving at the end of the 1980s. Like Brown in the past, McIntosh was both a farmer – he went on to be President of the KwaZulu-Natal Agriculture Union in the 1990s – and a politician. Having served a term in Parliament for the United Party in the 1970s, he eventually defected to the Progressive Federal Party (PFP) when the writing was on the wall for the UP, and became the PFP MP for Pietermaritzburg in 1981. A Christian conservative, McIntosh's subsequent political career took a lurch back to the right: having failed to secure a return to Parliament with the Democratic Alliance in 2004, he joined the African Christian Democratic Party.

McIntosh told Brown that AFRA was 'less relevant than it once was', and that it 'could do much more useful work if it endeavoured to follow the example of the Rural Foundation rather than concentrating on dealing with grievances and resettlement'.[85] In fact, AFRA should concentrate on 'facilitating the painful process of urbanisation' and ensure that communities 'condemned to a life of rural slum existence' should either be decently developed or 'assisted to voluntarily resettle themselves in a more viable economic environment'.

Brown agreed that urbanisation was part of the long-term solution to population distribution but felt there was another problem which threatened future political stability. This was 'the enormous discrepancy in access to land between white and black'.[86] 'When,' he asked, 'is anybody going to start seriously applying their minds to bringing about changes in this situation which will protect the environment and which do not seriously undermine productivity?'

To illustrate his case, Brown turned to Weenen, where the eviction of black farm workers continued unabated. McIntosh had a farm in the area, and he was one of the landowners issuing summonses for eviction.[87] The previous year, Brown had written to the Chairman of the Tugela Basin Regional Development Association, calling for the suspension of evictions and the expropriation of white-owned farmland to be given to black farm workers facing eviction.[88] He added:

> We ... believe that a solution based on a negotiated development and conservation plan for the Weenen district, in which black residents have participated fully, and which would enable them to continue to live in this area, which they regard as their ancestral home, would go a long way towards establishing harmonious race relations in a district which has experienced considerable tension in the past.

Brown reiterated his position to McIntosh, conceding that the local Emergency Camp should be upgraded and recognised as a permanent settlement. Industry, too, should be introduced into the area. But that would not happen for a long time, and even if it did, there was unlikely to be enough jobs for everyone in the Emergency Camp. A more workable solution was to expropriate white-owned farms where the landlords were absent: 'We [AFRA] suggest that these be taken over and administered, with the involvement of the people at present living on them, as black areas.'[89] Of course, there would be problems: given the conservative nature of the people involved, it would be difficult to get them to adopt modern farming techniques. Nevertheless, Brown believed this was an 'imaginative proposal' that 'might at last start us on a new tack which could contribute something, at least, towards starting to resolve the question of land redistribution'. He concluded: 'No amount of urbanisation will satisfy the present black bitterness over the distribution of land and it is surely time that somebody started, however modestly, to address the question?'

With some degree of foresight, in the late 1980s Brown raised the kinds of questions about land reform and redistribution that would come to gnaw at policy-makers in post-apartheid South Africa. Under his chairmanship, AFRA now began to apply itself seriously to these matters. In 1989, Richard Clacey, AFRA's field worker at the time, prepared a paper on the objectives, structure and function of the organisation. Interestingly, he stressed that the need for such an assessment was driven by 'operational and managerial imperatives rather than any deep rooted differences about the organisation's policies or ideological positions'.[90] Clacey traced AFRA's roots back to the Liberal Party's involvement with the ANC in the Northern Natal African Landowners' Association in the 1950s, the upshot of which was a 'management style [that] reflects a specific political and humanitarian tradition with its own values and modus operandi'. Politically astute and sensitive to the feelings of the Liberal old guard, unlike those earlier committee members who had branded AFRA a 'small, amateur, do-gooder organisation', Clacey called for management to be professionalised. He also recommended that AFRA turn itself into 'a kind of quasi Department of Rural Affairs and Land Settlement in the making', and craft a land reform policy that would ensure a 'viable socio-economic agrarian transformation'.

Paul Graham, later the Executive Director of the Institute for Democracy in South Africa (IDASA), was brought in as an outside consultant to consider Clacey's scheme. He interviewed all AFRA's staff members and Brown, and reported back that everyone he spoke to saw merit in Clacey's document.[91] In the end it was Brown who moved for the adoption of Clacey's proposal at the annual general meeting in 1989.[92] At the same meeting, he was re-elected as chairman.

Although to some extent he saw AFRA as a reincarnation of the NNALA, and believed that it should concentrate on raising awareness about forced removals and opposing them, Brown was able to adapt to the shifting political context. Once removals were permanently suspended in 1990, he urged AFRA to mount a campaign to help rural communities with the resources for development they had been denied throughout their history. He also posited that, '[f]urther into the future it might be possible to contemplate a campaign urging the return to their lost homes of communities previously resettled'.[93] In his final report before standing down as chairman in 1990, Brown called for AFRA to lay greater emphasis on farm workers' rights.[94] In his attention to land redistribution and restitution before the transition to democracy, Brown was certainly in advance of his contemporaries – liberal and otherwise – most of whom directed little thought to land reform in post-apartheid South Africa. He wrote editorials and invited contributions on the subject in *Reality* as early as 1980.[95] Today, as an independent NGO, AFRA continues to perform vital work in promoting land rights and agrarian reform. Brown helped give strategic direction to the organisation from its inception and throughout the 1980s, when the stranglehold of Inkatha over rural communities in Natal made it difficult for AFRA to carry out its work independently. As hostilities flared between Inkatha and the UDF, Brown insisted that AFRA should strike a neutral pose. This displeased many of AFRA's younger committee members and employees. They supported the UDF; they wanted AFRA to engage in politicising work; and they found Inkatha to be violent and obstructive. Brown was no admirer of Inkatha, but he stuck to his guns. In his report to the annual general meeting in 1989, Brown said: 'AFRA's role will continue to be to pursue a course of trying to work with and for communities as a whole without becoming involved in local politics.'[96] In part, this reflected his belief that AFRA could achieve more by remaining non-aligned; in part, it signalled his apprehension about the actors on the political scene in the 1980s, so different from what he had known during his earlier years of activism. And to some extent, his reluctance to back one over the other was due to his hope, as he confided to Cherryl

Walker, that AFRA might yet 'play some kind of reconciliatory role'. By occupying the middle ground, Brown hoped to facilitate the politics of compromise. It was an approach that led to his formation of the Liberal Democratic Association in 1986, and his participation in the Five Freedoms Forum during the late 1980s and early 1990s.

PART
FOUR

LIBERALISM IN THE TRANSITION:
THE LIBERAL DEMOCRATIC ASSOCIATION
AND THE FIVE FREEDOMS FORUM
1984-1994

From the mid-1980s, South African politics were marked by a cycle of vicious state repression and violent resistance. PW Botha, who had succeeded Vorster as Prime Minister in 1978, crafted a 'total strategy' to counteract the 'total onslaught' on the apartheid state. This strategy targeted both the so-called neighbouring 'front-line states' that were home to ANC and PAC safe houses, and domestic opponents. Brown's editorials in *Reality* consistently condemned the state's cross-border raids into Angola, Mozambique and Namibia. They also denounced the State of Emergency which Botha declared on 20 July 1985 on the pretext that 'ordinary law and order was inadequate' to deal with protests in the townships, and which he declared for the second time – and now applied to the whole country – on 12 June 1986. In addition, *Reality* unfailingly drew attention to the staggering number of deaths in detention, acts of police brutality and political assassinations of prominent anti-apartheid activists like Griffiths Mxenge, who was murdered in 1981. *Reality* rejected the constitutional proposals that led to the creation of the Tricameral Parliament in 1984, which gave Coloureds and Indians voting rights and representation in separate parliamentary chambers. Brown privately told Hamm that the proposals were a 'certain recipe for disaster',[1] and publicly disagreed with Paton on the subject. *Reality* urged whites to reject them in the referendum of November 1983, arguing that if they didn't, they would be committing themselves and all other race groups to 'an apartheid straitjacket for as far into the future as any of us can see'.[2] The Progressive Federal Party (PFP) – as the Progressives had been renamed in 1977 – likewise campaigned for a 'No' vote.

Buoyed by their improved showing in the 1981 election (they gained 9 seats in Parliament, taking their tally up to 26), the Progressives called throughout the 1980s, like the Liberal Party before them, for a national convention to devise a constitution for a united, non-racial, democratic South Africa. *Reality* welcomed the Progressives' call and their electoral performance, but cautioned:

> The PFP has made a breakthrough, but time is short, and the momentum must be maintained. The Party's task now is not only to win more recruits from outside its ranks for a programme of negotiated change but to keep reminding those within its ranks of what that change is likely to involve. In particular they must be conditioned to the fact that the constitutional guarantees the party advocates for minorities, desirable as they may be, will only get support from a new National Convention if they are clearly seen as an attempt to guarantee rights and not to entrench privileges … In short, white voters must be prepared for the fact that, whatever constitutional guarantees the National Convention accepts, the society which it ushers in will be very different from today's. Keeping this fact before white voters will help build PFP credibility in black eyes, and on that credibility, as much as on white votes, will depend its capacity to influence the future.[3]

By the mid-1980s, as the inadequacy of Botha's haphazard reforms became clearer and the prospect of a full-blown racial war became more likely, some of the old Liberals began to wonder whether the PFP alone could meet the challenge that *Reality* had posed: winning black support for negotiated change and making whites understand what that change would entail. Others believed that the time was ripe for former Liberals to come together, take stock of the years since the Party had closed down, and plot a way forward for liberals (whatever their party affiliation) to act as facilitators of a negotiated settlement. It was in this context that Liberals gathered for a Liberal Party Workshop in Grahamstown in 1985.

Organised by Peter Vale, who was then the Director of the Institute of Social and Economic Research at Rhodes University, and funded largely by Brown, the workshop was held between 17 and 19 July and attended by about fifty delegates.[4] It was chaired by Jack Spence and opened by Alan Paton, who spoke on 'The meaning of liberalism for me'. On the second day, Brown gave an overview of the history of the Liberal Party – a condensed version of the chronological account he had written in Leslie Weinberg's house during his ban. Tony Mathews, the former LP national committee member who was now a Professor of Law at the University of Natal, prepared a speech on 'The Liberal Party: What it was and what it tried to do', that was read in his absence (due to ill health) by David Welsh. Norman Bromberger addressed the final session on 'The liberal dilemma in South Africa today'.

The air was thick with nostalgia as speaker after speaker listed the Liberal Party's achievements: it had spoken with moral force against institutionalising racial injustice, exposed abuses of state power, given concrete expression to non-racialism and carried the torch for liberal ideas like individual freedom and the rule of law in a time of darkness. But not all was self-congratulation. Mathews argued that the Party had 'failed to put forward a viable alternative policy for securing racial justice and racial peace in a divided society' because of its scepticism of safeguards for group rights.[5] Liberals, he suggested, should concentrate on devising a political system in which liberal values would triumph over simple majoritarianism. Bromberger outlined four possible roles for Liberals: actively opposing the government's policies in specific areas, such as removals; raising awareness about the destructive effects of anti-apartheid violence; building support for the government's reform initiatives; and formulating alternative policies for the post-apartheid state.[6]

Although there was no great appetite at Grahamstown for reviving the Liberal Party, delegates did feel that there should be some kind of follow-up to the workshop. Bunny Curran moved that there should be follow-up meetings in Cape Town, Johannesburg, Grahamstown, Durban and Pietermaritzburg, and convenors were appointed for each area. Brown took overall control of the process, keeping delegates from around the country informed of what was happening in other parts.

He explained the rationale to Audrey Cobden, a former Liberal Party secretary: 'The predominant view, I think, which is certainly my view, is that there is not enough room on the political spectrum for another organisation, but that there may be room for one competing in the realm of ideas, arguing the case with the various contestants, for basic Liberal concepts to be incorporated in the new society.'[7] His idea was to form a 'think-tank' that could put forward 'a compromise deal of some sort' when Afrikaner and African nationalists reached a stalemate.[8]

The upshot of this was the Liberal Democratic Association of South Africa (LDA), which sprung into existence at a meeting at Shinglewood on 31 May 1986. The LDA aimed to promote liberal democratic principles such as the rule of law, the independence of the judiciary, individual rights and freedoms, open and accountable government and a free civil society. It also advocated a 'just' economic system that took into account 'socio-economic injustices produced by the discriminatory economic policies of the past which can be addressed by competent and intelligent government intervention'.[9]

Always a small organisation with limited reach, the LDA in the 1980s was active in two centres, Pietermaritzburg and Johannesburg, but from the outset there were sharp differences of opinion over what the emphasis of the association should be. Ernie and Jill Wentzel were the leading lights in the Johannesburg LDA. They adopted a strong anti-communist stance, argued that the LDA should concentrate on condemning the violent tactics employed by the liberation movement, and punted the Inkatha leader, Mangosuthu Buthelezi, as the liberals' black saviour.[10]

The Pietermaritzburg LDA, by contrast, among whose members were left-leaning former Liberals like Colin Gardner now sympathetic to the UDF, held no particular brief for Buthelezi or Inkatha. They were dismissive of the *rooi gevaar*, and favoured formulating proposals for the transfer of power together with liberal policies for a non-racial democratic post-apartheid society. Early on, Brown warned the Wentzels against Buthelezi:

Buthelezi presents us with a particular problem. Much of what he says is very good but I think his commitment to what I call democracy is quite superficial. The Inkatha hit-squads are very active here and are as bad as their opponents. Their main function is to see that there *are* no opponents in Buthelezi territory. Opposition is intolerable to Buthelezi, in my opinion, and he won't want it in a non-racial society any more than he wants it in KwaZulu.[11]

And when Brown was told by David Everatt, an Oxford DPhil student researching his thesis on non-racial politics in the 1950s, that Jill Wentzel had described the LDA's mission as 'socking the left', Brown wrote to her reprovingly:

I know that this is what you and several other Transvaal [members] feel should be the primary task of the Association but most of the rest of us do not want to get involved in a public slanging match with the Left. We want to put forward Liberal principles, and policies based on them, in a positive way, in the hope that we can build up support for them to the extent that they can have some influence on the shape of the future.[12]

Early in 1987 Brown reiterated this to another prominent LDA member in Johannesburg, Peter Horwitz. He argued that for the LDA to see its primary role as attacking the left would be 'not only quite wrong, but disastrous'; this would be true 'whatever the circumstances', but was 'even more so under the circumstances of the State of Emergency'.[13]

As for the Wentzels' preoccupation with revolutionary violence, Brown tended to share the views of Tony Morphet, an academic who had joined the Liberal Party while studying in Pietermaritzburg in the 1950s. Brown had hoped that Morphet would get the LDA up and running in Cape Town, but Morphet was uncomfortable with the Johannesburg LDA's stance on violence, and decided to cut his ties with the association. He explained to Brown that one had to 'accept the logic of the ANC argument that they reached violence as a last resort … So to denounce violence comes to mean asking Blacks to diffuse and weaken their battle'.[14] Brown sympathised with Morphet, and hoped that he might be able to persuade the Johannesburg LDA 'into more sensible directions than the ones they now seem set on'.[15]

At the time the LDA was formed, Jill Wentzel was beginning to formulate her critique of what she perceived to be 'the liberal slideaway'.[16] The slideaway manifested itself in a departure from core liberal principles, an accommodation with the forces of Marxism and a quickness to condone the violence of the liberation movement. In March 1986, the South African Institute of Race Relations hosted a symposium, and Wentzel delivered a paper, on the theme. As far as Wentzel was concerned, most liberal organisations, including the PFP, NUSAS and the Black Sash (with which she was intimately involved as an organiser) were 'on the slides'. She even detected 'signs of slideaway' in the LDA, and warned that unless its aims and objects clearly resolved to try 'to avoid violent revolution', she saw 'no purpose in its formation'.[17] Just about the only liberal organisation that held the line in her opinion was the South African Institute of Race Relations, and she singled out its director, John Kane-Berman, for special praise. In fact, Wentzel, whose husband had been instrumental in getting Kane-Berman appointed to the Institute, wanted Kane-Berman to play a leading role in the LDA. But Brown demurred: Kane-Berman had closed down the institute's satellite structures in Natal, and many Liberals resented the imperious manner in which he had done it.[18]

Although Jill Wentzel was a cherished friend, who remained devoted to Brown's memory after his death, Brown was deeply uneasy with her preoccupation with slideaway liberals and her loathing of the left. He later confided to Peter Horwitz that 'one of the problems' he had with the LDA was its 'rightwing bias' in Johannesburg, and he acknowledged that 'that was partly the cause of the lack of liaison between the two centres'.[19] This may explain why Brown, who chaired the Pietermaritzburg LDA until 1990, was never really enthusiastic about the LDA, and why nothing much came of it in the run-up to the dramatic events of that year, when Botha's successor, FW de Klerk, announced the impending release of Nelson Mandela and other political prisoners, and unbanned the ANC, PAC and SACP. The LDA continued to operate in the 1990s, initially with Leslie Weinberg as its chairman, and did some important work. For example, in 1991 it organised a very useful and successful conference, which Brown co-sponsored, on 'Implementing a Bill of Rights in South Africa', with papers by eminent constitutional scholars and lawyers, which were eventually published in a booklet.[20]

Certainly, Brown failed to put the LDA on the national map in the 1980s. While the LDA served an ancillary social function as a sort of rallying point for the dwindling band of Liberal Party faithful, it failed to attract a significant number of new converts to liberalism – and very few black members at that. It failed to emerge as a serious broker between the ANC and the National Party, and its success in putting forward liberal policy alternatives for the post-apartheid order was muted. In part, that was because there was very little internal cohesion in the LDA: Brown and Wentzel and their respective sympathisers were pulling in opposite directions, and this prevented the association from becoming a national force to be reckoned with. Added to that, there were many other pressure groups vying to occupy the same space in the late 1980s. As the decade wore on, the extra-parliamentary terrain became increasingly crowded with organisations offering their services as political bridge-builders, 'dialogue facilitators' and negotiations mediators.

One of the most important of these organisations was the Institute for a Democratic Alternative in South Africa (IDASA). IDASA's aim was to find an alternative way to reduce the polarisation between black and white South Africans, and its mission was to help broker a peaceful transition to democracy while fostering and strengthening a culture of democratic rights. It was formed by Frederik van Zyl Slabbert after his decision in 1986 to quit Parliament and the leadership of the official opposition PFP. Slabbert's resignation sent shockwaves through the liberal community and created much resentment against him in his own party, which felt abandoned by him. Helen Suzman didn't speak to him for years. But Slabbert was convinced that the time had come to go. He was frustrated with the slow parliamentary process of constitutional change designed to maintain white supremacy – something that the Liberals had expressed decades before – and believed that he could achieve more outside Parliament.

Brown's view was that Slabbert had done 'something terrible to his Party', but disagreed with Paton's assessment which he related to Hamm: 'Alan's feeling [is] that he did something unforgivable to his Party and that, if you can do something like that, there is something flawed in you which will prevent you from ever doing anything of great consequence.' Brown continued: 'I don't share that view. I think he did something terrible to his Party, but I think it will survive it, which I also think is important. This is not to say that I think his Party is great but I do think it helps to have them in Parliament, questioning and exposing.'[21]

Brown welcomed Slabbert's new initiative. He wrote to Slabbert in January 1987, explained the genesis of the LDA, and told him that he wanted the Association to be 'complementary to, rather than in competition with, IDASA'.[22] Brown also offered to act as point of contact between IDASA and the PFP, 'if that is a problem'. Slabbert responded: 'My sentiments are very strongly with you concerning the promotion of liberal ideals and anything I can do to help I will.'[23]

There wasn't a close cooperation between the LDA and IDASA, although in 1989 IDASA convened a conference on the ANC's 'Constitutional Guidelines and Proposals', which Brown attended. The LDA submitted a memorandum prepared by Brown and a fellow committee member (and good friend of his), Francis Antonie, which 'welcomed the ANC's proposals and interpreted them as an indication of the ANC's bona fides in relation to ... establishing ... a non-racial democracy in South Africa'.[24] Its members supported the ANC's proposals and had 'no serious or major objections' to those 'policy goals, such as ... redistribution of land, the mixed economy, affirmative action, etc'. In fact, the LDA placed on record that '[t]he principle of affirmative action is accepted by our membership and should be applied to help overcome the historical iniquities that have accumulated'. On the issue of land, the LDA went to so far as to suggest that '[w]here appropriate, farms at present owned by Whites should be expropriated (not confiscated) by the State for re-allocation to landless Black people'. However, the LDA felt that several issues needed to be clarified or reconsidered. For example, the ANC's proposals favoured a unitary state, and the LDA argued that a federal system would be preferable in order to diffuse power, promote accountability and bring democracy closer to the people. The LDA acknowledged that calls for a federal system could be interpreted as a 'ploy' to perpetuate white privilege, but deemed that other mechanisms – primarily a Bill of Rights – could be used to 'accomplish the goals of non-racism and non-discriminatory socio-economic practices'. Finally, the LDA was concerned that the courts should have a testing right over the Bill of Rights.

* * *

Between 1986 and 1988, some petty apartheid laws were repealed. Botha warned white South Africans that they must 'adapt or die' to these reforms, but despite promising to 'cross the Rubicon' and announce more substantial reforms – which would have meant unbanning the ANC and PAC and releasing Nelson Mandela and other political prisoners from jail – Botha never delivered. His dilatoriness served to stoke political violence and cripple the economy. By 1987, the rate of economic growth had declined to among the lowest in the world. Industrial unrest intensified: that same year, about 200 000 members of the National Union of Mineworkers staged the longest strike (three weeks) in South African history. Meanwhile, the state cracked down even harder on its opponents: in 1987, the State of Emergency was extended for another two years, and the following year the UDF was banned.

All of this led to a growing sense of desperation among those South Africans who realised that there would have to be a negotiated transfer of power from the NP to the ANC soon, in order to prevent the 'explosion' which Brown had presaged in the 1940s.

The result was a number of clandestine meetings between the ANC in exile and domestic advocates of change. In 1987, Slabbert organised a group of academics, businessmen, clerics, journalists and politicians to attend a three-day meeting with senior ANC leaders in Dakar. Brown, too, was eager to make contact with the ANC in exile. He made two trips to Lusaka, the second one in 1989 when he attended a four-day conference, opened by Oliver Tambo, at the Intercontinental Hotel on the subject of 'Whites in a changing society'. Brown reported back to Hamm that one of the impressions he had gained from his two visits to Lusaka was the 'far greater sophistication of the ANC in exile than that of the MDM [Mass Democratic Movement] at home'. He explained: 'From being out in the world they have a far greater perception of how it works and what is possible and what is not, so that they are ready to make compromises about how to get to the post-apartheid state.'[25]

The second Lusaka conference was organised by a body called the Five Freedoms Forum (FFF). The genesis of the FFF occurred in November 1986, when Rev Beyers Naudé, then general secretary of the SACC, together with Geoff Budlender, the Transvaal director of the Legal Resources Centre, and Zwelakhe Sisulu, editor of New Nation, called together a broad range of organisations, including the Black Sash, the End Conscription Campaign, NUSAS and the PFP, to discuss a unified response to the latest State of Emergency. They formed a loose coalition, tackling issues as they arose and organising campaigns such as the 1986 'Christmas against the Emergency' campaign and a campaign against censorship in the 1987 election. In March 1987, the coalition eventually formed the Five Freedoms Forum, which styled itself as an 'extra-parliamentary, anti-apartheid organisation striving for a non-racial democracy'. The 'five freedoms' to which the name referred were: freedom from want; freedom from fear; freedom from exploitation and discrimination; freedom of conscience; and freedom of speech and association. The organisation's two main aims were to conscientise white South Africans and draw them into the process of change, and to facilitate the interaction between white parliamentary structures and extra-parliamentary organisations.[26]

Brown told Peter Horwitz in 1992 that although he remained on the committee of the Pietermaritzburg LDA, 'much more of my energy is going into the local Five Freedoms Forum', which he chaired, and whose work he described as 'getting blacks and whites of various political persuasions or none to get together to discuss the future in education, local affairs, the environment, health and on land and agricultural policy'.[27] He added: 'It seems to me that if you can get farmers and farm workers talking to each other on the basis of equality to discuss the transition process to the future, while doing the same sort of thing in other fields, it can only help.'[28]

Brown's other main interest, *Reality*, was forced to close in 1993 due to falling circulation and funds drying up, despite its fresher look and more crisply packaged content under the editorship of Ian Wyllie.[29] Brown's concern with agricultural policy, land reform and farm workers' rights in the FFF dovetailed with his work in AFRA, and this became his principal enthusiasm in the last decade of his active involvement in public life, until 1994, when he scaled back his activities. In the 1990s, under the auspices of the FFF, Brown organised a number of workshops on improving race relations between black freehold farmers and white commercial farmers,[30] and on land rights.[31] So any role Brown might have played – or that former Liberals might have wanted him to play – as a political mediator between the ANC and the NP in the late 1980s, or in the engine room of the negotiations process at the Convention for a Democratic South Africa (CODESA) in the 1990s, didn't materialise.

There were a number of explanations for this. Firstly, Brown's time had passed: his ban had removed him from the national stage and he never quite found his way back, or seemed to want to. He saw no good reason to revive the Liberal Party, especially after the Democratic Party (DP) was formed in 1989 through a merger of the PFP, Denis Worrall's Independent Movement and Wynand Malan's National Democratic Movement. Brown had 'serious reservations about Worrall' and thought some of the Progressives were 'pretty conservative', but he was glad that an opposition party to the left of the NP had managed to draw Afrikaner support.[32] Brown helped the DP ferry voters to the polls in the 1989 election, and found the Party 'much less equivocating than the PFP had often seemed to be'.[33]

Secondly, any attempts to position the LDA as a national vehicle for steering the transition in a liberal direction were hamstrung by its parochialism and the conflicting priorities of its branches in Pietermaritzburg and Johannesburg. In the end, Brown found it easier to work through organisations like the Five Freedoms Forum and AFRA, and to focus on specific issues like land reform.

Thirdly, Brown was caught somewhat off guard by the sudden-ness with which De Klerk announced his sweeping reforms on 2 Feb-ruary 1990 and the inexorable momentum which they proceeded to gather. In 1987, Helen Suzman had complained to Brown that '[w]e liberals are very much an endangered species' and be-moaned the fact that 'we have a limited role to play in this country of extremes'.[34] Yet, by the end of the decade both the NP and the ANC had grudgingly come to realise that liberal principles and values would be what drew them onto the middle ground; that these ideas would provide the tools for a negotiated settlement and the building blocks of a non-racial democratic society with a Con-stitution as the supreme law. Soon after De Klerk made his ground-breaking speech and Mandela was set free, Brown wrote to Wolf Hamm and asked: 'What do you do when the NP and the ANC start claiming Liberal policies as their own?' He put forward two options: 'You can decide to join one or other of them and "work from within", or you can stay outside and keep challenging both of them to practise what they now say they believe in.'[35] Brown chose to stay outside and take on the challenger's role.

* * *

Alongside his work for *Reality*, AFRA, the LDA and Five Freedoms Forum, Brown continued to maintain his social contacts at home and abroad. He continued to visit Winnie Mandela in Brandfort, the Free State town to which she was banished under 'house arrest' between 1977 and 1985. Brown had first visited Winnie with Alan Paton on the way back from Robert Sobukwe's funeral in 1978, and he tried to visit her as regularly as he could thereafter. He kept up a correspondence with her throughout the 1980s, and after her release she thanked him for making her days more 'bearable': 'You will probably never guess just how much your visits meant to me,' she wrote to him. 'On each occasion it was as if I had a new lease of life and I was able to face each lonely day ahead courageously.'[36]

In November 1986, Brown went on his first trip overseas since being unbanned. Pride and adherence to democratic principle had stopped him from applying for a new passport in the intervening twelve years, but with Vanessa having given birth to a granddaughter, Grace, in August, Brown was eager to travel to England. He and Phoebe spent the first week with Vanessa and then set off on a tour of England and Scotland, visiting old Liberal friends. They started with the Hains in Putney, and then spent time with Hans Meidner in Stirling. They also saw David Craighead, Derick Marsh in Stratford and dined with Bill Hoffenberg at the Royal College of Physicians.[37]

At home, Brown kept up his farming operations. In the early part of the 1980s, his son, Chris, took over the running of a farm that his father had acquired in Nottingham Road, and Brown senior showed him the ropes – a case of 'the blind leading the blind', he joked to Bill Hoffenberg.[38] He busied himself with his duties as a trustee of King's School and took a keen interest in the establishment of the Alan Paton Centre (since renamed the Alan Paton Centre & Struggle Archives) at the University of Natal, which was officially opened in May 1989. The Centre, which includes an exact replica of Paton's study with his desk and books, also houses Paton's manuscripts and documents, as well as those of other individuals and institutions involved in the struggle against apartheid. Brown thought the Centre would be a fitting tribute to Paton, who died on 12 April 1988, and he was a generous benefactor.

Paton's death was naturally a great loss for Brown. He had been Brown's mentor and father figure in a way, his confidant, his nearest ally in the Liberal Party and his closest friend during the long years of his ban. Anne Paton believed that of all Paton's friends, Brown 'filled the number one slot'. She wrote to him after Alan's death:

> You had a great influence over his thinking, and he really valued your friendship above all others. In the latter years, when he had withdrawn considerably, you were one of the few people who could stimulate him and arouse his enthusiasm. But I guess you know this.[39]

Jonathan Paton, Alan's younger son, who had a complicated relationship with his father, told Peter and Phoebe that they were the '*real* legacy I have inherited from my father'.[40] For his part, Brown acknowledged to Anne that Alan had been his 'most important and constant support during the banning years, as well as on many occasions before and after that time', and added, 'the gap he has left in our lives isn't one that anyone else will ever fill'.[41]

Brown read from Paton's favourite psalms and prayers at his memorial service in Pietermaritzburg, as did Elliot Mngadi and John Mitchell. He was also the main speaker at Paton's memorial service in St Paul's Cathedral in London in June, which was organised by Randolph Vigne. He recalled with fondness Paton's visits to him during his ban, and captured something of their bantering relationship, saying of Paton:

> He invariably spent the night, and after dinner we would sit sipping a drink, and engage ourselves for an hour or two in putting the world to rights. On most occasions when people are putting the world to rights, an air of solemnity prevails. Not on these. Jokes would intervene. Alan was a great one for jokes and he told them very well. If I told a joke, he would chuckle away at it. And if he told a joke, he would chuckle away for longer.[42]

Brown also praised Paton's endeavours to bring about a democratic common society and his 'fearless and eloquent statement of ... Liberal concepts at a time when most other people were keeping quiet'. It was a source of sadness for Brown that Paton did not live to see the changes that, by 1988, Brown thought were inevitable. Another two of Brown's political confidants and friends, Selby Msimang and Ernie Wentzel, didn't live to see the fruits of their lives' work either: they died in 1982 and 1986, respectively. As Brown approached his three score and ten in 1994, and the moment to which his whole life's work had been directed – the first democratic election in which South Africans of all races could exercise their right to vote – thoughts of his own contribution to public life, and mortality, couldn't have been far off.

THE FINAL DECADE
1994-2004

In the late 1980s and early 1990s, Brown was actively involved in organisations like the LDA and the FFF, which sought to facilitate the transition to democracy and ensure that whatever political settlement was reached between the ANC and the apartheid government would be based on liberal principles. Both Brown and these two organisations were bit players in this drama. After President de Klerk announced his far-reaching reforms in 1990, the nuts and bolts of the negotiated settlement were put together at CODESA and in the Multiparty Negotiating Forum between 1991 and 1993.

Brown observed developments keenly from the sidelines, but he took no part in the negotiation process. The liberal ideas which he had championed since the 1950s were put forward by a younger generation of people involved in formal party politics – principally the DP – and contemporaries like Colin Eglin, who had fought a long and hard battle in Parliament for liberalism. However, it was a deeply moving experience for Brown to see his life's work – the struggle for non-racial democracy – culminate in the first democratic election on 27 April 1994.

Brown was one of 22 million South Africans who went to the polls that day, and stood in queues that snaked around for kilometres, to make their mark on the ballot paper and celebrate the end of years of oppression and the beginning of a new dawn. He thought the election was a 'miraculous occasion', and described to Wolf Hamm his sense of wonderment on voting at Nottingham Road where the atmosphere was almost festive:

Nobody quite knowing what might happen at the polling station, we decided to go early, and arrived about half an hour before it opened. There was already a queue about 100 yards long and it grew steadily all the time we were there. It was quite extraordinary to see vehicle after vehicle arriving, driven by a farmer and loaded to the hilt with his workers being brought to vote. Out they piled and, all together, went into the queue, shouting greetings to friends and relations already there. Once polling started we were finished within half-an-hour. I went in immediately behind an old man who is completely illiterate and usually becomes petrified at the sight of a pen. This time he sailed through with an enormous grin all over his face. And so it seemed to be with everyone else. In one day the atmosphere of the whole country seemed to change.[1]

Having dedicated his life's work to bringing about the change that was ushered in that day, Brown remained a keen observer of South Africa's consolidation as a constitutional democracy after the ANC took power.

He welcomed the reconciliatory thrust of Nelson Mandela's presidency, although he worried in 1995 that the Truth and Reconciliation Commission 'could do untold harm to what has been a remarkable record of reconciliation so far'. He explained to Hamm:

So far the Afrikaners have behaved remarkably well since 1990 and have shown themselves much more willing to accept their loss of real power than anyone could have expected. I don't believe in raking over the past, however awful it might have been, if that is going to threaten what has been achieved so far, and I very much fear that we may be embarking on a course which will ... exacerbate not only Afrikaner-ANC tensions but black-white tensions as well. I hope I am wrong.[2]

Later in the decade, Brown was disturbed by what he felt was a 'trend towards falling back on racially-tainted statements when anyone who isn't black criticises the government'.[3] One of the lessons from Robert Mugabe's Zimbabwe, he believed, was that 'our transformation must be much more rapid than his ever was', and that the 'white structures of business and agriculture' must come to the party. However, he cautioned that 'if either the government or their opponents start bandying charges of racism about, we may be in for a rough ride'.

Brown was critical of Mandela's successor, Thabo Mbeki: he found it 'difficult to have much faith in Mbeki as the custodian of our future' when Mbeki's government had, in his view, failed to 'get a grip on the things which really matter – crime, unemployment and, above all, Aids'.[4] If racial reconciliation had set the tone for Mandela's presidency, then Mbeki's administration was far more concerned with racial transformation. Brown didn't object to transformation insofar as affirmative action was concerned. He believed that affirmative action was 'fine in principle' and had to be 'seen to be happening … from the political point of view', though he worried that if it was implemented indiscriminately it would lead to a flight of skilled whites. Brown's concern about transformation was that it tended to racialise public discourse and fuel a tendency towards 'playing the race card'. He also objected to transformation when it was used as a cover for the over-concentration and centralisation of state power, and as an argument to keep the ruling party in power in perpetuity. A few months before he died in 2004, Brown told Hamm: '… I increasingly share [the] sense that Mbeki doesn't see the transition from a government dominated by the predominant liberation party to a position where there is a chance of it losing out in a full democratic society, as an altogether desirable thing.'[5] Yet Brown was critical of the liberal opposition too. He thought the DP had 'made a complete cock-up of its relations with the ANC',[6] and that its successor party, the Democratic Alliance, ran a 'very unattractive' campaign in 2004 – 'a mixture of bluster and nasty compromise'.[7]

* * *

Although Brown reduced his public commitments from 1994, he remained engaged in the causes which he thought were interesting and important. Like his father before him, he donated money to many good civic and individual causes, although often anonymously, so the actual extent of his charity will never be known. Brown was closely involved with the Alan Paton Centre at the University of Natal in Pietermaritzburg, and delivered the second Alan Paton Lecture in 1995 on 'Alan Paton: The Man and the Politician'. He was concerned that the contribution made by the Liberal Party to the coming of democracy should not be forgotten, and he invited Randolph Vigne, his friend who had gone into exile after the African Resistance Movement was blown open in 1964, to write its history. In fact, the idea had first been mooted at the Liberal Party Workshop in 1985. For many of the delegates there, the obvious candidate for the job seemed to be Brown, who had already produced a lengthy chronological history during his ban. When Paton caught wind of this, he apparently snarled: 'Brown? But he can't write!'[8] Jill Wentzel relayed the story to Brown at the time: 'Paton growled at me that you couldn't write, had no sense of drama, the jealous old bastard. So now you've *got* to write it.'[9] Vigne's book, *Liberals against Apartheid: A History of the Liberal Party of South Africa, 1953-1968*, was published in 1997, and Brown was the main speaker at its launch at the Reform Club in London.

The Browns travelled frequently to the United Kingdom in the last decade of Peter's life, to visit Vanessa and old Liberal Party friends who had gone into exile. Vigne would always rally a corps of South African exiles, including Colin and Margaret Legum, Donald and Wendy Woods, and Paul and Adelaide Joseph, when Brown visited. Until around 2000, after which he declined, Brown would speak to them about what was happening in South Africa. As Vigne notes, 'He had retired, though he remained true to his local commitments and was always a keen observer of the bigger picture.'[10]

One of his private commitments was to his prize-winning herd of Hereford cattle, which he farmed at Lion's Bush after selling up at Nottingham Road in the early part of the new century. From 1997, Brown, who was always keen to see land used productively, became actively involved with emerging African farmers in Mooi River, teaching them how to farm cattle and dairy. This project was eventually taken over by the Midlands Community College, on whose farm advisory committee Brown served. He also made over the surrounding land on which his Giant's Castle cottage stood to occupants of the neighbouring reserve, and helped them to farm cattle.

For his public commitments, Brown received some recognition in his final decade. Nelson Mandela had already publicly praised Brown at a rally in Durban shortly after his release from prison – Brown, coincidentally, had gone along to listen to him that day – and in 1994 he invited Brown to attend a luncheon in honour of 'veterans of the struggle', which he did, along with other liberals like Helen Suzman. In 1997, the University of Natal awarded Brown an honorary doctorate. In 2000, the Pietermaritzburg-Msunduzi Transitional Local Council presented him with a civic certificate of commendation in recognition of his work.

Brown continued to see his Liberal friends. In 2000, his old cellmate Derick Marsh and his wife spent three weeks visiting Peter and Phoebe, and they took a trip around the country. They started off in the Drakensberg where they called on Mike Ndlovu (Elliot Mngadi's right-hand man in the black spot campaigns), then went onto Excelsior in the Free State where they saw Jean van Riet, and ended with a few days in the Hluhluwe Game Reserve. In his last years, Brown kept up his forty-year-long correspondence with Wolf Hamm in England, regularly visited the Weinbergs and the Robertses, as well as other members of the Pietermaritzburg Liberal network, and saw as much of his grandchildren – Grace, Cameron, Alistair, Antonia and Peter – as he could.

Although he was fit and travelled with ease, Brown had in fact been diagnosed with prostate cancer in 1997. In 2001, the cancer began to spread and Brown became frailer. In January 2004, he cracked his pelvis and had to walk with the aid of a cane. A few months later, a brain surgeon picked up that he had a tumour and told him that he had four months to live. Vanessa came out from England to say her goodbyes. On the morning of 28 June 2004, while his unwavering partner of fifty-four years, Phoebe, and son, Anton, were at home, Brown collapsed in the passage after a massive heart attack. Within ten minutes he was dead.

* * *

What, then, to make of Brown's life and work? Delivering the eulogy at Brown's memorial service at the Cathedral of the Holy Nativity in Pietermaritzburg on 9 July 2004, Colin Gardner remarked on the fact that Brown was a 'natural liberal and democrat, a person who took for granted without any fuss or rhetoric that all people are equal, that every South African has the same kinds of needs, hopes and fears'. Those may seem like unremarkable qualities now, but in the 1950s they were rare indeed for a white South African.

Peter Brown grew up in an extremely affluent Old Natal Family, to parents whose political outlook was very much circumscribed by the conservative norms of contemporary white English-speaking settler society. When he visited Adams College as a schoolboy, his eyes began to open: in his own words, the visit shattered the accumulated stereotypes about black people with which he had grown up. From an early age, Brown sensed that there was something fundamentally unjust about the South African racial order. The feeling gnawed away at his conscience throughout the period of his active service in the Second World War, but it was only as a student at Cambridge in 1947 that the scales fell from his eyes. He heard Peter Abrahams, the Coloured South African novelist, attack the injustices of segregated South Africa, and it was, he wrote home, 'a revelation of our own blindness'. Brown realised then that his life's work must focus on building better race relations between black and white so as to avert the 'explosion' which he knew would otherwise occur.

To be sure, Brown's early efforts to this end, and his particular brand of liberalism in the early 1950s, were shaped by a racially more enlightened form of what he identified in his own parents as 'benign paternalism'. He believed in a qualified franchise. He believed that evolutionary change would come from the all-white Parliament. However, his conversion to a more radical liberalism was swift. This liberalism, which the Liberal Party championed under Brown's chairmanship between 1958 and 1964, considered universal suffrage non-negotiable, emphasised extra-parliamentary activism in black communities on issue-driven campaigns, like the one against black spot removals, and pitted a commitment to social justice and equity alongside civil rights. It was way ahead of its time in South Africa, and it was way ahead of the liberalism espoused by the Progressive Party when it was formed in 1959.

As leader of the Liberal Party, Brown was utterly dedicated and consistent. It was once said of Leo Marquard that he was like a piece of fine wood – all of one grain. Brown, too, was all of one grain, but he was not without his imperfections as a political leader. Always understated, both in his public and private lives, he failed to glamorise or dramatise the Liberal Party's campaigns and causes. Selby Msimang, who Brown first met at Edendale in 1951, acknowledged after the Party was forced to disband in 1968 that one of the reasons for its failure to attract mass African member-ship was the absence of something dynamic and emotional in its programme. Brown did not provide it, but then that was not his style. As Randolph Vigne recalls, Brown was 'no gladhanding, baby kissing politician': he could appear distant and offhand, since he was utterly without sham or simulation, but he had outstanding leadership qualities and inspired real trust and devotion in those who shared his political views.[11]

For years after the Liberal Party disbanded, right up until his death, Brown continued to express his care and concern for the party faithful, often through anonymous financial support along-side acts of friendship. He would root out old Liberals all over the country and gather them. As ever, Phoebe was by his side. She con-tinued to handle with calmness and composure the many larger-than-life characters who had frequented Shinglewood during Peter's years of active politics. Throughout their marriage, Phoebe provided the bedrock of domestic stability and emotional support that sustained her husband and allowed him to exert a positive influence in so many spheres.

The Liberal Party achieved something very important in the fif-teen years of its existence, and Brown made a significant contribu-tion to that achievement. The Party championed the principles and values that, decades later, would constitute the foundations of non-racial, democratic, post-apartheid South African society: uni-versal suffrage, the rule of law, the legal protection of basic civil lib-erties and social justice. In the 1960s, it was the only party in the electoral arena to do so. Outside the electoral arena, in the Congress movement, Marxist orthodoxy made many anti-apartheid activists suspicious of the liberal precepts which now underpin the South African constitutional order.

After his banning orders lapsed in 1974, Brown kept these liberal ideas alive in a variety of different institutions and through the magazine *Reality*. His decade of banishment exacted a toll, however: he never returned to active political life, and the role he played in the formal negotiated transition to democracy in the late 1980s and early 1990s was marginal and modest. Yet his work in organisations like the Liberal Democratic Association and the Five Freedoms Forum was not without consequence. In a small way, these organisations added to the growing chorus of voices calling for change.

Perhaps, after 1974, Brown's greatest contribution was in the field of rural advancement and land rights. In some ways a natural progression from his work with the Northern Natal African Landowners' Association against black spot removals in the 1950s, his involvement with AFRA helped empower farm workers and labour tenants. Brown also drew attention to the need for land redistribution and restitution before the transition to democracy, which was not something that many of his liberal contemporaries did.

Peter Brown made an important and lasting contribution to the liberal tradition in South Africa. He helped, in his own way, to guide us into the non-racial democratic society we inhabit today. For that he deserves recognition and respect. What did Brown think of the prospects for South African liberalism before he died? Interviewed by Norman Bromberger in 1996, Brown predicted:

> There may come a time when the ANC starts to disintegrate or to produce factions ... and ... perhaps as the economy improves and so on ... there will be an opportunity to form a fully non-racial Liberal Party again. Something which will absorb the DP [now the Democratic Alliance] and elements from other political organisations ...[12]

From the vantage point of 2010, Brown's views seem prescient. Time will tell if he is proved right.

NOTES

ABBREVIATIONS

APC   Alan Paton Centre and Struggle Archive, University of KwaZulu-Natal
BI   Borthwick Institute for Historical Research, University of York
JWP   Jill Wentzel Papers, in private possession of Jill Wentzel, Johannesburg
PBP   Phoebe Brown Papers, in private possession of Phoebe Brown, Pieter-
maritzburg
UCT   University of Cape Town Manuscripts and Archives
UNISA   University of South Africa Archives
WHP   Wolf Hamm Papers, in private possession of Wolf Hamm, London
Wits   University of the Witwatersrand Department of Historical Papers

PROLOGUE

1   Nelson Mandela, Address to rally in Durban, 25 February 1990. At
www.anc.org.za/ancdocs/history/mandela/1990/sp900225-1.html. See also
N Mandela, *Long Walk to Freedom* (Johannesburg: Macdonald Purnell,
1994), p 566 and A Sampson, *Mandela: The Authorised Biography* (London:
HarperCollins, 2000), p 437.

2   The invitation to the event, on 23 July 1994, is in the University of KwaZulu-
Natal, Alan Paton Centre and Struggle Archive (APC), Peter Brown Collection (PC16), PC16/5/4/7/6.

3   RW Johnson, 'The Rainbow Nation paints out the whites', *Sunday Times*,
London, 27 July 2003.

4   See, for example, Chris Barron, 'Peter Brown: Twice-banned Liberal Party
stalwart', *Sunday Times*, 4 July 2004; Howard Donaldson, 'Death of a man of
conscience', *Sunday Tribune*, 4 July 2004; Michael Gardiner, 'Adieu to "a particular kind of liberal"', *Mail & Guardian*, 2-8 July 2004; Douglas Irvine,
'Peter Brown: a pioneering democrat', *Sunday Independent*, 4 July 2004; 'A
man of honour', *Natal Witness*, 2 July 2004; Randolph Vigne, 'Obituary:
Peter Brown', *The Independent*, 6 July 2004.

5   Peter McKenzie Brown: Matters relating to the award of a civic certificate
of commendation, Pietermaritzburg-Msunduzi Transitional Local Council,
7 February 2000.

6   APC, PC16/5/3/3/92, Winnie Mandela to Brown, 15 January 1982.

7   A Luthuli, *Let My People Go* (Cape Town: Tafelberg/Mafube, 2006 [1962]),
p 132.

8   Commission reports and draft resolutions, ANC national policy conference,
27-30 June 2007, Gallagher Estate. At www.anc.org.za/ancdocs/policy/
2007/conference/commission.html.

9   K Asmal, L Asmal and RS Roberts, *Reconciliation through Truth: A Reckoning of Apartheid's Criminal Governance* (Cape Town: David Philip, 1996). For a discussion of Asmal's criticisms, see M Lipton, *Liberals, Marxists, and Nationalists* (London: Palgrave Macmillan, 2007), pp 138-144.

10 'Apartheid is the real enemy', The Long View, *Contact*, 13 June 1959. Duncan's open letter appeared in *Contact*, 2 May 1959.

11 'Why I support the boycott', The Long View, *Contact*, 6 February 1960.

12 Cited in R Vigne, *Liberals Against Apartheid: A History of the Liberal Party of South Africa, 1953-1968* (London: Macmillan, 1997), p 112.

13 C Eglin, *Crossing the Borders of Power: The Memoirs of Colin Eglin* (Cape Town: Jonathan Ball, 2007), p 200.

14 R Segal, *African Profiles* (Harmondsworth: Penguin, 1963), p 28.

Chapter 1 – Origins and childhood

1   APC, 96 APB3, Interview with Peter Brown by Norman Bromberger, 14 August 1995, p 3.

2   Elizabeth Brown, Personal memoirs, in possession of Phoebe Brown.

3   APC, 96 APB3, Interview with Peter Brown by Norman Bromberger, 14 August 1995.

4   Donald C McKenzie and John R McKenzie (eds), *Polo in South Africa* (Dargle, 1999), pp 28-29; pp 384-385.

5   *Natal Witness*, 23 August 1935.

6   APC, 96 APB3, Interview with Peter Brown by Norman Bromberger, 14 August 1995, p 2.

7   The term 'Byrne settlers' refers to those emigrants brought to Natal by the company, JC Byrne & Co. They arrived between 1849 and 1851 and settled on allotments in the Byrne valley, near Richmond.

8   Interview with Pat McKenzie, Pietermaritzburg, 7 May 2007.

9   APC, 96 APB3, Interview with Peter Brown by Norman Bromberger, 14 August 1995.

10 APC, 96 APB3, Interview with Peter Brown by Norman Bromberger, 14 August 1995.

11 APC, 96 APB3, Interview with Peter Brown by Norman Bromberger, 14 August 1995.

Chapter 2 – Michaelhouse

1   P Randall, *Little England on the Veld: the English private school system in South Africa* (Johannesburg: Ravan, 1982).

2   APC, 96 APB3, Interview with Peter Brown by Norman Bromberger, 14 August 1995, p 5.

3   APC, 96 APB3, Interview with Peter Brown by Norman Bromberger, 14 August 1995, p 5.

4   E Brookes, *A South African Pilgrimage* (Johannesburg: Ravan, 1977), p 6.

5   Brookes, *A South African Pilgrimage*, p 19.

6   Brookes, *A South African Pilgrimage*, p 35.

7   P Rich, *White Power and the Liberal Conscience: Racial Segregation and South African Liberalism, 1921-1960* (Johannesburg: Ravan Press, 1984), pp 33-4. Curiously, there is still no full-length biography of Brookes, but see his autobiography, *A South African Pilgrimage* (Johannesburg: Ravan, 1977), and Chapter 3: 'Edgar Brookes and the "Lie in the Soul" of Segregation' in P Rich, *Hope and Despair: English-Speaking Intellectuals and South African Politics, 1896-1976* (London: British Academic Press, 1993).

8   P Brown, 'Some Thoughts About Edgar Brookes, South African Liberalism and the Future', Delivered at the University of Natal, Pietermaritzburg, 16 August 1979, p 2.

9   APC, 96 APB3, Interview with Peter Brown by Norman Bromberger, 14 August 1995, p 6.

10 *St Michael's Chronicle,* Vol IX, No 4 (December 1942), p 22.

11 *St Michael's Chronicle,* Vol IX, No 1 (May 1941).

12 *St Michael's Chronicle,* Vol IX, No 2 (December 1941).

13 *St Michael's Chronicle,* Vol IX, No 1 (May 1941).

14 APC, PC2/9/11/1, Brown to the Governors, Rector and Staff of Michaelhouse, 6 August 1963.

15 APC, PC2/9/11/1, Brown to Rev Bishop Inman, Chairman of the Michaelhouse Board of Governors, 11 August 1965.

16 APC, PC2/9/11/1, Brown to Tommy Norwood, Rector of Michaelhouse, 15 November 1966.

17 APC, PC16/5/3/1/46, Brown to the Secretary of the Board of Governors of Michaelhouse, 4 July 1979.

18 *St Michael's Chronicle,* Vol IX, No 3 (September 1942).

19 APC, 96 APB3, Interview with Peter Brown by Norman Bromberger, 14 August 1995, p 8.

20 *St Michael's Chronicle,* Vol. IX, No. 3 (September 1942).

21 *St Michael's Chronicle,* Vol. IX, No. 4 (December 1942), p 11.

22 AM Barrett, *Michaelhouse: 1896-1968* (Michaelhouse Old Boys Club, 1969), p 120.

23 APC, 96 APB3, Interview with Peter Brown by Norman Bromberger, 14 August 1995.

24 APC, 96 APB3, Interview with Peter Brown by Norman Bromberger, 14 August 1995, p 8.

CHAPTER 3 – WAR

1   Cited in Rich, *White Power and the Liberal Conscience*, p 74, and Rich, *Hope and Despair*, p 187. See also P Walshe, *The Rise of African Nationalism in South Africa: The African National Congress 1912-1952* (London: C Hurst & Co, 1970), pp 268-71.

2   (DL Smit), *Report of the Inter-departmental Committee on Social, Health and Eco-nomic Conditions of Urban Natives* (Pretoria: Government Printer, 1942).

3   See, for example, Chapter 29, 'Planning a New World', in A Paton, *Hofmeyr* (Cape Town: Oxford University Press, 1964).

4   Phoebe Brown Private Papers [PBP] Brown to his mother, no date but stamped 26 October 1942.

5   APC, 96 APB3, Interview with Peter Brown by Norman Bromberger, 14 August 1995.

6   PBP, Brown to his mother, 13 January 1943.

7   PBP, Brown to his mother, 7 March 1943.

8   PBP, Brown to his mother, 3 May 1943.

9   PBP, Brown to his mother, 9 May 1943.

10   PBP, Brown to his mother, 26 December 1943.

11   APC, 96 APB3, Interview with Peter Brown by Norman Bromberger, 14 August 1995.

12   APC, 96 APB3, Interview with Peter Brown by Norman Bromberger, 14 August 1995.

13   APC, 96 APB3, Interview with Peter Brown by Norman Bromberger, 14 August 1995.

14   PBP, Brown to his mother, 6 February 1944.

15   PBP, Brown to his mother, 2 January 1944.

16   Burger [Leo Marquard], *The Black Man's Burden* (London: Victor Gollancz, 1943), p 244.

17   Burger, *The Black Man's Burden*, p 251.

18   PBP, Brown to his mother, 7 May 1944

19   PBP, Brown to his mother, 13 February 1944.

20   PBP, Brown to his mother, 17 November 1944.

21   PBP, Brown to his mother, 13 February 1944.

22   PBP, Brown to his mother, 25 May 1945.

23   PBP, Brown to his mother, 5 June 1945.

24   PBP, Brown to his mother, 25 June 1945.

25   PBP, Brown to his mother, 5 September 1945.

26   APC, 96 APB3, Interview with Peter Brown by Norman Bromberger, 14 August 1995.

27   PBP, Brown to his mother, 7 October 1944.

28   PBP, Brown to his mother, 20 October 1944.

29   APC, 96 APB3, Interview with Peter Brown by Norman Bromberger, 14 August 1995.

30   PBP, Brown to his mother, 12 January 1945.

31   PBP, Brown to his mother, 5 August 1945.

32   PBP, Brown to his mother, 8 September 1945.

33   APC, 96 APB3, Interview with Peter Brown by Norman Bromberger, 14 August 1995.

CHAPTER 4 – CAMBRIDGE AND THE AFRICAN AWAKENING

1   APC, 96 APB3, Interview with Peter Brown by Norman Bromberger, 14 August 1995.
2   PBP, Brown to his mother, 29 September 1946.
3   PBP, Brown to his mother, 6 October 1946.
4   PBP, Brown to his mother, 12 October 1946.
5   PBP, Brown to his mother, 20 October 1946.
6   PBP, Brown to his mother, 20 October 1946.
7   PBP, Brown to his mother, 10 November 1946.
8   PBP, Brown to his mother, 19 January 1947.
9   PBP, Brown to his mother, 30 November 1946.
10   Interview with Chris Carlisle, Kloof, 9 May 2007.
11   PBP, Brown to his mother, 19 January 1947.
12   APC, 96 APB3, Interview with Peter Brown by Norman Bromberger, 14 August 1995.
13   APC, 96 APB3, Interview with Peter Brown by Norman Bromberger, 14 August 1995.
14   PBP, Brown to his mother, 2 March 1947.
15   PBP, Brown to his mother, 2 March 1947.
16   PBP, Edgar Brookes to Maisie Brown, 7 May 1947.
17   PBP, Brown to his mother, 25 May 1947.
18   PBP, Brown to his mother, 14 June 1947.
19   PBP, Brown to his mother, 23 June 1947.
20   PBP, Brown to his mother, 31 October 1947.
21   PBP, Brown to his mother, 21 December 1947.
22   PBP, Brown to his mother, 21 December 1947.
23   PBP, Brown to his mother, 26 December 1947.
24   PBP, Brown to his mother, 17 January 1948.

CHAPTER 5 – INTO 'NATIVE AFFAIRS': THE UNIVERSITY OF CAPE TOWN

1   PBP, Brown to his mother, 12 March 1948.
2   PBP, Brown to his mother, 19 April 1948.
3   PBP, Brown to his mother, 19 April 1948.
4   Interview with Bill Hoffenberg, Cape Town, 16 March 2007.
5   APC, 96 APB3, Interview with Peter Brown by Norman Bromberger, 21 August 1995.
6   APC, 96 APB3, Interview with Peter Brown by Norman Bromberger, 21 August 1995.
7   PBP, Brown to his mother, 13 June 1948.
8   PBP, Brown to his mother, 26 November 1948; 28 November 1948.
9   APC, 96 APB3, Interview with Peter Brown by Norman Bromberger, 21 August 1995.

10   APC, 96 APB3, Interview with Peter Brown by Norman Bromberger,
      21 August 1995.
11   Communication with Phoebe Brown, 19 August 2009.
12   PBP, Brown to his mother, 30 August 1948.
13   PBP, Brown to his mother, 5 September 1948.
14   PBP, Brown to his mother, 26 November 1948.

CHAPTER 6 – EDENDALE

1   M Epprecht, 'Good and bad: history matters', 22 March 2007. At www.
      queensu.ca/sarc/ecohealth/downloads/Good%20and%20bad%20History
      %20Matters.pdf
2   RP Seymour, 'A Local Health Study: Public Health Area of Edendale and
      District', Report prepared at the invitation of Dr JJ du P le Roux, Union
      Secretary of Health, for presentation to the United Nations World Health
      Organisation (The Natal Press: no date). In APC, PC16/1/1/1/17.
3   APC, 96 APB3, Interview with Peter Brown by Norman Bromberger,
      21 August 1995.
4   APC, 96 APB3, Interview with Peter Brown by Norman Bromberger,
      21 August 1995.
5   APC, PC16/1/1/2/1, 'The YMCA in Edendale', no date.
6   APC, PC16/1/1/2/2-4, Brown to Master Builders Association of Pieter-
      maritzburg, 5 and 20 November 1951.
7   APC, PC16/1/1/2/78, Revenue and Expenditure Account for the Year
      Ended 30 September 1952.
8   APC, PC16/1/1/2/36, Doris Campbell (Secretary to the Rector of Michael-
      house) to Brown, 13 March 1952.
9   APC, PC16/1/1/2/78, Revenue and Expenditure Account for the Year
      Ended 30 September 1952.
10   Second Alan Paton Lecture, University of Natal, Pietermaritzburg,
      6 September 1995.

CHAPTER 7 – THE PIETERMARITZBURG LIBERAL GROUP AND THE
FORMATION OF THE LIBERAL PARTY

1   Vigne, *Liberals Against Apartheid*, p 10.
2   APC, 96, APB3, Interview with Peter Brown conducted by Norman Brom-
      berger, 14 August 1995, Interview 1, p 12.
3   Interview with Neville Rubin, Cape Town, 17 January 2007.
4   APC, 96 APB3, Interview with Peter Brown conducted by Norman Brom-
      berger, 21 August 1995, Interview 2, p 9.
5   APC, PC2/6/8/2, P Brown, unpublished 'Chronological History of the
      Liberal Party of South Africa, 1953-1966', pp 9-10.

6   S Dubow, *Racial Segregation and the Origins of Apartheid in South Africa, 1919-1936* (London: Macmillan, 1989), pp 21-50.

7   A Paton, *Hofmeyr* (Cape Town: Oxford University Press, 1964), p 165.

8   PS Thompson, *Natalians First: Separatism in South Africa, 1909-1961* (Johannesburg: Southern Books, 1990).

9   APC, 96 APB3, Interview with Peter Brown conducted by Norman Bromberger, 21 August 1995, Interview 2, p 9.

10 APC, 96 APB3, Interview with Peter Brown conducted by Norman Bromberger, 21 August 1995, Interview 2, p 9.

11 APC, PC2/2/1/4, Untitled TS, 21 June 1952.

12 APC, PC2/2/8/2, pp 9-10.

13 APC, PC2/2/8/2, pp 9-10.

14 APC, PC2/2/1/4, [Notes on] Liberal Group [meeting], 7 July 1952.

15 A Paton, *Cry, the Beloved Country: A Story of Comfort in Desolation* (New York: Scribner, 1948).

16 A Paton, *Too Late the Phalarope* (New York: Scribner, 1953).

17 APC, PC2/3/6/1, Alan Paton to Brown, 14 November 1952.

18 P Alexander, *Alan Paton: A Biography* (Oxford: Oxford University Press, 1994), p 286.

19 A Paton, *Journey Continued: An Autobiography* (Cape Town: David Philip, 1988), p 90.

20 APC, PC2/6/8/2, pp 8-9; Vigne, *Liberals Against Apartheid*, p 11.

21 A Keppel-Jones, *When Smuts Goes: A History of South Africa from 1952-2010* (Pietermaritzburg: Shuter & Shooter, 1953).

22 Ballinger was heard saying this by Randolph Vigne on a public platform, either in 1954 or 1955. Personal communication with Randolph Vigne, 8 April 2008. See also A Mouton, *Voices in the Desert – Margaret and William Ballinger: A Biography* (Pretoria: Benedic Books, 1997).

23 Cited in Vigne, *Liberals Against Apartheid*, p 14.

24 APC, PC2/3/6/1, Julius Lewin to Brown, 21 November 1952.

25 APC, PC2/2/1/1, Oscar Wollheim to Alan Paton, 15 November 1952.

26 APC, PC2/2/1/1, Oscar Wollheim to Alan Paton, 15 November 1952.

27 APC, PC2/2/1/1, Brown to Alan Paton, 20 November 1952.

28 APC, PC2/2/1/1, Oscar Wollheim to Brown, 25 November 1952.

29 APC, PC2/2/1/1, Oscar Wollheim to Brown, 25 November 1952.

30 APC, PC2/2/1/4, [Minutes of] Inaugural meeting of the Pietermaritzburg Liberal Group held in conference room, City Hall on Monday 8 December 1953 [1952].

31 APC, PC2/2/1/4, Brown's speaking notes for the inaugural meeting of the Pietermaritzburg Liberal Group held in conference room, City Hall on Monday 8 December 1953 [1952].

32 APC, PC2/6/8/2, p 15.

33 APC, PC2/2/1/1, Brown to Alan Paton, 6 January 1953.

34 APC, PC2/6/8/2, p 11.

35 APC, PC2/2/1/4, Unidentifiable sender to Brown, 9 December 1952.

36   APC, PC2/2/1/4, A Allsopp to Brown, 9 December 1952.

37   APC, PC2/2/1/4, Unidentified sender to Mr [Simon?] Roberts, 9 December 1952.

38   APC, PC2/2/1/1, Brown to Alan Paton, 6 January 1953.

39   Derick Marsh, Unpublished memoir, received by personal communication, 25 September 2006, p 111.

40   Royal Society of Edinburgh, Obituary: Hans Meidner. At www.royalsoced. org. uk/fellowship/obits/obits_alpha/meidner_anton.pdf.

41   APC, 96 APB3, Interview with Peter Brown conducted by Norman Bromberger, 27 September 1995, Interview 5, p 3; Vigne, *Liberals Against Apartheid*, p 16; Telephone interview with Olga Meidner, June 2007.

42   APC, PC2/2/1/1, Alan Paton to Brown, 5 March 1953.

43   APC, PC2/2/1/1, Alan Paton to Brown, 5 March 1953.

44   APC, PC2/6/8/2, p 23.

45   APC, PC2/2/1/3, Leo Marquard to Brown, 27 December 1964.

46   For Durrant's objections to the formation of a Liberal Party and suggestions that plans for an alternative Torch Commando-linked party might be afoot, see University of Cape Town Manuscripts and Archives (UCT), Leo Marquard Papers (BC 587), E2.18, Geoff Durrant to Marquard, 29 April 1953.

47   APC, PC2/2/3/1, Minutes: South African Liberal Association Council Meeting, 8-9 May 1953.

CHAPTER 8 – CONSOLIDATING THE HOME BASE: NATAL PROVINCIAL SECRETARY

1   M Ballinger, *From Union to Apartheid: A Trek to Isolation* (Cape Town: Juta, 1969), p 403.

2   Ballinger, *From Union to Apartheid*, p 403.

3   She unsuccessfully moved to substitute 'non-violent' for 'constitutional' at the 1954 Congress. APC, PC2/2/4/3, Minutes: National Congress, 10-12 July 1954.

4   APC, PC2/5/1/3, Brown to Walter Stanford, 1 July 1959.

5   APC, 96 APB3, Interview with Peter Brown conducted by Norman Bromberger, 27 September 1995, Interview 5, p 23. (The emphasis is mine.)

6   APC, PC2/2/3/1, 'Statement issued to the Press', 9 May 1953.

7   Walter Sisulu to the Chairman of the South African Liberal Association, 4 June 1953, cited in Vigne, *Liberals Against Apartheid*, p 25.

8   APC, PC2/6/8/2, p 34.

9   APC, PC2/6/8/2, p 33 (emphasis in original).

10   APC, PC2/6/8/2, p 35.

11   APC, PC2/6/8/2, p 36.

12   APC, PC2/2/4/1, 'Franchise policy', no date [1953].

13   APC, PC2/9/22/1, Report on the First National Conference of the South African Liberal Party, 11-13 July 1953.

14 APC, PC2/9/20/1, Minutes: Interim committee of the Pietermaritzburg branch, 30 July 1953.

15 APC, PC2/9/20/1, Minutes: Interim committee of the Pietermaritzburg branch, 21 September 1953; Interview with Simon Roberts, Pietermaritzburg, 7 May 2007.

16 Alan Paton to Margaret Ballinger, 18 June 1953, cited in Vigne, *Liberals Against Apartheid*, p 29.

17 APC, PC2/6/8/2, p 49.

18 APC, PC2/6/8/2, p 50.

19 APC, PC2/2/4/3, Minutes: National Congress, Report of Franchise Commission, 10-12 July 1954.

20 APC, PC2/2/4/3, Minutes: National Congress, Report of Franchise Commission, 10-12 July 1954.

21 APC, PC2/1/3/4, Franchise & Union Constitution Policy, adopted by National Congress, July 1954.

22 APC, PC2/6/8/2, p 52.

23 APC, PC2/9/22/1, Report on the First National Conference of the South African Liberal Party, July 1953.

24 APC, PC2/6/8/2, p 36.

25 APC, PC2/9/3/1, Minutes: Natal Provincial Congress, 1953.

26 APC, PC2/9/3/3, Secretary's report to the Natal Provincial Congress, Pietermaritzburg, 1-2 November 1957.

27 D Moffatt, 'From "Conscience Politics" to the Battlefields of Political Activism: The Liberal Party in Natal, 1953 to 1968' (MA dissertation, University of Natal, 1999), p 60.

28 APC, PC2/9/14/1, Walter Stanford to Brown, 11 October 1955.

29 *Contact*, August 1954; *Contact*, October 1954.

30 Interview with Walter and Adelaine Hain, London, 21 June 2007.

31 Interview with Walter and Adelaine Hain, London, 21 June 2007. See also P Hain, *Sing the Beloved Country: The Struggle for the New South Africa* (London: Pluto, 1996), p 10.

32 APC, PC2/6/8/2, p 36.

33 APC, PC2/9/9/1, Maggie Rodger to Brown, 3 July 1953.

34 APC, PC2/6/8/2, p 39.

35 APC, PC2/9/9/3, Brown to JZ Chamane, 16 October 1954.

36 APC, PC2/9/9/3, PL Khanyile to Brown, 19 October 1954.

37 APC, PC2/9/9/3, A Maphanga to Brown, 20 October 1954.

38 APC, PC2/9/9/3, Mary Lee to Brown, 24 October 1954.

39 Moffatt, 'From "Conscience Politics" to the Battlefields of Political Activism', p 62.

40 APC, PC16/6/1/1/1-11, Minutes of meetings of the Phoenix Settlement Trust, 1 August/1962 to 28 July 1963.

41 'Mahatma Gandhi Memorial Lecture', Given by P Brown at Phoenix, 19 October 1975. Reprinted in *Reality* (January 1976), p 5.

42 *Contact*, October 1953.

43   *Contact,* December 1953.
44   An incomplete set of the early *Contacts* and its successors, *Sokhel'-Umlilo* and *Umhlanganisi,* are kept in APC, PC2/6/10 and PC2/6/11.
45   APC, PC2/6/2/1, Margaret du Manoir to Brown, 2 February 1954.
46   APC, PC2/6/2/1, Brown to Oscar Wollheim, 10 February 1954.
47   *Contact,* January 1954.
48   'Searchlight on the Liberal Party', *Liberation,* June 1953.
49   *Fighting Talk,* July 1953.
50   *Natal Witness,* 21 May 1953.
51   *Rand Daily Mail,* 26 June 1953.
52   Paton, *Journey Continued,* p 68.
53   APC, PC2/3/6/1, Statement by the Dundee Branch of the Natal Indian Congress, 5 July 1953.
54   *Contact,* October 1953.
55   *Contact,* November 1953.
56   APC, PC2/6/8/2, p 43.
57   APC, PC2/9/10/1, Brown to JE Stanley, 4 February 1955.
58   APC, 96 APB3, Interview with Peter Brown conducted by Norman Bromberger, 21 August 1995, Interview 2, p 14.
59   J Robertson, *Liberalism in South Africa, 1948-1963* (Oxford: Clarendon Press, 1971), p 166.
60   APC, 96 APB3, Interview with Peter Brown conducted by Norman Bromberger, 21 August 1995, Interview 2, p 8.
61   Interview with Phoebe Brown, Pietermaritzburg, 13 December 2006.
62   P Alexander, *Alan Paton: A Biography,* p 289.
63   APC, 96 APB3, Interview with Peter Brown conducted by Norman Bromberger, 21 August 1995, Interview 2, p 14.
64   'Municipal By-Election, Ward 9, Johannesburg, November 18th, 1953 – An Analysis by the Chairman of the Transvaal Provincial Division', *Contact,* January 1954.
65   Leader, 'Deeds as well as words', by ASP [Alan Paton], *Contact,* January 1954.
66   APC, PC2/2/4/1, Minutes: National Conference, 11-13 July 1953.
67   APC, PC2/3/1/1, Alan Paton to Brown, 15 March 1954.
68   *Contact,* April 1954.
69   Interview with Sam Chetty, Pietermaritzburg, 17 August 2006.
70   APC, PC16/4/1/1/4, Speech by Archie Gumede, no date [1954].
71   University of South Africa Archives (UNISA), United Party Collection (UP), Natal, Constituencies, Pietermaritzburg South, Provincial Election 1954, Maj-Gen AR Selby, Manifesto.
72   *Natal Witness,* 13 May 1953.
73   UNISA, UP, Natal, Constituencies, Pietermaritzburg South, Provincial Election 1954, Maj-Gen AR Selby, Manifesto.
74   APC, 96 APB3, Interview with Peter Brown conducted by Norman Bromberger, 21 August 1995, Interview 2, p 16.
75   APC, PC16/4/1/1/1, Election speech, St Alphege's, 29 April 1954.

76 APC, PC16/4/1/1/1, Election speech, St Alphege's, 29 April 1954.

77 APC, PC16/4/1/1/1, Election speech, Cygnet Theatre, 11 June 1954.

78 APC, 96 APB3, Interview with Peter Brown conducted by Norman Bromberger, 21 August 1995, Interview 2, p 16.

79 APC, PC2/3/1/1, National Action Council of the Congress of the People to the Liberal Party, 6 July 1954.

80 T Karis and G Carter (eds), *From Protest to Challenge: A Documentary History of African Politics in South Africa, 1882-1964 – Volume 3, Challenge and Violence, 1953-1964* (Stanford: Hoover Institution Press, 1977), p 126.

81 APC, PC2/2/8/3, Minutes: National Committee meeting, 27-28 February 1954.

82 APC, PC2/2/8/3, Minutes: National Committee meeting, 9-12 July 1954.

83 APC, PC2/9/9/3, Brown to Violaine Junod, 1 October 1954.

84 APC, PC2/9/23/2, Minutes: Combined meeting of the Pietermaritzburg and Edendale branches, 12 October 1954.

85 APC, PC2/2/8/3, Minutes: National Committee meeting, 30-31 October 1954 (emphasis in original).

86 Cited in Vigne, *Liberals Against Apartheid*, p 48.

87 APC, PC2/6/8/2, p 63.

88 This was certainly Jack Unterhalter's view, according to his widow, Beryl. Interview with Beryl Unterhalter, Johannesburg, 21 August 2007.

89 APC, PC2/2/8/3, Minutes: National Committee meeting, 30-31 October 1954.

90 Paton, *Journey Continued*, p 135.

91 Cited in Vigne, *Liberals Against Apartheid*, p 47.

92 APC, PC2/9/10/1, Brown to Miss AM Wilson, 4 February 1955.

93 Paton, *Journey Continued*, p 135.

94 APC, 96 APB3, Interview with Peter Brown conducted by Norman Bromberger, 31 August 1995, Interview 3, p 2.

95 APC, 96 APB3, Interview with Peter Brown conducted by Norman Bromberger, 31 August 1995, Interview 3, p 3.

96 Vigne, *Liberals Against Apartheid*, pp 46-47.

97 R Segal, *African Profiles*, p 28.

98 APC, PC16/5/3/4/82, Brown to Mafika Gwala, 11 December 1983.

99 APC, 96 APB3, Interview with Peter Brown conducted by Norman Bromberger, 31 August 1995, Interview 3, p 4.

100 E-mail communication with Catherine Shallis [Brubeck], 1 August 2008.

101 Interview with Peter Brown by Deborah Moffatt, 25 March 1998, cited in Moffatt, 'From "Conscience Politics" to the Battlefields of Political Activism', p 73, footnote 167; e-mail communication with Catherine Shallis [Brubeck], 1 August 2008. Brown's widow, Phoebe, does not recall Brown expressing himself either way.

102 *Drum*, January 1965. See also D Everatt, 'The Politics of Non-racialism: White Opposition to Apartheid, 1945-1960' (unpublished DPhil thesis, University of Oxford, 1989), p 253.

103 Paton, *Journey Continued*, p 136.
104 APC, PC2/6/8/2, p 66.

CHAPTER 9 – ONTO THE NATIONAL STAGE

1   University of Cape Town Manuscripts and Archives [UCT], Leo Marquard Papers [BC 587], E2.62, Margaret Ballinger to Leo Marquard, 19 June 1954.
2   APC, PC2/6/8/2, p 71.
3   Margaret Ballinger to Oscar Wollheim, 19 November 1955, cited in Vigne, *Liberals Against Apartheid*, p 42.
4   APC, PC2/6/8/2, p 72.
5   APC, PC2/6/2/2, Michael O'Dowd to Brown, 14 February 1956.
6   CJ Driver, *Patrick Duncan: South African and Pan-African* (Cape Town: David Philip, 2000), p 128.
7   P Duncan, 'Thoughts on the Provincial Congress of the Liberal Party in Natal, 1955', *Contact*, November 1955.
8   University of York, Borthwick Institute [BI], Patrick Duncan Papers [DU], DU 8.16 6, Patrick Duncan to Brown, 21 January 1956.
9   BI, DU 5.75 15, Patrick Duncan to Dorrie Paton, 20 February 1956.
10 Interview with Liz Pitman [later Franklin], Cape Town, 19 March 2007. The contrast between Paton and Brown's oratorical styles was highlighted by most of the Liberals I interviewed.
11 Personal communication with Catherine Shallis [later Brubeck], 10 June 2008.
12 *Natal Witness*, 5 July 2004; Telephone interview with David Evans, 26 June 2007.
13 Luthuli, *Let My People Go*, p 132.
14 Interview with John Carlyle Mitchell, Nottingham Road, 29 November 2006.
15 Interview with Liz Pitman [later Franklin], Cape Town, 19 March 2007.
16 A Paton', 'The Crusader on a Polo Pony: Peter Brown', *Contact*, 5 April 1958.
17 APC, 96 APB3, Interview with Peter Brown conducted by Norman Bromberger, 27 September 1995, Interview 5, p 19; p 21.
18 APC, PC2/11/6/2, Walter Stanford to Brown, 18 May 1956.
19 University of the Witwatersrand [Wits], Department of Historical Papers [DHP], A410, B.2.11, File 3, Ballinger to Brown, 5 June 1956.
20 Cited in Driver, *Patrick Duncan*, p 101.
21 APC, PC2/11/6/2, Brown to Bunny Curran, 29 May 1956.
22 *Contact*, May 1956.
23 BI, DU 8.16 27, Brown to Patrick Duncan, 8 May 1956.
24 APC, PC2/9/7/1, Minutes: Natal Provincial Executive Committee, 18 May 1956.
25 APC, PC2/6/8/2, p 76.
26 Paton, *Journey Continued*, p 140.
27 APC, PC2/6/8/2, p 77.

28 Luthuli, *Let My People Go*, p 155.

29 D Herbstein, *White Lies: Canon Collins and the Secret War against Apartheid* (Cape Town: HSRC Press, 2004).

30 Paton, *Journey Continued*, pp 124-125.

31 APC, PC2/3/9/2, Brown to Canon John Collins, 11 June 1963.

32 APC, PC2/6/2/1, Margaret du Manoir to Brown, 17 October 1954.

33 APC, PC2/6/2/1, Brown to Margaret du Manoir, 8 November 1954.

34 APC, PC2/6/8/2, p 78.

35 APC, PC2/9/7/1, Minutes: Natal Provincial Committee, 22 August 1954.

36 APC, PC2/9/3/1, Minutes and resolutions: Natal Provincial Congress, Pietermaritzburg, 4 December 1954.

37 A Paton, *The Charlestown Story* (Pietermaritzburg: Liberal Party of South Africa, no date), p 25.

38 APC, PC2/9/14/1, Brown to Walter Stanford, 31 August 1955.

39 APC, PC2/6/8/2, p 70.

40 APC, PC2/9/7/1, Minutes: Natal Provincial Committee, 21 March 1956.

41 APC, PC2/9/7/1, Minutes: Natal Provincial Executive Committee, 6 December 1956.

42 Drawn from APC, PC16/3/1/5/3, 'Elliot Mngadi', unsigned but written by Brown, no date; P Brown, 'A visit to an old friend', *Reality*, November, 1976; Vigne, *Liberals Against Apartheid*, p 92.

43 APC, PC2/9/14/1, Jeremiah Mkhwanazi to Brown, 11 February 1956.

44 APC, PC2/6/8/2, p 122.

45 Vigne, *Liberals Against Apartheid*, p 91.

46 APC, PC2/9/3/3, Minutes: Natal Provincial Congress, 17-18 October 1958.

47 APC, PC2/9/12/1, Chief Luthuli to Brown, 22 September 1958.

48 APC, PC2/9/12/1, Brown to Chief Luthuli, 26 September 1958.

49 Cited in J Robertson, *Liberalism in South Africa, 1948-1963* (Oxford: Clarendon Press, 1971), p 178.

50 Paton, *Journey Continued*, p 142.

51 APC, PC2/9/3/3, Secretary's report to the Natal Provincial Congress, Pietermaritzburg, 17-18 October 1958.

52 P Brown, 'The Liberal Party: A Chronology with Comment', Unpublished paper delivered to the Liberal Party Workshop, Grahamstown, 17-19 July 1985.

53 BI, DU 8.16 13, Brown to Patrick Duncan, 6 February 1956.

54 BI, DU 8.16 16, Brown to Patrick Duncan, 9 February 1956.

55 APC, PC2/9/3/2, Minutes: Natal Provincial Congress, 27 October 1956 (emphasis is Brown's).

56 APC, PC2/6/2/2, Brown to Jordan Ngubane, 7 November 1956.

57 Brown, 'The Liberal Party: A Chronology with Comment', p 21.

58 APC, PC2/11/6/3, Brown to Walter Stanford, 13 February 1958.

59 APC, PC2/11/6/3, Brown to Bunny Curran, 7 May 1958.

60 APC, PC2/7/2/2, HM D'Ommet to Brown, 12 February 1958.

61 Derick Marsh, Unpublished memoir, received by personal communication, 25 September 2006.

62   APC, PC16/4/1/2/15, Speech at Hilton Road, 17 March 1958.

63   APC, PC2/7/2/3, 'Pietermaritzburg District: Vote for Peter Brown', no date [1958].

64   APC, PC2/7/2/3, 'I always vote U.P. ...', no date [1958].

65   Cited in Vigne, *Liberals Against Apartheid*, p 75.

66   APC, PC2/2/9/1, Minutes: National Committee, 31 May 1958.

67   APC, PC2/7/2/2, Brown to Miss JH Elder, 18 April 1958.

68   Paton, *Journey Continued*, p 175.

69   APC, PC2/3/4/1, Brown to Leslie Cooper, 14 November 1961.

70   APC, PC2/11/6/3, Brown to Bunny Curran, 7 May 1958.

71   APC, PC2/2/9/1, Minutes: National Committee, 31 May 1958.

72   P Brown, 'Union has never had "true parliamentary government"', The Long View, *Contact*, 16 May 1959.

73   APC, PC2/11/7/1, Oscar Wollheim to Brown, 5 May 1959.

74   APC, PC2/11/7/1, Brown to Oscar Wollheim, 19 May 1959.

75   APC, PC2/11/7/1, Oscar Wollheim to Brown, 26 May 1959.

76   P Brown, 'Not to boycott is to surrender', The Long View, *Contact*, 8 August, 1959.

77   *The Observer*, 13 December 1959.

78   APC, PC2/4/11/3, Signed statement on the boycott by Albert Luthuli and Peter Brown (signed by E Wentzel), 20 February 1960.

79   *The Times*, 25 November 1959.

80   APC, PC2/11/7/3, Oscar Wollheim to Brown, 7 March 1960.

81   APC, PC2/11/7/2, Brown to Walter Stanford, 31 July 1959.

82   APC, PC2/11/6/3, Brown to David Lang, 11 February 1958.

83   APC, PC2/11/7/3, Brown to Peter Hjul, 26 January 1960.

84   APC, PC2/11/7/1, Brown to Oscar Wollheim, 22 June 1959.

85   APC, PC2/11/7/1, Brown to Jack Causton, 8 June 1959.

86   APC, PC2/11/7/1, Jack Causton to Brown, 14 June 1959.

87   APC, PC2/11/7/1, Peter Hjul to Brown, 15 June 1959.

88   APC, PC2/7/11/2, Peter Hjul to Brown, 10 July 1959.

89   APC, PC2/10/14/4, Brown to Jack Unterhalter, 24 June 1959.

90   Interview with Helen Suzman, Johannesburg, 29 January 2007.

91   Vigne, *Liberals Against Apartheid*, pp 111-112.

92   P Brown, 'Progressives and the Liberal Party', The Long View, *Contact*, 5 September 1959.

93   P Brown, 'Why Liberals are not opposing Progressives', The Long View, *Contact*, 3 October 1959.

94   APC, PC2/10/14/5, Brown to Jack Unterhalter, 22 October 1959.

95   APC, PC2/2/7/3, National Chairman's Report for the months of September, October and November 1959.

96   P Brown, 'Progressives will accept Liberal idea', The Long View, *Contact*, 12 December 1959.

97   *The Star*, 16 November 1960.

98   APC, PC2/11/7/2, OD Wollheim, 'Future Tactics of the Liberal Party',

Confidential memo for discussion at Cape Provincial Committee, 22 October 1959.

99 APC, PC2/11/7/3, Oscar Wollheim to Brown, 7 March 1960.

100 APC, PC2/11/7/3, Brown to Margaret Ballinger, 14 March 1960.

101 UCT, Oscar Wollheim Papers [BC 627], D2.120, Oscar Wollheim to Margaret Ballinger, 10 September 1960.

102 APC, PC2/10/14/5, Brown to Jack Unterhalter, 4 December 1959 (emphasis in original).

103 Brown, 'The Liberal Party: A Chronology with Comment', p 61.

104 Brown, 'The Liberal Party: A Chronology with Comment', p 29.

105 APC, PC2/6/8/2, pp 134-135 (parenthesis is Brown's).

106 APC, PC2/11/7/1, Peter Hjul to Brown, 23 April 1959.

107 APC, PC2/11/7/1, Brown to Peter Hjul, 4 May 1959.

108 APC, PC2/10/14/4, Brown to Jack Unterhalter, 4 May 1959.

109 APC, PC2/10/14/4, Brown to Jack Unterhalter, 24 June 1959.

110 For an anthology of Paton's 'Long View' columns, see E Callan (ed), *The Long View* (London: Pall Mall, 1968).

111 BI, DU 5.14.10, Patrick Duncan to Brown, 14 November 1958.

112 APC, PC2/11/6/3, Brown to Oscar Wollheim, 6 December 1958.

113 BI, DU5.14 10, Brown to Patrick Duncan, 26 November 1958.

114 BI, DU 5.14 11, Patrick Duncan to Brown, 16 December 1958.

115 *New Age*, 1 January 1959.

116 'An Open Letter to Chief Luthuli', *Contact*, 2 May 1959.

117 Cited in Driver, *Patrick Duncan*, p 161.

118 APC, PC2/11/7/1, Brown to Patrick Duncan, 9 May 1959.

119 BI, DU 5.14 44, Brown to Patrick Duncan, 29 May 1959.

120 P Brown, 'Apartheid is the real enemy', The Long View, *Contact*, 13 June 1959.

121 Driver, *Patrick Duncan*, p 167.

122 Brown, 'The Liberal Party: A Chronology with Comment', pp 33-34.

123 APC, PC2/6/8/2, p 167.

124 Brown, 'The Liberal Party: A Chronology with Comment', p 34.

Chapter 10 – The State of Emergency

1 APC, PC2/6/8/2, p 167.

2 APC, PC2/4/12/3, Affidavit submitted in application to render unlawful and invalid the conditions imposed on Peter Brown as conditions of his release from detention, 4 August 1960.

3 Derick Marsh, Unpublished memoir, received by personal communication, 25 September 2006, p 93.

4 Derick Marsh, Unpublished memoir, received by personal communication, 25 September 2006, p 104.

5 Derick Marsh, Unpublished memoir, received by personal communication, 25 September 2006, p 102.

6   APC, 96 APB3, Interview with Peter Brown conducted by Norman Bromberger, 31 August 1995, Interview 3, pp 18-19.
7   Derick Marsh, Unpublished memoir, received by personal communication, 25 September 2006, p 112.
8   Brookes, *A South African Pilgrimage*, p 122.
9   Derick Marsh, Unpublished memoir, received by personal communication, 25 September 2006, p 108.
10   APC, PC2/4/12/3, Affidavit submitted in application to render unlawful and invalid the conditions imposed on Peter Brown as conditions of his release from detention, 4 August 1960.
11   APC, PC2/4/12/3, Personal release certificate, stamped 1 July 1960 and signed by Secretary for Justice, AP Ellis.
12   APC, PC2/4/13/2, Sue Spence to Marion Friedmann, 11 April 1960.
13   J Ngubane, *An African Explains Apartheid* (London, 1963), p 197.
14   Interview with Jack Spence, Cape Town, 3 November 2006.
15   APC, 96 APB3, Interview with Peter Brown conducted by Norman Bromberger, 31 August 1995, Interview 3, p 17.
16   Personal communication with Phoebe Brown, 15 August 2008.
17   APC, 96 APB3, Interview with Peter Brown conducted by Norman Bromberger, 31 August 1995, Interview 3, pp 20-21.
18   Interview with Phoebe Brown, Pietermaritzburg, 13 December 2006.
19   Interview with Vanessa Brown, Brighton, 27 June 2007.
20   Various conversations with Christopher Brown and Anton Brown, 2006-2008.
21   APC, 96 APB3, Interview with Peter Brown conducted by Norman Bromberger, 31 August 1995, Interview 3, p 21.
22   APC, PC16/5/2/4/6, Brown to Hans Meidner, 2 March 1974.
23   APC, PC16/5/2/1, Brown to Jack Unterhalter, 18 July 1960.
24   APC, PC16/5/2/1, Brown to Leslie Rubin, 15 July 1960.
25   APC, PC16/5/2/1, Brown to Leslie Rubin, 15 July 1960.
26   APC, PC16/5/2/1, Brown to Peter Hjul, 19 July 1960.
27   P Brown, 'After five months', The Long View, *Contact*, 10 September 1960.
28   APC, PC2/4/13/2, Media statement issued by Peter Brown, 1 September 1960.
29   *Contact*, 8 October 1960.
30   APC, PC2/9/11/1, Fort Hare Report, September 1960.

Chapter 11 – Towards the Ban

1   APC, PC2/11/7/4, Brown to Peter Hjul, 21 September 1960.
2   APC, PC2/9/11/1, Brown to Ernie Wentzel, 6 January 1961.
3   T Karis and G Carter (eds), *From Protest to Challenge: A Documentary History of African Politics in South Africa, 1882-1964 – Volume 3, Challenge and Violence, 1953-1964* (Stanford: Hoover Institution Press, 1977), p 354.

4   APC, PC2/9/11/1, Brown to Ernie Wentzel, 6 January 1961.
5   Brown, 'The Liberal Party: A Chronology with Comment', p 38.
6   Cited in Brown, 'The Liberal Party: A Chronology with Comment', p 38.
7   APC, PC2/6/8/2, p 213.
8   APC, PC16/5/2/1, Creina Bond to Brown, 28 March 1961.
9   *Natal Witness*, 27 March 1961.
10   APC, PC2/9/11/1, Brown to Peter Hjul, 1 June 1961.
11   APC, PC16/4/1/1/1, Election speech, St Alphege's, 29 April 1954.
12   P Brown, 'Alternative to apartheid', The Long View, *Contact*, 5 November 1960.
13   APC, PC2/9/5/1-3, Natal Convention, 17-19 April 1961.
14   APC, PC2/9/5/2, President's Opening Address: Natal Convention, 17 April 1961.
15   APC, PC2/9/5/2, Fact Paper 1, Political Aspects by Mr KA Heard; Fact Paper 2, Social Aspects by Prof Leo Kuper; Fact Paper 3, Economic Aspects by Mr IK Allen. recommendations were made to abolish all racial legislation;451451 APC, PC2/9/5/2, Recommendations from the Natal Convention.
16   APC, PC2/9/5/2, Report on the Natal Convention, 17-19 April 1961.
17   *Proceedings of the Natal Convention held in the University of Natal, Pietermaritzburg on 17th to 19th April, 1961* (Natal Convention Committee, 1961).
18   P Brown, 'The Natal Convention', The Long View, *Contact*, 4 May 1961 (emphasis is Brown's).
19   APC, PC2/6/4/1, Brown to Patrick Duncan, 27 September 1961.
20   APC, PC2/9/11/1, Brown to Peter Hjul, 11 April 1961.
21   Brown, 'The Liberal Party: A Chronology with Comment', p 40.
22   Brown, 'The Liberal Party: A Chronology with Comment', pp 40-41. Vigne explains the reasons for Lang's flight, and its financial repercussions, in *Liberals Against Apartheid*, pp 147-148.
23   APC, PC2/6/8/2, p 237.
24   P Brown, 'Votes for the few', The Long View, *Contact*, 3 December 1960.
25   *Contact*, 17 December 1960.
26   APC, PC2/6/4/1, Brown to Patrick Duncan, 9 January 1961.
27   *Contact*, 28 January 1961.
28   APC, PC2/6/4/1, Brown to Patrick Duncan, 20 January 1961.
29   APC, PC2/2/9/1, Minutes: National Committee, 21-22 October 1961.
30   APC, PC2/10/15/4, Brown to Jock Isacowitz, 26 October 1961.
31   APC, PC2/10/16/1, Brown to Ernie Wentzel, 16 March 1962.
32   Interview with Wolf Hamm, London, 18 June 2007.
33   Wolf Hamm Papers [WHP], Brown to Wolf Hamm, 29 November 1961.
34   *Liberal Opinion*, December 1961.
35   APC, PC2/11/8/ Brown to Michael Nuttall, 27 September 1961.
36   APC, PC2/11/8/1, Brown to Terence Beard, 9 September 1961.
37   APC, PC16/5/2/1, Geoff Luffingham to Brown, 11 June 1961.
38   APC, PC16/5/2/1, Brown to Geoff Luffingham, 22 June 1961.

39   Cited in Brown, 'The Liberal Party: A Chronology with Comment', pp 41-42.

40   APC, PC16/7/1/1/3, List of original trustees and committees of the SA Foundation, December 1959.

41   APC, PC16/7/1/1/2, List of SA Foundation committee members, campaign chairmen and campaign leaders as at 30 April 1962.

42   APC, PC16/7/1/1/1, Brown to Guinevere Ventress, 8 February 1963.

43   APC, PC2/6/4/1, Brown to Patrick Duncan, 10 November 1961.

44   WHP, Brown to Wolf Hamm, 29 November 1961.

45   APC, PC2/2/7/3, National Chairman's report, December 1962 to 30 April 1963.

46   See Chapter 16, 'Transkei Victory', pp 165-182 in Vigne, *Liberals Against Apartheid.*

47   Cited in Vigne, *Liberals Against Apartheid,* p 170.

48   *Liberal Opinion,* December 1963.

49   P Brown, 'Bantustans: New Vision is Mirage', The Long View, *Contact,* 21 February 1959.

50   APC, PC2/2/7/3, National Chairman's report, December 1962 to 30 April 1963.

51   APC, PC2/9/6/2, Brown to Jack Unterhalter, 21 March 1963.

52   P Brown, 'What Transkei Chiefs Voted for – Serfdom, Rightlessness in "White" Areas', The Long View, *Contact,* 31 May 1963.

53   APC, PC2/2/7/3, National Chairman's report, 16 November 1963 to 15 April 1964.

54   P Brown, 'Transkeian opposition will fight apartheid', The Long View, *Contact,* 10 January 1964.

55   Vigne, *Liberals Against Apartheid,* p 182.

56   Vigne, *Liberals Against Apartheid,* p 165.

57   APC, PC2/3/4/2, Albert Luthuli to Brown, 23 March 1962.

58   Cited in Mandela, *Long Walk to Freedom,* p 274.

59   Cited in *Reader's Digest Illustrated History of South Africa: The Real Story* (Cape Town: Reader's Digest Association, 1995), p 411.

60   P Brown, 'Poqo is a product of white racialism', The Long View, *Contact,* 19 April 1963.

61   APC, PC2/10/16/1, Ernie Wentzel to Helen Suzman, 22 May 1962.

62   Cited in Vigne, *Liberals Against Apartheid,* p 161.

63   Brown, 'The Liberal Party: A Chronology with Comment', p 45.

64   APC, PC2/6/8/2, p 269

65   APC, PC2/3/4/3, Brown to MB Yengwa, 4 March 1963.

66   Interview with Neville Rubin, Cape Town, 17 January 2007.

67   P Brown, 'Africans simply cannot live on their starvation wages', The Long View, *Contact,* 7 March 1959; 'On skinning Africans alive', The Long View, *Contact,* 23 January 1960; 'Welcome rise is not enough', The Long View, *Contact,* 13 November 1963.

68   P Brown, 'Riots were due to grinding poverty', The Long View, *Contact,* 25 July 1959.

69   P Brown, 'After 10 Years: Liberals will go on fearlessly', The Long View, *Contact*, 14 June 1963.

70   Interview with Neville Rubin, Cape Town, 17 January 2007.

71   UCT, BC 587, E2.78, Brown to Leo Marquard, 2 May 1963.

72   APC, PC2/3/4/3, Brown to Leo Marquard, 28 May 1963.

73   Interviews with Jill Wentzel, Johannesburg, 13 September 2006, and Beryl Unterhalter, Johannesburg, 21 August 2007.

74   APC, 96 APB3, Interview with Peter Brown conducted by Norman Bromberger, 27 September 1995, Interview 5, p 23.

75   Wits, Ernest Wentzel Papers [A1931], 'A': Memoirs, pp 67-68.

76   Wits, A1931, 'A': Memoirs, pp 66-67.

77   APC, PC2/10/16/1, Brown to Jock Isacowitz, 9 January 1962.

78   APC, PC2/2/9/2, Minutes: National Committee, 7-8 April 1962.

79   APC, PC2/3/4/2, Brown to Ernie Wentzel, 27 July 1962.

80   APC, PC2/3/4/2, Brown to Ernie Wentzel, 9 August 1962.

81   APC, PC2/3/4/2, Ernie Wentzel to Brown, 30 July 1962.

82   APC, PC2/2/9/2, Minutes: National Congress, 5-7 July 1963.

83   Wits, A1931, 'A': Memoirs, pp 153-154.

84   Interviews with Neville Rubin, Cape Town, 17 January 2007, and Bill Hoffenberg, Cape Town, 16 March 2007.

85   APC, PC2/2/9/2, Minutes: National Congress, 5-7 July 1963.

86   APC, PC2/2/9/2, Minutes: National Congress, 5-7 July 1963.

87   APC, PC2/6/4/1, Brown to Patrick Duncan, 26 July 1962.

88   APC, PC2/6/4/1, Patrick Duncan to Brown, 21 July 1962.

89   Driver, *Patrick Duncan*, p 208.

90   Driver, *Patrick Duncan*, p 209.

91   BI, DU 5.14 102, Brown to Patrick Duncan, 11 May 1962.

92   BI, DU 5.14 104, Brown to Patrick Duncan, 28 May 1962.

93   BI, DU 5.14 117, Patrick Duncan to Brown, 13 December 1962.

94   BI, DU 5.14 118, Brown to Duncan, 14 January 1963.

95   BI, DU 5.14 119, Patrick Duncan to Brown, 10 February 1963.

96   BI, DU 5.14 120, Brown to Patrick Duncan, 25 February 1963.

97   BI, DU 5.14 121, Patrick Duncan to Brown, 10 March 1963.

98   BI, DU5.75 49, Patrick Duncan to Alan Paton, 10 March 1963.

99   BI, DU5.75 50, Alan Paton to Patrick Duncan, 27 March 1963.

100   BI, DU 5.14 122, Brown to Patrick Duncan, 11 March 1963.

101   Vigne, *Liberals Against Apartheid*, p 202.

102   Brown, 'The Liberal Party: A Chronology with Comment', p 43.

103   APC, PC2/10/15/4, Jock Isacowitz to Brown, 10 November 1961.

104   APC, PC2/10/15/4, Brown to Ernie Wentzel, 14 November 1961.

105   Paton, *Journey Continued*, p 222.

106   Brown, 'Nearer the end', The Long View, *Contact*, 14 January 1961.

107   APC, PC2/9/11/1, Brown to Antoinette Swart, 21 December 1961.

108   *Liberal Opinion*, March 1962.

109   Interview with Pat McKenzie, Pietermaritzburg, 7 May 2007.

110 Telephone interview with David Evans, 26 June 2007.

111 APC, 96 APB3, Interview with Peter Brown conducted by Norman Bromberger, 11 September 1995, Interview 4, p 14.

112 Paton, *Journey Continued*, p 223.

113 Personal communication with Randolph Vigne, 29 July 2008.

114 APC, 96 APB3, Interview with Peter Brown conducted by Norman Bromberger, 11 September 1995, Interview 4, p 14.

115 Interview with Neville Rubin, Cape Town, 17 January 2007.

116 APC, 96 APB3, Interview with Peter Brown conducted by Norman Bromberger, 11 September 1995, Interview 4, pp 15-16.

117 Paton, *Journey Continued*, p 227.

118 APC, PC16/9/1/1/1 and PC16/9/1/1/2, Receipts for books, documents and pamphlets confiscated, signed by Detective Sergeant van Rensburg and PM Brown, 4 July 2004.

119 APC, PC2/9/11/1, Elliot Mngadi to Brown, 20 March 1964.

120 APC, Department of Justice Security Files on Peter McKenzie Brown, Commissioner of Police to Secretary of Justice, 16 June 1964.

121 APC, Department of Justice Security Files on Peter McKenzie Brown, Memorandum on Peter McKenzie Brown, 10 June 1964.

122 APC, Department of Justice Security Files on Peter McKenzie Brown, 'Secret: The Secretary/Minister [of Justice]', Restrictions: Peter McKenzie Brown', 22 July 1964.

123 APC, 96 APB3, Interview with Peter Brown conducted by Norman Bromberger, 11 September 1995, Interview 4, pp 19.

124 APC, PC16/9/1/1/3, TS marked 'A', 'Notice in terms of sub-section (1) of Section Nine of the Suppression of Communism Act, 1950', 22 July 1964; APC, PC16/9/1/1/4, TS marked 'B', 'Notice in terms of paragraph (a) of sub-section (1) of Section Ten of the Suppression of Communism Act, 1950', 22 July 1964; APC, PC16/9/1/1/5, TS marked 'C', 'Notice in terms of sub-section (1) of Section Ten Quat of the Suppression of Communism Act, 1950', 22 July 1964.

125 *Rand Daily Mail*, 25 July 1964.

126 UCT, BC587, C17.1, Brown to Leo Marquard, 17 August 1964.

127 APC, PC16/9/1/1/3, TS marked 'A', 'Notice in terms of sub-section (1) of Section Nine of the Suppression of Communism Act, 1950', 22 July 1964.

128 APC, PC16/9/1/1/5, TS marked 'C', 'Notice in terms of sub-section (1) of Section Ten Quat of the Suppression of Communism Act, 1950', 22 July 1964.

129 APC, PC16/9/1/1/4, TS marked 'B', 'Notice in terms of paragraph (a) of sub-section (1) of Section Ten of the Suppression of Communism Act, 1950', 22 July 1964.

CHAPTER 12 – THE BANNED YEARS

1 APC, PC2/5/2/4, Statement by Alan Paton and Edgar Brookes, no date [July 1964].
2 APC, PC2/3/5/1, Message from Alan Paton and Edgar Brookes, with covering letter from Mary Corrigal to Marian Lurie, 7 August 1964.
3 *Contact*, 18 August 1964.
4 A Paton, 'Peter Brown', The Long View, *Contact*, 28 August 1964.
5 Vigne, *Liberals Against Apartheid*, p 190.
6 Paton, *Journey Continued*, p 236.
7 APC, PC2/3/9/2, Brown to Marion Friedmann, 14 October 1964.
8 APC, PC2/3/9/2, Brown to Hans Meidner, 15 October 1964.
9 WHP, Brown to Wolf Hamm, 15 October 1964.
10 Interview with Walter and Adelaine Hain, London, 21 June 2007.
11 Paton, *Journey Continued*, p 237,
12 APC, PC2/9/11/1, Walter Hain to Phoebe Brown, 5 December 1964.
13 Maritz van den Berg to the Editor, *The Independent*, 31 October 1995. See also responding letters from Ann Wolfe (John Harris's widow) and Paul Trewhela, 2 November 1995
14 APC, PC2/3/9/2, Brown to Marion Friedmann, 25 October 1964.
15 APC, PC2/3/9/2, Brown to Marion Friedmann, 18 November 1964.
16 APC, PC2/3/9/2, Brown to Hans Meidner, 5 November 1964.
17 APC, PC2/3/9/2, Brown to Hans Meidner, 5 November 1964.
18 APC, PC2/9/11/1, Brown to Ruth Hayman, 1 December 1964.
19 APC, PC2/3/9/2, Brown to Marion Friedmann, 18 November 1964.
20 APC, PC2/3/9/2, Brown to Derick Marsh, 29 November 1964.
21 Paton, *Journey Continued*, p 237.
22 Paton, *Journey Continued*, p 235.
23 Paton, *Journey Continued*, p 236.
24 APC, PC16/5/4/5/6, Brown to Derick Marsh, 3 February 1988.
25 APC, PC2/3/9/2, Brown to Derick Marsh, 5 February 1965.
26 APC, PC2/9/11/1, Brown to Bill Hoffenberg, 9 March 1965.
27 APC, PC2/9/11/1, Bill Hoffenberg to Brown, 25 Feb. 1965
28 APC, PC2/9/11/1, Thomas Ngwenya to Brown, 9 March 1965.
29 APC, 96 APB3, Interview with Peter Brown conducted by Norman Bromberger, 11 September 1995, Interview 4, p 20.
30 APC, PC2/3/9/2, Brown to Derick Marsh, 5 February 1965.
31 APC, PC2/9/11/1, Brown to Jack Unterhalter, 20 January 1966.
32 APC, Department of Justice, Security Files on Peter McKenzie Brown, Commissioner of Police to Secretary of Justice, 8 February 1966.
33 APC, Department of Justice, Security Files on Peter McKenzie Brown, 'Geheim, Die Sekretaris/Minister, Beperkings: Peter McKenzie Brown', 19 April 1966.
34 APC, PC16/9/1/1/6, TS entitled 'Variation of Notice Issued in Terms of Paragraph (a) of Sub-Section (1) of Section Ten of the Suppression of Communism Act, 1950', 25 April 1966.

35 Personal communication with Phoebe Brown, 30 August 2008.

36 National Archives, Pretoria [NA], Directorate of Security Legislation, 2/4/2/40, Liberal Party, 8 September 1966.

37 APC, PC16/9/1/3/3, Brown to the Chief Magistrate of Pietermaritzburg, 26 March 1966.

38 APC, PC16/9/1/3/4, Chief Magistrate of Pietermaritzburg to Brown, 4 April 1966.

39 APC, PC16/9/1/3/10, Brown to the Chief Magistrate of Pietermaritzburg, 2 October 1966.

40 *The Friend*, 7 October 1966.

41 APC, Department of Justice, Security Files on Peter McKenzie Brown, Memorandum, 16 April 1969.

42 APC, 96 APB3, Interview with Peter Brown conducted by Norman Bromberger, 11 September 1995, Interview 4, p 20; Interview with Leslie and Pessa Weinberg, Pietermaritzburg, 30 November 2006.

43 P Brown, 'A History of the Liberal Party of South Africa, 1953-1966'. Various drafts of the text are kept in APC, PC2/6/8/1 to APC, PC2/6/8/3. All references in this biography are to the copy filed under APC, PC2/6/8/2.

44 The correspondence from Brown's research is kept in APC, PC2/2/2/2.

45 A Paton, *Hofmeyr* (Cape Town: Oxford University Press, 1964).

46 APC, PC2/3/9/2, Marion Friedmann to Brown, 11 February 1965.

47 WHP, Brown to Wolf Hamm, 5 February 1965.

48 APC, PC2/3/4/1, Brown to Leslie Cooper, 14 November 1961.

49 Alexander, *Alan Paton*, p 329.

50 M Cardo, '"Fighting a Worse Imperialism": White South African Loyalism and the Army Education Services during the Second World War', *South African Historical Journal* 46 (May 2002), 141-174.

51 UCT, BC587, B1.505, Leo Marquard to Nell Marquard, 24 October, 1943.

52 APC, PC2/4/17/1, Memorandum submitted to the Commission on the Prohibition of Improper Interference Bill, 18 November 1966.

53 UCT, BC 587, C17.3, Brown to Leo Marquard, 20 January 1968.

54 L Marquard, *The Peoples and Policies of South Africa* (Cape Town: Oxford University Press, 1952); *The Story of South Africa* (London: Faber & Faber, 1966).

55 Editorial: 'Two Great South Africans', *Reality*, May 1978; Rene de Villiers, 'Leo Marquard: A Memoir', *Reality*, May 1978; David Welsh, 'A Tribute to Leo Marquard', *Reality*, May 1978.

56 Interview with Christianne Carlisle, Kloof, 9 May 2007.

57 APC, PC16/5/2/3/9, Brown to Hans Meidner, 6 June 1973.

58 UCT, BC 587, C17.7, Brown to Leo Marquard, 7 November 1968.

59 APC, PC16/5/1/1/47, Brown to Jack Clouston, 11 July 1969.

60 APC, PC16/9/1/1/7, Notice in Terms of Section 9(1) of the Suppression of Communism Act, 1950, 14 May 1969; APC, PC16/9/1/1/8, Notice in Terms of Section 10(1)(a) of the Suppression of Communism Act, 1950, 14 May 1969; PC16/9/1/1/9, Notice in Terms of Section 10 Quat (1) of the Suppression of Communism Act, 1950, 14 May 1969.

61 APC, Department of Justice, Security Files on Peter McKenzie Brown, Commissioner of Police to Secretary of Justice, 18 April 1969.

62 *Natal Mercury*, 9 August 1969; *Natal Mercury*, 14 August 1969.

63 Wits, Alan Paton Papers [AD1169], D15, Speech by Alan Paton at a meeting of the Black Sash in Durban, 13 August 1969. A similar text was subsequently published in *Reality*: A Paton, 'Peter Brown – Rebanned', Speech delivered in Pietermaritzburg on 8 August, reprinted in *Reality*, September 1969.

64 UCT, BC 587, C17.2, Brown to Leo Marquard, 21 October 1967.

65 Interview with Walter and Adelaine Hain, London, 21 June 2007; Interview with Bill Hoffenberg, Cape Town, 16 March 2007.

66 UCT, BC 587, C17.2, Brown to Leo Marquard, 21 October 1967.

67 UCT, BC 587, C17.2, Brown to Leo Marquard, 21 October 1967.

68 UCT, BC 587, C17.4, Brown to Leo Marquard, 27 April 1968.

69 UCT, BC 587, C17.9, Brown to Leo Marquard, 24 August 1969.

70 *Sunday Tribune*, 9 December 1979.

71 APC, PC16/9/1/4/1-20, Applications/permits to visit farms in Mooi River and adjoining districts, and elsewhere, 28 February 1967 to 11 September 1970.

72 APC, 96 APB3, Interview with Peter Brown conducted by Norman Bromberger, 11 September 1995, Interview 4, p 21.

73 Wits, Helen Suzman Papers [A2084], Ac1.1, Helen Suzman to the Minister of Justice, 22 August 1969.

74 Wits, A2084, Ac1.1, Brown to Helen Suzman, 29 August 1969.

75 Wits, A2084, Ac1.1, OA de Meyer [Private Secretary: Minister of Justice] to Helen Suzman, 4 November 1969.

76 Wits, A2084, Ac1.1, Private Secretary: Minister of Justice to Helen Suzman, 20 January 1970; Private Secretary: Minister of Justice to Helen Suzman, 16 February 1970.

77 M Cardo, Chapter 4: 'South Africanism and Liberalism: the Case of the National Union of South African Students, 1924-1945' (PhD thesis, University of Cambridge, 2002), pp 88-127.

78 'Black Souls in White Skins', *Frank Talk*, August 1970.

79 Ibid. See also S Biko, *I Write What I Like* (London: Heinemann, 1978), p 24.

80 Biko, *I Write What I Like*, p 51.

81 *Sunday Tribune*, 9 December 1979.

82 APC, 96 APB3, Interview with Peter Brown conducted by Norman Bromberger, 17 October 1995, Interview 6, p 20.

83 APC, Department of Justice, Security Files on Peter McKenzie Brown, GC Tomlinson to the Minister of Justice, PC Pelser, 24 July 1972.

84 APC, Department of Justice, Security Files on Peter McKenzie Brown, Commissioner: South African Police to the Secretary of Justice, 10 August 1972.

85 APC, Department of Justice, Security Files on Peter McKenzie Brown, Head: Ministerial Services to GC Tomlinson, 7 September 1972.

86 APC, Department of Justice, Security Files on Peter McKenzie Brown, Memo, 27 June 1974.

87 APC, Department of Justice, Security Files on Peter McKenzie Brown, Commissioner: South African Police to the Secretary of Justice, 18 June 1974.

88 Vigne, *Liberals Against Apartheid*, p 196.

89 APC, Department of Justice, Security Files on Peter McKenzie Brown, Secretary of Justice to Commissioner: South African Police, 18 July 1974.

90 *Rand Daily Mail*, 2 August 1974.

91 WHP, Brown to Hamm, 1974 [no date; letter suggests March 1974].

CHAPTER 13 – THE DEPENDANTS' CONFERENCE AND *REALITY*

1   Wolf Hamm Private Papers [WHP], Brown to Wolf Hamm, 1974 [no date; letter suggests March 1974].

2   WHP, Brown to Wolf Hamm, 31 October 1974.

3   Sam Chetty dates the first such occasion back to 1956; John Carlyle Mitchell puts it at 1954. Interviews with Sam Chetty, Pietermaritzburg, 17 August 2006 and John Carlyle Mitchell, Nottingham Road, 29 November 2006.

4   Interview with John Carlyle Mitchell, Nottingham Road, 29 November 2006.

5   See, for example, APC, PC16/5/3/2/46, Brown to Mrs M Leibrandt [Secretary of the Parents' Association at King's], 13 July 1980.

6   Interview with David Welsh, Cape Town, 26 October 2006.

7   D Welsh, *The Roots of Segregation: Native Policy in Colonial Natal, 1845-1910* (Cape Town: Oxford University Press, 1971).

8   Interview with David Welsh, Cape Town, 26 October 2006. This anecdote is also related in Alexander, *Alan Paton*, p 418.

9   *Natal Witness*, cutting, no date.

10 APC, PC16/5/2/5/4, Brown to Derick Marsh, 30 January 1975.

11 Alexander, *Alan Paton*, p 294.

12 Communication with Phoebe Brown, 22 July 2008.

13 Interview with Sam Chetty, Pietermaritzburg, 17 August 2006.

14 Cited in Alexander, *Alan Paton*, p 359.

15 APC, PC16/5/2/5/4, Brown to Derick Marsh, 30 January 1975.

16 Interview with Colin Gardner, Pietermaritzburg, 22 November 2006.

17 E-mail correspondence, Colin Gardner to Michael Cardo, 18 November 2006.

18 WHP, Brown to Wolf Hamm, 8 July 1975.

19 APC, Department of Justice, Security Files on Peter McKenzie Brown, Commissioner of Police to the Secretary of Justice, 16 June 1964.

20 C Gardner, 'Cathedral Tribute to Peter Brown', Cathedral of the Holy Nativity, Pietermaritzburg, 9 July 2004, attached in e-mail correspondence, Colin Gardner to Michael Cardo, 16 November 2006.

21 Interview with John Carlyle Mitchell, Nottingham Road, 29 November 2006.

22 A Boraine, *A Life in Transition* (Cape Town: Zebra Press, 2008), p 302.

23 APC, PC16/13/1/2/17, Minutes: AFRA committee meeting, 27 February 1980.

24 APC, PC16/5/2/5/10, Jean Sinclair to Brown, 23 March 1975.

25 Telephone interview with Pat McKenzie, 25 July 2008.

26 Heribert Adam, 'The Rise of Black Consciousness in South Africa', *Race*, XV, 2 (October 1973), p 158.

27 APC, PC16/11/1/3, Duchesne Grice to Brown, 28 May 1975.

28 APC, PC16/11/1/4, Deed of Trust, no date [1937]; APC, PC16/11/1/9, Suggestions for grant disbursements, no date, but attached to APC, PC16/11/1/8, Grice to Brown 24 June 1977; APC, PC16/11/1/19, Balance Sheet for the year ended 31 March 1979.

29 'The Man in the Race Relations Hot Seat', *The Star*, 6 May 1972.

30 Eglin, *Crossing the Borders of Power*, p 135.

31 Interview with Helen Suzman, Johannesburg, 29 January 2007.

32 WHP, Brown to Wolf Hamm, 31 August 1973.

33 APC, PC16/14/1/2/9, Brown to Angela Pringle, 29 January 1976.

34 APC, PC16/14/1/2/10, Angela Pringle to Brown, 6 February 1976.

35 APC, PC16/14/1/2/80, Detainees' Hire-Purchase Commitments, no date.

36 APC, PC16/14/1/2/74, Brown to Marianne Knappstein, 11 August 1976.

37 A Paton [C Gardner (ed)], *Knocking on the Door: Shorter Writings* (Cape Town: David Philip, 1975).

38 APC, PC16/14/1/3/33, Brown to C Berglind-Dehlin, 5 August 1977.

39 APC, PC87 [Bunty Biggs Collection], PC87/1/1/13-PC 871/1/15; Fylippa Cumming, 'A plea for younger women to help in welfare work', *Natal Witness*, 22 Jan 1974.

40 APC, PC16/14/1/4/4, Minutes of a meeting held on 24 January [1978], Pietermaritzburg Council of Churches [PCC], Justice and Reconciliation Commission [JRC].

41 APC, PC16/14/3/4/21, Brown to the Secretary of Pietermaritzburg Council of Churches [PCC], 22 December 1991.

42 See, for example, APC, PC16/14/1/7/57, Minutes: PCC/JRC meeting, 3 November 1981.

43 APC, PC16/14/3/1/7, Minutes: PCC DCC [Dependants' Conference Committee] meeting, 30 March 1988.

44 Suzman refers to Brown's original letter, dated 17 May 1988, in her response: APC, PC16/14/3/1/18, Helen Suzman to Brown, 2 June 1988.

45 APC, PC153, Index to the Marie Dyer Collection.

46 APC, PC16/10/1/1/2, Document setting out proposed board members, names and policy, no date [1969].

47 Interview with Colin Gardner, Pietermaritzburg, 22 November 2006.

48 *Reality*, March 1969.

49 APC, PC16/10/1/1/48, Jane Lundie to Brown, 13 November 1974.

50 APC, PC16/10/1/4/2, Minutes: *Reality* board meeting, 21 January 1975.

51 Alexander, *Paton*, p 394; A Paton, *Towards the Mountain* (Cape Town: David Philip, 1980).

52 APC, PC16/10/4/2/107, Alan Paton to Brown, 27 November 1983.

53   APC, PC16/10/1/4/11, Minutes: *Reality* board meeting, 11 March 1975.

54   APC, PC16/10/3/2/54, Minutes: *Reality* board meeting, 8 April 1980.

55   APC, 96 APB3, Interview with Peter Brown conducted by Norman Bromberger, 3 November 1995, Interview 7, p 18.

56   APC, 96 APB3, Interview with Peter Brown conducted by Norman Bromberger, 3 November 1995, Interview 7, p 19.

57   Alexander, *Alan Paton*, p 367.

58   APC, PC16/10/2/1/20, Income & expenditure for the nine months ended 31 March 1976.

59   APC, PC16/10/2/1/20, Income & expenditure for the nine months ended 31 March 1976.

60   APC, PC16/10/2/1/35, Minutes: *Reality* board meeting, 11 May 1976.

61   APC, PC16/10/2/1/78, Minutes: *Reality* board meeting, 10 August 1976.

62   APC, PC16/10/2/1/92, Minutes: *Reality* board meeting, 7 September 1976.

63   APC, PC16/10/2/1/65, Minutes: *Reality* board meeting, 13 July 1976.

64   APC, PC16/10/3/2/54, Minutes: *Reality* board meeting, 8 April 1980.

65   APC, 96 APB3, Interview with Peter Brown conducted by Norman Bromberger, 3 November 1995, Interview 7, p 20.

66   APC, PC16/10/2/2/11, Ernie Wentzel to Brown, 15 January 1977.

67   Cited in Rich, *Hope and Despair*, p 113.

68   P Randall (ed), *Education beyond Apartheid: Report of the Education Commission* (Johannesburg: SPRO-CAS, 1971); *Towards Social Change: Report of the Social Commission* (Johannesburg: SPRO-CAS, 1971); *Power, Privilege and Poverty: Report of the Economics Commission* (Johannesburg: SPRO-CAS, 1972); *Law, Justice and Society: Report of the Legal Commission* (Johannesburg: SPRO-CAS, 1972); *South Africa's Political Alternatives: Report of the Political Commission* (Johannesburg: SPRO-CAS, 1973).

69   P Randall (ed), *Apartheid and the Church: Report of the Church Commission* (Johannesburg: SPRO-CAS, 1972).

70   Alan Paton to Leo Marquard, 21 August 1970, cited in Alexander, *Paton*, p 387.

71   E Brookes, 'Federalism – Opportunity or Evasion', *Reality* (March 1975).

72   *Reality* (September 1977), pp 4-6.

73   APC, PC16/10/2/2/82, Edgar Brookes to Alan Paton, 8 September 1977.

74   APC, PC16/10/2/2/90, Alan Paton to Edgar Brookes, 20 September 1977.

75   APC, PC16/10/2/1/72, Alan Paton to Brown, 27 July 1976.

76   APC, PC16/10/2/1/78, Minutes: *Reality* board meeting, 10 August 1976.

77   WHP, Brown to Wolf Hamm, 1974 [no date; letter suggests March 1974].

78   APC, PC16/5/2/5/178, Brown to Wolf Hamm, 19 November 1977.

79   APC, PC16/5/24/19, Brown to Henry Hewett, 25 March 1974 (emphasis in the original).

80   WHP, Brown to Wolf Hamm, no date [1974].

81   'The White Political Scene', *Reality* (September 1975), p 1.

82   APC, PC16/10/2/1/10, Edgar Brookes, 'False Dawns', no date, enclosed with APC, PC16/10/2/1/9, Edgar Brookes to Brown, 14 February 1976.

83 APC, PC16/10/2/1/9, Edgar Brookes to Brown, 14 February 1976.
84 APC, PC16/10/2/1/11, Brown to Edgar Brookes, 28 February 1976.
85 APC, PC16/10/2/1/14, Edgar Brookes to Brown, 6 March 1976.
86 APC, PC16/10/2/1/131, Minutes: *Reality* board meeting, 14 December 1976.
87 WHP, Brown to Hamm, 4 July 1977.
88 APC, PC16/10/2/3/29, Edgar Brookes to Brown, 4 March 1978.
89 APC, PC16/10/2/3/30, Brown to Edgar Brookes, 9 March 1978.
90 APC, PC16/10/2/3/34, Minutes: *Reality* board meeting, 14 March 1978.
91 Interview with David Welsh, Cape Town, 26 October 2006.
92 Cited in Vigne, *Liberals Against Apartheid*, p 221.
93 Cited in Vigne, *Liberals Against Apartheid*, p 221.
94 P Brown, 'Some Thoughts About Edgar Brookes, South African Liberalism and the Future', Delivered at the University of Natal, Pietermaritzburg, 16 August 1979, p 1.
95 P Brown, 'Some Thoughts About Edgar Brookes, South African Liberalism and the Future', Delivered at the University of Natal, Pietermaritzburg, 16 August 1979, p 2.
96 Brookes, *A South African Pilgrimage*, p 122.
97 Paton, *Journey Continued*, p 62.
98 WHP, Brown to Wolf Hamm, 17 November 1970.
99 *The Times*, 22 July 1971.
100 WHP, Brown to Wolf Hamm, 30 July 1971.
101 'Politics and morality in South Africa – Alan Paton clarifies his attitude to apartheid', *The Times*, 30 July 1971.
102 'Inkatha', *Reality* (November 1975).
103 APC, PC16/5/2/3/2, Brown to Wolf Hamm, no date [1971].
104 *Daily News*, 13 July 1978.
105 APC, PC2/6/8/2, p 349.
106 'An Open Letter to Alan Paton', *Reality* (September 1978), p 6.
107 'Alan Paton Replies', *Reality* (September 1978), p 7.
108 APC, PC16/10/2/3/67, Minutes: *Reality* board meeting, 8 August 1978 and APC, PC16/10/2/3/77, Minutes: *Reality* board meeting, 12 September 1978.
109 APC, PC16/10/2/3/73, Edgar Brookes to Brown, 7 September 1978, enclosing PC16/10/2/3/74, a letter to the Editor regarding the Aitchison/Paton correspondence, which Brookes submitted for publication in the following issue of *Reality*.
110 APC, PC16/10/2/3/78, Brown to Edgar Brookes, 19 September 1978.
111 APC, PC16/10/4/4/7, Brown to Dot Cleminshaw, 8 January 1985.
112 See, for example: S Biko, 'Black Consciousness and the Quest for Humanity', *Reality* (March 1972); A Paton, 'Black Consciousness', *Reality* (March 1972); L Marquard, 'Black Consciousness', *Reality* (September 1973); S Mkhatshwa, 'The Black Renaissance Convention', *Reality* (May 1975); 'Black Renaissance Convention Declarations and Resolutions', *Reality* (May 1975).

113 APC, PC16/5/2/5/156, Brown to the Editor, [unspecified publications], 14 September 1977.

114 'Inkatha', *Reality* (November 1975).

115 APC, PC16/10/1/4/42, Brown to Mangosuthu Buthelezi, 19 June 1975.

116 'The National Cultural Liberation Movement', *Reality* (September 1975).

117 'Inkatha', *Reality* (November 1975).

118 'Inkatha', *Reality* (March 1976), p 10.

119 APC, PC16/5/2/3/2, Brown to Wolf Hamm, no date, but postmark suggests November 1971. The letter was a reply to one sent by Hamm in September. See APC, PC16/5/2/3/1, Wolf Hamm to Brown, 26 September 1971.

120 APC, PC16/5/2/6/21, Brown to Wolf Hamm, no date, but filed between March and April 1978 in both APC, and Wolf Hamm's private papers in Harpenden.

121 APC, PC16/5/3/1/25, Brown to Adelaine and Walter Hain, 2 April 1979.

122 APC, PC16/5/4/1/22, Brown to Mafika Gwala, 10 April 1984.

123 P Brown, 'Reflections on Graaff-Reinet', *Reality* (May 1978).

124 B Pogrund, *How Can Man Die Better: The Life of Robert Sobukwe* (Cape Town: Jonathan Ball, 1990), p 376.

125 *Daily News*, 16 May 1978.

126 APC, PC16/5/2/6/27, Brown to the Editor, *Daily News*, 17 May 1978.

127 WHP, Brown to Wolf Hamm, no date [1978].

128 APC, PC16/5/2/6/48, Mangosuthu Buthelezi to Brown, 20 September 1978.

129 APC, PC16/10/3/2/139, Brown to Oscar Dhlomo, 11 September 1980.

130 APC, PC16/10/3/2/142, Oscar Dhlomo to Brown, 19 September 1980.

131 APC, PC16/10/3/2/146, Brown to Oscar Dhlomo, 27 September 1980, and APC, PC16/10/3/2/145, Brown to Mafika Gwala, 27 September 1980.

132 APC, PC16/5/3/4/78, Mafika Gwala to Brown, 16 November 1983.

133 APC, PC16/5/3/4/82, Brown to Mafika Gwala, 11 December 1983.

134 *Reality* (November 1972).

135 Paton, *Alexander*, p 381.

136 D Maughan-Brown, 'On the Unbanning of the Banned – David Philip's Africa South Series', *Reality* (September 1983).

137 APC, PC16/10/4/2/107, Alan Paton to Brown, 27 November 1983.

138 APC, PC16/10/4/2/109, Brown to Alan Paton, 5 December 1983.

139 APC, PC16/10/4/3/15, Brown to Alan Paton, 19 February 1984. The article was: C Hamilton, 'Retrieving the Colonial Past: A Review of Wright and Manson's *The Hlubi Chiefdom in Zululand – Natal, Reality* (March 1984).

140 Wits, A1931, E, Alan Paton to Ernie Wentzel, 15 March 1984.

CHAPTER 14 – BACK TO THE LAND: THE CHURCH AGRICULTURAL PROJECT

1   R Malan, *My Traitor's Heart* (London: Vintage, 1991), p 348.

2   APC, 96 APB3, Interview with Peter Brown conducted by Norman Bromberger, 17 October 1995, Interview 6, p 1; Telephone interview with Olga Meidner, London, 26 June 2007.

3   Malan, *My Traitor's Heart*, p 348.

4   APC, PC2/9/7/2, Minutes, Natal Provincial Committee, LPSA, 8 August 1961; PC2/9/8/4, 'Suggestions re organisation of the Liberal Party', no date [1961?].

5   APC, PC2/6/8/2, p 278.

6   APC, 96 APB3, Interview with Peter Brown conducted by Norman Bromberger, 17 October 1995, Interview 6, p 3.

7   Chizuko Sato, 'Forced Removals, Land NGOs and Community Politics in KwaZulu-Natal, South Africa, 1953-2002' (DPhil thesis, University of Oxford, 2005), p 79.

8   Cited in APC, PC2/6/8/2, p 278.

9   Malan, *My Traitor's Heart*, p 350.

10   APC, 96 APB3, Interview with Peter Brown conducted by Norman Bromberger, 17 October 1995, Interview 6, p 6.

11   Sato, 'Forced Removals, Land NGOs and Community Politics in KwaZulu-Natal', pp 73-74; PB Rich, 'Bernard Huss and the Experiment in African Cooperatives in South Africa, 1926-1948', *The International Journal of African Historical Studies*, Vol. 26, No. 2 (1993), pp 313-317, and F Schimlek, *Against the Stream: Life of Father Bernard Huss, CMM. The Social Apostle of the Bantu*, Mariannhill Mission Press: Mariannhill, 1949.

12   Cited in Sato, 'Forced Removals, Land NGOs and Community Politics in KwaZulu-Natal', p 82.

13   APC, 96 APB3, Interview with Peter Brown conducted by Norman Bromberger, 17 October 1995, Interview 6, p 7.

14   APC, PC16/12/1/1/20, Brown to Neil Alcock, 20 August 1974.

15   APC, PC16//1/1/1 [sic], Brown to Paul Henwood, 24 September 1974.

16   APC, PC16/12/1/1/30, Paul Henwood to Brown, 23 October 1974.

17   APC, PC16/12/1/1/34, Duchesne Grice to Chief Buthelezi, 29 October 1974.

18   APC, PC16/12/1/1/40, Douglas Blausten to Brown, 7 November 1974.

19   APC, PC16/12/1/1, Brown to Douglas Blausten, 6 December 1974.

20   APC, PC16/12/1/1/41, Brown to Archbishop Hurley, 7 November 1974.

21   APC, PC16/12/1/1/38, Brown to Paul Henwood, 7 November 1974.

22   APC, PC16/12/1/1/38, Brown to Paul Henwood, 7 November 1974.

23   APC, PC16/12/1/2/9, Brown to Douglas Blausten, 19 January 1975.

24   APC, PC16/12/1/2/9, Brown to Douglas Blausten, 19 January 1975.

25   APC, PC16/12/1/2/7, Report on a visit to the farms Lorraine, Spring & ..?.. [sic], no date [1975].

26   APC, PC16/12/1/1/20, Brown to Douglas Blausten, 17 February 1975.

27   APC, PC16/12/1/2/31, Neil Alcock to Brown, 6 March 1975.

28   APC, PC16/12/1/2/30, Alcock to CAP Directors and Farm Advisory Committee, 5 March 1974.

29   APC, PC16/12/1/2/37, Brown to Neil Alcock, 20 March 1975.

30   APC, PC16/12/2/1/5, Douglas Blausten to Brown, 29 January 1976.

31   APC, PC16/12/2/1/25, Brown to Douglas Blausten, 18 February 1976.

32   APC, PC16/12/1/2/35, March 1975.

33   Sato, 'Forced Removals, Land NGOs and Community Politics in KwaZulu-Natal', p 90.

34   APC, PC16/12/2/1/70, Brown to Douglas Blausten, 20 May 1976.

35   APC, PC16/12/2/1/70, Brown to Douglas Blausten, 20 May 1976.

36   APC, PC16/12/2/1/70, Brown to Douglas Blausten, 20 May 1976.

37   CAP newsletter, December 1975, p 4, cited in Sato 'Forced Removals, Land NGOs and Community Politics in KwaZulu-Natal', p 91.

38   APC, PC16/12/2/1/70, Brown to Douglas Blausten, 20 May 1976.

39   APC, PC16/12/2/1/70, Brown to Douglas Blausten, 20 May 1976.

40   APC, PC16/12/2/1/116, Brown to Douglas Blausten, 7 December 1976.

41   APC, PC16/12/2/1/70, Brown to Douglas Blausten, 20 May 1976.

42   APC, PC16/12/2/1/70, Brown to Douglas Blausten, 20 May 1976.

43   APC, PC16/12/2/1/105, Brown to Elliot Mngadi, 26 October 1976.

44   APC, PC16/12/2/2/42, Pat Macdonald to Brown, 11 September 1977.

45   APC, PC16/12/2/2/55, Neil Alcock to Directors, Donors and Members of the Advisory Committee, Memo on Administration, 31 October 1977.

46   Sato, 'Forced Removals, Land NGOs and Community Politics in KwaZulu-Natal', pp 91-95.

47   Cited in Malan, *My Traitor's Heart*, p 378.

48   APC, PC16/5/3/4/77, Elsie Bond to Brown, 4 November 1983.

49   APC, PC16/12/4/3/22, Brown to Marc Alcock, 9 August 1985.

50   Cited in Sato, 'Forced Removals, Land NGOs and Community Politics in KwaZulu-Natal', p 111.

51   APC, PC16/12/2/3/10, Neil Alcock to Brown, 27 March 1978.

52   APC, PC16/12/2/3/10, Neil Alcock to Brown, 27 March 1978.

53   APC, 96 APB3, Interview with Peter Brown conducted by Norman Bromberger, 17 October 1995, Interview 6, p 11.

54   P Brown, 'Neil Alcock: A Tribute', *Reality* (November 1983), p 3.

55   APC, PC16/5/2/5, Brown to Hans Meidner, 12 November 1976.

56   APC, PC16/5/3/3/105, Brown to Bunty Biggs, 21 March 1982.

57   APC, PC16/12/1/1/21, Neil Alcock to CAP Directors, 7 September 1974.

58   APC, PC16/5/3/1/4, Neil Alcock to Brown, no date, but internal clues strongly suggest either November or December 1979.

59   APC, PC16/5/3/1/1, Brown to Neil Alcock, no date [1979].

CHAPTER 15 – BACK TO THE LAND: THE ASSOCIATION FOR RURAL
ADVANCEMENT

1   Mandela, *Long Walk to Freedom*, p 130.
2   L Platzky and C Walker, *The Surplus People: Forced Removals in South Africa*
     (Johannesburg: Ravan, 1985), p 10.
3   APC, 96 APB3, Interview with Peter Brown conducted by Norman Brom-
     berger, 17 October 1995, Interview 6, p 20.
4   Paton, *The Charlestown Story*; P Brown, 'The Destruction of Charlestown',
     Reality (September 1977), pp 7-9.
5   P Brown, 'A visit to an old friend', *Reality* (November 1976), p 12.
6   P Brown, 'A visit to an old friend', *Reality* (November 1976), p 12.
7   APC, PC16/12/3/1/23, Brown to Ray Swart, 9 August 1979.
8   APC, 16/13/1/1/18, Notes of a meeting of concerned people dealing with
     the Natal rural situation, 4 October 1979. See also A Harley and R Fother-
     ingham (eds), *AFRA: 20 years in the land rights struggle* (Pietermaritzburg:
     AFRA, 1999).
9   C Desmond, *The Discarded People: An Account of African Resettlement in South
     Africa* (Harmondsworth: Penguin, 1971).
10   See APC: KZN-OHP, Interview transcript: Peter Kerchhoff, 10 February
     1998; and L Levine (ed), *Hope Beyond Apartheid: The Peter Kerchhoff Years of
     PACSA, 1979-1999* (Pietermaritzburg: PACSA, 2002).
11   APC, 96 APB3, Interview with Peter Brown conducted by Norman
     Bromberger, 17 October 1995, Interview 6, p 14
12   APC, PC16/3/1/1, Minutes: the Natal Rural Scene, 24 November 1979.
13   AFRA constitution, adopted 24 November 1979, cited in Harley and Fother-
     ingham (eds), *AFRA: 20 years in the land rights struggle*, p 85.
14   APC, PC16/13/1/1/21, Minutes: Meeting of AFRA *ad hoc* committee,
     5 December 1979.
15   APC, 96 APB3, Interview with Peter Brown conducted by Norman Brom-
     berger, 17 October 1995, Interview 6, p 15.
16   APC, PC16/13/1/2/5, Minutes: Meeting of AFRA *ad hoc* committee, 28 Jan-
     uary 1980.
17   When interviewed in later years, Brown said of AFRA: 'There was no direct
     link, but it was a continuation of what the old Liberal Party and the Northern
     Natal African Landowners' Association had been doing.' APC, 96 APB3,
     Interview with Peter Brown conducted by Norman Bromberger, 17 October
     1995, Interview 6, p 16.
18   APC, PC16/13/1/2/28, Minutes: AFRA committee meeting, 12 April 1980.
19   APC, PC16/13/1/2/17, Minutes: AFRA committee meeting, 27 February
     1980.
20   APC, PC16/13/1/2/53, Report on a trip through Northern Natal, July
     1980.
21   APC, PC16/13/1/2/20, Brown to Ray Swart, 4 March 1980.
22   APC, PC16/13/1/1/17, Brown to Ray Swart, 27 October 1979.

23   APC, PC16/13/1/2/52, Brown to Mangosuthu Buthelezi, no date. The fact
     that this letter had been sent is referred to in the AFRA committee minutes
     for 12 April 1980. See APC, PC16/13/1/2/29.

24   APC, PC16/13/1/2/48, Mangosuthu Buthelezi to Brown, 12 June 1980.

25   The Commission's report was published as: *The Requirements for Stability and
     Development in KwaZulu and Natal,* Volumes 1 & 2 (Durban: H & H Publi-
     cations, 1982).

26   APC, PC16/13/1/2/48, Mangosuthu Buthelezi to Brown, 12 June 1980.

27   APC, PC16/13/1/2/86, Minutes: AFRA committee meeting, 4 November
     1980.

28   APC, PC16/13/1/3/2, Notes on a meeting of the sub-committee on farm
     evictions, 21 January 1981.

29   APC, PC16/13/1/3/2.

30   APC, PC16/13/1/3/3, Notes on a meeting of an *ad hoc* discussion group,
     23 January 1981.

31   Cited in Harley and Fotheringham (eds), *AFRA: 20 years in the land rights
     struggle,* p 106.

32   APC, PC16/13/1/3/52, Brown to Bishop Philip Russell, 14 May 1981, and
     APC, PC16/13/1/3/56, Handwritten notes on Brown's visit to Kwa-Pitela,
     no date.

33   APC, PC16/13/1/3/90, Minutes: AFRA committee meeting, 29 July 1981.

34   APC, PC16/13/1/3/86, Brown to Bishop Philip Russell, 24 July 1981.

35   APC, PC16/13/1/3/107, Brown to Bishop Philip Russell, 13 September
     1981.

36   APC, PC16/13/1/3/26, Report on Petros Majozi, no date. Brown men-
     tioned his memorandum in a letter to Neil Alcock dated 29 March 1981:
     PC16/12/3/3/4.

37   APC, PC16/13/1/3/33, Frank Mdlalose to the Bishop of Natal, [Philip
     Russell], 5 April 1981.

38   APC, PC16/13/1/3/81, Brown to Bishop Desmond Tutu, 1 July 1981
     (emphasis in original).

39   APC, PC16/13/1/3/82, Bishop Desmond Tutu to Brown, 7 July 1981.

40   J Allen, *Rabble-rouser for Peace: The Authorised Biography of Desmond Tutu*
     (Johannesburg: Random House, 2006).

41   Malan, *My Traitor's Heart,* p 379.

42   APC, PC16/13/2/1/37, Statement by Peter Brown for Pierre Cronje,
     18 June 1982.

43   APC, PC16/13/2/1/36, Organiser's report for AFRA AGM, 15 June 1982.

44   Surplus People Project, *Forced removals, Volume 4: Natal* (Cape Town: SPP,
     1983).

45   Harley and Fotheringham (eds), *AFRA: 20 years in the land rights struggle,* p 97.

46   'Group calls for end to forced removals', *Natal Witness,* 9 November 1981;
     'Big Natal plea to end removals', *Rand Daily Mail,* 10 November 1981; APC,
     PC16/13/1/3/120, Report on AFRA workshop on the law and removals,
     7 November 1981.

47   APC, PC16/13/2/2/29, Brown to the Editors of the *Witness, Rand Daily Mail, Mercury* and *Daily News*, 5 April 1983.

48   APC, PC16/13/2/2/53, Minutes: AFRA AGM, 29 June 1983.

49   APC, 96 APB3, Interview with Peter Brown conducted by Norman Bromberger, 17 October 1995, Interview 6, p 22.

50   APC, PC16/13/2/2/53, Minutes: AFRA AGM, 29 June 1983.

51   APC, PC16/13/3/2/165, Chairman's report for 1986.

52   Cited in Sato, 'Forced Removals, Land NGOs and Community Politics in KwaZulu-Natal, South Africa, 1953-2002', p 140.

53   APC, PC16/13/2/3/85, Laurine Platzky to Brown, 9 October 1984.

54   APC, PC16/13/2/3/88, Brown to Laurine Platzky, 18 October 1984.

55   APC, 96 APB3, Interview with Peter Brown conducted by Norman Bromberger, 17 October 1995, Interview 6, p 22.

56   APC, PC16/3/3/1/36, Minutes: Meeting of the National Committee Against Removals, Cape Town, 17-18 May 1985.

57   APC, PC16/13/3/2/51, Minutes: AFRA AGM, 20 March 1986.

58   APC, PC16/13/3/2/13, Brown to Cherryl Walker, 2 February 1986.

59   APC, PC16/5/2/6/21, Brown to Wolf Hamm, no date, but filed between March and April 1978.

60   APC, PC16/5/4/4/27, Brown to Archie Gumede, 20 May 1987.

61   APC, PC16/5/4/1/35, Mangosuthu Buthelezi to Archie Gumede, 22 May 1984.

62   APC, PC16/5/4/1/36, Brown to Archie Gumede, 17 June 1984.

63   APC, PC16/5/4/5/47, Brown to Derick Marsh, 31 May 1988.

64   APC, PC16/3/3/1/52, Minutes: Special meeting of the AFRA committee to evaluate AFRA's work, 28 July 1985.

65   APC, PC16/3/3/1/33, Minutes: AFRA AGM, 9 May 1985.

66   APC, PC16/3/3/1/76, Report of AFRA sub-committee on administration, 26 September 1985

67   APC, PC16/13/3/3/31, 'Some thoughts for the AFRA evaluation', 14 March 1987.

68   APC, PC16/13/3/3/60, Susan Mathieson to [AFRA] Committee Members, April 1987.

69   APC, PC16/13/3/3/38, Minutes: AFRA, 26 March 1987.

70   APC, PC16/13/3/2/26, Minutes: AFRA committee meeting, 13 February 1986.

71   APC, PC16/13/2/3/9, Minutes: AFRA committee meeting, 29 February 1984.

72   See, for example, APC, PC16/3/3/1/8, Brown to Chris Mann, 3 February 1985; and APC, PC16/13/3/2/26, Minutes: AFRA committee meeting, 13 February 1986.

73   APC, PC16/13/3/2/132, Minutes: AFRA committee meeting, 11 September 1986.

74   APC, PC16/13/3/3/1, P Brown, 'Steincoalspruit – visit of 3rd January 1987'.

75   APC, PC16/13/3/3/5, Minutes: AFRA committee meeting, 15 January 1987.

76   Harley and Fotheringham (eds), *AFRA: 20 years in the land rights struggle*, p 91.

77   Sato, 'Forced Removals, Land NGOs and Community Politics in KwaZulu-Natal, South Africa, 1953-2002', p 135.

78   Cited in Harley and Fotheringham (eds), *AFRA: 20 years in the land rights struggle*, p 91.

79   APC, PC16/3/3/1/33, Minutes: AFRA AGM, 9 May 1985.

80   Sato, 'Forced Removals, Land NGOs and Community Politics in KwaZulu-Natal, South Africa, 1953-2002', p 136.

81   APC, PC16/3/3/1/94, Minutes: AFRA committee meeting, 5 December 1985; and APC, PC16/3/3/1/95, Brown to Secretary of the Consolidation Commission, 7 December 1985.

82   APC, PC16/13/3/2/1, Minutes: AFRA committee meeting, 8 January 1986.

83   APC, PC16/13/3/2/3, 'Before the Commission', unidentified author, 16 January 1986.

84   APC, PC16/13/3/2/7, Minutes: AFRA committee meeting, 23 January 1986.

85   APC, PC16/13/4/1/88, Graham McIntosh to Brown, 25 July 1988.

86   APC, PC16/13/4/1/105, Brown to Graham McIntosh, 24 August 1988.

87   APC, PC16/13/4/1/132, Minutes: AFRA legal subcommittee report, 8 November 1988.

88   APC, PC16/13/3/3/96, Brown to Mr Viljoen [Chairman of the Tugela Basin Regional Development Association], 19 October 1987.

89   APC, PC16/13/4/1/105, Brown to Graham McIntosh, 24 August 1988.

90   APC, PC16/13/4/2/13, Position paper on the possible reorganisation of AFRA and its objectives, February 1989.

91   APC, PC16/13/4/2/29, AFRA: A report on future development, commissioned by JJW Aitchison and prepared by PM Graham, 31 March 1989.

92   APC, PC16/13/4/2/33, Minutes: AFRA AGM, 1 April 1989.

93   APC, Gerard Mare Collection, PC126/1/3/1/2, AFRA Annual Report, 1989-1990.

94   APC, Gerard Mare Collection, PC126/1/3/1/2, AFRA Annual Report, 1989-1990.

95   Editorial, 'Land Redistribution', *Reality* (September 1980); N Bromberger, 'Land Reform in South Africa', *Reality* (July 1980); T Lodge, 'Land Reform in South Africa', *Reality* (September 1980), pp 4-6.

96   APC, PC16/13/4/2/36, Chairman's report to the AFRA AGM, 1 April 1989.

CHAPTER 16 – LIBERALISM IN THE TRANSITION: THE LIBERAL
DEMOCRATIC ASSOCIATION AND THE FIVE FREEDOMS FORUM

1   WHP, Brown to Wolf Hamm, 9 August 1983.
2   'The referendum', *Reality* (November 1982).
3   'The election', *Reality* (July 1981).
4   For the programme, see APC, PC16/15/1/1/1, Programme – Liberal Party
    Workshop – July 1985.
5   APC, PC16/15/1/1/4, AS Mathews, 'The Liberal Party: What it was and
    what it tried to do', 15 July 1985.
6   APC, PC16/15/1/3/45, P Brown, 'Follow-up to the Grahamstown work-
    shop', 28 July 1985.
7   APC, PC16/5/4/2/39, Brown to Audrey Cobden, 11 August 1985.
8   APC, PC16/5/4/2/49, Brown to Audrey Cobden, 8 September 1985.
9   APC, PC16/15/2/1/2, Constitution of the Liberal Democratic Association
    of South Africa, no date; APC, PC16/15/2/1/1, Leaflet: 'Statement of
    Liberal Democratic Principles', August 1997.
10 See, for example, APC, PC16/15/1/4/44, Minutes: Meeting of the Trans-
    vaal LDA, 28 June 1986; APC, PC16/15/1/4/64, Minutes: Meeting of the
    Transvaal LDA, 16 August 1986.
11 APC, PC16/15/1/3/76, Brown to Jill and Ernie Wentzel, 7 September
    1985.
12 Jill Wentzel Papers [JWP], Brown to Jill Wentzel, 16 January 1987.
13 APC, PC16/15/2/3/9, Brown to Peter Horwitz, 15 January 1987.
14 APC, PC16/15/1/4/34, Tony Morphet to Brown, 15 June 1986.
15 APC, PC16/15/1/4/61, Brown to Tony Morphet, 6 August 1986.
16 J Wentzel, *The Liberal Slideaway* (Johannesburg: South African Institute of
    Race Relations, 1995).
17 APC, PC16/15/1/4/88-96, J Wentzel, 'The Liberal Slide-away', Paper
    delivered to the South African Institute of Race Relations, 21 March 1986.
18 APC, PC16/5/4/3/82, Brown to Jill Wentzel, 18 August 1985.
19 APC, PC16/15/2/6/44, Brown to Peter Horwitz, 9 September 1992.
20 M Cowling and T Barrett (eds), *Debating a Bill of Rights* (Pietermaritzburg:
    Natal Witness, 1991).
21 APC, PC16/5/4/3/24, Brown to Wolf Hamm, 9 March 1986.
22 APC, PC16/15/2/3/10, Brown to Frederik van Zyl Slabbert, 20 January
    1987.
23 APC, PC16/15/2/3/25, Frederik van Zyl Slabbert to Brown, 1 March 1987.
24 APC, PC16/15/2/5/18, 'Memorandum on the ANC's constitutional guide-
    lines and proposals submitted to IDASA by the Liberal Democratic
    Association', no date.
25 WHP, Brown to Wolf Hamm, 14 February 1990.
26 APC, PC5/1/1/1, 'Five Freedoms Forum: Aims and objectives, structures,
    activities, events', 1989.
27 APC, PC16/15/2/6/44, Brown to Peter Horwitz, 9 September 1992.

28 APC, PC16/15/2/6/44, Brown to Peter Horwitz, 9 September 1992.

29 APC, PC16/10/6/1(b)I, Minutes: *Reality* board meeting, 27 January 1993.

30 APC, PC5/5/2/1.

31 APC, PC5/5/6/1-2.

32 WHP, Brown to Wolf Hamm, 8 February 1989.

33 WHP, Brown to Wolf Hamm, 12 November 1989.

34 APC, PC16/5/4/4/38, Helen Suzman to Brown, 28 July 1987.

35 WHP, Brown to Wolf Hamm, 14 February 1990.

36 APC, PC16/5/4/3/72, Winnie Mandela to Brown, 12 November 1986.

37 APC, PC16/10/5/1, Brown to Tony Morphet, 28 November 1986.

38 APC, PC16/5/4/1/13, Brown to Bill Hoffenberg, 12 February 1984; Interview with Chris Brown, Pietermaritzburg, August 2006.

39 APC, PC16/5/4/5/41, Anne Paton to Brown, 13 May 1988.

40 APC, PC16/5/4/5/35, Jonathan Paton to Peter and Phoebe Brown, 23 April 1988 (emphasis in original).

41 APC, PC16/5/4/5/44, Brown to Anne Paton, 19 May 1988.

42 WHP, Peter Brown, [Speech for] 'Alan Paton Memorial Service', St Paul's Cathedral, 28 June 1988.

CHAPTER 17 – THE FINAL DECADE

1   WHP, Brown to Wolf Hamm, 18 June 1994.

2   WHP, Brown to Wolf Hamm, 3 November 1995.

3   WHP, Brown to Wolf Hamm, no date [handwritten insertion states '1998' (early)].

4   WHP, Brown to Wolf Hamm, 18 September 2000.

5   WHP, Peter Brown to Wolf Hamm, 15 January 2004.

6   WHP, Brown to Wolf Hamm, 25 September 1999.

7   WHP, Brown to Wolf Hamm, 26 March 2004.

8   Interview with Jill Wentzel, Johannesburg, 13 September 2006.

9   APC, PC16/15/1/3/50, Jill Wentzel to Peter Brown, 8 August 1985.

10 Personal communication, April 2009.

11 Personal communication, 27 August 2009.

12 APC, 96 APB3, Interview with Peter Brown conducted by Norman Bromberger, 11 March 1996, Interview 8, p 13.

INDEX